Managing the Research University

Managing the
Research University

DEAN O. SMITH

OXFORD
UNIVERSITY PRESS

Oxford University Press, Inc., publishes works that further
Oxford University's objective of excellence
in research, scholarship, and education.

Oxford   New York
Auckland   Cape Town   Dar es Salaam   Hong Kong   Karachi
Kuala Lumpur   Madrid   Melbourne   Mexico City   Nairobi
New Delhi   Shanghai   Taipei   Toronto

With offices in
Argentina   Austria   Brazil   Chile   Czech Republic   France   Greece
Guatemala   Hungary   Italy   Japan   Poland   Portugal   Singapore
South Korea   Switzerland   Thailand   Turkey   Ukraine   Vietnam

Published by Oxford University Press, Inc.
198 Madison Avenue, New York, New York 10016

www.oup.com

Oxford is a registered trademark of Oxford University Press

Library of Congress Cataloging-in-Publication Data
Smith, Dean O., 1944-
   Managing the research university / By Dean O. Smith.
      p. cm.
   Includes bibliographical references and index.
   ISBN 978-0-19-979325-9 (cloth : alk. paper) 1. Universities and colleges–United States–
Administration. 2. Research institutes–United States–Administration. I. Title.
   LB2341.S54   2011
   378.1'07–dc22   2010039993

1 3 5 7 9 8 6 4 2
Printed in the United States of America
on acid-free paper

CONTENTS

PREFACE

In recent years, the federal government and private industry have entrusted universities to conduct an increasingly growing portion of their research portfolio. Research expenditures at U.S. universities and colleges have doubled within the past ten years—from $27 billion in 1999 to $55 billion in 2009. Furthermore, these amounts are expected to increase at a comparable pace into the foreseeable future. The 2007 congressionally commissioned report on American competitiveness, *Rising Above the Gathering Storm: Energizing and Employing America for a Brighter Economic Future*, calls for increased federal support of basic research in the nation's universities. Academic research has become an engine of economic development as well. In 2008, academic inventions in medicine, plant genetics, and alternative energy generated $2.3 billion in licensing revenue and spawned 543 new companies.

The magnitude and importance of the academic research economic enterprise call for knowledgeable, responsible management—for strong academic research leadership. Many, but certainly not all, university research administrators come from the faculty ranks, and many have had little or no formal training in this role. More often than not, they learn the profession "on the job." I'm no different. As a young associate professor at the University of Wisconsin-Madison, I stumbled into research administration without any meaningful idea about the position. Now, after thirty-six years as a faculty member, and twenty-one of those years as a research administrator at one level or another at three very different research universities, I have learned the job and want to share this knowledge with the next generation of academic research administrators.

Some facets of research administration require either simply common sense or personal experience as a research-active faculty member. However, there are many other aspects that benefit from formal training. These include the historical and legal backgrounds of many institutional and federal policies and regulations. *Managing the Research University* aims to fill that void by providing a comprehensive background and a discussion of the issues and challenges of managing a university's research enterprise. In a sense, this book serves as a surrogate mentor who provides advice and guidance on the various topics.

The underlying premise of this book is that the administration of academic research becomes enlightened leadership through an understanding of the thinking behind the policies and decisions. Therefore, the goal is to provide the historical and cultural background of the main issues and challenges faced by research administration. From this knowledgeable platform an administrator can more readily interpret policies and regulations. And, more important, he or she can understand diverse points of view about various issues.

Managing the Research University is targeted to anybody involved directly or indirectly in research administration. Within academe, chief research officers, provosts, their associates, deans, center and institute directors, and department chairs will find answers to myriad questions that pop up daily on the job. In that sense, it will serve as a comprehensive introduction to the topic and a subsequent reference book. Numerous faculty members have also expressed an interest in *Managing the Research University's* inside view of research-university administration. Furthermore, other senior-level administrators, such as chief executive officers (presidents and chancellors), chief financial officers, and governing board members who themselves have not been active researchers, will find this to be a source of informative insights into the realm of research administration. Industry and government officials who oversee grants and contracts with academic institutions may also find this book interesting. It will provide them with a comprehensive overview of academic research from the university's perspective.

The book may also be of considerable interest to international markets. As countries such as India, China, South Korea, South Africa, and Russia invest in their research universities, they may appreciate the insights gained from administering complex American research institutions. Likewise, European Union countries are expanding their research efforts, and they, too, may benefit from this guide to administrative "best practices." In general, *Managing the Research University* provides the essential framework for building a strong leadership infrastructure serving an expanding research enterprise.

Managing the Research University is also suited as a higher education textbook. By presenting the professional standards of academic research administration, it provides a good didactic introduction to the field. Moreover, the content has been thoroughly researched and vetted by experts to ensure accuracy and timeliness. It could be required reading for either advanced undergraduates or graduate students in higher education administration or in research management in a college of education or business school. In addition, the book may also be a supplementary resource for research-administration workshops.

The complexities of research administration vary according to the size and scope of the university. At the University of Wisconsin-Madison, for example, the job dealt with a broad spectrum of academic disciplines, ranging from the surgery department in the medical school to the piano program in the music school. As a vice president for research at both the University of Hawaii and Texas Tech University, I also discovered that these medium and smaller research universities face unique challenges not found at a large institution like the University of Wisconsin. And vice versa. In other words, one size does not fit all. Thus, drawing from my experiences at these three, very dissimilar institutions, I have addressed issues arising at different-size universities.

The main objective of *Managing the Research University* is to provide the tools needed for good management of complex research organizations. To accomplish this primary goal, the book analyzes the four main elements of research administration: personnel, finance, regulatory compliance, and investments. Several chapters on personnel set the framework for effective management. The book concentrates on clearly defined reporting lines that effectively couple responsibility and authority. Moreover, it stresses the need and legal requirements for proper training in assigned areas of responsibility. And foremost, *Managing the Research University* provides guidance in developing an environment conducive to researcher productivity.

The financial aspects of academic research are examined in considerable detail. The funding sources and restrictions on their expenditure are analyzed from an accounting perspective. In addition, methods for increasing the amount of funding supplement this analysis. Furthermore, three chapters focus on the commercialization of university-owned intellectual property. This includes an examination of the legal and financial aspects of patenting and licensing intellectual property and of spin-off businesses based on university-owned patents.

To protect public health and national security, and to ensure proper accountability, the federal government has promulgated myriad rules and regulations that academic research institutes must obey. Thus, throughout the book *Managing the Research University* concentrates on regulatory compliance. In general, the ethical basis and rationale for the various regulations are explored to provide a deeper understanding of this important element of research administration.

Investment comprises the fourth main element of research administration. How can administrators maximize returns from the federal, state, private, and institutional investments in the academic research enterprise? This recurrent theme weaves through nearly all chapters in *Managing the Research University*. Attention centers primarily on creating an environment that inspires researchers to increase productivity. Ultimately, success in this effort defines academic research leadership.

Organizationally, *Managing the Research University* is divided into seventeen chapters that cover all of the main issues confronting an academic research administrator's portfolio of responsibilities. Each chapter presents and discusses policies, regulations, and procedures encountered in research administration. Formal discussions are supplemented by "rules of thumb," best practices, and other advice gleaned from many years of personal experience.

The first two chapters introduce the personnel responsible for academic research administration. Chapter 1 examines the chief research officer's position within the organization, reporting lines, authority and responsibilities, and early career considerations. It also gets to the nuts and bolts of organizing and staffing the office. Moreover, it discusses the protocol and etiquette of relations with various internal constituencies, including other senior executives and governing board members. And it ends appropriately with a brief discussion about gracefully leaving the office. The second chapter looks at relationships with various external constituencies, including reporters, state legislators and members of Congress, corporate executives, and labor union officials. It focuses on not only the common topics discussed with these groups but also the rules of protocol and etiquette attendant to these communications.

The next five chapters analyze strategies for obtaining and investing the financial resources needed to support the university's research enterprise. Chapter 3 discusses the development and implementation of a strategic plan for the university's research investments. Chapters 4, 5, and 6 analyze financial aspects of research administration. Chapter 4 examines the available resources necessary to conduct research—namely, money, space, and students—and various restrictions governing their use. In that context, chapter 5 then explores ways to increase the financial resources needed to build research capacity. Investing these resources effectively can pose unexpected challenges and pitfalls, which are discussed in chapter 6. Chapter 7 concludes this section by focusing on centers and institutes. As a major venue for interdisciplinary research programs, these have become an increasingly vital component of the overall research environment—and often are a strong magnet for large grants and contracts.

The next section, chapters 8 through 13, addresses managerial duties and responsibilities specific to all academic research programs. The core duty is administration of sponsored research grants and contracts—the topic of chapter 8. Basic tasks include grants and contract support, indirect cost recovery, and accountability reporting. Chapters 9 through 11 discuss regulatory compliance. This includes compliance with all rules and regulations in the realm of research ethics, conflicts of interest, hazardous materials (including recombinant DNA and select agents), and restricted research (for example, classified research). This section concludes with chapters 12 and 13, analyzing federal regulations guiding the use of human and animal subjects in research, respectively. In general, these six chapters cover the chief research officer's bread-and-butter managerial responsibilities.

The following three chapters discuss a dominant feature of modern research universities: technology transfer, or moving the products of academic research into the commercial marketplace. As an introduction, chapter 14 analyzes intellectual property ownership from a legal perspective. This is followed in chapter 15 by a discussion of the basic elements of technology transfer: patents and licenses. Chapter 16 concludes this section with an examination of the university's role in economic development. This includes a discussion of the mechanisms for establishing and financing spin-off companies based on university-owned patents, the tax consequences of using university facilities for private business, and the utility of university-affiliated research parks.

The book concludes with a discussion of evaluation and assessment—chapter 17. How is success measured? Unless that question is answered clearly, strategic investments can be widely misdirected. The emphasis is on information-driven decision making.

As a vehicle for discussing more controversial aspects of some topics "off the record," and expressing arguable opinions about others, I have woven conversations between two hypothetical chief research officers, K and Smith, into each chapter. In general, these brief conversations complement the pedagogical text. They convey the gist of numerous casual discussions with colleagues over the years of our common interest: the art of academic research leadership.

In retrospect, I should like to acknowledge my numerous mentors and collaborators over the years. It all started with my Ph.D. adviser, Dr. Donald Kennedy, who demonstrated that a superb scientist could also be an enlightened administrator. This was followed by an equally influential colleague, Dr. Arnold "Bud" Brown, former dean of the University of Wisconsin Medical School in Madison, who enlisted me to become chair of the Medical School Research Committee. After several years in that role, I was appointed associate dean of the Graduate School. In those days, the dean of the Graduate School was also the university's chief research officer. Thus, in that role I was also a de facto associate chief research officer. The dean to whom I reported was the late Dr. Robert M. Bock, who had been in the position for about twenty years when I came on board. He taught me the trade. Like all true mentors, Dr. Bock tutored me in both the theory and the art of research administration.

My formal training was enhanced considerably by Dr. Kenneth P. Mortimer, who, as president of the University of Hawaii, recruited me to become senior vice president for research and graduate education at the flagship Manoa campus. As a scholar of university administration, Dr. Mortimer introduced me to the theory behind many policy issues. After nearly three years as vice president for research, I became the university's senior vice president and executive vice chancellor. As the chief academic and operating officer, to whom the senior vice president for research reported, I gained an appreciation of the chief research officer's position from a higher level perspective. In addition, I learned the protocol and etiquette for interactions with labor union leaders and members of the state legislature, the governor's office, the Board of Regents, and the federal congressional delegation. Likewise, I was introduced to the formalities of international research agreements and consortia. As vice president for research at Texas Tech University, I discovered the unique challenges of building research capacity at smaller universities. They call for capacity-building strategies quite different from those of larger, more established research universities.

I should also like to extend my heartfelt thanks to numerous friends who have graciously read and provided invaluable comments at various stages of the manuscript preparation. Their thoughtful suggestions ranged from emendations of style to corrections of factual errors. Most important of all, I thank my many colleagues of the last thirty-six years—faculty members and staff who inadvertently served as a living laboratory where I learned and practiced my trade.

Managing the Research University

CHAPTER 1

The Chief Research Officer

K: Strong leaders inspire their colleagues to higher performance levels. How does the chief research officer provide this inspiration?

Smith: There have been books and books written about leadership. Some people have the gift of inspiring leadership and some people don't. I'm not sure that it boils down to a learned skill.

K: Maybe, but aren't there ways that even an uninspiring chief research officer can provide leadership?

Smith: Fortunately, yes. In a nutshell, they involve understanding the mechanics of research administration and making the researchers feel that the institution values them.

Leadership

For centuries, scholars have debated the qualities of leadership, and many books, movies, and tales extolling an individual's unique leadership qualities have been produced. They include mythical (Ulysses) as well as real (Eleanor Roosevelt, Nelson Mandela, Knute Rockne) heroes. Some people simply have the gift of inspiring leadership. For many others, however, leadership evolves from another source: recognizably competent management.In his classic book *The Practice of Management*, Peter Drucker elaborates on the evolution of leadership from good management:

> Leadership is of utmost importance. Indeed, there is no substitute for it. But leadership cannot be created or promoted. It cannot be taught or learned... management cannot create leaders. The supply of leadership is much too limited and unpredictable to be depended upon for the creation of the spirit the business enterprise needs to be productive and to hold together. Management must work on creating the spirit by other means. These means may be less effective and more pedestrian.

But at least they are available and within management's control. In fact, to concentrate on leadership may only too easily lead management to do nothing at all about the spirit of the organization.[1]

An institution may get lucky and hire a chief research officer with the rare gift of leadership to elevate "common" people to "uncommon" people that Drucker asserts is so rare. Hedging its bets, however, the institution might seek an individual who understands the basic principles of academic research management. This candidate, then, has the prerequisites for the kind of academic leadership that creates a research environment conducive to increased faculty productivity. Through competent management, an aspiring chief research officer can inspire faculty members to more satisfying and more productive research careers. This inspiration is the essence of leadership.

Within this introductory context, the remainder of this book explores the responsibilities and challenges of research leadership. Because the federal government and private industry have entrusted universities to conduct a considerable portion of their research portfolio in recent years, the emphasis will be on the academic setting—on academic research leadership. However, the managerial principles and practices apply just as well to all other research settings, as do the laws and regulations. The titles and organizational structure may change, but these factors remain relatively constant.

Job Description

The institution's chief research officer usually has a lengthy and diverse job description that can be reduced to a simple phrase: cultivate and maintain a healthy research environment. But hidden behind those seven words is a jungle of detailed tasks and responsibilities needed to accomplish that mission. Most posted job descriptions share a common list of expectations: promote graduate-level scholarship, enhance extramural funding, represent researchers' interests in institutional and external forums, ensure regulatory compliance, oversee the use of animals and humans in research, and administer the university's technology-transfer and economic-development activities. Each of these topics will be discussed in subsequent chapters. Likewise, the job description usually requires candidates to have a distinguished record of scholarly achievements, including substantial grant support, several years of experience in academic administration, knowledge of technology transfer, and myriad other talents.

The chief research officer also serves as a member of the university's senior management team. This role may not be stated explicitly in the job description, but it is a de facto responsibility. In this capacity, the chief research officer participates in high-level managerial policy and decision making. And this often involves issues not related directly to research, such as setting undergraduate tuition levels and campus parking policies. In that context, public (or student) approval or disapproval of a policy is directed to the university management as a whole, and that includes the chief research officer. As in all managerial settings, the chief research officer must abide by the "team" decisions, regardless of personal or professional opinion.

The extensive lists of duties and responsibilities and of desired qualifications in most posted job descriptions might seem daunting. How could any faculty member ever meet these expectations and remain a productive scholar? Interestingly, executive search firms estimate that there are usually twenty-five to thirty-five applicants for a chief research officer's opening at major research universities. In some cases, the number may be much higher. And about half are qualified for serious consideration. So, the position attracts numerous qualified candidates.

Reporting Line

The actual title of the chief research officer varies from one institution to another. The most common variation is vice president or vice chancellor, depending on the university's convention. To facilitate discussion, the term "vice president" (or VPR) will be used in this specific context. As a vice president, the reporting line is, by definition, directly to the president. A priori, that would seem to be quite desirable for an aspiring chief research officer; why not report right to the top? True, this organizational arrangement guarantees that the chief research officer sits on the highest level decision-making committees and has personal access to the chief executive officer. But there can be a major downside to this otherwise appealing reporting line.

In most universities, the chief executive officer delegates the academic budget and authority to the chief academic officer—the provost. In contrast, the chief research officer usually has direct control of little or no academic personnel budget; it is certainly unusual for a chief research officer to have any discretionary influence on the allocation of faculty positions or the salary of new faculty recruits. Consequently, for a vice president for research to succeed with any plan that requires new faculty appointments, he or she must necessarily have the provost's support—programmatic and budgetary. As a corollary, the provost does not necessarily have a vested interest in seeing a vice president for research succeed. Even in the best of situations, the provost and the chief research officer compete for resources such as money and faculty time, and that can cause subtle friction in their working relationship.

Therefore, an alternative reporting arrangement has evolved in numerous large and small research universities—namely, the vice-provost for research. In this structure, the chief research officer works directly for and with the provost, who now has a clear interest in seeing this immediate staff member succeed.

Another variation on this arrangement is for the chief research officer to be a dean, such as dean of research. As a dean, he or she reports to the provost. Some institutions try to have it both ways; in their organizational charts, the chief research officer reports directly to the chief executive officer via a solid line and to the provost via a dotted line, or vice versa. However, dotted-line reporting arrangements are inherently weak and usually meaningless. The dotted lines can lead to confusing responsibilities and an uncoupling of authority and responsibility. Thus, the straightforward vice-provost for research title (no dotted lines) is a very pragmatic and effective alignment.

In many settings, the chief research officer also is the dean of the graduate division. The rationale is that the Ph.D. is a research degree. Combining these two positions facilitates the integration of research and instruction at the graduate level. University policies affecting research also affect doctoral-level graduate studies and vice versa. For example, if the graduate dean increases the base stipend level for research assistants, this will impact the individual investigator's research budget. If the chief research officer is also the dean of graduate studies, then he or she must report to the provost in one way or another, preferably directly. Obviously, if the positions are split, the chief research officer must work closely and collaboratively with the graduate dean. Often the graduate dean controls funding for graduate-student stipends, which complements the other resources available to the chief research officer.

Negotiations

Having been offered the job, the prospective new chief research officer faces three personal issues that require negotiation. The first deals with salary: what is a fair offer? This is the easiest of the three to resolve. The annual College and University Professional Association for Human Resources (CUPA-HR) *Administrative Compensation Survey* is a widely recognized benchmark.[2] Salaries of chief research officers (and many other executive positions) are tabulated according to university type (for example, doctoral versus master's level) and to annual research expenditures. These reports can be expensive to buy (several hundred dollars), but most university human resources offices have institutional copies available for faculty and staff use. With that as a common reasonable starting point, further negotiations usually proceed smoothly.

If negotiations stall over salary issues, deferred compensation plans often resolve differences between the job candidate (the chief research officer) and the university (usually the chief executive officer). In their simplest form, known as a "rabbi trust,"[3] on a monthly basis the university deposits some amount of money into an interest-bearing account that it controls. After a certain period in the position, such as five years, the candidate (now the chief research officer) gains access to the accumulated funds and may withdraw them for personal use.

As an example, suppose for some reason the university must cap its salary offer for a chief research officer at $200,000 per year, but the desired candidate insists on $212,000. Using funds contributed by local donors (such as industries or hospitals), the university agrees to deposit $1,000 per month into an account that earns 5 percent interest annually, thus bringing its offer to the required $212,000 per year. The candidate must remain in the position for five years before he or she can withdraw the money, which then equals $68,000 including accumulated interest. If the candidate leaves voluntarily before five years, he or she forfeits the entire amount. Therefore, this plan constitutes a "golden handcuff." If he or she leaves involuntarily, the money usually reverts to the institution, although this could become a negotiation point. In general, there are numerous professional firms specializing in these "executive compensation" plans. Usually they charge on an hourly basis at prevailing legal-fee rates.

The second issue deals with a personal research program. Many chief research officer candidates may be expected to have ongoing research programs of their own. During the interview process, the question will inevitably arise: "Do you plan on continuing your own research program while serving as chief research officer?" The probable answer is yes. Most successful researchers hesitate to give up their programs. Unless the new chief research officer is an in-house appointment, this leads to a discussion about laboratory space, moving equipment, start-up funds, transferring grants, and even relocating the candidate's business ventures.

It pays to understand the implications of this decision to continue a personal research program. On the positive side, it is always better to lead by example. Moreover, the chief research officer gets an inside look at his or her office at work and is thus better informed about troublesome bottlenecks. Importantly, the research program also provides an occasional refuge from the office and its commotion. However, there is also a negative side. Most obviously, the demands of the job may be so time-consuming that there is realistically little productive time left for personal research. Yes, a trustworthy technician, postdoctoral fellow, or graduate student can keep a scholarly career somewhat productive. However, while the chief research officer is spending most of his or her time thinking about research administration, competitors (namely, fellow full-time investigators in the same discipline) are thinking about their own research. In the short run, this may not be a serious mismatch. But after several years, the chief research officer will inevitably fall behind as colleagues move forward. This slippage may not be evident until it is too late to recover: "Well, that won't happen to me." Maybe not, but the odds aren't favorable. And finally, the institution is being asked to divert resources from promising young faculty members to the chief research officer's program. Some governing boards have policies prohibiting senior executive officers, including the chief research officer, from engaging in any activity other than administration: "We hired you to run this place. Let the faculty members do the teaching and research." (Of course, a board can always grant exceptions to its own policies.)

A third negotiating issue deals with discretionary funds for program development. This is usually far more difficult to resolve. Axiomatically, the chief research officer must control the budgetary resources needed to meet the obligations and expectations of the job, which run the gamut from start-up packages to cost-sharing to emergency bridge funds. How much is needed to be effective? As they say, "way too much is not nearly enough." However, the general rule of thumb is that the chief research officer should have discretionary control over an amount equal to about 5 percent of the institution's overall research expenditures. So, if the annual research expenditures are $100 million, then the chief research officer should control about $5 million of that amount. This percentage should be treated as a starting point for further negotiations. Each university has unique requirements and expectations that ultimately will influence the actual budget available to the chief research officer.

By the way, chief research officers are commonly required to get a security clearance as a condition of employment. This is necessary if anybody within the university has access to information classified by the federal government.[4] Because the chief research officer may at some time find it necessary to know something about these projects, he or she must have the clearance. Of course, the investigators also must have security clearance.

Legacy

After obtaining the position, the newly appointed chief research officer should ask the following personal question: "What do I want my legacy to be?" This is a question to ponder from the outset, although it may not be answered until some time (such as one or two years) has been spent on the job. Will it be measured in terms of institutional research expenditures, construction of a sorely needed research building, or development of a new program or research unit? Or will the legacy be of some less tangible value? For example, were the faculty members recognizably inspired to greater levels of performance because of the chief research officer's leadership? Did the institution's scholarly prestige increase demonstrably? The answers to this battery of questions will depend on institutional culture and needs, as well as on personal career goals. And of course, fate—more accurately, luck—will play a major role. Nonetheless, a clearly defined notion of legacy will serve as a subconscious guide during decision making along the career pathway.

There is a related, equally personal question: "Why do I want to leave a legacy?" The answer to this question, which depends on personal aspirations, will shape the legacy's framework. For example, if the chief research officer considers the job to be a stepping-stone in the career path to a higher position in academic administration, then the legacy will rest on an academic foundation—a new building, increased research expenditures, and so forth. On the other hand, if the personal ambition is name recognition (that is, fame), then the legacy will have a more public basis—leadership in economic development or public policy venues, for example.

> K: *Who defines a legacy? Is it based on colleagues' perceptions of the chief research officer's performance or is it really more personal?*
>
> Smith: *Most people want to be respected by their colleagues for their contributions, so in that sense their perceptions predicate the legacy. The personal legacy question is usually something like, "What do I want to be remembered for?" "Remembered by whom?" Usually, this reverts to colleagues' perceptions.*
>
> K: *Regardless, shouldn't there be some inwardly personal sense of legacy?*
>
> Smith: *Yes. Ideally, a personal legacy would be positive attributes such as "inspired leadership" and "forward-thinking resource management." In contrast, it would be a real shame if the personal legacy devolved to negative attributes such as "getting rid of those scoundrels" or "cleaning up this place."*

Office Staffing

Shortly after moving into the new office, the chief research officer faces the next major challenge: setting up the office. At a bare minimum, the core staffing includes a secretary, financial officer, associate chief research officer, director of sponsored research, director of animal care, human-subjects committee chair, and director of technology transfer. Many of these positions can be part time; in fact, only the secretary must be full time. Of course, large universities have many more research-administration personnel with expertise in these fundamental areas or ancillary areas. The additional, ancillary positions include a biosafety officer, radiation safety officer, research integrity officer, government relations officer, and veterinarian, among others.

One of the most important colleagues is the secretary. At this level, secretaries are often referred to as "administrative assistants." Unless they have had prior major administrative experience, many professors have little experience in using a secretary effectively. And at this executive level, most of the secretaries are very competent. Their professional goal is to ensure their supervisor's success; they look good if the boss looks good. In the executive secretary's universe, there are several unwritten rules of the office for the chief research officer to follow. First, always be predictable. The secretary should know when to expect the chief research officer to be in the office and where he or she is going when leaving the office. And the chief research officer must always be in contact with the office. Cell phones make this communication quite easy these days. Second, delegate all calendar functions to the secretary. When a colleague suggests, "Let's meet in my office next Wednesday at 2 p.m.," the answer should always be, "Please check with my secretary." Personal control is ceded. But only then can the embarrassing and often chaotic consequences of double-booked time commitments or missed meetings be avoided. Third, don't throw any paperwork away. Put it in the "outbox," and let the secretary decide which file it goes into—circular or sliding drawer.

The second equally valuable colleague is the financial officer, also known as the business officer, the manager of financial and administrative services, and other variations on the theme. This is the individual who keeps the books, manages accounts, issues purchase orders, pays bills, prepares and submits required financial reports, and responds to auditors' requests for information. In that latter context, the chief research officer usually learns very quickly to listen attentively to what the financial officer has to say about money issues, such as balances, commingling, and permissible expenditures of specific funds and to follow his or her advice. These individuals, who bear major fiscal responsibilities, must occasionally say no to some faculty member's requested expenditure. The chief research officer should be prepared to defend the financial officer in those situations, regardless of whether he or she agrees with the decision. Differences of opinion between the chief research officer and the financial officer should be resolved privately, in a way that does not undermine public perceptions of the financial officer's authority.

The chief research officer typically has one or more associate research officers who oversee specific areas. These may be arranged by function, such as faculty development, government affairs, clinical affairs, animal care, pre- and/or postgrant awards, and so forth. Or, less commonly some very large universities like the University of Wisconsin-Madison organize the office by discipline—life sciences, physical sciences, social sciences, and humanities. In general, associates who interact with the faculty on academic issues should themselves be faculty members. This is a matter of faculty governance, as well as a practical concern. In the faculty member's universe, administrators are on the "dark side." This inherent mistrust of administrators is at least minimized when faculty members are dealing with their own kind. The usual conventions for faculty service apply: the faculty associates should be tenured full professors, well regarded professionally, and willing to compromise. Equally important for the research office, the associates should come from diverse backgrounds. Ideally, they do not share the same discipline as the chief research officer.

In this context, faculty members in the social sciences and the humanities sometimes feel disadvantaged because they are not in fields that have access to large amounts of extramural funding. That can be especially true in universities that are trying to improve their national rankings, which are often weighted heavily on research and development expenditures. Since the chief research officer's domain includes all forms of scholarly activity—not just laboratory research—they must be sensitive to this perception. A common solution is to appoint an associate research officer specifically assigned to the social sciences and the humanities. Because the private sector may offer more funding opportunities in these areas than the federal government, this associate may be expected to work closely with the university's development (fund-raising) office in the quest for resources. In some cases, the development office may assign an individual specifically to the research office to coordinate efforts. This is an important symbiotic relationship between the two offices.

When hiring faculty members into administrative positions, it is important to protect their professional careers. Thus, appointments are usually for three years with an option for extensions. Moreover, many institutions also limit the administrative appointment to 50 percent of the time. The remaining half of the time is with the home department. This arrangement helps ensure that the individual remains productive as a faculty member and also relates to fellow colleagues. For those with nine-month faculty appointments, the research office pays half of that salary plus 100 percent of the summer salary—although the actual administrative workload remains at 50 percent through the summer as well.

In addition, it is advisable to provide these associates with research funding to offset their reduced time available to write grant proposals and to work on research. As a rule of thumb, this should equal approximately half of the associate's annual salary. The funding should be split between the associate's home department (which has realized a half-year's worth of salary savings because of the appointment) and the research office. Why should the home department be asked to contribute? Most importantly, this ensures that they still have a vested interest in seeing the associate remain academically productive. The department is not expected to contribute the entire salary savings—just half. The other half remains in the department for other uses. Likewise, the chief research officer also has invested in the individual, thus reinforcing his or her interest in the associate's academic success while serving in the administration. The main objective is to keep productive faculty members productive, not to draw them into the administration, take advantage of their talents for several years, and then to discharge them in the form of "dead wood" back to the faculty ranks.

The need for faculty status among the other, more technical associates is optional. Often, some faculty member will have a specific talent or interest in some area, such as animal care or clinical trials. All else being equal, it is usually advisable to hire these individuals, but the same "care and feeding" guidelines apply—namely, half-time appointment and research support. Usually, however, all else is not equal. The more technical positions typically require career professionals. Sponsored-projects directors must have experience in grants and contract administration, animal-care directors must understand veterinary issues (and may even be a licensed veterinarian), technology-transfer directors must understand patent law and marketing, and so forth. The list of additional staff positions varies, depending on the devilish details of each specific university organization. These professionals are generally "inherited;" they hold long-term university staff appointments and may belong to a labor union. Nonetheless, sooner or later, the chief research officer may have to replace one of them, for one reason or another. The office of human resources should always be consulted well in advance of any dismissal, resignation, or hiring in this category.

Effective managers look ahead. One important aspect of this forward-looking approach is to groom future managers. If a key staff member leaves the institution for whatever reason, there should always be somebody else in the pipeline to take over his or her duties with minimal disruption—a back-up person. The chief research officer should heed this good advice and insist that each of his or her major associates and directors prepares a plan of professional development for potential successors: a succession plan. And, of course, the chief research officer must also abide by this directive.

Inevitably, occasions will arise when in-house personnel do not have the requisite skills or knowledge to handle a situation competently. The chief research officer should always remain alert to this possibility. In those cases, he or she should not hesitate to seek outside help—hire a consultant. Many experienced chief research officers are quite liberal in this sense; they recognize the need for, and the often immense value of, an expert consultant or consulting firm. "But how do I find a knowledgeable consultant?" Ask colleagues such as chief research officers at other institutions, faculty members, governing board members, granting-agency program directors, lobbyists. A word of caution is in order: many universities have policies limiting the amount of money that can be paid to a consultant without prior governing board approval. Likewise, some states require the attorney general's approval before outside legal counsel can be retained. Thus, the chief research officer should be familiar with these potential restrictions before signing a consulting contract.

Two protocol matters warrant attention. First, for efficient management it is important to establish clean, consistent lines of delegated authority and responsibility within the office. Specific issues should be assigned routinely to the same individual. This develops consistency in policy implementation and expertise among the various office personnel. Of course, more than one person should be familiar with specific tasks for back-up. As a corollary, all incoming correspondence to the research office should be directed to the secretary, who will log it in and then forward it to the appropriate staff member. The chief research officer may or may not be in the loop at this stage when the secretary makes that initial routing decision. However, the staff member receiving correspondence via the secretary may also decide to inform the chief research officer about an issue. Furthermore, the secretary must receive a copy of all correspondence leaving the office to ensure its availability for future access.

Second, the chief research officer and the associate research officers should not communicate directly with faculty members about an institutional resource or personnel issue without first informing their dean about both the topic to be discussed and the time. Of course, a dean may say, "Please call whomever you want whenever you want." Regardless, the dean's office should be informed, mainly to minimize confusion. A faculty member (or, vice versa, a research officer) may hear what he or she wants to hear and not necessarily what the other person actually said. Depending on the situation, this may lead to a misunderstanding that ultimately erodes trust between the various parties—the faculty member, the dean, and the research officer. And that does nobody any good.

Internal Relations

As a senior member of the university administration, the chief research officer interacts with various campus constituencies. These include faculty members, deans, other upper level administrators, and the governing board. Many of these interactions occur informally at receptions, lunches, or spontaneous encounters. The usual rules of social etiquette apply to these meetings. In addition, these meetings occur under more formal circumstances as part of the job. The nature of these formal interactions can be quite different from informal gatherings.

Faculty members constitute a challenging constituency. As most experienced administrators know, faculty members often harbor an inherent mistrust of "the administration." Although many administrators, including the chief research officer, have deep roots in the faculty, they are often perceived to have betrayed this heritage by stepping into "the dark side." As in any labor-management environment, this mistrust evolves from higher paid administrators (managers) making decisions that affect lower paid faculty members (workers). Not all decisions are popular among all of those affected by their consequences, especially when their rationale has not been clearly and transparently presented. And this fuels mistrust and sometimes anger.

In this context, the newly appointed chief research officer may detect a change—often a more or less respectful "distance"—in his or her relationship with faculty colleagues. Furthermore, social occasions frequently become an opportunity for faculty members to tout their program, seek "inside" information, or ask for money. Over time, the chief research officer reflexively limits the duration of these social interactions and guards against saying anything that might be misinterpreted. In these circumstances, conversation often centers on the faculty member's self-interests. Ultimately, this distance transforms friendships. These behavioral changes are not unique to academe. They are universal; as the adage states with some exaggeration, "it's lonely at the top."

When communicating with the faculty on a formal basis, the chief research officer must choose the right audience and venue. The governing board at most universities empowers a single body—the faculty senate (or some variation on the name)—to represent faculty interests. In that capacity, the faculty senate plays an active role in the university's governance. Consequently, the chief research officer should consult routinely with this formally recognized group on matters affecting faculty members and explain the reasoning behind major policy decisions. And conversely, he or she should always consider attentively their expressed concerns. This may entail meaningful debates on an issue. Failure to communicate effectively and forthrightly with the faculty senate exposes the administration to potentially embarrassing censures. Other faculty organizations may also proffer advice on various subjects. And they should be listened to with courtesy. In addition, the chief research officer may assemble a "kitchen cabinet" of trusted faculty members for informal advice. However, if these individuals or groups are not authorized by university policy to represent the faculty, their informal advice must be considered as just that—informal advice.

Deans are an important constituency. For the chief research officer, they can be either an invaluable ally or a dreaded opponent, depending on the issue. Fortunately, a dean's position on any particular issue is generally quite easy to predict. As "captains" of the university's academic enterprise, the deans have a singular loyalty to their college's well-being. Unlike the chief research officer whose dominion extends across the entire campus, deans are hired explicitly to do one thing: protect their college's interests. Politically, groups of deans may unite on a particular issue, but only when it ultimately benefits each dean's own college. Because they control faculty appointments, space, and discretionary research funding, the deans' cooperation is crucial to the chief research officer's efforts to enhance the overall research environment. And vice versa; the deans depend on the chief research officer for institutional support—both material and moral.

Consequently, the chief research officer and the deans meet regularly in various settings. Generally, the chief research officer joins the deans ex officio in regularly scheduled meetings with the provost. This venue offers the chief research officer an opportunity to comment on specific topics under discussion and to generate enthusiasm for a shared vision of the university's research objectives. However, most interactions with the deans occur ad hoc in an informal setting and focus on specific day-to-day topics, such as start-up packages, space allocations, corporate alliances, and the like. In addition, associate research officers meet routinely with associate deans for research to iron out details of particular arrangements. All in all, effective communication with the deans is a major determinant of the chief research officer's success on the job.

The chief research officer's relationship with the provost is absolutely crucial to successful research leadership. As chief academic officer, the provost controls the academic budget and faculty positions available to the deans. Because the deans report to the provost, he or she has a strong influence on their relationships with the chief research officer. Moreover, the provost usually has frequent direct access to the chief executive officer and members of the governing board. Thus, without the provost's support, the chief research officer faces very difficult odds against successful leadership.

The nature of the relationship between the provost and the chief research officer depends in some part on the institution. In universities with well-established research traditions and ample resources, a benign relationship generally evolves: the two offices co-exist in harmony. However, in universities with less mature research traditions and scarcer resources, the provost and the chief research officer may compete for programmatic, as well as budgetary support. In this context, "programmatic" refers to teaching versus research; "Are we a teaching or a research university?" These tensions can be mitigated somewhat if the chief research officer reports directly to the provost. But if the reporting line leads directly to the president, bypassing the provost, the competitive tensions can be subtly destructive.

Regardless of the organizational reporting lines, the chief research officer must meet and communicate regularly with the provost. The venues should include the provost's regularly scheduled meetings with the deans and the chief executive officer's meetings with other senior administrators. More importantly, the chief research officer should meet individually with the provost on a regular basis— at least once or twice per month—to discuss campus research issues. If nothing else comes from these get-togethers, they strengthen the working relationship between the two.

Communication with the chief executive officer takes on a different tone. Both formal and informal meetings revolve around more general topics, such as overall research productivity, large grants and contracts, and economic development initiatives. Importantly, they are also the occasion for informing the chief executive officer about emerging situations that may draw public attention, such as biosafety violations, ethical misconduct cases, or major scientific breakthroughs. The chief executive officer and members of the governing board dislike learning about campus affairs like these from reading the newspaper or watching a television newscast. They can be embarrassed if a member of the public questions them about a news report and they are not fully informed. The chief research officer must alert them beforehand. Indeed, that is an unwritten sine qua non for success.

Ideally, the chief research officer should have regularly scheduled interactions with the institution's governing board. According to protocol, these are generally arranged by the chief executive officer. They may involve regular briefings at board meetings on significant research outcomes since the last meeting, occasional presentations to the board on timely research issues, or even little more than attendance at receptions or dinners where board members are also present. At the University of Hawaii, for example, at every governing board meeting the chief research officer makes an oral report on the past month's grant and contract awards, highlighting particularly noteworthy ones, and then introduces a university researcher who makes a ten-minute presentation of his or her research project in layman's terms. These presentations are well received, and they engage board members in the overall research enterprise.

Why is this access important? In most cases, governing board members have only a limited understanding of the inner workings of a research university. They may be quite knowledgeable about educational and financial issues, since they most probably are all college graduates. Thus, they can relate to many items raised by the chief executive officer, provost, and chief financial officer. Not to mention the athletic director. But the realm of academic research is murkier, and the chief research officer should be entrusted to enlighten the board. Of course, the provost or chief executive officer could probably handle this assignment, and for the sake of parsimony, they might be tempted to exclude yet another administrator from an already packed board agenda. But if the chief research officer is to be held responsible for maintaining a healthy research environment, his or her voice should be heard in person by those making institutional policy.

These internal constituencies—the faculty members, deans, provost, chief executive officer, and governing board members—set the foundation for the chief research officer's mission to cultivate and maintain a healthy research environment. Internal relationships based on trust are critical for success as a chief research officer. Indeed, failure to establish trust leads almost inevitably to frustration and compromised effectiveness on the job. Thus, he or she must always refrain from comments or actions that can be perceived as disingenuous. Furthermore, borrowing a rule of thumb from the business world, "the customer is always right." If a promise or a deal is made—verbally or written—it must be honored.

Realistically, relations with one or more of these groups or individuals may at times be worse than with others. Or to state this more positively, relations may be better with one or more of these constituents. These positive constituents form what is referred to as a "power base." Pragmatically, a power base must be cultivated because this is the group that the chief research officer can turn to for support during difficult times. For example, if the chief executive officer and the governing board are unhappy with some aspect of the chief research officer's performance, the faculty's and deans' strong support—the power base in this case—may be sufficient to mitigate the situation. Stated bluntly, a strong power base gives critics a reason to pause before taking any adverse action against an individual. Most seasoned administrators are keenly aware of the importance of cultivating a strong power base.

The Limits of Authority

According to the job description, the chief research officer may have considerable authority in numerous dimensions. And, as some people say, "authority not used is authority wasted." Indeed, strong, effective leadership requires the chief research officer to make decisions based on his or her authority. Conversely, weak leadership is often characterized by indecisiveness and inability to make the tough call. Furthermore, once a decision is made, it is usually a mistake to reverse or even to modify it. The only exception to this general rule is when some very important piece of information becomes available that simply makes the original decision look ridiculous. Leadership and respect for authority can be seriously compromised by flip-flopping. "Why should we pay attention to this latest decision by the chief research officer when we know that it will be changed tomorrow?" (By the way, the same goes for the provost, the chief executive officer, and the members of the governing board.)

There are further limitations to authority. The chief research officer may make a decision that results in some specific action by colleagues (for example, faculty members) or issue a work assignment to staff members. In reply, the colleagues or staff members may smile and say yes. But beware: that may not mean "Yes, I'll follow your orders." Instead, the reply's real meaning may be, "Yes, I heard what you said." And then nothing ever happens; the order goes unheeded. Why not? The answer is that the colleagues or staff members do not agree with the decision or assignment. They exercise passive resistance—do nothing. Authority is effectively neutralized. Of course, this can quickly become very frustrating. To avoid this neutralization of authority, the chief research officer must consult those affected by a particular decision or assignment beforehand and listen attentively to any objections or alternatives. "The boss is always the boss" and retains the authority of the office, but the disruptive power of passive resistance cannot be overestimated.

A common mistake committed by newly appointed executive officers is to overstep the boundaries of authority when hiring or establishing a program. For example, an enthusiastic chief research officer may single-handedly recruit a new center director without appropriate consultation. After all, the job description states that the center directors report to the chief research officer. However, this authority does not preclude consultation with colleagues and, importantly, with members of the faculty. Likewise, an overzealous but well-intentioned administrator may declare the founding of a new research center without consulting the appropriate faculty members. Without proper consultation, faculty support and cooperation can be very difficult to rally, thus jeopardizing the newly formed center's chances for success. Ultimately, faculty governance always prevails. Experienced administrators, including chief research officers, demur reflexively to faculty governance via direct consultation in all academic matters that ultimately affect the faculty members.

Of course, when hiring a new director, for example, consultation carries the risk that the faculty members put forth a candidate unacceptable to the chief research officer. For the chief research officer, there are two choices: reject the nomination or unhappily accept the recommendation. Neither option is desirable. To minimize the chances of encountering this dilemma, the usual tactic is to request a list of three (plus or minus) unranked nominees—all acceptable to the faculty members—from which the chief research officer will choose one. These are standard search and selection procedures in most universities.

Now for the most insidious limitation to authority: patronage. This occurs when some higher authority, such as the chief executive officer, the governing board, a legislator, the state's governor, or a generous donor, imposes the hiring of an individual onto the university, and in this context, onto the chief research officer's office. Unfortunately, this happens all too often. A typical scenario would be for the governor's office to "suggest" that the university hire a former congressman, staff member, or political establishment member. Likewise, a chief executive officer might unilaterally assign a former provost or other loyal staff member to the research office. There are many variations on this theme, and all of them are equally undesirable. Patronage like this shows disrespect for the research administration office and the chief research officer. By extrapolation, this could raise questions about the overall commitment to the university's research mission.

Unfortunately, not much can be done when this happens. If the patronage assignment came from the governing board or outside the university, such as the governor's office, then the chief executive officer should be enlisted to register any objection. Alternatively, the chief research officer can resign in protest. But that usually isn't a desirable outcome. If "reason" doesn't prevail, the best bet is simply to accommodate the new appointee with as much courtesy as can be mustered.

A similar assault on authority occurs when some higher level individual, such as a member of the governing board or a state legislator, asks for a special, personal favor. Examples include requests for help in getting a relative admitted to a university program, funding for a particular research project that benefits a colleague, hiring or firing a dean or center director for political reasons, and other easily imaginable situations. In all cases, the chief research officer should politely inform the requestor that he or she "is not in the position" to comply with the request. "My authority does not extend that far." Then, he or she should promptly inform the provost and the chief executive officer about the conversation and its outcome. Depending on the details of the case, the chief executive officer may inform the governing board chair about the request and explain why the university cannot acquiesce to these kinds of personal requests: "It would erode institutional integrity."

Stepping Down

The time eventually comes when the chief research officer relinquishes the position. This occasion is often called "returning to the faculty," and it may be done either voluntarily or involuntarily. The reasons for stepping down are myriad, and there are few unifying themes, thus precluding any sage analysis. However, several aspects warrant attention.

Most chief research officers hold a tenured faculty position at the university. Consequently, unless he or she is leaving for a job at another institution or simply retiring, there is a secure fallback position. The question of salary inevitably arises. In some cases, the faculty salary level will have been part of the original appointment negotiations. Regardless of any pre-negotiated fallback salary, the chief research officer usually wishes to keep the higher administrative salary, adjusted for a nine-month appointment if that is the case and less any special perks, such as a car allowance and club membership dues. And it is not unusual for this to be granted—although certainly not in all cases. The old adage, "If you don't ask, you don't get" is good advice. Ironically, the probability of maintaining the higher administrative salary level is generally greater when the chief research officer is fired; it's, "Just take the money and get out of here." From a cynical viewpoint, there may be pecuniary—but not professional—advantages to getting fired relative to resigning.

Newly appointed chief executive officers may choose to replace the provost, the chief financial officer, and the chief research officer in order to build a loyal team. Likewise, if the chief research officer reports to the provost, he or she should be prepared to be replaced if a newly appointed provost comes on board. Of course, these personnel changes may not necessarily occur, or they may take place gradually over a year or two. In some institutions, the standard protocol requires the senior staff members, including the chief research officer, to submit his or her resignation whenever the top leadership changes. These resignations may or may not be accepted. The main point is that the chief research officer should be prepared for these changes in leadership and not be caught off guard when they occur. Importantly, they should not be considered a harsh judgment of work performance. The new leader most probably wants to appoint his or her immediate staff members simply to engender loyalty—the kind of loyalty that accompanies the hiring process.

Occasionally, a chief research officer will seek a higher position within the institution, such as provost or chief executive officer. In-house candidates often have distinct advantages, but there may be unwelcome consequences if they don't get the position. Of course, there is the disappointment, which is normal and expected. The unexpected consequence may be the need to step down as chief research officer. Again, it is a matter of loyalty. As a contender for the position, the chief research officer may be perceived as a threat to the newcomer's authority and as a potentially uncooperative team member. Firing may not be imminent. But authority, and therefore job responsibilities, may be gradually shifted to other staff members. In fact, that is a tell-tale sign of unwelcome presence on the job. Ultimately, the chief research officer should be prepared for another job whenever declaring an in-house candidacy for a higher level position—either in the same institution as the successful candidate or at another university as the ousted opponent.

> K: Wouldn't you think that an incoming chief executive officer would prefer to keep an experienced chief research officer on board? After all, he or she has institutional knowledge.
> Smith: True, experience and connections are built up over time in the office. However, a newly appointed chief executive officer usually has a fresh agenda, including research priorities. Rather than hope that the incumbent "gets with the program," it's often preferable to recruit a new, loyal chief research officer. Unfortunately, as they say, "nobody is irreplaceable."

K: *In that case, is it better to resign shortly after the new chief executive officer's appointment or wait until asked to step down?*

Smith: *Idealists would probably offer to resign early on and then hope to be retained for a while. But human nature probably favors waiting until asked. In that case, a graceful response might be "Okay. I'll step down at your convenience. By the way, may I ask for your support when looking for a similar position at another institution?" The answer will almost always be yes.*

Notes

1. P. F. Drucker, *The Practice of Management* (New York: HarperCollins, 1954), pp. 158–9.
2. College and University Professional Association for Human Resources (CUPA), *Administrative Compensation Survey, 2009–10* (Knoxville, Tenn.: CUPA, 2010).
3. Internal Revenue Service, *Revenue Procedure 92-64* (Washington, D.C.: Government Printing Office, 1992).
4. Defense Security Service, "Personnel Security FAQs," 2010, https://www.dss.mil/GW/ShowBinary/DSS/psco/ps_faqs.html (accessed January 4, 2011).

CHAPTER 2

External Relations

K: Universities have such diverse constituencies—students, their parents, alumni, and lawmakers, among many others. How do they orchestrate communications with these external relations?

Smith: A well-funded public relations office generally coordinates all formal communications with the news media, usually quite effectively. Nonetheless, high-level administrators, including the chief research officer, frequently encounter impromptu situations when they must represent the university to the public—often with minimal time for preparation or forethought.

K: Is that so bad?

Smith: Not if they have prepared to handle these situations. Like anything else in life, it's not so bad if you're prepared for the unexpected.

Press Releases

Immediately after formal appointment to the position, the chief research officer becomes the university's primary spokesperson on research issues. This entails press releases, interviews, testimonies, speeches, and meetings with public- and private-sector organizations. These ongoing public relations obligations are among the first assignments of the job. Often they arise before he or she has become familiar with the topics to be discussed. Nonetheless, the university willingly complies with requests for information. Indeed, it takes advantage of every opportunity to inform the public about noteworthy accomplishments. The immediate goal is to enhance the university's public image. Ultimately, the goal is more mercenary: to generate goodwill that garners more funding through gifts, state appropriations, or grants and contracts.

Consequently, universities continuously provide information about various achievements, especially in the research arena, to the interested members of the public. Press releases are a frequently used conduit of information. In many university settings, public relations personnel produce a constant stream of articles highlighting faculty members' noteworthy research accomplishments. These press releases are issued to targeted audiences. Usually, they include local and regional news media, and if the story has state or national interest, Associated Press (AP) correspondents who provide broader coverage. To reach more targeted audiences, universities commonly subscribe to news-media databases, such as MEDIAtlas, which contains "fully searchable contact details of hundreds of thousands of journalists from around the world."[1] Thus, if a story involves flowers, it can be sent to journalists specializing in flower stories. In addition, in-house publications including alumni magazines, stand-alone research-highlight magazines, and university Web sites provide coverage.

Although the university's public relations office usually writes and produces these articles, they rely heavily on the chief research officer for help in identifying new story material. Thus, he or she regularly forwards noteworthy items to them. Furthermore, the chief research officer may be asked for a quotable comment on a particular research item. Quite commonly, the public relations office "ghostwrites" these remarks in concert with a university's news release. Although the chief research officer generally has the opportunity to preview these comments attributed to him or her, they usually pass without significant emendation into the public domain.

These myriad publications and Web sites are expensive to produce and maintain. The production expenses vary depending on the numbers produced. Typical costs range from $2 to $3 per page, which includes production (photography and design), printing, and postage. Therefore, for 1,000 copies of a sixteen-page, three-color brochure, the expenses may exceed $40,000. Are they worth the cost? After all, this funding could otherwise be invested in basic research. Evidently, the answer is yes. Although many may lie unread on a coffee table, when done properly these publications (including Web sites) lucidly portray the results of taxpayers' investment and, it is hoped, will generate enthusiasm for continued generous support of the university's research efforts. In addition, some chief research officers astutely include detailed research budget information, including their office budget, in publications that highlight various research efforts. Thus, when asked for budget information by an auditor, governing board, legislator, or other interested party, the chief research officer can respond at least in part with a document that also demonstrates the benefits accruing from the budgeted expenditures.

In this general vein, the chief research officer is often asked to address a symposium, conference, site visit, group of distinguished visitors, or other meeting in the community or on campus. These invitations are almost never turned down, even if the chief research officer is totally clueless about the topic to be discussed. Therefore, the chief research officer usually asks the meeting organizer to draft his or her comments beforehand: "Please tell me what to say." Of course, the organizers will accept the invitation to prepare these introductions quite readily because of the opportunity to tout their program's accomplishments. It is always a good idea for the chief research officer to read these prepared remarks carefully before stepping up to the podium.

Interviews

Reporters routinely ask senior administrators, including the chief research officer, for comments about some university-related issue. Indeed, most universities encourage the local news media (newspapers, television, and radio) to contact university personnel for comments on national and international news stories, especially those benefiting from an expert's opinion or analysis.

Interviews, such as those produced for the nightly local television news or the newspaper, offer more spontaneity than prepared material. This also provides the chance to make a point favorable to the university or, conversely, a blunder that requires follow-up damage control. Typically, the reporter asks for the interview in advance, thus allowing the chief research officer the chance to prepare background information and remarks. Secretaries typically screen reporter's telephone calls. They ask what the call concerns and then say that the chief research officer will be returning the call promptly. This allows time to prepare for the interview. Also, experienced administrators know when to expect an interview request, and they think about possible questions and answers beforehand. A new facility dedication, a governing board meeting, a major conference opening session, and similar events usually attract reporters and therefore interview opportunities.

During these interviews, most reporters are quite courteous and respectful. Moreover, they are often in a hurry to move onto the next assignment. (University activities compete with major traffic accidents, crippling snow storms, government scandals, and other interesting stories for audience attention.) Nonetheless, experienced reporters have a good nose for news and can evoke a remark that cannot be taken back. Thus, it is important not to "think out loud," conjecture wildly, make brash promises, speak derogatorily about anyone, or for that matter, make jokes during an interview. Importantly, whenever the chief research officer feels the need to qualify a statement, he or she can stipulate in advance that a subsequent comment will be "off the record." In that context, the key words are "in advance." Without this a priori qualification, a remark cannot be retracted gracefully. Many embarrassed interviewees have learned this lesson the hard way.

If an off-the-record remark, misquote, or factual error appears in print or on the air, the chief research officer should resist the temptation to contact the reporter directly. Assuming that the slipup is worth correcting, the more prudent recourse is to refer the situation to the public relations office. They generally have good working relationships with members of the news media and can resolve the situation professionally. Often the best course of action is to let it go; making an issue of it just keeps the news alive and in the public eye.

Especially difficult interview sessions can occur in the context of research-animal care and use. Occasionally, individuals or groups opposed to the use of animals in research organize demonstrations, picket lines, or other activities that attract news coverage. The chief research officer can expect questions whenever this occurs. And a slight provocation can trigger volatile debates, which amplify the arguments against the university's use of research animals. Thus, he or she should always prepare informative, noninflammatory remarks ahead of time and rehearse expected questions and answers. This preparation is so important that the National Association for Biomedical Research (NABR) offers its members "analyses of issues, sample responses, and suggested strategies" for communications about the use of animals in research.[2] A chief research officer should attend these sessions at least once to become familiar with the gravity of the animal-use debate.

Some universities provide formal training in public speaking for their senior administrators. Both in-house and outside public relations consultants coach groups and individuals on various aspects of public communication, with particular emphasis on news-media interviews. In addition, myriad books, workshops, and formal courses have advice on how to be an effective public speaker. Insights provided by this kind of formal training can be quite useful for an inexperienced chief research officer, especially if he or she has not had extensive classroom teaching experience. By the way, it pays to watch a seasoned politician carefully during an interview, speech, or debate. For the most part, the individual has learned how to avoid traps and to engage an audience. For example, the person usually steps away from the podium and moves forward to speak, thus removing that physical barrier between him or her and the audience.

Less formal but often more challenging requests for information come from individual members of the public. As a general rule, these inquiries should always be answered. Sometimes, this is easy: "No, the university doesn't have a goat dairy-management program." These simple answers should always offer a brief, courteous explanation. In contrast, some questions may be a bit more demanding: "Why do universities spend so much money studying ancient Chinese philosophy and not a dime on solving my problem right here at home?" Or still more complex: "How can a public university support research on human embryonic stem cells when half of the state residents oppose that?" Fortunately, most questions of this nature come in writing, which allows the chief research officer the time to prepare a thoughtful and respectful answer. He or she may delegate preparation of a reply to a colleague, but this should always be with the understanding that a courteous answer will be provided, regardless of the inquiry's nature.

Legislative Testimony

Taxpayer money pays for a major fraction of the research efforts at most universities, public and private. Nationwide, nearly 65 percent of science and engineering research is supported by federal funds. Another 6 percent is supported by state and local funds. And in public universities, state funds usually pay faculty member and graduate research assistant salaries—at least that portion not covered by grant funds. Even endowed professorships cost the taxpayer indirectly through the donors' gift-tax deductions. Not surprisingly, taxpayers want to know how universities spend their money. In this context, "taxpayers" refers not only to single individuals but also to the taxpayers' representatives: state legislators, members of Congress, governors, and governing boards.

Because they receive funding from state and federal government agencies, universities must account for its use. In addition to the usual written documents (progress reports and financial statements), this frequently entails public hearings conducted by a legislative or congressional committee (or subcommittee). This is especially the case at the state level, where public university officials are routinely asked to appear at hearings of one sort or another. These sessions may focus ostensibly on programmatic issues, but ultimately they hone in on money. Chief executive officers, provosts, chief financial officers, and chief research officers usually represent the university. They are accompanied by support staff members, such as executive assistants and budget officers, who provide expertise. Because these are usually open sessions, members of the public may also attend. They may be waiting for the next hearing on the agenda and have little interest in the university. Nonetheless, they serve as silent witnesses to the proceedings. Reporters may also attend, and they may ask questions after the session.

These state legislative hearings usually proceed rather smoothly. Often only a few members of the committee show up; sometimes, only the chair is present. Others may come and go, depending on floor votes and other competing obligations. This is par for the course, and a university official should not worry or become offended when a committee member gets up and leaves without a word. Also, timing is seldom exact, for one reason or another. For example, preceding hearings may drag on past their scheduled end times, thus tying up the room. Or committee members caught up in floor votes and other legislative business may appear late. Seasoned administrators are accustomed to waiting patiently.

The usual procedure calls for university administrators to present written testimony to committee members prior to the hearing. Executive assistants, experienced associates, or lead persons on the subject at the university prepare these documents, keeping in mind that most legislators (including members of Congress) come from a business or legal background and have only a rudimentary understanding of university administration. Routinely, testimonies are proofread carefully and discussed by senior administrators before the hearings. The usual discussion venue is the chief executive officer's senior staff meeting, which typically includes the provost, chief financial officer, chief research officer, legal counsel, and others. The goal is to ensure accuracy and "consistency of message" among all university officials. During the hearings, the appropriate university administrator reads the testimony into the record. Commonly, the committee members have not read the testimony beforehand, although their staff members may have. Thus, many committee questions arise spontaneously from the oral testimony.

After the testimony has been read, the committee questioning begins. Again, this can be quite routine. But there is always the potential for the ensuing discussion to become contentious and uncomfortable for university administrators. Several rules of protocol can mitigate this potential. First, veteran administrators seldom contradict committee members in public; this carries the risk of an embarrassing rebuke. Second, if the administrator does not know the answer to a question, he or she can openly ask an associate for the answer. For example, the chief executive officer cannot be expected to know detailed budget information, so understandably he or she must defer to the chief financial officer. If the question still cannot be answered with authority, the standard reply is, "We'll get that information to you promptly." And that promise must be kept to maintain institutional integrity.

Third, experienced administrators seldom offer elaborate answers that stray from the point of the question. They feel, "The more you say, the greater the chance of getting into trouble." Indeed, experts advise to "get in and get out." The fourth protocol rule is very important: do not respond to provocation. What does this cryptic commandment mean? On rare occasions, for whatever reason, a committee member may challenge an administrator's competence, sincerity, integrity, or honor. That can be very unsettling, and a natural defensive instinct is to contest the allegation. However, this can only inflame the situation in public and make a bad situation worse. The best response is to accept the criticism and hope that other committee members will quickly forward the discussion beyond this uncomfortable point.

Personal visits to key legislators (committee chairs, in particular) before committee hearings usually lessen any tensions that might otherwise surface during hearings. Here, too, there are a few unwritten guidelines. Most universities have a government relations officer who routinely interacts with legislative staff members. It helps when this individual accompanies the senior administrator on these visits because he or she knows the protocol, the staff members, and in most cases, the legislators. And as a matter of courtesy, a small gift such as food is usually given to the legislator's office staff members. (In Hawaii, the standard gift was a box of *manapua*—barbecued pork-filled steamed dumplings.)

These private meetings allow for a preview of university issues and, importantly, a forewarning about any problematic topics "off the record." Problem areas may resurface during the public session, but at least the conversation has already begun. Importantly, the university administration has been alerted to any negative sentiments and can prepare responses for otherwise difficult questions. Thus, prior face-to-face contact with legislators reduces the probability of going into public session "cold"—unaware of potentially troublesome issues. What might be a "problematic topic?" As an example relevant to the chief research officer, legislators may wonder why deans are allowed to keep multimillion-dollar start-up fund reserve accounts when the university is asking for more state funding just to meet basic needs.

In the political realm, both university officials and the legislators benefit from these personal visits. As politicians, the legislators get to know important, highly visible members of the university administration. Politically, this can be beneficial for them. Likewise, university officials befriend the legislators. And that can be quite advantageous. In general, the more presence the chief research officer establishes at the legislature, the better—regardless of whether he or she speaks or interacts with legislators. Just being there indicates that the legislators' activities are important to the university and worthy of the chief research officer's presence. That's one reason senior university administrators, including chief executive, academic, research, and financial officers, spend so much time at the legislature. Not all of this time is spent on meetings and lobbying; they are just being visibly present.

Federal Relations

Relations with the federal government have a different nature. With rare exceptions, accountability reports are addressed routinely to granting agencies such as the National Institutes of Health (NIH), National Science Foundation (NSF), and the U.S. Department of Defense. In the absence of major aberrations, members of Congress seldom become involved in this aspect of federal relations. What constitutes an aberration? These rare situations usually pivot around a serious breach of confidence in university management of federal funds. A frequently cited example is the 1990 congressional audit and subsequent hearing that investigated Stanford University's indirect cost-reimbursement claims. In a particularly contentious atmosphere, Stanford President Donald Kennedy appeared before the congressional Subcommittee on Oversight and Investigations of the House Commerce Committee, chaired by Representative John Dingell. Support staff included not only the chief research officer and chief financial officer but also legal counsel. Stanford was cleared ultimately of any wrongdoing, but the hearing and associated negative publicity tarnished the university's reputation. In his book *Academic Duty*, Kennedy elegantly documents these proceedings.[3] Other universities found themselves swept into this investigative maelstrom, subject to congressional scrutiny, and called to congressional hearings.

Most relations with the federal government involve far less acrimony. Congressional offices regularly consult university officials on policy and legislative issues. The venue may be formal hearings or informal visits. The procedures and protocol resemble those for state legislative hearings and visits. For hearings, the university provides well-prepared written testimony, which the university official reads verbatim to the committee members, and questioning follows. Although the topics are generally at a "higher level," such as the nation's health-care or energy policies, political concerns understandably lurk under the surface. For example, during the questioning delegates from coal-rich states may predictably "fish" for testimony that is supportive of coal-based energy. University testifiers, or course, can anticipate politically tainted questions and prepare for them.

As always, objective, unbiased answers must prevail to preserve university integrity.

Senior university officials, including the chief research officer, visit members of the congressional delegation in Washington, D.C., regularly. They are often accompanied by the institutional government relations officer, who may also be a lobbyist. University chief executive officers and chief research officers usually take every opportunity to meet with members of their home-state delegation—or at the very least, with senior members of their staff—whenever they are in the Washington, D.C., area. And they are usually well received, especially by representatives from the university's congressional district. During these visits, the university's research agenda is a frequent topic of discussion. As usual, the ultimate goal is to court support for a particular piece of legislation favoring the university. Large health-science centers and land-grant universities may predictably wish to influence budget appropriations for agencies such as the NIH and U.S. Department of Agriculture (USDA), respectively. Equally predictable, most visits also involve a pitch for earmark support for specific university programs.

In this context, the basic relationship between members of Congress and their home states or districts warrants comment. They represent their specific constituency—namely, the voters in that state (in the case of the Senate) or district (in the case of a member of the House of Representatives), but nobody else. When parlaying support for a particular issue such as an earmark, there is always the wish for reinforcement from Congress members representing another state or district. Unless there is some tangible advantage to their constituency, this wish will remain a pipe dream. Savvy chief research officers recognize this limitation. If additional out-of-state support is essential, they will somehow forge a beneficial collaboration with an institution in the other state to gain the desired help.

Several associations represent university interests at the national level at a less personal and politically charged level. Examples include the Council on Government Relations (COGR), the Association of American Universities (AAU), American Council on Education (ACE), and the Association of Public and Land-grant Universities (APLU). Each has its own characteristic areas of concentration and membership criteria. Although they differ substantially in many ways, various combinations of two or more of these organizations often collaborate to influence a particular federal policy.

These associations, which retain well-informed professional management personnel, prepare letters to government agencies and members of Congress based on the best interests of their constituents. Often template letters supporting a particular federal policy or piece of legislation are sent to university chief executive officers, who are asked to prepare and submit a supportive letter under their signature. These templates may be rerouted to the chief research officer, for example, for review to ensure that they accurately favor the university's interests—which they usually do. More often than not, there is some urgency to submission of these supportive letters. Logistically, shuttling draft letters among offices on campus for review (for example, chief executive officer to chief research officer to chief of staff and back to chief executive officer) causes delays that can preclude getting the letter to Washington, D.C., in time to be relevant. To be an effective participant in this process, the institution must develop speedy, efficient pathways to prepare and submit these letters. Since a great many of these efforts involve research, the chief research officer should actively seek to minimize turnover time of these requests for supportive letters.

Incidentally, insistence by the governing board, the chief executive officer, or the provost on previewing all communications concerning university interests prepared by the chief research officer, including these association-drafted "template" letters to members of Congress, may characterize mistrust of his or her abilities to handle the job. Indeed, it is diagnostic of a lack of confidence in the chief research officer's leadership skills. And it flouts the tenets of delegated authority. In these situations, the chief research officer must discuss the reasons for this untrusting micro-management with his or her superior (the chief executive officer or provost), for it undermines the university's overall managerial performance.

> K: *Realistically, how much does a letter from one university influence federal policymaking or legislation?*
> Smith: *Like any other political process, that all depends on who signed the letter. All else being equal, a letter from the president of a prestigious major university probably has more clout than a letter from a smaller, less prestigious institution.*
> K: *That could be rather discouraging for a smaller institution.*
> Smith: *Not always. As former Speaker of the House "Tip" O'Neal said, "all politics is local." Less prestigious universities from states or districts with powerful members of Congress can exert inordinate influence nationally. It may take no more than a letter from the local university's chief executive officer to unleash that political power.*

Industry Relations

Industry relations take on another guise. Typically, they constitute a business partnership with several possible dimensions. Examples include basic or applied research collaborations, licensing agreements, and federal research-facility operating partnerships. The size of the industrial partner and the scope of the collaboration vary across a broad spectrum. But there are common elements that characterize university–industry relations.

The universal communications backbone of these arrangements is a carefully worded contract prepared by the chief research officer (via the office of sponsored research or technology transfer) on the university side and the legal office on the industry side. Ideally, they cover all potential sources of conflict; the more salient issues deal with intellectual property and liability. Stated simplistically, the terms for intellectual property simplify to "what our people invented is ours, what your people invented is yours, and what our people invented jointly will be negotiated." Liability and indemnification also reduce to relatively straightforward terms; the university is liable for acts or omissions of only its own employees, officers, or agents. It does not accept third-party liability. And likewise for the industrial partner; it accepts liability for only its own employees. Parenthetically, state universities may be exempt from liability owing to sovereign immunity. In this context, they may be immune to tort liability, which is failure to meet a contract's legal requirements using a prudent degree of care.

Another skeletal communications aspect is the need for clearly defined university policies regulating its relations with private business. Industry leaders may not agree with a university's policies, such as the imperative to publish research results promptly and reluctance to accept indemnification clauses. However, if these rules are stated clearly and enforced consistently, then industry partners can and usually will adapt to them. Conversely, ambiguous or inconsistent policies undermine the chances for a good working relationship between universities and industry. Many chief research officers prepare simple, brief pocket-size brochures outlining university policies that relate to partnerships with industry for handing out at meetings, workshops, conferences, and other venues. Furthermore, some chief research officers prepare more inclusive notebooks documenting not only university policies but also services advantageous to industry partners, such as animal-care facilities, grant-proposal assistance, and other core sources of support.

The usual contact protocol rules within academe apply to industry. In most cases, initial talks between university and industry representatives do not include senior executives from either party. Faculty members and deans (or associate deans) generally meet with industry technical-staff members to iron out operational details of a partnership. Upon completion of the technical framework, senior executives join the discussions and ultimately finalize the deal. In this context, "senior executives" refers to the chief research officer and his or her industry counterpart, who usually carries the title "director" or "vice president" with some modifier. Note: some industry firms have a "director of academic relations." This individual's responsibilities may focus on graduate-student affairs and not necessarily on research collaborations. Thus, he or she may not be the appropriate representative to forge an effective research partnership. When launching a partnership, the chief research officer should ensure a priori that he or she is meeting with the right person. Indeed, this preparatory "surveillance" should extend beyond just that; the chief research officer should study the partner's organizational structure (who reports to whom), research mission, and other academic partnerships. Most of this information is available on the Internet.

To belabor the obvious, academic and industry cultures differ significantly. If these differences are not fully appreciated, they have the potential to constrain constructive relationships. Some are definitional, such as nonprofit versus for-profit tax status and basic research versus product-directed research orientation. Others are more subtle and must be recognized by the chief research officer if he or she is to communicate effectively with industrial partners. For example, a Ph.D. degree is usually a minimum qualification for top-level academic administrative positions, including the chief research officer and provost. In contrast, a doctoral degree is much less relevant for advancement to senior executive positions in industry. It goes beyond saying that an effective chief research officer must never underestimate the qualifications and skills of his or her counterpart in industry because of this difference; it would be arrogantly presumptuous and foolhardy.

Another noticeable difference is industry's propensity for confidentiality. Unlike the university's penchant for open communication, industry tends toward more reticence about its research efforts. Consequently, the chief research officer and all other university participants in a cooperative venture are asked routinely to sign a confidentiality (also called a "nondisclosure") agreement. These are not meant to stifle open communication between the two parties. On the contrary, they enable both university and industry partners to discuss proprietary issues freely among themselves without worrying that they will be leaked to competitors. Thus, university representatives, including faculty members and administrators, do not hesitate to sign these agreements. Nonetheless, as a matter of course the chief research office should examine the agreement carefully before signing to ensure that some unexpected clause (for example, one that restricts publication) does not slip by unnoticed.

Incidentally, whenever possible, the university should try to exempt students working in partnership with industry from signing confidentiality agreements. By signing an agreement, students cannot freely discuss what they are doing with university faculty advisers—unless they are working on the same project. Nor can they necessarily publish the results of their work without restrictions. There are, of course, trade-offs to be considered. Without a confidentiality agreement in place, the student may not participate meaningfully in a joint project. Thus, the chief research officer, graduate dean, and faculty members should weigh these considerations carefully and make decisions about the extent of student participation on a case-by-case basis.

Labor Unions

In some universities, another inquisitive party takes an interest in how the institution spends its money—namely, labor union officials. This occurs because labor unions have become a common feature on the academic landscape. In the United States, nearly half of the universities have faculty unions.[4] In addition, about fifty universities have graduate-student unions.[5] And in recent years, three major universities have launched postdoctoral unions—namely, the Connecticut

Health Sciences Center, the University of California system, and Rutgers University. From the chief research officer's perspective, these numbers aren't necessarily daunting. However, they presage a trend toward unionization.

The right to organize unions varies from state to state. Public-sector employees, including state university faculty members, have the right to unionize in some states but not others. Moreover, some "right to work" states rule that individual employees have the option not to join a union. Each state has a labor relations office that oversees union activities, including charges of unfair labor practices, or violations of state labor laws. For private universities, the federal National Labor Relations Board (NLRB) enforces the provisions of the National Labor Relations Act, which defines and protects the rights of private-sector employees to bargain collectively through elected representatives. Unions appeal unfair labor practices with the NLRB.

To converse knowledgeably about unions, it helps to know the union vocabulary. Unions arise when a group of employees decide voluntarily to function as a group to improve their working conditions. A core group, known as the "organizing committee," takes the lead in establishing the organization, often by affiliating with a large national labor organization, such as the American Federation of Teachers (AFT), the National Education Association (NEA), or the American Association of University Professors (AAUP). Some of these (for example, the AFT) are affiliated in turn with much larger national organizations such as the AFL-CIO.

To become the employees' legally recognized representative, the new union must "gain recognition." This process varies from state to state. But the most common is for prospective union employees to vote via an "authorization card," which is equivalent to a ballot. This election is held under the auspices of a state labor board or the NLRB for public and private institutions, respectively. If the majority of authorization cards favor the union's establishment, it gains formal recognition ("certification") to represent the employees. The union then writes its bylaws, sets dues, and elects a "bargaining committee" from among its members. If it is affiliated with a larger organization (such as the AFT), the union is known as a "local." It derives political and bargaining support from the larger union organization but maintains full autonomy over its own staff and sets its own policies. Employers generally have the option to recognize a nascent union voluntarily, which may mitigate the union's need to gain formal certification.

The bargaining committee meets with management representatives to negotiate a contract that defines working conditions. These negotiations comprise so-called collective bargaining. In most situations, management is required by law to engage in good-faith collective bargaining with a union that has been certified as representing that organization's employees. If negotiations stalemate, they reach an impasse—the point at which no further progress can be made toward a contract agreement. "Impasse resolution" may involve arbitration (an impartial third party rules on disputed contract issues), mediation (a third party does not issue a ruling but simply attempts to bring both sides to agreement through compromise), and fact finding (a third party reviews each side's supporting evidence and then issues an advisory opinion in favor of either side's package of proposals). Laws on the procedures for impasse resolution vary from state to state.

The contract defines explicitly all anticipated working conditions, ranging from base salary, pay raises, vacation allowances, and pension plans to working hours. It is a binding legal document. If the employer—namely, the university—fails to abide by the terms of the contract, a union member can file a grievance with the employer. Importantly, the contract describes procedures for resolving a grievance. Usually, this is accomplished within the university without recourse to outside litigation.

Note the subtle language changes: the union bargaining committee meets with management. In these terms, management comprises the individuals representing the university in any negotiations about union members' working conditions. The conversation now involves collective bargaining between labor and management.

The introduction of organized labor to university campuses brought with it a new set of rules governing administrators' communications with union members. For employees as a collective class, any discussions concerning their employment or working conditions—salary, fringe benefits, pay raises, working hours, tenure and promotion, and so on—must be directed to union leadership. Of course, these issues may be discussed one on one by the employer and employee, but the terms of an individual's employment must conform to the contractual agreement between the university (employer) and the collective employees who are represented by the union. A union member's dissatisfaction with some working condition that was not articulated in the collective bargaining agreement, such as an employer's post hoc request for working in the evening or on weekends, may be filed by the employee with the union, which then negotiates a resolution on the employee's behalf. In particularly contentious disputes with an employer, an employee files a formal grievance with the union, and this triggers a negotiated sequence of actions to resolve the disagreement. In many settings, these interactions between the unionized employee and the employer take on the adversarial qualities inherent in contract-law disputes.

Graduate-student unionization has generated considerable concern about faculty-student relationships. Union organizers argue that graduate teaching assistants—and many research assistants—are, indeed, employees who deserve the same collective-bargaining rights as other more traditional university employees. Opponents worry that unionization erodes the fundamental mentoring relationship between graduate students and faculty advisers. In a union context, the faculty members take on the role of managers, thus pitting them implicitly against their employees, the graduate students.

In a 2000 landmark case that set conditions for union membership, the NLRB ruled that some but not all graduate students at New York University (NYU) are employees and are therefore covered under the National Labor Relations Act.[6] Specifically included in the bargaining unit are "all teaching assistants [TAs], graduate assistants [GAs], research assistants [RAs] ... employed by New York University." Importantly, research assistants funded by external grants in the Physics, Biology, Chemistry and the Center for Neuroscience (CNS) departments are not included in the unit because they:

> have no expectations placed upon them other than their academic advancement, which involves research. They receive stipends and tuition remission as do other GAs, RAs, and TAs, but are not required to commit a set number of hours performing specific tasks for NYU .... The research they perform is the same research they would perform as part of their studies in order to complete their dissertation, regardless of whether they received funding. The funding ... therefore, is more akin to a scholarship.[7]

In contrast, research assistants who are assigned specific tasks under the direction and control of a faculty member are not excluded. In summary, union membership is available to graduate students who teach or perform specific research assignments but not to those who do dissertation research. Moreover, union eligibility does not depend on salary funding source.

The unionization of postdoctoral scholars has raised similar concerns about their mentoring relationship with faculty advisers.[8] With only three recognized postdoctoral unions, however, there is insufficient evidence for judgments about the impact of unionization. From a practical point of view, the major differences are that pay and benefits have become subject to negotiations that do not involve the principal investigator of a grant. Significantly, terms and conditions of a grant or contract are not subject to negotiations. Thus, the amount of postdoctoral salary awarded by the granting agency is not negotiable. Although federal agencies have not published specific policies, grant budgets requesting postdoctoral salary levels set by collective bargaining as they are for unionized faculty member salaries would seem quite justifiable.

Do unions affect a university's research efforts? The answer seems to be no. Faculty members are unionized at numerous research universities that have quite respectable research programs. There are few anecdotal situations where union activities might have impacted university research. In a worst-case scenario, University of Hawaii faculty members went on strike in 2001 following an unresolved impasse in contract negotiations. Human-health–related workers (primarily medical school clinical faculty members) and faculty members who could document a convincing need to care for research animals or facilities were exempt from the strike. Except for clinicians, few researchers could justify an exemption. Nonetheless, despite picket lines and some harsh words, there were no blatant attempts to hinder researchers' access to their laboratories. And their research continued unabated, although perhaps at a reduced intensity. Many faculty members met with their graduate students off-campus to avoid crossing picket lines. (Incidentally, faculty members were not paid their salary during the strike. However, when a contract agreement was finally reached, it contained a provision for retroactive payment of the foregone salary.) Conceivably, unionization could improve a university's research infrastructure if the unions negotiated lighter teaching loads, thus providing faculty members with more time for scholarly activities.

Moreover, there is little evidence that graduate-student unions have had a deleterious impact on faculty-student mentoring relations. Despite the rancor surrounding some graduate-student organizing efforts, there has not been a flood of anecdotal breaches between student and teacher in the academic realm. Collective bargaining has focused on work issues such as salaries, numbers of students in class, child care and other fringe benefits, and maximum number of work hours but not on academic issues. Furthermore, in a 2000 survey, "results show that faculty do not have negative attitudes toward graduate student bargaining and believe that student bargaining does not interfere with their ability to advise, instruct, and mentor their graduate students."[9]

The chief research officer has a low profile on the union landscape. Indeed, he or she has little visibility in contract negotiations. Commonly, the university's bargaining team consists of financial and human resources personnel with negotiating experience. They may seek advice from the chief research officer on a particular issue, but that is generally the extent of his or her involvement. Moreover, as a member of management, the chief research officer must limit conversation with union members regarding terms under negotiation. Any comment—even inadvertent—disparaging union activities could be construed as an unfair labor practice in violation of the Labor Relations Act. Although a single, isolated remark will not trigger a grievance, persistently vocal opposition may constitute a violation.

> *K: A union contract covers pay raises for all employees. How can an employer like a university dean or departmental chair reward merit under that system?*
> *Smith: True, the unions must represent all employees. However, they aren't by nature opposed to rewarding merit. A contract could specify that a percentage of an overall pay raise package is set aside for merit-based pay increases. For example, an average 3 percent pay raise may be allocated with 2 percent across-the-board and the remaining 1 percent according to merit.*
> *K: Suppose a disgruntled employee files a grievance that has no obvious basis. Does the union have to represent the employee under these circumstances?*
> *Smith: Yes. The union dares not ignore an employee's grievance, no matter how frivolous it might appear to be. Otherwise, the union may be cited for nonrepresentation, which is a violation of the National Labor Relations Act.*

Notes

1. PR Newswire "Welcome to MEDIAtlas," January 2, 2011, http://mediatlas.prnewswire.com/mediatlas/Login.aspx?LanguageID=1033&RedirectLink (accessed January 2, 2011).

2. National Association for Biomedical Research, "Member Services," 2010, http://www.nabr.org/About-NABR/Member_Services.aspx (accessed January 2, 2011).

3. D. Kennedy, *Academic Duty* (Cambridge, Mass.: Harvard University Press, 1997).

4. National Education Association, "Frequently Asked Questions: Collective Bargaining in Higher Education," 2010, http://www.nea.org/home/35275.htm (accessed January 2, 2011).

5. C. M. Wickens, "The Organizational Impact of University Labor Unions," *Higher Education,* 56 (November 2008): 545–64.

6. National Labor Relations Board, "New York University and International Union, United Automobile, Aerospace and Agricultural Implement Workers of America, AFL-CIO, Case No. 2-RC 22082." *National Labor Relations Board Decisions* 332, (2000): 1205–22.

7. Ibid., p. 1220.

8. B. L. Benderly, "Can Labor Unions Work for Postdocs?" *Science Careers,* October 3, 2003, http://sciencecareers.sciencemag.org/career_development/previous_issues/articles/2590/can_labor_unions_work_for_postdocs (accessed January 4, 2011).

9. G. J. Hewitt, "Graduate Student Employee Collective Bargaining and the Educational Relationship Between Faculty and Graduate Students," *Journal of Collective Negotiations,* 29, no. 2, pp. 153–66.

CHAPTER 3

Strategic Planning

K: *How important is a strategic plan in guiding your decisions?*
Smith: *We all have a strategic plan. As the famous American baseball player*
Yogi Berra said, "If you don't know where you are going, you might wind
up someplace else." But its actual usefulness is sometimes compromised
by external events.
K: *You do try to rely on it, don't you?*
Smith: *Usually. But not always.*

Preparation of a Strategic Plan

Yogi got it right: the university should have a strategic plan that sets goals for the institution, including its research enterprise. The six regional associations that accredit public and private schools, colleges, and universities in the United States agree. They require universities to have strategic plans and to show adherence to them. For example, the Western Association of Schools and Colleges (WASC) sets specific criteria for the "strategic thinking and planning" process, the alignment of priorities and resource allocation, and the assessment of these efforts in their *Handbook of Accreditation* 2008:[1]

> The institution periodically engages its multiple constituencies, including faculty, in institutional reflection and planning processes which assess its strategic position, articulate priorities, examine the alignment of its purposes, core functions and resources, and define the future direction of the institution. The institution monitors the effectiveness of its plans and planning processes, and revises them as appropriate.

The other five accrediting associations have similar standards. And they all take this seriously. Failure to provide convincing evidence of a functional plan can jeopardize accreditation reaffirmation, as a few institutions sadly learn each year.

As the WASC states, the university develops its strategic plan in consultation with its "multiple constituencies." They include the chief research officer, who may be expected to orchestrate preparation of the plan's research component. However, his or her actual influence over the plan's content will depend on the institutional culture. At universities with strong faculty governance, the chief research officer's input may be more administrative than directional. Faculty committees will do the planning and the writing. That is not an insult; it is a welcome corollary to an active research faculty. In sharp contrast, at universities with a limited number of research-active faculty members, the chief research officer may be expected to prepare the plan's initial draft singlehandedly. In either case, the draft plan must be vetted through extensive consultation with multiple constituencies, including the faculty members, usually represented by a faculty senate, the deans, and fellow senior administrators such as the provost and the chief executive officer.

Where does the strategic planning effort begin? To find the starting line, it's necessary to back up a step. If the university is part of a multicampus system, the system presumably has an overall strategic plan that defines the relationships between campuses and their separate missions. Individual campus planning derives from the system plan, and this mainly involves elaborating and refining the system plan. Importantly, the campus plan must adhere to the tenets of the system plan, although the system's planning assumptions may be modified to suit an individual campus's unique character. These assumptions cover axiomatic topics such as commitments to general education, diversity, state-of-the-art information technology, need-based financial aid, fiscal responsibility, and continual quality improvement. For the chief research officer, it is important to ensure that the assumptions also include a commitment to research. Within this framework, the chief research officer can then begin to prepare the campus plan's research component.

For starters, the plan should reinforce the importance of research to campus academics. This may seem to be self-evident, but it bears mentioning. Even in the most mature research universities, there may be faculty members who question this priority: "Our job is to educate students." This generally means undergraduates—not research-active graduate students. Or, "our job is to serve the citizens of the state." This often means in terms of service, such as agricultural extension or teacher training. And in less research-intensive institutions, there may be a cadre of faculty members who were not necessarily expected to do research as a condition of employment or were not provided the resources necessary to maintain a productive program. They, too, will gravitate to the undergraduate teaching or service universe. These individuals may play a very important and valuable role within the university, but their voices may drown out a call for research. Furthermore, the strategic plan will become a public document. It never hurts to reiterate the university's research mission in every possible forum.

There are many members of the general public who share the view that the university's sole job is to educate undergraduates (and to field a winning football team). This generally reflects unfamiliarity with the academic research mission. Thus, the chief research officer should seize the strategic-planning opportunity to educate and inform the public about the importance and benefits of research and its role in the university. In this context, the plan will ideally include an introductory statement that all faculty members are expected to maintain an independent research program. This may also assert the importance of including undergraduates in research endeavors.

Specificity

The remainder of the research plan addresses specific goals. Specificity comes in several forms. The most straightforward is numerical. In their strategic plans, many universities set goals to increase research activity by a certain amount. Two examples are, "The university will strive to rank in the top fifty public institutions in research expenditures by 2015;" or alternatively, "The university's research annual expenditures will increase to $450 million by fiscal year 2015." Other numeric goals seen in strategic plans (posted on the Internet) are "The number of National Academy members will increase to twelve by 2016" and "All of the university's research programs will be ranked in the top 25th percentile by 2018." From the chief research officer's perspective, it is relatively easy to come up with these numeric goals and to incorporate them into the plan. Consensus in this regard among the various constituencies comes fairly easily because specific academic programs are not singled out. The goals are lofty, and everybody benefits. Nobody has been left out, but nobody in particular is accountable, either.

Another form of specificity identifies high-priority areas. This can be an extremely difficult planning section to prepare because of its implications for future resource allocations. Nearly every discipline or organizational unit will inevitably make its case for preferential consideration. To help navigate through this stormy sea, it is useful a priori to emphasize the university's commitment to maintaining its existing highest quality and most productive programs. Of course, this just makes good sense: "do no harm." Disruptive tension between academic programs competing to achieve recognition as a high-priority area can be mitigated further by focusing the plan on areas where the institution has a comparative advantage owing to geography, location, history, ethnic or cultural features, and local economic conditions, to name a few. This makes good sense, too: "play from strength."

With this broad framework of comparative advantages, it may prove easier to identify programmatic specializations. Examples include astronomy in Hawaii, dairy science in Wisconsin, alpine ecology in Colorado, oceanography in Rhode Island, and petroleum engineering in Texas. This level of specificity may be unfeasible politically without broad compromises that greatly expand the list of priority areas. That should be no surprise. However, this expansion is generally acceptable to the chief research officer and the provost if the outcome is a list of specifically identified priority areas that they can then refer to during the plan's implementation.

To be an effective tool for future decision making, the final plan must have buy-in. This is an extremely important point. Otherwise, the plan's legitimacy can, and most probably will, be called into question: "I don't like your decision." "But it adheres to the strategic plan." "Whose strategic plan? I was never asked for input." That kind of questioning will seriously compromise the plan's usefulness. Therefore, the importance of extensive consultation cannot be overemphasized.

Responsibility for ensuring adequate consultation usually lies in the chief executive's office, who may delegate it to the provost. A working draft is often made public, and comments are solicited from a broad constituency, including members of the general public. As part of this effort, the chief research officer should seize every opportunity to seek input on the research component. This cannot be an insincere exercise. The chief research officer should not be surprised to receive telephone calls, e-mails, and personal visits touting the importance of some specific discipline or program from members of not only the university community but also the general public. The draft plan must be amended (usually by the chief executive's office) to accommodate meaningful input from these multiple constituencies.

As a consequence, whatever programmatic specificity that was built into the original draft will usually be diluted through this process. The list of high-priority areas may become so long that the only practical outcome is to revert to generalities: "The university will invest in high-priority areas." Ultimately, some plan will emerge, and it may lack any programmatic specificity. In this case, the art in preparing the final version of the research component lies in the chief research officer's ability to craft general guidelines that allow for future preferential resource allocations to programs that can convincingly be called high priority.

The balance between buy-in and specificity merits further comment. Ultimately, buy-in trumps specificity. That cardinal premise raises a penetrating question: what good is a watered down plan that doesn't identify specific high-priority areas for future investment? In an ideal world, specific priority setting is the whole point of strategic planning, for it sets definitive guidelines for programmatic investment. But, from a practical perspective, buy-in is far more important than specificity. With experience, an administrator can usually decide if a programmatic area adheres to a well-constructed plan that favors something general like comparative advantages, but he or she can never gain post hoc acceptance of these decisions without initial buy-in to the plan in general. Clearly, an administrator such as the chief research officer can't flout the strategic plan and interpret it however he or she wants. That would be disingenuous. But if the final plan doesn't name specific priority areas, the operational goal in decision making is to try to honor the plan's spirit.

The planning process epitomizes the role of "shared governance" in university administration. Many people representing various constituencies have a say in the planning effort. That is good. Ultimately, however, the chief research officer will be held accountable for the research component's success or failure. Governance is no longer shared at this juncture. Therefore, the chief research officer (like the other top-level executives) must be granted some flexibility in interpreting and implementing the plan. That does not mean that he or she has a license to ignore the plan; on the contrary, the plan must be followed. The accrediting associations (and many observant faculty members and deans) keep an eye on that. Whenever major decisions are based on the plan, the chief research officer must prepare a justification of the alignment of this action with the plan's goals. And that is where reasonable flexibility must be allowed and, indeed, expected by the watchful observers. That is generally not a significant problem if there has been meaningful consultation right from the beginning.

Often, individual colleges, departments, and offices within a university prepare their own, more focused strategic plan as part of the overall campus-planning effort. Although these must adhere to the campus plan, they can be much more specific when dealing with internal priorities and operating procedures. And they can be long. Indeed, the Strategic Plan FY2009-FY2013 of the Office of the Senior Vice President for Research at Penn State is a fifty-eight-page document that combines planning with assessment.[2] Or they can be short. The UCLA Strategic Research Web site is about one page, with links to the university's six priority thematic research areas.[3] The preparation of these plans follows the same guidelines and process as the broader, campus-wide efforts.

> K: *Since the chief research officer will be held accountable for decisions based on the strategic plan's research components, does he or she have the authority to impose a plan without heeding stakeholder opinions?*
> Smith: *Technically yes. This authority accompanies the responsibility and accountability for the institution's research endeavours.*
> K: *Then why should a chief research officer willingly compromise the plan's specificity by seeking input from a broad constituency?*
> Smith: *The written document is only part of the strategic planning process. In fact, it may just sit on the shelf. The planning process with its extensive consultation serves a broader purpose: the opportunity to articulate the chief research officer's vision of the research enterprise. Stakeholder feedback provides clarity to this vision.*

Implementation of the Strategic Plan

It bears repeating that the strategic objectives and priorities should be aligned with the institution's resource allocations. Indeed, that alignment is a performance standard monitored by the accreditation associations. For example, WASC requires that: "Planning processes at the institution define and, to the extent possible, align academic, personnel, fiscal, physical, and technological needs with the strategic objectives and priorities of the institution."[4] This is often much easier said than done. In a textbook world, the chief research officer would develop a goal-oriented plan to implement the strategic research objectives. This would be accompanied by dollar amounts, task assignments, and timelines. Moreover, the chief research officer and the provost would agree to coordinate the distribution of funding, faculty hires, fund-raising priorities, and other resources, such as space, according to plan priorities. Some university strategic plans include this coopera-tion between the provost and the vice president for research in the plan's imple-mentation as a strategic goal. (This may be consequent to previous failures of the two officers to work synergistically, as discussed in the section on reporting lines in chapter 1.) As a matter of good management, the chief research officer, the provost, and usually the chief finance officer must make a genuine and transparent effort to fulfill these idealistic implementation plans. After all, they will be held accountable in this regard by the chief executive officer, the governing board, and the accreditation associations.

Unfortunately, reality quickly takes control of even the best-laid plans. Most strategic plans extend forward for five years or more. During that time period, changes in top leadership—the chief executive officer, composition of the govern-ing board, even the governor—can often trigger development of a new strategic plan before the old one has run its course. New leadership may expound novel, dif-ferent priorities that do not fall within one of the broad categories of the existing plan. Or they may propose quite different ways to achieve the existing plan's goals. These changes can have a serious impact on the university's overall research direc-tion and can thoroughly disrupt ongoing implementation efforts. The chief research officer must be keenly alert to these possibilities whenever there is a major change in leadership and must be prepared to either adapt quickly or get out of the way.

Numeric goals are intrinsically elusive. Although they are easy to incorporate into a strategic plan, many factors complicate their attainment. Targets based on performance relative to other institutions, such as breaking into the top fifty universities, are particularly difficult to achieve, because most other universities have a similar goal: to improve their standing in national rankings. For example, consider the goal of reaching $450 million in research expenditures by 2015. By that date, competing universities will also have increased their expenditures, so unless the institution's growth rate is faster than theirs, it has actually fallen behind relative to them. The university may have successfully implemented its strategic plan. It increased its overall research activity, which is the true spirit of the strategic plan, but it didn't move forward. Unfortunately, there is no such thing as altruism in this business—even between two institutions in the same system. Thus, success in achieving this kind of numeric goal depends not only on the chief research officer's efforts—no matter how valiant—but also on the success of competing institutional efforts. And that is not something that the chief research officer can easily influence.

Likewise, achieving a targeted amount of research expenditures depends on uncontrollable factors. Federal funding priorities may shift away from an institution's strengths, the overall amount of extramural funding may drop (or not increase), one or more highly productive researchers may leave the university, to name a few. It takes little imagination to think up numerous other additions to this list. Most seasoned administrators recognize that it is not worth worrying too much about things like this that cannot be controlled.

Technically, two pathways lead to increased research expenditures. The first is broad; many faculty members travel it. To accomplish this, the university hires additional productive faculty members and increases the productivity of those already on board in numerous disciplines across campus. Investments according to the strategic plan may favor specific academic areas, but the ultimate goal is to enhance a broad spectrum of research programs. In contrast, the second pathway is narrow; few faculty members travel it. The university concentrates resources on only a few lucrative research programs to maximize expenditure numbers. That strategy accomplishes the goal—research expenditures are up—but it does not necessarily improve the university's overall scholarly performance. Because of the necessity for broad-based buy-in, most strategic plans point down the broad pathway. However, zealously goal-oriented implementation of a broad-based plan may drift toward the narrow pathway.

Incidentally, if an institution's strategic plan calls for increasing the number of faculty members in the national academies (science, medicine, or engineering) to some target amount, it may find that goal equally elusive. There are two ways to accomplish this: grow your own or bring them in from the outside. The former is by far the cheaper way to go about this, but it requires talented faculty members with the credentials necessary for this kind of recognition. The chief research officer must be prepared to support these individuals in any way possible without alienating other faculty members.

Of course, selection to a national academy ultimately depends on recognition of the candidate's merits by peers. But the home institution can help matters in subtle ways. Professional reputations are boosted whenever an individual receives a formal award based on his or her research. Local awards beget national awards, and national awards beget international awards. Thus, the chief research officer should always work with the deans to nominate qualified faculty members for an award. Moreover, the institution can help itself by increasing the number of in-house research awards, including named professorships; the chief research officer and the university's development officer can play a major role in this regard. There is some risk involved here. As a faculty member's fame increases, so does the attention of other aspiring universities. The chief research officer and the provost must always respond to any serious outside offers to these star faculty members.

And that introduces the other way of increasing the number of national academy members: bring them in from the outside. In all likelihood, this will be expensive. The price tag will vary from one case to another, and there is little way of predicting a priori what it will cost eventually. But the final number may exceed $10 million in unusual cases. To put the cost in perspective, many universities are offering young assistant professors start-up packages in excess of $1 million these days, and that number just keeps getting larger with time. Furthermore, any university with an academy member on its faculty will also most probably counter an outside offer from another institution, thus upping the price. The chief research officer and the provost must carefully calculate the return on investment when considering this kind of hire.

The wisdom of recruiting national academy members or other "superstars" benefits from further reflection. The issue of money can become more complicated. The initial costs of hiring highly successful researchers can be daunting and out of reach for many institutions. But they enhance institutional prestige, and that may attract more private donations and institutional research grants. Also, some national rankings factor in the number of national academy members on the faculty, thus elevating institutional attractiveness. So, on that score, the institution may recoup its large initial investment. If an institution can afford these expensive national-academy level hires, an internal debate usually focuses quickly on whether it might be a better long-term investment to recruit two or three young or mid-career researchers for the same or considerably less money.

In comparison to these numeric goals, implementing a plan that invests in specific high-priority academic programs can be fairly straightforward. That is, in the best of conditions. The generally acknowledged protocol is for the chief research officer to respond to initiatives submitted by the faculty. A good catalyst for innovative ideas is a university-wide competition with a broadly disseminated call for proposals that are compatible with the strategic plan. For example, "Money is available for creative projects that support the university's high-priority initiatives. Submit your application by the deadline." Most universities have one or more faculty committees that review these applications and recommend those to receive an award. This process is standard fare and is generally immune to serious objection. The results, of course, may be questioned by those who were not funded. Thus, the decision-making process must be transparent and well documented.

Alternatively, the chief research officer, perhaps together with the provost, may choose to allocate resources directly to a high-priority area without meaningful faculty consultation or participation: "After all, the faculty members were consulted when the strategic plan was written; now we're implementing their directives." For the chief research officer, this is an appealing argument, for it provides considerable discretion in any decision making. And it might be argued that this method for plan implementation is far more effective because the resources can be focused for maximal impact. In reality, most chief research officers would probably prefer this flexibility, but they must balance this against the need to maintain the faculty members' respect and trust.

Two major shortcomings can complicate hiring aspects of implementing a strategic plan. The first involves money. It is no mystery that not much can be accomplished if money is in short supply. Since that is usually the case at most universities, progress may be slow, and patience is required. Bit by bit, however, incremental investments can generate meaningful results over time.

The second involves size of the faculty and therefore the number of discretionary hiring opportunities. If a strategic plan calls for building up expertise in a particular area, the number of available faculty positions to be filled can become rate-limiting. Large universities will have an advantage over their smaller counterparts in this situation. For example, the physiology department may have been awarded the funds to hire into a campus-wide high-priority area such as stem-cell research. But, unfortunately, the department desperately needs somebody to teach renal physiology to first-year medical students. The department's and the university's priorities do not match in this case. In a large university, the provost may be able to solve the dilemma by providing a second position to fill the teaching need, thus preserving the option to hire a high-priority stem-cell researcher according to the strategic plan. This solution may not be available at smaller universities. Less prestigious institutions may also encounter serious difficulties in attracting qualified faculty members in popular fields.

There is an additional subtle aspect of faculty hiring that involves money. If the university recruits celebrated faculty (no matter what their rank) into its high-priority areas, their starting salaries may significantly exceed those of the existing faculty members. This all-too-common phenomenon is called "salary compression." It raises the "equity" issue, which the provost usually cannot just dismiss with a shrug of the shoulders. The human resources office, the faculty union, or the governing board policies may insist on rebalancing an entire department's salary structure to relieve compression. How this is handled depends on the case and the university's culture. However, it is not unusual in these situations for the university to conduct a department-wide (if not even wider) salary study to ensure that the existing faculty members are treated equitably. And this can cost additional salary money. Incidentally, *equity* does not necessarily mean "equality;" equity studies take merit, time in service, and other factors into consideration.

Curiously, the most subtle impediment to implementing a strategic plan may be opportunism. Despite the strategic goal to hire into some specific high-priority area in their department, the faculty members may prefer to hire some highly qualified individual in a totally different field. The rationale is that "we should always hire the best individual available in our overall discipline." For example, although the posted job opening was for a high-priority stem-cell researcher, a well-funded, highly regarded membrane biophysicist just became available. For many administrators, that is a difficult argument to counter. This is especially true for the chief research officer who may be attracted by the thought of more research expenditures from somebody who is well funded, regardless of the strategic plan.

Ultimately, implementation of the strategic plan's research component and the attendant complications illustrate the need for a tight, cooperative working relationship between the provost and the chief research officer. Indeed, it is critical to any successful effort. This is well known by any savvy chief executive officer, who undoubtedly will be keeping an eye on how well they work together in this context. The ability to maintain a well-coordinated working relationship between the provost and the chief research officer in this context can be a major test of the chief executive officer's leadership skills.

> K: *Opportunism is an interesting concept. Why should a university simply hire the best person available in a broadly defined area, regardless of the strategic plan? Why bother making a research plan if that's what you're going to do?*
>
> Smith: *Good question. But as Yogi said, you need to have some vision of where you're going, even if you don't always stay on the pathway. Again, big universities have all the advantages here. They have more hiring options. Smaller and less prestigious universities will often be tempted to jump at opportunities when they come along, regardless of any strategic plan. In my opinion, that's not such a bad practice.*
>
> K: *So you advocate that getting good faculty members takes precedence over the focused hiring into high-priority areas identified in the strategic plan?*
>
> Smith: *Yes. If the opportunities arise, grab them. In the long run, I think that you end up with a better quality faculty. And for me, that is paramount.*

Notes

1. Accrediting Commission for Senior Colleges and Universities, *Handbook of Accreditation,* Standard 4.1 (Alameda, Calif.: Western Association of Schools and Colleges, 2008), p. 21.
2. Pennsylvania State University, Office of the Senior Vice President for Research, "Strategic Plan FY2009-FY2013," 2008, http://www.research.psu.edu/about/documents/strategicplan.pdf (accessed January 16, 2011).
3. University of California, Los Angeles, Office of the Vice Chancellor for Research, "Strategic Planning," 2008, http://www.ovcr.ucla.edu/index.php?section=pages&id=149 (accessed January 16, 2011).
4. Accrediting Commission, Standard 4.2, p. 21.

CHAPTER 4

Resources

K: What resources do you have available to accomplish the strategic plan's goals?
Smith: For the chief research officer and nearly everyone else in the university,
the term "resource" most often means money. So the usual answer is
money, perhaps coupled with the power of persuasion.
K: Surely there must be other resources. How about space and students?
Smith: Yes, those, too. Obtaining each of these resources poses challenges in an
ironic order of increasing difficulty: money, space, and students.

Money

Money means different things to different people. For the cell biologist, it means laboratory supplies and equipment. For the English scholar, it means time— usually available by buying out of teaching obligations. And for the anthropologist, it means travel. For all faculty members, however, money means student salaries. Money becomes extremely important in this context because of the pivotal role played by graduate students in most academic research programs.

In another dimension, money means summer salary for many faculty members. In the chief research officer's eyes, that is important because summer is when the nine-month faculty members can devote their attention to research. Parenthetically, for medical school and agricultural-college faculty members, summer salary is usually not a concern; they have annual appointments. This occurs because the medical curriculum extends throughout the year, including summer, to take advantage of all available clinical opportunities for students. And illness doesn't take a vacation. Also, most agriculture appointments are annual because summer is the primary growing season, and that is when crop-oriented field studies take place.

To be effective, the chief research officer must have an appreciation of the different meanings of money for various faculty disciplines. Some individuals are naturally aware of these differences because of circumstances in their own background. Say, for example, that the chief research officer is a biochemist, his or her mother is a music professor, father is a lawyer, and older sister is an engineer. Variations on this eclectic environment are easily imagined. But other individuals may not have been exposed to these various perspectives on the meaning of money. It is hoped that they recognize this early in their career as chief research officers because they can then adapt by appointing associates with sensitivity and understanding complementary to their own.

For the chief financial officer, money comes in different forms. In general, funds used for current university operations are called "current funds," and they are divided into "restricted" and "unrestricted" categories. By definition, restricted funds have explicit restrictions imposed by an external entity, such as a federal agency or a private donor. For example, research grant funds must be spent in support of the funded project. Or a donor may earmark a gift to support a named professorship in cell biology. In these cases, the money cannot be used for any other purposes. The primary sources of restricted funds are sponsored projects and gifts. These restrictions often cause confusion among the general public, including legislators. They may see a large pool of restricted university money and, not knowing about the restrictions, assume falsely that it can be used in an unrestricted manner.

In contrast, unrestricted funds have no restrictions imposed on them by entities outside the university. Understandably, from the university's perspective, including the chief research officer and all faculty members, the most useful money is unrestricted. Common sources are endowed gifts, patent-generated revenue, clinical income, and interest earned on various components of the university's budget (such as tuition). In reality, these funds are not truly free of restrictions, for they are still subject to university and perhaps state spending regulations. For example, alcohol may be bought only in certain circumstances; preferred contract vendors, including travel agencies, must be used; and three bids may be required for purchases exceeding a threshold amount. Moreover, some sources of revenue are linked to their expenditures. For example, tuition and fee income is generally spent on items benefiting the students. Similarly, revenue from a self-supporting activity such as an animal-care unit is used to pay expenditures incurred by that unit.

The source of money also dictates its usefulness. In public universities, money from the state's general fund may be unrestricted for accounting purposes, but it must be spent within the constraints of state guidelines. Commonly, unspent balances cannot be carried forward from one year to the next. Furthermore, there may be limitations on travel, especially international travel. Of course, all money is valuable regardless of source, but these two constraints limit the usefulness of state money for the university researcher. In some cases, though, state money can be very useful for personnel salaries. In many states, the salaries become part of the ongoing state budget and a de facto recurring resource over time. Also, many states pay fringe benefits out of a separate pool, thus sparing the university that cost from its appropriated budget. This is a significant asset. For example, if the fringe benefit rate is 33 percent of the salary, the value of the state money increases by a third when used for salaries.

To take advantage of this state-funded fringe-benefit "bonus" if it is available, university financial officers try to fund as many personnel as possible with state general funds. Thus, they try to adjust their budgets to shift personnel costs to state funds. This is a powerful way to enhance the usefulness of state money. Moreover, there may be swapping of funds between offices to maximize use of these state funds for salaries: "I'll give you $100,000 in nongeneral funds to buy a piece of equipment if you'll give me $100,000 in general funds to cover my personnel costs. That way, I save $33,000 in fringe benefit costs that the state pays." In that example, the exchange rate is $1.33 in nonstate money for $1 in state money.

The chief research officer should occasionally survey whether any of these cost transfers involve personnel whose salaries are included in an externally funded grant budget. Transferring salary expenditures—or even a portion of a salary—from the grant to a state source (or any other source, for that matter) may at first glance seem like a good idea; this frees up salary money on the grant that can be rebudgeted to some other needy purpose. If this amount exceeds 25 percent of the budgeted salary on most federal awards, though, prior agency approval will be required. Also, if the committed effort remains the same, the transfer means that the university is now voluntarily sharing the cost of the research project. This could be a significant concern for two reasons. First, the voluntary cost sharing may reduce the amount of money that the university receives in indirect costs from the federal government. Second, this transfer may reduce the amount of research expenditures, and that may affect some aspect of state support. Thus, the chief research and financial officers should calculate the financial benefit of these cost transfers. Although they may seem like "good business" prima facie, there is a potential for subtle negative consequences.

Private universities operate with many fewer fiscal restrictions. Generally, they derive operating revenue from three main sources: tuition, endowment income, and indirect costs on extramural grants (which will be discussed below). The only meaningful limitations on spending these funds are those specified by an endowment donor. Otherwise, all money from these three sources can be treated as if they were in a single pool. The university's balance sheets will itemize the sources of revenue, but the spenders of the money (the provost, the chief research officer, and so forth on down the line) may never know the detailed source of their allocated funds. To them, it doesn't make any difference. Of course, if they receive state support in return for providing specific services, private universities may have to deal with imposed spending limitations on the state funds.

Funds for Sponsored Projects

Funds for sponsored projects come from federal, state, and local governments; private corporations; and gifts to support financially some research and other university activities. They may be in the form of grants, contracts, or gifts, and they are always restricted. The restrictions associated with these funds vary by fund source. For example, federal research grant funds must be spent on the research project described explicitly in the proposal. Alternatively, gift funds may sponsor research in a broadly defined area with relatively flexible project constraints.

The source of sponsored-projects funds—namely, sponsored research— requires further clarification. What is sponsored research? Backing up yet another step, why is it important to know exactly what is meant by the term "sponsored research?" Because the university must adhere to acceptable accounting standards and distinguish a sponsored-research grant or contract from a gift.

But to answer the original question, in its simplest form, sponsored research is research that is funded by a grant like those awarded by the NSF or NIH. Indeed, all federal grants and contracts are by nature sponsored research. The grant proposal contains a list of specific aims to be accomplished (or hypotheses to be tested), a timeline for achieving those aims, and a budget. Moreover, the principal investigator is required to submit an annual report to the granting agency that documents progress toward achieving the specific aims. This includes publications, patents, and copyrights arising from the research. In addition, the university provides the granting agency with periodic reports on how the grant money was spent (the financial status report). Most research-active faculty members know this procedure well. If they have a grant or contract, they are conducting sponsored research. In this context, the granting agency is the sponsor and is actually buying the research and its results. And the principal investigator is providing a "deliverable" in the form of the annual report. Agreements for sponsored projects also usually include terms and conditions for the disposition of tangible or intangible properties such as equipment, data, and intellectual property. The presence of these terms and conditions in a grant or contract define the activity as a sponsored project.

Incidentally, the terms "grants" and "contracts" have been used as if they were the same. Both grants and contracts constitute sponsored research, but technically they're not the same. And, for legal reasons, the federal government goes to great length to distinguish between the two in the Federal Grant and Cooperative Agreement Act.[1] In their terms, a grant is awarded to accomplish a specific goal. The usual purpose is to enhance knowledge about a topic or to provide services or training for the recipient's or public's benefit. Responsibility for the performance of the project rests primarily with the principal investigator, with little or no involvement of the granting agency. If a federal-granting agency, such as the NIH, intends to play a significant role in a grant's programmatic activities, the award is redefined as a "cooperative agreement."

In contrast, a contract is a legally binding procurement relationship between the sponsor and the recipient. Unlike a grant, the results (service or product) of a contract benefit the contracting agency. The contract obligates the principal investigator to furnish a project outcome or service that is defined in detail in the written contract, and it binds the sponsor to pay for it. From a legal perspective, contracts differ significantly from grants. A contractual agreement but not a grant is enforceable by law; the contractor may recover damages if the recipient fails to deliver the promised performance. Because of these legal ramifications, the chief research officer usually has one or more staff members with expertise in the distinction between grants and contracts.

Direct Costs

Typically, sponsored-project budgets contain direct and indirect costs. Direct costs are those that are budgeted specifically to achieve a grant's objectives. In the research context, this is the money available to the principal investigator to conduct the research. It includes funds for salaries, expendable supplies, equipment, travel, consulting services, and other project-related expenses. In its guidelines for spending federal grant and contract funds, known as circular A-21[2] or A-122[3] for educational or nonprofit institutions, respectively, the federal Office of Management and Budget (OMB) documents constraints on the use—the "allowability"—of direct-cost funds. Most importantly, they must be reasonable, allocable, and allowable. Or, in the eyes of a prudent person, the direct-cost expenditures must be necessary (reasonable) to conduct a specific project (allocable) and in compliance with university, sponsor, and federal guidelines (allowable).

Most researchers understand the concept of direct costs, although they occasionally misunderstand specific allowability criteria. For example, the federal granting agency may not allow food purchases with grant funds, yet a principal investigator charges dinner costs incurred for a visiting consultant to the grant. This is not an allowable expense and cannot be paid with grant funds. In egregious cases of direct-cost misuse, the chief research officer often mediates a resolution to the situation, usually together with the principal investigator and his or her dean. Of course, any money spent on an unallowable item (such as food or liquor) must be returned to the funding agency. Consequently, the cost must be transferred to some other fund for payment where it is allowable. This can cause difficulties if the investigator and the department don't have other sources of unrestricted money to cover this obligation. At that point, the dean and perhaps the chief research officer may be asked for help. In those cases, the chief research officer may lend the money with a pre-arranged payback agreement (over three years, for example). However, he or she seldom gives the money outright; that would be bad policy, for it rewards mismanagement.

Indirect Costs

Indirect costs, also called "facilities and administrative (F&A) costs," are budgeted to pay for facilities and administrative (F&A) expenses incurred by the university on behalf of the project. Importantly, through the F&A costs the sponsor reimburses the institution for expenses that have been already paid to support the infrastructure needed to conduct the sponsored project. Generally, the actual amount of these costs for a specific sponsored-research project cannot be determined readily. For example, a specific project's fraction of a laboratory building's air-conditioning, hot and cold water, and electricity costs cannot easily be ascertained. And if the project is conducted in two or more buildings, the exact reckoning becomes even more complicated. Consequently, the university calculates the total F&A costs incurred for all of its research activities for reimbursement claims and then estimates the amount attributable to an individual project. Because the F&A costs for specific projects are based on the entirety of the university's research expenditures—not just those of a single grant—they tend to be an average of the overall research portfolio, ranging from small awards from the National Endowment for the Humanities (NEH), for example, to large NIH program-project grants.

In their guidelines for determining F&A costs, the OMB refers to pools of university-incurred indirect costs. They identify nine suggested categories (also called "cost pools"), such as university operations and maintenance, libraries, facilities depreciation, departmental administration, sponsored-project administration, and so forth (circular A-21, sec. F). The word *suggested* is used because OMB allows institutions to add additional categories. These nine suggested pools sort into two fundamental pools: (1) facilities (such as operations and maintenance, depreciation, and libraries) and (2) administration (such as departmental administration, and sponsored projects administration). The expenses incurred in these two pools combined are called logically the "total F&A costs." Thus, the university calculates how much it spent on the research infrastructure needed to support its sponsored research and assorts it into separate cost pools.

The estimated fraction of the overall institutional F&A costs assignable to an individual project is based on its direct-cost budget relative to the university's overall sponsored-research direct costs. Significantly however, for these F&A calculations, some direct costs are excluded from both the individual project and the university total budgeted direct costs, mainly because they don't incur significant facilities or administrative costs or they are instructional in nature. The main exclusions are equipment items costing more than $5,000; capital expenditures; charges for patient care and tuition remission (including graduate-student health insurance); scholarships; and fellowships, as well as the portion of each subgrant and subcontract in excess of $25,000. The excluded scholarships and fellowships are defined more specifically as financial aid paid to university students or postdoctoral scholars as stipends, or dependent allowances. (Fellowships that pay salaries and wages or honoraria in contrast to stipends are not excluded.) These exclusions modify the budgeted direct-cost numbers. Thus, these modifications result in what is known as the modified total direct costs (MTDC) for a project and the overall university budget. Therefore, stated more accurately, an individual project's F&A costs are based on its MTDC budget relative to the university's overall MTDC budget.

F&A Rate Calculations

To simplify estimates of the F&A costs attributable to a single project, the university calculates an institutional F&A rate. This rate is the percentage of the overall F&A costs relative to the institution's overall MTDC. An individual project's F&A costs are then calculated by multiplying the institutional F&A rate times the project's budgeted MTDC. Stated algebraically,

$$\text{F\&A rate} = \frac{\text{total F\&A costs for research}}{\text{MTDC}}$$

$$= \frac{\text{total F costs}}{\text{MTDC}} + \frac{\text{total A costs}}{\text{MTDC}}$$

Conceptually, this is simply the ratio of the institutional expenses over the sponsors' awarded expenses (modified to exclude equipment and other items). Knowing the F&A rate, an experienced chief research officer can look at a grant budget and quickly calculate the expected F&A costs in a grant proposal or award.

To reinforce the notion that an individual projects F&A costs are based on its MTDC budget relative to the university's overall MTDC budget, the individual project's F&A costs can be expressed more formally:

$$\text{project F\&A} = \text{F\&A rate} \times \text{project MTDC}$$

$$= \frac{\text{institutional F\&A costs}}{\text{institutional MTDC}} \times \text{project MTDC}$$

$$= \text{institutional F\&A costs} \times \frac{\text{project MTDC}}{\text{institutional MTDC}}$$

Three details merit attention. First, the F&A rate has two components derived from the facilities (F) and the administrative (A) cost pools. According to OMB, the administrative component cannot exceed 26 percent. In most universities, that component is usually higher than 26 percent, but because of the cap they can only recover the 26 percent. Second, in contrast, the facilities component has no cap. This is good news to the university, for according to circular A-21, "Institutions may be compensated for the use of their buildings, capital improvements, and equipment, provided that they are used, needed in the institutions' activities, and properly allocable to sponsored agreements. Such compensation shall be made by computing either depreciation or use allowance."[4] Using a straight-line depreciation method, an institution can cover the costs of a newly constructed building within the time frame of the depreciation schedule. For example, if the building's useful lifetime is fifty years, then 2 percent of its cost can be recovered through

F&A reimbursement per year, and the building's cost is paid off with federal grant F&A funds in fifty years. Alternatively, the university may claim use allowance for an amount not exceeding 2 percent of the acquisition cost; thus, the building could be paid off in fifty years by this method. Facilities costs can also include interest on loans that financed a building's construction costs.

Enterprising universities take advantage of this provision to recover most but not all of the costs of constructing a new research building as part of their growth and modernization strategy. In each of these cases, F&A reimbursement can be claimed for only the fraction of the building that is actually used for research— not auditoriums, lecture halls, hallways, and other nonlaboratory, general-use space. A typical research building will have about 80 percent of its assignable space in laboratories. So, assuming that the researchers occupying the building generate sufficient grant income, the associated F&A recovery will pay for 80 percent of the building's construction costs—and continuing maintenance as well. Similarly, the depreciation or use allowance and the interest expenses incurred in the acquisition or maintenance of major equipment items used exclusively in sponsored research costing more than $10,000 are allowable for F&A reimbursement. All in all, circular A-21 has a long list of allowable and unallowable expenses that are well worth studying.

Notably, some teaching or other instructional activities unrelated to research within the building must be deducted from the F&A cost pool. Research training— that is, activities involving the training of individuals in research techniques—is an allowable cost. Likewise, student research sponsored by a federal training grant is allowable. However, all other instructional activities are not eligible for F&A reimbursement. Consequently, the percentage of the building used for these instructional activities must be calculated and subtracted from the F&A cost pool. From a practical perspective, this means that the presence of students in a research building will most probably reduce the institutional F&A rate.

Third, F&A recovery applies to only the first $25,000 of a subcontract. Therefore, if a grant budget includes $100,000 to be paid to some other institution for contracted work, the university can claim F&A costs only on $25,000, not the whole $100,000. Incidentally, if the institution receiving the subcontract expects to receive F&A reimbursement on the value of the subcontract ($100,000, in the example), this F&A amount must be included in the subcontract budget (in the example, it comes out of the $100,000). Consequently, this subcontract F&A cost is in the main grant direct-cost category. For universities that frequently subcontract grant-related activities to other institutions, this $25,000 cap can be costly. The expenses of administering these subcontracts usually far exceed the recoverable F&A costs for them.

Occasionally, a federal department may deviate from this standard F&A rate formula. For example, in 2008, the Department of Defense capped F&A costs for many of its grants and contracts, including basic research grants, at 35 percent of the total budget (direct costs plus indirect costs). Initially, most universities objected vociferously. But on closer inspection, they discovered that the impact was minimal; indeed, only those institutions with MDTC-based F&A rates higher than 53.8 percent would be affected. Why? Under these limitations, F&A costs cannot exceed 35 cents for every dollar expended. Therefore a ratio of 35 cents of F&A costs to 65 cents of direct costs, which equals 0.538, translates to a conventional 53.8 percent F&A rate based on MTDC. Ironically, many universities with lower negotiated F&A rates (based on MTDC) actually gained—at least on paper—as a result of this apparent cost-cutting measure.

Private universities usually have higher F&A rates than do public universities. Unlike private universities, public universities often benefit from the state's payment of building and other infrastructure costs. These costs, which can be substantial, aren't included in the F&A rate calculations. Private universities don't receive this state support; they must pay these costs themselves. Consequently, they charge the federal government for these infrastructural costs through F&A reimbursement, and this raises their F&A rate. For example, building depreciation and interest costs can add a lot to the F&A rate. Importantly, institutions with higher F&A rates don't necessarily have better research infrastructure.

The federal government assigns its F&A cost negotiations to a so-called cognizant agency. According to circular A-21:

> Cost negotiation cognizance is assigned to the Department of Health and Human Services (HHS) or the Department of Defense's Office of Naval Research (DOD), normally depending on which of the two agencies (HHS or DOD) provides more funds to the educational institution for the most recent three years. Information on funding shall be derived from relevant data gathered by the National Science Foundation. In cases where neither HHS nor DOD provides Federal funding to an educational institution, the cognizant agency assignment shall default to HHS.[5]

Ideally, the two cognizant agencies should follow similar negotiation guidelines, and therefore it shouldn't matter which one a university deals with. However, there are anecdotal reports of potentially significant differences. For example, the Office of Naval Research purportedly allows higher percentages for the library cost pool.

Incidentally, the word *negotiations* accurately describes how F&A rates are determined by the cognizant agency. In principle, the university's cost pools prepared according to circular A-21 guidelines should accurately reflect actual expenditures, thus making F&A rate calculations quite straightforward. Realistically, however, it seldom works out that simply. The cognizant agency frequently reduces or disallows some costs claimed by the university. And the university may dispute these changes. Ultimately, after sometimes lengthy negotiations, a final F&A rate is established.

Granting agencies vary in how they award these F&A funds. The NIH adds them to an award, separate from the direct-cost budget. Indeed, the indirect costs do not appear in the direct-cost budget, and an inattentive principal investigator may not know or even care about the size of the F&A award component. In contrast, the NSF and most other federal and private funding organizations include the indirect costs as a line in the overall grant budget, where it is quite visible to the principal investigator. Although these differences may not seem important, they can easily pose problems for the chief research officer.

The problem arises from the university's natural desire to recoup as much money as it can from the granting agencies as reimbursement for its expenses incurred in supporting the research mission. (Incidentally, these institutional expenses are well documented and are subject to annual federally mandated audits.) Therefore, higher F&A rates are favored from the chief financial officer's perspective. For the investigator with an NIH grant, this makes no difference; the F&A award is simply tacked onto the award separately from the direct-cost budget, so it doesn't really matter how large or small the actual F&A amount might be. The F&A component does not reduce the direct-cost award available to the principal investigator. In sharp contrast, however, most other granting agencies, including the NSF, incorporate the F&A costs as a line in the award budget. Therefore, if the total award is for a fixed amount, higher F&A rates translate to a larger F&A bite out of the budget amount available to the investigator; the investigator gets a smaller fraction of the budget for the project. For example, if the direct costs simplistically equal the modified total direct costs in a $1 million NSF award with a 50 percent F&A rate, the actual amount available to the investigator is only $666,667 because of the $333,333 in institutional F&A costs. Consequently, principal investigators whose funding usually comes from NSF or the Department of Defense, for example, strongly favor lower institutional F&A rates. In this context, the chief research officer is often drawn into the center of a debate among faculty members about the magnitude of the F&A rate.

> K: I understand why a faculty member would prefer the lower F&A rate if it means more money in direct costs. Most researchers prefer the money in their hands—not the administration's—so they can control how it's spent.
>
> Smith: It goes beyond that. F&A costs cut into a granting agency's total amount of grant money. If there were no F&A reimbursement—that is, the rate is zero—the agency could spend all of its money on awards. From that perspective, higher F&A rates necessarily reduce the number of awards that can be made. That's another reason most faculty members are generally opposed to high F&A rates. And, if the truth be told, I'll bet that most granting-agency program directors also oppose high F&A rates because they want to fund as many grants as possible.
>
> K: With such opposition, why don't the federal agencies impose further limitations on allowable F&A costs?
>
> Smith: They try to do that now and then. But this is tantamount to requiring the university to share more of the costs of federally sponsored research. That is

*equally unpopular among university administrators who claim that, if the
government wants the research done, then they should pay the full costs of
doing it. Ultimately, it boils down to a politically charged public-policy issue.*

F&A Funds Distribution

What happens to F&A money when it comes into the university? Again, this
depends on state and institutional policies. In all cases, the F&A reimbursement
funds are no longer considered federal money from an accounting perspective.
Thus, they have relatively few spending constraints; indeed, from an accounting
perspective, they are generally considered unrestricted funds. In that sense, they
are quite valuable to the university.

Although the money is deposited originally into a university account, some
states do not allow the institution itself to spend it—or at least not all of it. In
most cases, a public university can spend only what the legislature allows it to
spend via an appropriation, regardless of the money's source. For example, if the
university collects $100 million in F&A costs but the legislature authorizes only
$70 million in expenditures from this source, the remaining $30 million cannot
be spent until the state increases the spending limit. And that usually requires
legislation. (The chief financial officer must accurately predict future F&A cost
recovery to avert this situation.) Or, the legislature uses F&A costs to cover part
of the university's state general-funds budget. Understandably, this is not considered a desirable situation by university administrators because they have little or
no control over how these F&A funds can be spent; the legislature does. In states
where this occurs, the chief research and the chief financial officers will probably
be trying regularly to convince state legislators to allow the university to have full
control of the F&A cost return.

Universities that do control the F&A funds may have constraints imposed by
either the state or the governing board on how they may be used. The default is
to use these funds to cover the incurred costs that are being reimbursed. A small
fraction may be set aside for the chief research officer's discretionary use. In many
cases, the policies (or law) may stipulate that the F&A funds shall be used to
support research. (Note: in legislative jargon, the word *shall* differs from *will*.
Unlike *will*, which leaves some wiggle room, *shall* conveys force; without question,
the university must use the money to support research.) That is good policy because
it reinvests in the research effort that generated the money in the first place.

Within that guideline, the chief research officer might expect to control the
funds. However, it is not unusual for the provost and the chief financial officer also
to stake a claim to part, if not all, of the money. But this generally supports the
research mission indirectly. The provost may simply allocate the funds to the deans
in direct proportion to the amount they generated as part of their departmental
research budget or apply the money to new faculty member start-up packages, for

example. And the chief financial officer may use the money to pay for research-related services such as biohazard removal, purchasing personnel, utility bills, and so forth. These service expenditures support the research infrastructure, but they diminish the chief research officer's overall budget flexibility.

F&A and unrestricted funds can usually be carried forward from one fiscal year to the next, which amplifies their usefulness and attractiveness to the university. It is not unusual for a chief research officer, a dean, or a faculty member to build up sizable account balances "for a rainy day." *Sizable* is a loose word, but more than about $50,000 is a reasonable threshold. For a chief research officer, a dean, or a department chair, a common rationale is for future start-up packages, which can be very costly. Faculty members may hold money in reserve to cover loss of a grant, unexpected opportunities, and other emergencies.

These are among the many good reasons for setting aside this kind of reserve pool of money. But in times of budgetary stress, these reserves look very attractive to cash-hungry chief financial officers, legislative budget personnel, and governing board members. Unspent funds can be swept—taken away—to cover other university needs. These individuals may acknowledge that a sweep punishes what might seem to be solid conservative management by the account holders. However, in tight times, there may be few other alternative sources of cash to meet budgetary shortfalls. Experienced chief research officers routinely keep an eye on these unspent research-related balances and issue warnings about potential sweeps. One common defense against "the sweep" is to distribute unspent money into many smaller reserve accounts to reduce their visibility on the chief financial officer's radar screen.

> K: *But couldn't you also argue that allowing large reserves is bad management? After all, the money isn't being invested in the research program. It's just sitting there idly. And that will limit growth.*
>
> Smith: *Very good point. You want your money working for you, not sitting under a mattress. So the chief research officer should discourage the accumulation of large balances that sit unspent for more than two or three years.*
>
> K: *OK. Understanding that, if you were a dean, would you try to keep a big reserve?*
>
> Smith: *Hypocritically, I probably would. You never know when you'll need some big cash, and you can't trust the upper administration to help. They may have helped in the past, but there are no guarantees that they will in the future. I would want to be ready for that. So I would take my chances on having my reserves swept.*

Gifts

In academic parlance, a gift is a donor's contribution to a university of something with economic value, such as money or other asset. An individual, a corporation, or a nonprofit entity may be the donor. Importantly, there is no reciprocal economic benefit provided by the university in return. Furthermore, the award is typically irrevocable, with no specified time limit for its expenditure. And there is no formal fiscal accountability beyond periodic progress and expenditure reports to the donor. These progress reports are generally considered to be reports on stewardship and not performance. The essential point is that a gift may not have a "scope of work" or other deliverable. Thus, the benefactor receives nothing in return other than recognition and disposition of the gift in accordance with the donor's wishes. Recognition usually includes a thank-you note and, more important, a receipt for tax-deduction purposes.

Gift funds may be unrestricted or restricted, depending on the donor's wishes. A gift may be designated for general operations or restricted to a particular purpose, such as research in a defined area or support of a professorship or a program. The donor may stipulate the gift for specific purposes but may not have control over expenditures or over the work performed. Because there are no "deliverables," gifts from a private donor are not considered sponsored research, even if the donor calls the gift a grant or the gift is used in support of the research mission. Furthermore, a gift may be designated by the donor as expendable— immediately usable for current purposes—or as endowment to be invested with the investment returns available to support university purposes.

Parenthetically, when a donor gives something to the university, he or she usually intends to claim an income-tax deduction for the value of the gift. Not surprisingly, the Internal Revenue Service (IRS) has specific guidelines about what constitutes a gift that qualifies for this deduction:

> Generally, you can deduct your contributions of money or property that you make to, or for the use of, a qualified organization. A gift or contribution is 'for the use of' a qualified organization when it is held in a legally enforceable trust for the qualified organization or in a similar legal arrangement. The contributions must be made to a qualified organization and not set aside for use by a specific person.[6]

According to the last phrase, "not set aside for use by a specific person," if the donor specifies the intended recipient of gift funds (who may be himself or herself), the donation is not tax deductible. Indeed, the IRS has ruled that in these cases the ultimate recipient is realistically the specific person and not the university—even though the gift was given to the university: "The organization must have control and discretion over the contribution, unfettered by a commitment or understanding that the contribution would benefit a designated individual . . . . The donor's intent must be to benefit the organization and not the individual recipient."[7] Thus, the donor is not entitled to deduct the charitable contribution. Ultimately, it is the responsibility of the donor to ensure that a donation meets the definition to qualify as a charitable deduction for income-tax purposes, regardless of whether or not a gift receipt has been issued by the university.

The university's development office generally administers gifts. For their services, they charge a fee. The amounts and fee structure differ among institutions. However, a common charge is a one-time service fee—for example, 5 percent of the original gift amount. Alternatively, the charge may be an annual management fee, such as a percentage (for example, 2 percent) of the gift's current market value. In general, gifts that restrict the collection of a management fee will be assessed the charge out of some other source of funds.

To conform to IRS and standard accounting procedures, the university must distinguish between sponsored projects and gifts. As they come into the university, sponsored projects and gifts are usually identifiable as one or the other and are routed to the appropriate office. The chief research officer administers sponsored projects, and the chief development officer administers gifts. However, when ambiguities arise, the two offices must jointly decide whether it is a sponsored project or a gift. A subtle tension may lurk under the surface. The chief research officer naturally wants the university to bring in as many sponsored projects as possible; likewise, the chief development officer wants to maximize the number of gifts received by the university. However, competent staff members recognize this tension and do not allow it to cloud their judgment.

Incidentally, if the management fee for a gift is less than the F&A costs collected from a sponsored project, researchers may steer research support from private sources to the gift category, and vice versa. Ethically and legally, this poses no serious problems, but it can skew reporting data one way or the other.

K: Suppose I want to donate money to the university to support a particular professor's research program. Did you say that I can't do that?

Smith: The Internal Revenue Service states that you can't get a tax deduction if you do.

K: That strikes me as odd. It's my money, so I should be able to say who gets to use it.

Smith: You can. But if you do, you won't get the tax deduction. The usual solution is to make the donation to the university to support research in the specific area that your favored professor studies, such as stem-cell research. If your person is the only one at the university in that field, then he or she will get the money, fair and square. And you get the tax deduction. If there are several faculty members studying in that area, then the university will have to devise some way to distribute your money among them. But it isn't obligated to give your person any of it—the university may decide to give it all to one or more of the other researchers.

K: Couldn't I just narrow the area so much that only my professor would qualify for the money?

Smith: Yes, but be careful. The IRS has a low tolerance for that kind of manipulation. They may disallow your deduction if they suspect that you're violating the spirit of the law.

Endowments

Endowment income originates from the return on the investment of principal from a gift or bequest. There are three endowment types: permanent, quasi-, or term. Each can be either restricted or unrestricted, depending on the donor's wishes. Permanent (or true) endowments occur when the donor specifies that the principal is to be invested and maintained in perpetuity; only the income distributions may be expended. If the university rather than the donor determines that an account's funds are to be retained and managed like an endowment, the fund is called a quasi-endowment. The university may invest its own funds in a quasi-endowment, either as a sole donor or as a supplement to a private gift. Since quasi- endowments are established at the discretion of the institution rather than an external source, the principal may also be spent; these expenditures must also conform to the donor's wishes. If the donor specifies a time limit for an endowment's lifetime, it becomes a term endowment. At the end of the lifetime—for example, ten years—the university may expend the principal in its entirety according to the donor's wishes.

Endowment income comprises an important component of many universities' operating budgets. The payout rate—the percentage of the endowment that contributes to the operating budget—is the maximum amount of the endowment that can be spent in a given year. The governing board usually sets the payout rates based on a three- to five-year average of the endowment's market value. Generally, rates vary between about 3 and 10 percent; typically, they are about 4 to 5 percent. Ultimately, the goal is to maximize the payout while reinvesting a sufficient amount of the return as a safeguard against inflation. The actual payout rate depends heavily on the balance between investment performance and institutional need. An increased investment performance and a constant budgeted need (for example, $100 million per year) translate to a decreased payout rate and vice versa. Thus, counterintuitively, a university may report a lower payout rate during a time of lucrative investment returns. Depending on the circumstances, the university may increase the payout rate, thus reducing the reinvestment amount, or leave it constant, thus increasing the rate of principal growth.

Salary Savings

A common source of money to support research is salary savings. How does this work? Most federal and some private granting agencies allow the investigator to include some of his or her salary in the grant budget. The amount must conform to the investigator's effort on the project. For example, if the investigator claims to spend 25 percent effort on the project, then one-fourth of the salary (plus fringe benefits on that amount) may be included in the grant's budget. This frees up the corresponding amount of university-funded salary. In many institutions, the provost allows the college dean to keep most or all of these "salary savings" to use for his or her own purposes. Usually, the savings stay in the department, and some may even be given to the investigator. That is good policy, for it provides a strong incentive to generate this kind of income.

Some granting agencies limit the amount of salary that can be requested in a grant budget. For example, the NSF usually allows only two months of salary support. This may be used any time during the year. However, most faculty members are on a nine-month salary, and they use the grant support for summer salary. Consequently, this usually doesn't generate significant salary savings. The NIH policy doesn't have this limitation. However, they set an upper limit on the amount of salary that may be in the grant budget. In 2009, this cap was about $200,000, and the amount is adjusted periodically. So, if an investigator's annual salary is $250,000, the project effort is 40 percent, and the NIH limit is $200,000, up to $80,000 may be included in the grant budget. Since most medical-school faculty members are on annual appointments, these institutional salary savings from an NIH award can be sizable. Cautionary note: at some medical schools, the salary structure may provide only a fraction of the "official" university salary. The remainder must be obtained from research grants; if the researcher fails to get a grant with salary in its budget, then he or she doesn't get full salary. Therefore, in those cases, there are no salary savings.

These funds can be an important component of the overall research infrastructure support. At many universities, departmental budgets provide minimal resources—just enough to meet the teaching mission. Therefore, these salary savings can be used to hire additional research staff support (such as secretaries, fiscal officers, technicians, and workshop personnel), purchase office equipment (such as copy machines), pay graduate student salaries, and so forth. The chief research officer seldom has any access to these funds. Nonetheless, because of their importance in the research context, he or she generally takes an interest in maximizing this source of revenue. In that context, the chief research officer may find it necessary to educate fiscal officers, departmental chairs, and the faculty members about the availability and usefulness of these salary savings. That may sound unnecessary at universities with extensive research activity. However, at institutions with a less developed research culture, the concept of generating salary from extramural grants may be novel and not well understood. In those cases, the chief research officer should actively encourage the practice—even if it does not yield large amounts of revenue. The goal is to inculcate its benefits to the university's overall research enterprise.

Space

In many ways, space is a more valuable resource than money. Money can be obtained from numerous sources, but space availability can be quite limited. As in world history in general, the quest for laboratory and office space has catalyzed monumental disputes at one time or another within all universities.

Technically, the governing board controls all university space. The board delegates management to the campus chief executive officer, who usually delegates it further to the provost or the chief administrative officer, who then delegates it to the deans, directors, and maybe the chief research officer. Thus, the dean can assign a building or other block of space to a particular department and delegate its management to the chair. And the delegations go on down the line to the individual faculty member. At the upper levels of this delegation tree, things go fairly smoothly. But down at the department level, space problems can bring out the worst in anybody's personality. Usually, space disputes are resolved at the level of the department chair, although they may occasionally rise to the dean's level.

The chief research officer becomes involved indirectly or directly in several ways. In some universities, laboratory space is assigned strictly on the basis of research expenditures. The more research grant money a faculty member has, the more space he or she gets. These assignments are reviewed periodically and often are based on a rolling three- or five-year average of the research expenditures. According to protocol, the chief research officer should not interfere with these matters that are usually handled by the dean's office. The major exception would be if there were special circumstances about expenditure data that warrant consideration in specific instances. For example, a large fraction of some large grants may be subcontracted out to other universities; it may be inappropriate to assign laboratory space on the basis of these subcontracted research dollars.

A more menacing trap can be encountered when the chief research officer provides an investigator the funds to buy a major piece of equipment. What if the investigator doesn't have anywhere to put the equipment? "Why didn't you think of that in the first place?" This can be an expensive oversight. If the dean cannot identify suitable space, the chief research officer may be asked to cover the expenses of renting or renovating space to accommodate the new equipment. However, the chief research officer may counter that he or she has just contributed a large amount of money to this project, and the least the dean can do is to cover these unexpected costs. Ultimately, some deal will be negotiated.

There are variations on this scenario, such as the unexpected need for more electrical power or better air-conditioning. Most experienced chief research officers try to avert these situations by insisting that the department chair or the dean sign off on any request for large pieces of equipment. Supposedly, this ensures that they are aware of any special space requirements and are prepared to cover any extra costs. Unfortunately, most experienced chief research officers also know that it may not matter if the dean signs off on the request. If the extra costs are high, the chief research officer and maybe the provost will be asked to contribute anyway. And they usually do, although sometimes begrudgingly, mainly to protect their investment.

The chief research officer's biggest challenge is to ensure that the university provides adequate space for growth of the research enterprise. That includes not only assignable square feet but also adequate utilities, including computer support. If the university succeeds in its growth plans, research expenditures will increase every year. Historically (1953 through 2007), university research expenditures have grown by 10 percent per year; more recently (1998 through 2007), the growth rate has been about 8 percent per year.[8] Increased space needs accompany this steady growth in grant dollars. Together with the provost and the chief financial officer, the chief research officer must always anticipate the direction and the rate of this growth. This is serious business, mainly because buildings are so expensive and take so long to build. And, land may not be available on the main campus. Thus, the horizon may be at least ten years ahead. Predicting what kind of research buildings will be needed through either new construction or renovations is usually the chief research officer's responsibility. This is not done in a vacuum, of course. It requires thoughtful consultation with the deans and the provost.

Where to get the money for new buildings? This is usually the chief financial officer's or the provost's problem. However, the chief research officer should always know about potential extramural sources, such as the NIH and NSF. Indeed, the chief research officer should be ready to take the lead in preparing grant applications for these funds if they are available (which occurs now and then). Some institutions finance new research building costs by issuing bonds, usually tax-exempt, backed by the F&A cost-recovery revenue. (Thus, they are called "revenue bonds.")

Interestingly, the key to all of this is the inclusion of interest on construction costs in the F&A reimbursement, for it provides a revenue stream to back the bonds. (Likewise, they may finance instructional building costs through revenue bonds backed by tuition income.) Moreover, universities recover many of the construction costs via F&A funds. This arrangement pulls the chief research officer into the picture because he or she is responsible (right or wrong) for ensuring that there is adequate F&A generated to cover these obligations, which may extend for twenty years or more.

In some cases, universities must resort to leasing space off-campus to solve a space shortage. For nonacademic programs, such as medical clinics and business centers, this may prove acceptable in the long run, especially if the program has a revenue stream to pay the rent. However, for academic programs, off-campus rentals provide only short-term relief. Consequently, most universities resort to off-campus leasing for academically related programs only in the most desperate situations.

The chief research officer also works routinely with the chief information officer to ensure that the university's computer infrastructure is adequate. This includes not only large-scale facilities, such as clusters and supercomputers, but also bandwidth. The planning horizon is usually about three to five years ahead in these cases. Again, the chief research officer should be prepared to take the lead in any extramural grant applications, although the chief information technology officer may insist on being the principal investigator. And that would be quite appropriate.

> K: *Issuing bonds backed by future F&A revenue takes courage. It ties up the F&A for many, many years. What if research support decreases unexpectedly sometime in the future and F&A costs are insufficient to cover the bond expenses?*
>
> Smith: *The money would have to come from some other source. I wouldn't want to be in the chief financial officer's shoes if that happens.*
>
> K: *Given the risk, is that a good use of the F&A money?*
>
> Smith: *I think so. The university has to keep moving forward. As they say, "latecomers get the bones." It would be hoped that a new state-of-the-art building would provide the environment for even greater research productivity and therefore even more F&A revenue. You want to get into an upward spiral. Better facilities, more F&A reimbursement, even better facilities, even more F&A reimbursement.*

Specialized Facilities

Specialized facilities are also research resources. These include electronics and machine shops, large-scale computing facilities, transgenic mouse laboratories, music and drama studios, biotechnology core facilities, imaging centers, and various others. They also include the library, although it is usually within the provost's domain of responsibility.

In most cases, these specialized facilities are administered within a specific school or college, and their directors report to the dean. Nonetheless, the chief research officer can expect to be asked to contribute funds for their ongoing support, including the library. Because these facilities provide critical infrastructural support to a broad research community on campus, chief research officers seldom balk at providing some support, although they assuredly look very carefully at the size of the request. Generally, the requested amount of the contribution is proportional to the fraction of the facility's usage attributable to research, which should be well documented. These calculations are made by the facility director and should be available for public scrutiny. Indeed, the research usage will undoubtedly be included in the institution's F&A costs and in this context will be subject to occasional federally mandated audits.

Students

In many faculty members' opinion, good students are the most important resource for their research programs. Money and space can be found somehow, but top-quality students can be much more difficult to find. The chief research officer and the graduate dean are constantly expected to help attract and keep good students. And that is a major challenge, even at the elite research universities.

As usual, money helps. Thus, most universities try to assemble competitive financial-aid packages for their graduate students. The benchmark is four years of twelve-month salary support plus tuition remission and health insurance. That can be costly. Some institutions are now offering up to about $30,000 per year plus free tuition and health insurance for four years. However, this amount may vary among departments, with engineers and scientists usually getting more. Stipend levels in the $10,000 to $20,000 range are more common. And in some public universities, the student must pay in-state tuition. From the chief research officer's vantage point, the least desirable element of any financial-aid package is a teaching assistantship because that takes the student away from research. Nonetheless, some institutions must rely on this method of supporting graduate students, and some require a semester or two of teaching.

Money to finance these packages comes from various sources. Teaching assistantships are usually covered by institutional instructional funds derived from the state general fund, tuition, or endowment income. The more desirable positions—namely, research assistantships—are usually funded by extramural research grants, patent-generated income, graduate tuition, and other miscellaneous funds available to the university.

Commonly, faculty members include graduate student salaries in the form of scholarships or fellowships and tuition as direct costs in their research grant budgets. These are permissible costs as long as the support is limited to training graduate students working on the project and is approved beforehand by the granting agency. Significantly, according to circular A-21, the tuition must be reasonable compensation for the work performed, and "it is the institution's practice to similarly compensate students in non-sponsored as well as sponsored activities."[9]

An important point in all of this is that the salary amount must be reasonable. What's reasonable? According to the NIH, "In general, graduate student compensation will not be considered reasonable if in excess of the amount paid to a first-year postdoctoral scientist at the same institution performing comparable work."[10] As of 2010, that maximum stipend amount is $37,368. The NSF states simply that "Salaries requested must be consistent with the organization's regular practices."[11] Regardless, add the cost of tuition remission and health care, multiply by four years, and suddenly these become very expensive packages.

Furthermore, according to circular A-21, "it is the institution's practice to similarly compensate students in non-sponsored as well as sponsored activities."[12]

Prima facie, this suggests that students supported by grant income cannot receive more financial aid than those not supported by grants. Therefore, comparable support must be offered to students not covered by grants, and that money must come from other university resources. Realistically, most institutions interpret this provision to mean that all students within a specific discipline must be appointed at the same base-pay level. If there is insufficient funding to support a student at this base level, one strategy is to reduce the appointment level. For example, the base pay for first-year graduate students in a discipline such as civil engineering may be $32,000 annually for a standard 50-percent appointment; however, if the civil engineering department only has $25,600 available, the appointment level is reduced to 40-percent. To extend the example, the 50-percent-appointment base pay for first-year graduate students in the English department may be $20,000. A particularly desirable candidate may be offered $24,000 on a 60-percent appointment—assuming that the institution allows greater than 50-percent graduate-student appointment levels. In these examples, the base pay remains constant within the discipline, in apparent compliance with the intent of circular A-21.

Both the NIH and the NSF have grants specifically for graduate-student support. Two examples are the Ruth L. Kirschstein National Research Service Award (NRSA) from the NIH and the Integrative Graduate Education and Research Traineeship (IGERT) awards from the NSF. Interestingly, the NRSA graduate student stipend is set at $20,976. Therefore, if the institution's standard research-assistant award is for more than that, the university must supplement the NRSA award up to that standard level to comply with circular A-21. As a matter of policy, some universities use their own resources to bring all extramural stipends—even very small ones—to their standard support level. Clearly, the chief research officer and the graduate dean must cooperate to ensure that the university pursues every opportunity to offer competitive graduate-student recruitment packages.

Private endowments for graduate-student support are rare. Most focus on undergraduate educational opportunities. Thus, experienced development officers will tend to place graduate support low on their fund-raising priority list. It is a low-yield effort. The chief research officer and the graduate dean should not take this personally and as a failure of the institution to support the research mission. Development officers face the mandate of maximizing the gift funds raised from private sources, and they go where the money is. Rather than fret over this, the chief research officer can accomplish the same goal, raising private money for graduate student support, by emphasizing the importance of endowed professorships. Why? Because faculty members quite often use these funds to support graduate students. And endowed professorships are an easy sell for the development officer; the donor's name will be memorialized in the professor's title. Indeed, many capital campaigns place endowed professorships as one of the very top fund-raising priorities. The chief research officer and the graduate dean can sit back and smile about this because it strongly supports the university's research mission.

Other less mercenary factors also play a role in a graduate student's choice of university. Location, for example, can be quite important. A student may want to be near home, on the East Coast, down South, and so forth. Conversely, the student may not want to live in some part of the country or particular environment. The chief research officer and the graduate dean may have little influence over these matters, but they should work with the public relations office, the local chamber of commerce, and related organizations to develop the best case for their institution's location. Also, a student may wish to study with a specific faculty member or on a particular topic unique to some institution.

> *K: I'm glad that you mention these other factors. Do you really think that money is such an important issue for most students?*
>
> *Smith: Yes. Money is always a powerful attractant.*
>
> *K: Do you think that a good financial-aid package can overcome some negative aspect of a university's location?*
>
> *Smith: Yes. Sad to say, but money reigns supreme. That's why I think that it's so important for the chief research officer to develop a keen sense of smell for sources of graduate-student support and to devote a lot of time trying to get at it.*

Notes

1. Using Procurement Contracts and Grant and Cooperative Agreements, 31 U.S.C. §§ 6301–6308 (2006).
2. Office of Management and Budget, Executive Office of the President, Circular A-21, 2 C.F.R. Pt. 220 (2010).
3. Office of Management and Budget, Executive Office of the President, Circular A-122, 2 C.F.R. Pt. 230 (2010).
4. 2 C.F.R. Pt. 220, App. A, § J.14.a.
5. Ibid., § G.11.a.1.
6. Internal Revenue Service, *Charitable Contributions*, publication 526 (Washington, D.C.: Internal Revenue Service, 2009), p. 3.
7. Internal Revenue Service, "Letter Ruling Request Regarding a Charitable Contribution, no. 200250029, index no. 170.12-06", p. 4, 2002, http://www.irs.gov/pub/irs-wd/0250029.pdf (accessed January 16, 2011).
8. National Science Foundation (NSF), "R&D Expenditures at Universities and Colleges, by Source of Funds, FY 1953–2007," 2010, http://www.nsf.gov/statistics/nsf10311/pdf/tab1.pdf (accessed January 16, 2011).
9. 2 C.F.R. Pt. 220, App. A., § 45.a.5.
10. National Institutes of Health, "Graduate Student Compensation NOT-OD-02-017", 2001, http://grants.nih.gov/grants/guide/notice-files/NOT-OD-02-017.html (accessed January 16, 2011).
11. National Science Foundation, "Proposal and Award Policies and Procedures Guide, Part I: Proposal Preparation and Submission Guidelines", § II.C.g(i)(c), 2010, http://www.nsf.gov/pubs/policydocs/pappguide/nsf11001/nsf11_1.pdf (accessed January 16, 2011).
12. 2 C.F.R. Pt. 220, App. A, § J.45.a.5.

CHAPTER 5

Enhancing Research Resources

K: Chief research officers are expected to enhance the university's extramural funding. How would you go about doing that?

Smith: The chief research officer will inevitably be asked to devise a plan for increasing institutional research capacity.

K: Are we talking about the same thing? I said extramural funding and you said research capacity.

Smith: Maybe not exactly. But they're closely related. It takes money to make money. So getting more money is typically a key element of any effort to increase institutional research capacity. And the usual measure of research capacity is extramural funding—money.

Research Capacity

Chief research officers are expected to enhance the university's research resources, a task which falls under the more general topic of building research capacity. Indeed, early in their administrative career, they will inevitably be asked to devise a plan for increasing what is known as institutional research capacity. Before going much further into this topic, it may be helpful to answer this question by defining exactly what is meant by the term "research capacity" in the academic vernacular. Academe uses the phrase all the time but without precise definition. Does it translate simply into extramural funding or into something more involved? The term isn't in standard dictionaries. However, the British Department for International Development (DFID) provides a definition that verbalizes the common notion of research capacity: "the ability of individuals, organizations and systems to undertake and disseminate high quality research effectively and efficiently."[1] By inference, in the university context, research capacity refers to the institution's physical infrastructure, administrative services, incentives, and resource base that support its research endeavours. As a corollary, efforts to improve these support elements constitute "capacity building." Thus, in the chief research officer's lexicon, building research capacity means enhancing the institution's research administrative services, incentives, physical infrastructure, and most important, resource base.

The proper metric for enhanced research capacity should be a research program's impact in its discipline. If the institution's capability to generate high-quality research has gone up, its impact in the field should also increase. But since impact is often difficult to measure, a more convenient metric of research capacity is, perhaps not surprisingly, research expenditures. These data for all research universities are reported annually by the NSF.[2] Furthermore, the numbers are ranked from largest to smallest, thus providing a convenient measure for comparing institutions. And moving up the list by generating more institutional research expenditures is one commonly recognized criterion of increased research capacity. Therefore, to return to the earlier question, Does research capacity translate simply into extramural funding? Technically, the answer is no. But research expenditures have become such a frequently used measure of research capacity that the two are de facto synonymous. Consequently, most capacity-building efforts concentrate on increasing research expenditures.

Theoretically, there are two mutually dependent ways to accomplish this goal: adding to the institutional resource base and increasing the annual research expenditure growth rate. In a university setting, "adding to the base" means increasing the number of faculty members who generate research funding; and "increasing the expenditure growth rate" means increasing the average amount of research funding generated per faculty member. Quantitatively, the two methods for enhancing research capacity—adding to the base and increasing the research expenditure growth rate—can be quite interdependent. Additional, new faculty members who add to the base may stimulate more research grant applications by existing faculty members, with a consequent overall increase in expenditure growth rate. In contrast, expensive start-up costs for new faculty members may depress needed investments in ongoing research activities, thus reducing the growth rate.

Because of these interactions, the expected net impact of capacity-building efforts may not be intuitively obvious. Therefore, when planning capacity-building strategies, it is highly advisable a priori to construct a spreadsheet-style financial model that analyzes various investment scenarios based on several key parameters: the number of new faculty members to be added per year, predicted start-up costs, hoped-for grant revenue per faculty member, current and projected expenditure growth rate, inter alia. Furthermore, these planning models should adjust institutional growth rates for changes in the average growth rate of federal research funding to universities in the same way that economists adjust financial data for inflation. Without this kind of prior analysis, subsequent capacity-building efforts may prove to be surprisingly ineffective. The outcomes of this modeling, which depend on the planning assumptions, can be devilishly difficult to predict beforehand.

The two methods for building research capacity—adding to base and increasing growth rate—have different timelines. Ideally, adding to the base provides steady, predictable growth of research capacity over a long time. The timeline usually includes a three- or four-year lag to accommodate start-up times for new faculty members. However, more dramatic, short-term (that is, within five years or so) results can be obtained by concentrating on increases in the expenditure growth rate. Although this translates into higher average research funding per faculty member, the goal can often be attained relatively quickly by sharply focusing efforts on increased funding for only a few select programs in highly fundable fields. In this context, congressional earmarks have become a common way to jump-start expenditure growth rates. Sharply focused methods may increase research expenditures quickly, but they may not enhance overall institutional research capacity. Moreover, growth may prove to be unsustainable over a timeline of several years.

Additions to Base

Ultimately, adding to the base is the canonical method for capacity building. Stated more explicitly, increasing the number of research-active faculty members is the straightforward way to build research capacity. Simply hire new research-oriented faculty members who will bring in more grants. "Simply" is relative, of course. Adding more research-active faculty members is a simple matter of having more researchers at work. But being able to add enough new faculty members to make a measurable difference in research productivity is another matter entirely; it's not at all simple just to hire new people. A university's ability to expand the size of its faculty depends on many factors, such as enrollment, availability of funds, number of positions authorized by the state, and space suitable for research. Although most of these factors may seem at first glance to be beyond the chief research officer's control, he or she may have opportunities to influence them. For example, if lack of adequate space prevents the hiring of research-active faculty numbers, then the chief research officer should analyze what is needed and present the case for new space to the chief executive officer and, therefore, indirectly to the governing board. The same goes for any other limiting factor. Also, in some cases additional faculty members may be hired using funds derived from newly acquired large research grants and contracts, corporate alliances, or specialized research facilities. These opportunities may lie within the chief research officer's sphere of influence.

New faculty members do not necessarily have to be tenure-track or tenured appointments. Many research universities have provisions for nontenure-track research faculty members. Their titles are usually some variation on "research professor" or "research scientist." Most often, these are soft-money positions. That is, the research faculty members must generate their salary from external sources, although the university may pay their salary for up to about three years or so (if at all) to help them get started toward independence. That usually means that they depend on extramural grants for their paycheck. In many medical schools, research faculty members not on tenure track are paid by funds from clinical practice plans. As clinical faculty members spend more time in the university's clinics, they generate more revenue, and many clinical practice plans allocate some of this money to hire nonclinical, nontenure-track faculty members to oversee research programs. This is usually administered at the department level.

On a cautionary note, it bears mentioning that some institutions' personnel policies promote, and may even mandate, conversion of a nontenure-track academic staff appointment to a tenure-track appointment after several years of continuous employment. For example, the University of Hawaii faculty union contract calls for the university to "make every effort to convert temporary positions to tenure track status where . . . evidence of continuing need has been demonstrated by consistent funding of the position for seven (7) consecutive years that includes an average of at least seventy–five percent (75%) State general funding."[3] Texas Tech has a more permissive policy for research scientists and research professors. Although these faculty "do not acquire tenure, persons serving in these positions have academic freedom and, after six years, can only be dismissed for adequate cause . . . in accordance with the faculty grievance procedure."[4] These continuing appointments do not occur automatically; like any tenure decision, they require a majority vote of the academic department's tenured faculty and approval by the the dean and provost. Realistically, these individuals become de facto tenured employees—and continuous funding must be available to support them. The potential for these conversions, which may carry a hefty long-term financial obligation, must be kept in mind when recruiting research faculty members who would not be on tenure track.

All else being equal, there should be a linear relationship between the number of faculty members and the amount of research expenditures. On average, three faculty members should bring in three times more grant money than one faculty member would. But all things are seldom equal. The extramural research funding available in different disciplines varies widely, from very little in music to a lot via the NIH in biomedical sciences. Indeed, if bringing in grant funds were the only hiring criterion, every new faculty member would be in the biomedical sciences because that's where the money is. Except for stand-alone medical institutions, most universities cannot take such a mercenary approach to faculty hiring—even if they wanted to. Thus, the marginal benefit of adding new faculty members depends on their disciplines and, therefore, on their access to extramural funding. Furthermore, when calculating the net benefit of new faculty members, the investment costs such as start-up expenses, space remodeling, and salaries must be taken into consideration. Sometimes these calculations can be very startling, for they inevitably show that it takes a surprisingly long time (for example, up to ten years or so) before the marginal monetary benefits exceed the investment costs.

To amplify the impact of hiring new faculty members, many universities make "cluster hires." That is, they recruit several new faculty members who all work in the same area, such as nanophotonics, zebra-fish neurobiology, Southeast Asian drama, and so forth. The hope is that their common interests will catalyze interactions that boost research productivity. For example, as a group they may be eligible for large program project grants like those awarded by the NIH. If they successfully obtain these large grants, then the relationship between the new faculty members and the amount of research expenditures becomes nonlinear; for example, three faculty members studying different aspects of a common topic may bring in nine times more grant money than one working alone would.

Who decides what cluster areas to focus on? The best practice is a campus-wide call for proposals that are consistent with the university's strategic plan. This emanates from the provost's office. Usually the provost, typically in consultation with the chief research officer, then chooses the winner based on criteria specific to that institution. Bringing in a group of "rainmakers" is definitely not a routine hiring effort, so it transcends the usual departmental decision-making process. If the chief research officer discovers that he or she has not been included throughout the process, there may be cause for alarm. After all, the chief research officer is ultimately accountable for the cluster members' success in boosting research capacity. This responsibility must be coupled with corresponding authority over the hiring process.

Cluster hiring can have an important collateral benefit—retention. For example, a valued faculty member may threaten to leave the university for a job at another institution that has more colleagues—the critical mass—in his or her discipline. The promise of a cluster hire in that discipline by the home institution may be sufficient enticement to retain the faculty member. It would not be unusual for a provost to attach considerable significance to this retention strategy when selecting the areas for a cluster hire.

> K: Is there any proof that these cluster hires actually increase productivity nonlinearly?
> Smith: I've never seen a thorough analysis that looked at the overall academic benefits of cluster hiring. However, there are anecdotal stories about successes, and I've seen it work. In fact, I can't think of any downside except that a department's breadth may be sacrificed for depth. But, as they tritely say these days, "We can't be all things for all people."
> K: As a chief research officer, would you encourage cluster hiring?
> Smith: Oh, yes. There are very lucrative research-grant opportunities available for related groups of researchers, like the NIH program project grants or the various NSF center grants. They bring in big money and invaluable prestige to the university.

Congressional Earmarks

More and more universities have begun to rely on congressional earmarks to increase their research capacity. This is the academic version of pork barreling.

Another euphemism is "congressionally directed appropriation." Before discussing the ins and outs of this practice, it is interesting to know exactly what constitutes an earmark. Simply put, an earmark is a provision in congressional legislation that allocates funding for a specific purpose at the request of a member of Congress. Usually earmarked funds are for a project, program, or organization located in the congressional district. Thus, earmarks have been called "federal spending with a zip code attached."[5]

Interestingly, the Office of Management and Budget (OMB) defines earmarks as "funds provided by the Congress for projects, programs, or grants where the purported congressional direction (whether in statutory text, report language, or other communication) circumvents otherwise applicable merit-based or competitive allocation processes, or specifies the location or recipient, or otherwise curtails the ability of the executive branch to manage its statutory and constitutional responsibilities pertaining to the funds allocation process."[6] These are harsh words: "circumvents" the competitive allocation process; "curtails" the executive branch's abilities to manage constitutional responsibilities. They underscore the divisive opinions about earmarks in general and academic earmarks in particular.

To understand the rationale for the OMB's harsh comments, it helps to review briefly the federal budget process. This process starts when the President presents next year's proposed federal budget to Congress every February. The multi-volume document contains detailed budget proposals for each federal agency and, thus, reflects their spending priorities. Both the House of Representatives and the Senate refer the presidential budget to two of their committees, the budget committee and the appropriations committee. Separately, the House and Senate budget committees analyze the presidential budget and, after consultative hearings, arrive at a concurrent resolution that determines the amount of money needed to implement its proposed programs. Based on their analyses, the budget committees provide each appropriations committee with a budget (the so-called 302a budget) that covers mandatory entitlement allocations (for example, Medicare and Social Security payments) and discretionary allocations. The discretionary programs include those requested in the presidential budget.

Meanwhile, the House and Senate appropriations committees refer the presidential budget to their thirteen subcommittees responsible for the various federal activities, such as defense, energy and water development, and so on. Each subcommittee is also given its share of the overall appropriations committee's 302a budget (the so-called 302b budget). Within their budgetary constraints, the subcommittees draft the appropriations bills and report them to the full appropriations committees. The subcommittees are not obligated to honor any aspect of the presidential budget, although they usually pay close attention to it when drafting the final bill.

Importantly, under House and Senate rules, any appropriations must first be authorized by separate congressional legislation. Authorizing legislation permits a federal program or activity to begin or continue from year to year. It may limit the amount of budget authority to be provided subsequently or may authorize the appropriation of "such sums as may be necessary." Authorizing bills are not necessarily coupled to the budget calendar, but they are prerequisite to an appropriations bill. Indeed, an appropriation must fit into an account established in an authorization bill.

Earmarked appropriations may enter the federal budget at two main loci in this process: the authorizing committee or the appropriations subcommittee. Most frequently, earmarks originate in the appropriations subcommittee, in response to a formal request from a member of Congress to the subcommittee chair, who then decides which of many such requests to include as appropriations. Notably, these are seldom transparent, merit-based decisions; they may be politically based. At this point, the appropriations subcommittee chair may informally set aside some of the discretionary budget for its members' special-request projects. In that way, the committee "carves out" a portion of the discretionary budget for these congressionally directed appropriations (that is, earmarks). In practice, members of the majority party usually receive 60 percent of the earmark pool, and the minority party receives 40 percent—especially in the Senate.

Interestingly, the appropriation may occur directly or indirectly. Directly, legislation may be inserted into an appropriations bill under consideration by the House or the Senate. Occasionally, earmark language may be incorporated directly into an authorization bill. Indirectly, the earmark appropriation may be specified in the legislative report accompanying an appropriations bill. These reports convey congressional intent underlying the actual legislation. Most earmarks (80 to 90 percent) originate via this indirect method; they are not specified in the actual appropriations bill, just in the accompanying report. In that sense, the indirect earmarks do not carry the full force of law. Nonetheless, federal agencies customarily honor earmarks and other conditions contained in the legislative report, mainly because they rely on congressional goodwill for subsequent appropriations.

Because the congressionally directed earmarks are funded from the discretionary budget, the amount available for a federal agency's programmatic priorities as requested in the President's budget is decreased. For example, the Department of Energy's discretionary budget for competitive grant programs may be decreased because of the mandate to fund a congressionally directed earmark such as an ethanol-fuel facility in a particular Congress member's district. Because earmarks decrease the agency's overall programmatic budget, they are understandably very unpopular among federal agency administrators. And that explains the OMB's harshly stated definition of earmarks. (Note: the OMB is in the executive branch and reports to the President.)

Universities get their earmarks through members of their congressional delegation. In this context, the delegation refers to both Senate and House members representing the university's district. If the university has campuses (including field stations and so forth) in more than one congressional district, then the House members representing those other districts may also be considered part of the university's delegation. Predictably, the most influential earmark procurers are members of the appropriations committees, including their various subcommittees. Practically speaking, each member of Congress can expect to deliver only a limited number of earmarks per year. And they receive requests from numerous constituents. A university can expect to get no more than about five or six per session from each member of the delegation, and usually no more than two or three from any particular federal agency (for example, the Department of Energy). Often, several universities will collaborate on a request to garner support from more than one delegation; then, they divide the earmark according to a formula that they have agreed to beforehand. Notably, some members of Congress oppose earmarking as a matter of principle, and they may not entertain any requests.

Generally, the members of the delegation ask universities for a list of their earmark requests, along with a brief description, a proposed budget, and a summary of results obtained from previous earmarks for the same project. And they should be rank-ordered in terms of university priorities. The amount that can be requested depends on the delegation's political influence. The actual amount per project can vary widely; it may range from $1 million to $50 million or more, although the usual size is about $2 million. For the costlier items (which may be a building or a ship, for example), it may take several years before the earmark can be obtained. One strategy is to spread the cost over several years. Also, because of the 60:40 split of earmarked funds between majority and minority party members, changes in the majority party following an election will most probably affect the amount that the university might expect to receive from its earmark requests. Earmarks may be renewed; indeed, they usually are for several years. Most members of Congress balk at funding a particular project for more than six or seven years, although there is no legal limit to the number of renewals.

The chief research officer routinely oversees preparation of the earmark requests and their delivery to members of the delegation. Common practice is for the chief research officer to issue a call for proposals, with preparation guidelines to each dean or, in some cases, each member of the faculty. He or she then sifts through the proposals with an eye toward strategic priorities (the university's strategic plan) and, more important, the probability of funding from a political viewpoint. Proposed projects must have some political appeal to be successful. That important point—the need for political appeal—is poorly understood by many faculty members and university administrators, including deans. The chief research officer frequently needs to explain this aspect of political reality to disappointed colleagues whose earmark proposal has not been chosen for consideration. Most universities have staff members with expertise in government affairs to help with this political vetting process. In the end, a final list is prepared with the necessary documentation—description, budget, and so forth. Often, an attractive bound volume is printed for distribution to members of the delegation.

Importantly, universities must control the submission of earmark requests to members of the congressional delegation. The delegation members must recognize that the formal list prepared by the chief research officer unambiguously repre-sents the university's official, definitive request. Any other requests emanating from other sources, such as governing board members, deans, faculty members, alumni, or members of the general public, must be strongly discouraged because they may potentially confuse members of the delegation: "Is this a university priority? Does it replace something on the list?" Of course, any citizen may communicate freely with members of Congress and thus transmit an unofficial earmark request. Consequently, the chief research officer must diligently remind delegation members about the primacy of the officially submitted priority list. Realistically, when the chief research officer learns about a planned unofficial earmark request, he or she should not aggressively try to intervene. The better strategy is simply to alert the delegation about the forthcoming request and remind them about the official priority list.

Universities often retain professional lobbyists to help procure earmarks. There are several major firms with considerable experience in representing universities. For a medium-size university, their annual fees are in the $300,000 to $500,000 range—plus expenses such as travel and entertainment. Of course, everything is negotiable. It is also common for some institutions to hire former members of Congress or members of their staff to work with the lobbyists on specific projects. And some of the large universities and university systems maintain permanent lobbying staff members in Washington, D.C.

Working with the chief research officer, lobbyists typically assist in developing the call for proposals and vetting them from a political viewpoint. They also deliver by hand the final list and any other communications from the university to the members of Congress. This service can be quite helpful because it routinely takes nearly a month for mail delivery after it has been received in Washington. (Each incoming piece is inspected for security reasons.) Lobbyists' help goes well beyond that, of course. They communicate regularly with members of the delega-tion to answer questions about the university's request and to monitor progress. Furthermore, they occasionally help the congressional staff members write the legislation appropriating an earmark.[7]

If a requested earmark stalls, the lobbyist will usually step in and try to get it moving again. And after an earmark is awarded, the lobbyist tracks it to the funding agency (for example, a particular program in the Department of Energy) to ensure a timely award. This is not a trivial pursuit. Many federal agencies bristle at earmarks because they divert money from the agencies' high-priority programs. Thus, they use various tactics to thwart funding earmarks, sometimes successfully. In a related context, lobbyists can help obtain the appropriate program element (PE) number, which the Department of Defense uses in the budget process to identify each program, and other account information.

Are lobbyists worth the money? Each chief research officer asks that question every year when lobbying contracts must be renewed. The answer is elusive. Lobbyists will tabulate how much earmark funding the university has gained relative to the retainer cost. This ratio is usually quite large; forty- or fifty-fold is not unusual. However, could the university have garnered that much earmark funding independent of lobbyists? After all, university chief executive officers usually communicate regularly with members of the delegation and can effectively present the university's congressional funding priorities. And, anecdotally, many members of the delegation profess indifference to lobbyists in this context. Ultimately, if the university is seeking a large (for example, $50 million) complicated earmark such as a major research facility, building, or ship, a lobbyist's services probably warrant the cost. For "routine" $1 million or $2 million requests, many universities may not need a professional lobbyist. Investing the retainer costs in the research enterprise may be more effective use of the money.

Within academe, there are divergent opinions about earmarks (and about lobbyists). Yes, earmarks can provide a major boost to a university's research capacity. New programs can be launched with the hopeful expectation that they quickly become self-sustaining through competitive grants. And new facilities can be obtained to improve the overall research infrastructure. Furthermore, some proponents assert that the "people," via their members of Congress, know better how to spend public funds than "some federal agency bureaucrat."

Unfortunately, earmarks can also become lifelines for research programs that either cannot compete successfully for extramural funding or that are in disciplines where little federal funding is available. They may engender a sense of complacency and entitlement among recipient faculty members. Some opponents argue against earmarks because they circumvent a competitive, peer-reviewed process and subsequent accountability. To be fair, earmark recipients must submit a thorough accounting of how the funds were spent, and this is reviewed and audited by the funding agency. However, earmark opponents claim that this is not comparable to rigorous peer review; the quality of the research is not necessarily evaluated. In other words, earmarks entail no thorough accountability.

Not surprisingly, the most vocal opposition comes from universities with extensive peer-reviewed federal funding. The nation's most prestigious group of research universities, the Association of American Universities (AAU), issued a policy statement urging members to refrain from seeking or accepting earmarks: "AAU is concerned that Congressional earmarking of federal research funds may reduce the capacity of federal agencies that sponsor merit-based competitions to support the most promising research and will thereby impair the quality of our national research program. AAU institutions have a responsibility to support a strong research program based on merit and should refrain from seeking or accepting earmarks that put merit-reviewed funding at risk."[8]

They acknowledge that "not all federal research funds will be allocated according to strict, competitive merit-review criteria" and that "historically most U.S. Department of Agriculture research funding has not been awarded through competitive merit review." However, "These deviations from or exceptions to the primary process of allocating federal research funds by merit-reviewed competition should not be used by AAU institutions as a license to seek earmarks that could threaten the merit-based funding that is essential to sustaining the highest quality research and providing the most effective use of federal research dollars."[9]

Many of the AAU's sixty-three member institutions adhere to this policy. For example, the Massachusetts Institute of Technology (MIT) states explicitly that it is "MIT policy not to accept earmarks."[10] In contrast, the *Chronicle of Higher Education* reported that in 2008 another AAU member, Texas A&M University, ranked fourth nationally in the amount of earmarked money received ($31.3 million), and there are anecdotal reports that many more AAU members actively seek earmarks.[11] Indeed, one of the pioneers of major earmark legislation was Columbia University, a prestigious AAU member.[12] Moreover, the *Chronicle* analysis shows that legislators channeled more than 2,300 projects to 920 institutions, mostly for research, in the 2008 fiscal year.[13]

Earmarks may increase the university's extramural funding and its overall research capacity, but unfortunately, they may not help its academic reputation. In some academic circles, there is a stigma attached to earmarks. This negative attitude is expressed explicitly in a 2001 article on earmarking in *Science*: "Without the need to justify expenditures to expert reviewers, schools often spend earmarks on projects that do little to boost their competitiveness . . . . As a result . . . top earmarkers . . . rarely improve on their middling rank on a list of universities with the most federally funded research."[14] Thus, the chief research officer should consult with the provost and the chief executive officer about the merits of aggressively pursuing earmarked funds. There is a trade-off that ultimately defines the university's public image.

> K: *You don't seem to be very enthusiastic about earmarks.*
> Smith: *I'm not. In a certain sense, they are counter to the university's fundamental meritocracy. Success at getting earmarked funding often depends on a politician's skills, not just the faculty members' merits.*
> K: *But isn't that also the case for all federal funding agencies? Ultimately, their budgets are the product of political maneuvering. And I'm not sure that merit is the driving force there.*
> Smith: *Yes, politics play a significant role in all aspects of the federal budget and merit is seldom the driving force. But at least agencies like NIH and NSF allocate most of their appropriated funds by a peer-reviewed system.*
> K: *Isn't there politicking in that process as well?*
> Smith: *There is, of course. We live in a political world. Ultimately, if earmarking is the game, we have to play it. So play it well.*

Programs to Stimulate Competitive Research

The federal research-funding portfolio includes two noteworthy programs designed to stimulate competitive research capacity—the NIH Institutional Development

Awards (IDeA) and the NSF Experimental Program to Stimulate Competitive Research (EPSCoR). These two programs are designed to build research capacity in states that traditionally have not fared well in the arena of competitive grants. According to the NIH, the IDeA program "broadens the geographic distribution of NIH funding for biomedical and behavioral research. The program fosters health-related research and enhances the competitiveness of investigators at institutions located in states in which the aggregate success rate for applications to NIH has historically been low. The program also serves unique populations—such as rural and medically underserved communities—in these states."[15] Researchers in the twenty-three states plus Puerto Rico that received the least amount of NIH funding are eligible for funding through the IDeA program.

Similarly, the NSF's EPSCoR mission is to provide a mechanism "to strengthen research and education in science and engineering throughout the United States and to avoid undue concentration of such research and education."[16] EPSCoR's goals are "to provide strategic programs and opportunities for EPSCoR participants that stimulate sustainable improvements in their R&D capacity and competitiveness" and "to advance science and engineering capabilities in EPSCoR jurisdictions for discovery, innovation and overall knowledge-based prosperity."[17] The twenty-five states plus Puerto Rico and the U.S. Virgin Islands that received the least aggregate NSF funding over the previous three years are eligible for the EPSCoR program.

The benefits of being an IDeA or EPSCoR state are profound. Both programs provide large infrastructure grants designed to boost overall research competitiveness in a way that is available only to eligible states. Although applications are judged competitively, nearly every applicant state receives these grants within one or two submission cycles. A good example is the NIH IDeA Networks of Biomedical Research Excellence (INBRE) grant program. These awards, which are typically for about $15 million over a five-year period, provide funding for young investigators' research programs, bioinformatics resources, undergraduate- and graduate-student support, and other infrastructural items. Furthermore, these funds must be allocated to the various institutions—baccalaureate and doctoral—throughout the state. EPSCoR has similar infrastructure awards. Moreover, both agencies have so-called co-funding. In these cases, the agencies set aside money from their overall extramural grant budget to enable funding of proposals that were judged meritorious by established peer-review committees but that received priority scores below the fundable range. Thus, researchers in the IDeA and EPSCoR states have an advantage—a handicap, to use a golfing metaphor—in the grant-application peer-review process.

Predictably, the IDeA and the EPSCoR programs are unpopular among researchers in the ineligible states. "They're funding uncompetitive science at the expense of top-rate programs" and similar derogatory utterances tarnish the underlying merit of these programs. Those laments must be heard in proper context because, in reality, the overall IDeA and EPSCoR budgets amount to less than 1 and

2 percent of the agency overall budgets, respectively. It might also be argued that these programs benefit the disadvantaged baccalaureate institutions. One anecdote recants the story that, because of IDeA funding, a small baccalaureate college was able to replace an antiquated triple-beam balance with a modern electronic scale capable of microgram resolution. An NIH program director commented: "How else could these institutions provide a twenty-first-century education to their students?" In fact, that opinion encompasses the spirit of EPSCoR and IDeA: breed a new generation of scientists in the have-not states. Cynics would reply, Yes, but how about comparably disadvantaged colleges in non-IDeA states? The equitable solution to this conundrum is not soon forthcoming. From a political perspective, these programs are safe and justifiable. They help spread federal tax dollars more equitably among the fifty states, Puerto Rico, and the U. S. Virgin Islands. And proponents have about half of the Senate votes in support of these programs.

Major Facilities

Research capacity can increase significantly when a university takes over management of a large research facility. Two well-known examples of university-managed major facilities are the Jet Propulsion Laboratory and the Lincoln Laboratory, administered by California Institute of Technology (Caltech) and MIT, respectively. Like these two examples, fourteen other large facilities that conduct research for the federal government as so-called Federally Funded Research and Development Centers (FFRDCs) are administered by universities and colleges, either individually or as part of a consortium.[18] In addition, there are numerous university-administered facilities not on the FFRDC list that might be considered major because of their size, availability to researchers from other institutions, and research impact. A good example is the San Diego Supercomputer Center administered by the University of California, San Diego.

There is usually intense competition among universities for contracts to administer these facilities because of the expected benefits to the institution. The rewards are enhanced prestige and, more important, easy access for their own researchers, including students. In the latter case, research capacity goes up because of the addition of more staff investigators (additions to base) and an enriched environment (a stimulus to growth). These contracts are not easily won. To compete effectively, a university—that usually means the chief research officer—must assemble a team to prepare the proposal and enlist the support of the congressional delegation. Politics can play a significant role in the competitive process, and the chief research officer must be keenly aware of that. The university will probably have to make a considerable investment (maybe hundreds of thousands of dollars) on its own simply to mount a competitive effort and will probably be expected to contribute money (maybe tens of millions of dollars) and perhaps land if they are successful. But this is "big science", and it is generally worth the investment.

Sometimes, a university's unique location provides the opportunity to manage a large research enterprise and to increase research capacity along the way. Prime examples are the Mauna Kea observatories, a collection of thirteen independent telescopes located on state land managed by the University of Hawaii. The summit of Mauna Kea, a 13,803-foot-high shield volcano, offers one of the world's best locations for astronomical observations owing to nearly laminar wind flow across the mountain, clear air, and very low ambient lighting. The individual telescopes are owned and operated by various consortia comprising universities or government agencies of the United States and foreign countries. As the state-appointed landlord, the University of Hawaii manages the overall facility. For rent, the university gets between 10 and 15 percent of the observing time on each telescope that it does not own. No money changes hands, just observing time. And this observing time is invaluable, for it provides the university's faculty members and their students with generous access to the world's premier telescopes.

A university's existing facilities can attract similar installations because of the supportive, synergistic infrastructure. As an example, in 2009 the federal government (the Department of Homeland Security) chose to locate a major facility to house agents of infectious disease, the National Bio and Agro-Defense Facility (NBAF), on the Kansas State University (KSU) campus in Manhattan, Kansas. This followed an intense competition among seventeen applicants to host the facility. In their selection announcement, the Department of Homeland Security stated that "the site location near KSU provides site proximity to existing research capabilities that can be linked to NBAF mission requirements. Additionally, the site's proximity to the KSU College of Veterinary Medicine, KSU College of Agriculture, and the Biosecurity Research Institute is relevant to the NBAF mission and a significant strength."[19] As part of their proposal to attract this $650 million facility, the State of Kansas agreed to build a $105 million power plant, and Kansas State University agreed to provide the necessary land on campus—right next door to their existing Biosecurity Research Institute.

The university does not receive any significant direct monetary benefit from having the facility on its campus. However, the indirect benefits abound. Since the award announcement, the USDA has relocated its Arthropod-Borne Animal Diseases Research Unit from Laramie, Wyoming, to Manhattan. Moreover, Kansas State anticipates that its faculty members will reap access to biosecurity expertise through cooperation and collaborations with NBAF staff members. Further advantages, including money, may accrue if Kansas State is selected by the Department of Homeland Security to manage the facility. That managerial decision has not yet been made; however, as the host institution, Kansas State should be a strong candidate.

Characteristically for large-facility competitions, Kansas State enlisted letters of support from sixteen different partner institutions, such as Colorado State University, Iowa State University, and others, to bolster its original application. Typically, these letters document their institutions' expertise in the discipline and their commitments to lend technical and academic assistance to specific projects involving the facility and its ancillary programs. Like Kansas State, these consortium members receive no formal monetary benefit from the award. However, the projected rewards for their support will be subcontracts from subsequent grants and contracts received by Kansas State predicated on its housing the national facility.

Corporate Alliances

Over the past twenty years, private industries have been downsizing their research laboratories and contracting more and more of their research to universities. This provides industry access to the university's expertise and, conversely, enhances the institution's research capacity, for it introduces new opportunities for interdisciplinary research and development of intellectual property. Moreover, it provides opportunities for students to become familiar with industry and its operations.

Some of these corporate alliances have been colossal in size. One of the first large alliances was between Washington University in St. Louis and the Monsanto Corporation, also in St. Louis. In 1982, they signed an agreement that focused on one specific topic—namely, the role of proteins and peptides in cell-to-cell communication. Monsanto provided the university's medical school with $23.5 million, distributed over a five-year period; of this, 30 percent went to basic research and 70 percent to applied research. The total award was purposely kept at less than 10 percent of the medical school's overall research budget to minimize its potential influence on school policies. These funds were allocated to Washington University investigators by an internal peer-review process; all faculty members were eligible to apply. Importantly, all intellectual property would vest with Washington University. In return for its investment, Monsanto was guaranteed an exclusive license to any intellectual property arising from the joint venture, and its scientists and technicians were granted access to university laboratories and researchers, thus learning new techniques. Furthermore, Monsanto could request a thirty-day delay in any publications funded by their money, which gave them advanced access to the results.

But an even larger alliance was on the horizon. A 2007 agreement between British Petroleum (BP) and the Universities of California and Illinois shattered the mold. After a nationwide competition, BP selected the University of California, Berkeley, in partnership with Lawrence Berkeley National Laboratory (LBNL) and the University of Illinois at Urbana-Champaign, to lead a ten-year, $500 million research effort "to develop new sources of energy and reduce the impact of energy consumption on the environment."[20] A new institute, the Energy Biosciences Institute (EBI), was created, and BP agreed to pay $50 million annually to support research programs, help fund a new building to house the EBI, and hire seven new faculty members.

The EBI has two components: open and proprietary. The open component houses university faculty members whose research results can be published in academic journals as usual. In contrast, the proprietary component is staffed only by BP employees working on confidential BP projects. Although it is located adjacent to the open component, the proprietary component is closed to university personnel. The intellectual-property agreement is standard. Ownership belongs to the discoverer: BP owns what its employees discover, and the university owns what its employees discover. In addition, because of their investment, BP has the option to a nonexclusive, royalty-free license to any open-research intellectual property, plus first right of negotiation for an exclusive license. Although the BP alliance is exceptional because of the amount of money involved, it provides a good template for large corporate alliances.

Many universities have less grandiose agreements with corporate partners that also enhance the institutional research capacity. A fairly common model, sometimes called a university-industry research center, brings together researchers from industry and the university to work on projects of mutual interest. This may be applied research focusing on a particular industry project or more fundamental research in the general area. Often the collaborating partners sign an overarching agreement that acknowledges their shared interests in a particular topic, such as wind power, and that covers boilerplate issues such as intellectual property rights, confidentiality, liability and indemnification, and publication rights. Notably, these generalized agreements typically do not mention any specific research projects; instead, they usually state that these will be the subject of separate project-specific agreements.

Industrial affiliates may pay an annual fee to participate in these consortia. In return, they gain access to university expertise and resources. The fee amount depends on the specifics of the agreement. If the university agrees to conduct research on an industrial partner's particular project, the fee may be quite high (approaching $1 million). Guaranteed patent-licensing options, faculty consulting time, and other university-based services also raise the fee. In contrast, if the university agrees to less costly endeavors, such as sponsoring occasional workshops on topics of interest to the consortia members—for example, the merits of various industry-specific accounting software programs—the fees may be much less extravagant (perhaps about $20,000). In some agreements, neither party pays a fee. Instead, they agree formally or informally to apply as a consortium for federal funding to support a joint project.

These corporate alliances are not without controversy. Several issues raise concerns. The presence of a proprietary component closed to the general university community, which is not unusual in university-corporation partnerships, can become a flashpoint. It did in the BP alliance. The Foundation for Taxpayer and Consumer Rights in Santa Monica said that the BP agreement "compromises the university's commitment to public education by allowing secret corporate research on campus."[21] Another major concern is the potential influence of the generous corporate partner on traditional academic priorities: will they influence directly or indirectly the tenure and promotion decisions or faculty members' research directions? Furthermore, has the university ceded land or building space to the corporate partner that might have been more used more beneficially for some other core purpose (such as teaching)? And, has the university cheapened its reputation because it has "sold itself" to gain corporate money? These and other questions must be answered as part of any negotiated corporate partnership agreement.[22]

Where does the chief research officer come into all of this? Nearly everywhere. Although the corporate entities may initiate discussions about an alliance with an individual faculty member, a dean, a member of the governing board, or some other person affiliated with the university, the suggestion is usually referred very quickly to the chief research officer. He or she then organizes exploratory conversations with corporate representatives and interested university participants, usually faculty members. Importantly, throughout this process, the chief research officer must consult extensively with faculty members (typically through the faculty senate) to develop guidelines providing adequate protection of the university's academic interests. As negotiations proceed, other university administrators become involved, including the deans, the provost, the chief financial officer, and the chief executive officer. But the chief research officer usually remains the primary point of contact.

In larger cases, the closing deal is struck at the chief executive officer level—on both sides. The chief research officer may not be party to the final negotiations. In highly visible deals, state governors and members of the congressional delegation may also step into the picture. And, not unusually, publicity surrounding a successful agreement will be dominated by executives at the highest level. The chief research officer should not feel slighted; this is standard protocol. As a matter of fiduciary policy, most governing boards do not delegate the authority to approve contracts exceeding several million dollars. Thus, the final negotiations involving these sizable agreements move to their level—or at least to the chief executive officer. Indeed, the chief research officer will have succeeded if the chief executive officers of both the university and the industrial partner take ownership of the alliance. Getting the negotiations to their level should be a strategic goal for the chief research officer. Remember, however: after the agreement has been signed, a faculty member will probably be the alliance director, but the chief research officer will in all likelihood be held responsible for its success or failure. For that reason, he or she is usually an ex officio member of the alliance's governing body.

K: *If a corporation provides generous research funding in return for access to university expertise and facilities, I can understand the concerns about their influence on faculty research priorities.*

Smith: *I can, too. But researchers typically follow the money. Federal funding agencies like the NSF and NIH are continuously announcing "calls for proposals" to do research on this or that specific topic. Take cancer research, for example. And researchers routinely shift their interests in those directions, like plants growing toward sunlight.*

K: I suppose that you're right. At least, a faculty member always has the right not to do research on any specific topic.

Smith: Realistically, though, the researcher has little choice but to work on projects where funding is available. Without the necessary money, you can't do much. Academic freedom has its practical limitations in this respect.

Public and Private Consortia

A university can also enhance its research capacity by participating in consortia that include government agencies. These alliances among the state government, several universities, and private industries can be particularly effective at marshaling resources to address a specific aspect of economic development. For example, in 2007, the Texas governor's office prompted the establishment of a consortium comprising several universities (including Texas A&M, Texas Tech, the University of Houston, and others) and industrial partners (including Shell, BP, Vestas, and others) to develop the state's alternative-fuel industry. A similar statewide consortium focused on nanotechnology initiatives. These consortia are smaller versions of "big science."

Each member of the nanotechnology initiative was expected to contribute to the initial capitalization. This is the money needed to set up the office, prepare grant proposals, buy shared equipment, pay for cost sharing on grants and contracts, and other items. The amount varied, but it was in the $10 to $25 million range. Unlike a poker ante, each member did not contribute the same amount to the pool; wealthier universities were expected to contribute larger amounts. The relatively wealthy University of Texas at Austin and Texas A&M were asked to provide $25 million each, but the less wealthy partners such as Texas Tech were asked to pay $10 million in initial costs. Notably, the state contributed only indirectly through competitive research grants and contracts. Consortium members had to apply for these funds, but they generally had a clear advantage because of their combined resources and expertise. According to the business plans in each of these examples, government and private-industry grants submitted by various partners through the consortium were expected to provide revenue to fund ongoing operating costs (F&A costs), as well as direct research costs.

In these consortia, one member usually serves as the formal administrator, but the other members all contribute to the governance in one way or another. The usual method is via seats on the consortium's governing board. Seats are allocated according to the members' financial contributions. Thus, in the Texas nanotechnology example, the University of Texas and Texas A&M would each have had three seats (rounding up) on the governing board whereas Texas Tech would have had one.

The initial costs of joining these consortia—tens of millions of dollars in many cases—limit the number of universities capable of participating. Indeed, Texas Tech was ultimately unable to join the state's nanotechnology consortium because it could not afford the $10 million initial cost.

This example illustrates a more general impediment to building research capacity: the need for investment capital. As the adage states, "it takes money to make money." Most large research universities have access to sizable pools of money needed for these kinds of research investments. For example, the University of Texas and University of Wisconsin have access to oil revenue from land holdings, the so-called Permanent Fund, and patent-generated income through the Wisconsin Alumni Research Foundation (WARF), respectively. Other universities have large endowments that provide revenue for these purposes. And "the rich get richer" through participation in these relatively large-scale consortia. Consequently, a major research capacity-building goal of chief research officers at less pecuniary institutions must be to generate a pool of investment capital (at least $10 million) that can be used to join these potentially lucrative consortia.

In most of these arrangements, especially those involving private industry, the consortia organizes as a not-for-profit corporation under section 501(c)(3) of the Internal Revenue Service (IRS) code. This serves two purposes. First, it creates a separate legal entity distinct from the member institutions. Thus, the consortium is exempt from state procurement laws and other impediments. Second, it limits the financial and legal liability of the members. Importantly, most consortium bylaws obligate the member institutions to cover revenue shortfalls and other financial obligations incurred by the alliance. However, the individual members have the liability protection offered by the corporate veil. They are not personally liable for the consortium's debt and other obligations provided that business was conducted according to corporate laws. The articles of incorporation and the bylaws are drawn up mainly by legal counsel, although the chief research officer may be asked to provide guidance in their preparation.

Incidentally, according to the IRS, a 501(c)(3) corporation "may not attempt to influence legislation as a substantial part of its activities and it may not participate in any campaign activity for or against political candidates."[23] Thus, the consortium cannot engage in any political lobbying.

Under this structure, participating members may submit grant applications through the consortia, thus bypassing the university's control. This can be very tempting to faculty members and very troubling for the chief research officer. The faculty member may perceive that he or she can expect a greater return of F&A funds from the consortium. Moreover, the consortium is not subject to the university's often cumbersome procurement and hiring policies. There is another perceived advantage. In most universities, a faculty member is allowed one day per week for consulting. Income earned during that time is above and beyond anything paid by the university unless it comes from a federal grant. According to OMB circular A-21, federal grant money cannot be used to pay the investigator more than what the university pays. However, if the federal grant is awarded to the consortium, this limitation applies to the salary paid by the consortium, and that may be higher than what the university pays.

But what if the member institutions stipulate that the consortium cannot pay higher salaries than they do? There is still the opportunity to get a bigger paycheck. Technically, if the faculty member gets one day per week for consulting, that means that the university pays for only four workdays per week (not five). So, a day's pay is one-fourth of a weekly paycheck, not one-fifth. That's a 25 percent pay increase that can be justifiably built into the grant budget if it's submitted through the consortium instead of the university. This is such an attractive situation that some enterprising faculty members establish their own small corporations to administer their grants. Of course, they must not use university facilities or resources for any aspect of this venture, or they could be subject to criminal prosecution. Understandably, universities try hard to prevent faculty members from exploiting these consortia arrangements in these ways because they deprive them of F&A recovery and reportable research expenditures.

> K: *Can't the university establish a policy that punishes faculty members who take advantage of them like this?*
>
> Smith: *Not easily. It's very difficult to keep a watchful eye on everything that a faculty member does. And, you don't want to discourage faculty members from participating in otherwise very attractive consortia. Plus, I would find it a bit awkward to deprive faculty members of this opportunity if the university's policies made it notoriously difficult to do research.*
>
> K: *If that were the case—the university is just a tough place to do research— shouldn't you try to improve conditions? Reduce the incentive to go outside the university?*
>
> Smith: *Definitely, yes. The advantages of participating in these larger scale research consortia are so important that it is worth every effort to make them work, and that includes cleaning up in-house impediments to research.*

Notes

1. Department for International Development (DFID), "DFID Research Strategy 2008-2013: Capacity Building," p. 3, 2008, http://www.dfid.gov.uk/R4D/PDF/Outputs/Consultation/ResearchStrategyWorkingPaperfinal_capacity_P1.pdf (accessed January 6, 2011).
2. National Science Foundation, "R&D Expenditures at Universities and Colleges", 2010, http://www.nsf.gov/statistics/nsf10311/content.cfm?pub_id=3944&id=2 (accessed January 6, 2011).
3. University of Hawaii Board of Regents and the University of Hawaii Professional Assembly, "Conversion of Temporary Appointments to Probationary Status, Article XIII, B," agreement between the University of Hawaii Professional Assembly (UHPA) and the University of Hawaii Board of Regents (UH-BOR), Honolulu, Hawaii, 2009, p. 30.

4. Texas Tech University, "Approval of Faculty in Non Tenure-acquiring Ranks," Operating Policy and Procedure 32.34, Lubbock, Texas , 2006, p. 1.

5. R. Porter and S. Walsh, "Earmarks in the Federal Budget Process," Harvard Law School Federal Budget Policy Seminar, Briefing Paper no.16, Cambridge, Mass., 2006, p. 4.

6. Office of Management and Budget, 2010, "OMB Guidance to Agencies on Definition of Earmarks," http://earmarks.omb.gov/earmarks_definition.html (accessed January 6, 2011).

7. R. G. Kaiser, *So Damn Much Money: The Triumph of Lobbying and the Corrosion of American Government* (New York: Knopf, 2009).

8. Association of American Universities (AAU), "AAU Statement on Preserving Merit Review In Federal Funding of University Research," 2005, http://www.aau.edu/search/default. aspx?searchtext=earmarks (accessed January 6, 2011).

9. Ibid.

10. Massachusetts Institute of Technology, Office of Sponsored Programs, "Congressional Earmarks," 2003, http://osp.mit.edu/policies/congressional-earmarks (accessed January 6, 2011).

11. J. Brainard and J. Hermes, "Colleges' Earmarks Grow Amid Criticism," *Chronicle of Higher Education,* 54, no. 29 (2008): A1.

12. Kaiser, *So Damn Much Money*, p. 11.

13. J. Brainard and J. Hermes, 2008, p. A1.

14. D. Malakoff, "Lobbying: Hawaii Rides a Wave of Research Earmarks," *Science,* 292, no. 5518 (2003): 835.

15. National Institutes of Health, Institutional Development Award, 2011, http://www.ncrr.nih. gov/research_infrastructure/institutional_development_award/ (accessed January 6, 2011).

16. National Science Foundation, "About EPSCoR," 2009, http://www.nsf.gov/od/oia/programs/ epscor/about.jsp (accessed January 6, 2011).

17. Ibid.

18. National Science Foundation, "Federally Funded R&D Centers Master Government List," 2009, http://www.nsf.gov/statistics/ffrdc/start.cfm (accessed January 6, 2011).

19. Department of Homeland Security, "Science and Technology Directorate; Record of Decision for the National Bio and Agro-Defense Facility Environmental Impact Statement," *Federal Register,*74, no. 11 (2009): 3065-6.

20. R. Sanders, "BP Selects UC Berkeley to Lead $500 Million Energy Research Consortium with Co-Partners Lawrence Berkeley National Lab, University of Illinois," *UC Berkeley News,* February 1, 2007, http://berkeley.edu/news/media/releases/2007/02/01_ebi.shtml (accessed January 6, 2011).

21. C. Burress, "UC Berkeley, BP Finally Sign Contract for Research Project," *SFGate,* November 15, 2007, http://www.sfgate.com/cgi-bin/article.cgi?f=/c/a/2007/11/15/BAABTCDKK.DTL. ixzz0OkEKUQSS (accessed January 6, 2011).

22. J. Washburn, *University, Inc.* (New York: Basic Books, 2005).

23. Internal Revenue Service (IRS), "Organizations Lobbying Expenditures," § 501(c)(3), in publication no. 557, *Tax-Exempt Status for Your Organization* (Washington, D.C.: IRS, 2008), p. 44.

CHAPTER 6

Resource Investments

K: With the strategic plan as a guide, how do you actually allocate resources?

Smith: That's not as easy as it might seem to be. Things can go astray, sometimes with curious consequences, if there's a perception of unfair bias in resource allocations.

K: If the strategic plan favors specific programs, how can you avoid apparent favoritism?

Smith: You can't. But you can mitigate bad feelings by involving the faculty members in many funding decisions.

Faculty Investment

Axiomatically, research universities invest in their faculty members. From the moment that they are hired, faculty members receive start-up funding and suitable space to establish an independent research program. And this investment continues throughout a faculty member's productive career—although it may occur somewhat sporadically. The chief research officer plays a pivotal role in making these investments; indeed, it is a major responsibility. And, realistically, his or her entire discretionary budget (excluding office personnel and operational expenses) goes into faculty research.

In return for this investment, the university expects faculty members to generate revenue from research grants and contracts to support their research programs, as well as the institutional infrastructure. Some colleges and departments specify implicitly a required rate of return on their investment by requiring faculty members to generate a fraction of their salary from extramural sources. In these cases, the university sets a base salary but contractually provides salary for less than a 100 percent time appointment; the faculty members must obtain the remaining fraction (up to 100 percent) from other sources. To retain case-by-case flexibility, few institutions specify explicitly the number of extramural grant awards or dollars that must be generated. However, they may set informal guidelines, such as the need to obtain at least two NIH research grants to be eligible for tenure consideration or to generate three dollars from extramural sources for every one dollar of institutional investment. Note: unless these expectations are documented conditions of employment, they cannot be used formally as tenure or promotion criteria.

The simplest form of investment is to give research money directly to the faculty members. Usually, this occurs via a regularly scheduled, periodic competition. Even if the average amount is small (for example, less than $25,000), these institutional awards are extremely valuable. Many faculty members see them as the lifeline that keeps them afloat in hard times or the gateway to new research opportunities. If the competition precludes some applicants from receiving an award, emotions can run high when funding decisions are announced. So there has to be a well-respected, credible mechanism for making choices as to who gets what. As in the preparation of a strategic plan, the constituency (the faculty members in this case) must buy into the investment process. Otherwise, the result may be disappointment and even backlash.

Before discussing the mechanisms for achieving the necessary buy-in underlying the investment process, it is informative to determine who actually owns the university's resources.

Spending Authority

In nearly all universities, the governing board has authority over all financial matters, including money. This stewardship is established in the founding charter or the articles of incorporation of private universities and the state constitution or enabling legislation for public universities. Stanford University's founding grant provides a good example: "The Executive and Finance Committee [of the Board] shall have the management and control, subject to the approval of the Board, of the property, the finances, and the general business of the University."[1] This control extends to all funds administered by the university, including all research grants and gifts. The latter point may startle individuals who have written and submitted a grant application through the university. The governing board—not the principal investigator—retains the ultimate authority over the award money.

Although the governing board has the ultimate authority, many funds must be spent within the fiduciary controls established by an external entity. These include restricted funds appropriated by a state legislature, gifts and endowments, grants and contracts, and federal programs. Moreover, there are usually state laws governing the allowable uses of state money. So, the governing board technically owns the money but cannot spend it all on whatever it wants. Therefore, if the governing board can't, nobody else in the university can, either.

In nearly all universities, the governing-board policies delegate the money management downstream to the chief executive officer, who delegates to the chief financial officer, the provost, and the chief research officer. And these individuals have further authority to delegate management of funds under their control on down the organizational ladder to deans, department chairs, and individual faculty members. In the case of a grant or contract, the delegation routinely extends down this pathway to the principal investigator on the premise that he or she prepared the grant proposal on behalf of the university and is, therefore, uniquely qualified and responsible for its administration. The governing board seldom trumps its delegated authority. However, a department chair or dean may intervene in cases of a principal investigator's mismanagement of grant or contract funds, such as cost overruns, unallowable expenses, and failure to submit required financial reports.

As far as the chief research officer is concerned, he or she is given a budget and has the responsibility to spend it wisely. During normal day-to-day business, it may not matter that the money actually belongs to the governing board. Nonetheless, the chief research officer must always remember that the board has the ultimate authority over how the money is spent. Occasionally, a board may mandate a specific research initiative, and the chief research officer must comply, even if it takes resources from some other program or project. Protesting that this is unwanted micromanagement or that the requested expenditure is inconsistent with a board-approved strategic plan does little good, for the board has the final authority.

Although the governing board is assigned responsibility for university financial matters, in many states there is a caveat that allows the legislature to control some aspects of the university's money. For example, in its establishment of the University of California, the California State Constitution provides for legislative control over financial matters "as may be necessary":

> The University of California shall constitute a public trust to be adminis-
> tered by the existing corporation known as "The Regents of the University
> of California," with full powers of organization and government, subject
> only to such legislative control as may be necessary to insure the security
> of its funds and compliance with the terms of the endowments of the
> university and such competitive bidding procedures as may be made
> applicable to the university by statute for the letting of construction
> contracts, sales of real property, and purchasing of materials, goods, and
> services.[2]

More recently, Hawaii amended its constitution in 2000 to grant the university constitutional autonomy over its money management, but it left open the opportunity for legislative involvement: "The board shall also have exclusive jurisdiction over the internal structure, management, and operation of the university. This section shall not limit the power of the legislature to enact laws of statewide concern. The legislature shall have the exclusive jurisdiction to identify laws of statewide concern."[3] What might be of "statewide concern?" The most probable answer is "how money is spent." Consequently, in these situations, the chief research officer may discover that the legislature has decided to direct how some of the money ostensibly under his or her control will be spent.

In some states, the legislature has far greater control over money it appropriates to the university. This usually comes in the form of so-called line items in the university's budget. Often they are inserted by lawmakers to meet some state need, such as water-conservation research, alternative-energy development, and the like. Sometimes, a single legislator may insert the requirement to fund research on some project specific to his or her district or special interest. To the university administration's annoyance, an individual faculty member or even a dean may influence a legislator to insert a line-itemed mandate to fund a specific research project that is not in the university's requested budget. University policies generally prohibit lobbying like this, but it happens anyway. Although these line items may not be mentioned in the university's strategic plan, the university (including the chief research officer) has no choice but to support them.

Equally annoying to the university administration, the legislature may mandate funding of special-interest line items but not provide any additional money to accomplish this—the so-called unfunded mandate. University administrators, including the chief research officer, can do little more than swallow hard and comply. (When a faculty member or dean lobbies to get an unfunded mandate inserted into the university budget, one effective punishment is for the provost to instruct the dean to pay for the project out the college's general budget. That discourages but doesn't necessarily eliminate similar efforts in future years.)

In addition to line items, legislatures may pass resolutions instructing the university to fund a particular program. These can be easier to deal with because they are generally nonbinding. If both houses of a bicameral legislature pass the same resolution, the university may choose to comply, although it is not required to do so. However, if only one of the two legislative bodies (for example, the house or senate) passes the resolution, many administrators will not comply because there wasn't a full legislative directive. Before doing this, however, a cautious administrator will always inform the chief executive officer, who will, in turn, forewarn the governing board that the university doesn't intend to honor the resolution. Legislatures seldom challenge this resistance to a single-body resolution.

In all cases of line items and resolutions, the chief research officer should read the legislative wording carefully and, more important, refer to legislative notes to be sure that the spending is compliant with legislative intent. Those are two critical words: *legislative intent*. Often the underlying wishes of the legislature can be fathomed only in their notes, not in the actual legislative language. And the intent can be the most important aspect of the mandate.

K: *What would happen if the chief research officer, or for that matter, a dean or faculty member, simply refused to go along with these unfunded mandates?*

> Smith: An angry legislature or legislator can cause big problems. In the worst-case scenario, the legislature may revoke delegated authority of the university to spend major portions of its budget. For example, they could repeal any lump-sum budget authority, thus restricting the university's freedom to decide how it spends all state money. Everything would be line itemed. And they could exert pressure on the board or chief executive officer to fire a disobedient administrator. That's not quite so bad unless you happen to be the one who gets the axe.
>
> K: That sounds pretty harsh.
>
> Smith: It boils down to matters of trust. The university must continually work to maintain the legislature's confidence in how it spends public money. Occasionally that means acquiescing to an unwelcome legislative request.

Research Committees

Taking into account these various constraints on spending authority and the need for buy-in, the chief research officer must decide how to distribute the funds under his or her ultimate control. Right off the bat, the question arises: How much spending authority is the chief research officer willing to share with the deans or the faculty members? For that matter, is the chief research officer obligated to share this authority, or can he or she simply act alone? The answer, or course, varies according to institutional history and culture. But most frequently, both the deans and the faculty members participate in the decision-making process to determine how at least some institutional research funds are spent. That is good policy because the chief research officer's ultimate effectiveness depends on the engagement of the faculty members and the deans for the establishment and maintenance of a thriving research environment. This ethos is very difficult to maintain if the chief research officer, perhaps in cahoots with the provost or the chief financial officer, makes all of the decisions about how resources are allocated.

Therefore, most universities have a standing faculty committee that participates in the distribution of research funds. These are the so-called research committees, and they provide advice and funding recommendations to the chief research officer. Assembling a research committee generally follows the procedures that are routine in higher administration. However, there are a few special considerations that warrant attention.

As with all committees, there must be a manageable number of members to simplify scheduling of meetings. The "best practice" is about twelve members, although this is often insufficient to satisfy all constituencies across campus because each discipline must be represented in one way or another. There are usually too many different disciplines (as measured by the number of departments) to permit each one to have its own delegate on the committee. So, the campus must be divided into broader categories. At the University of Wisconsin-Madison, for example, the campus is divided into four divisions: life sciences (including agriculture), physical sciences (including engineering), social sciences, and arts and humanities. Using that as a model, the number of divisions may be modified by other universities to accommodate specific institutional cultures, size, and mission. Faculty members representing each division are chosen for the committee, and each division's members will constitute a subcommittee with the responsibility for representing their own constituents. Thus, in the Wisconsin model, there are four subcommittees, one for each division. Of course, some minor adjustments to who belongs in which division may be necessary. For example, agricultural economics may prefer to be lumped with the social and not the life sciences. Or the psychology department may wish to be split between the life and the social sciences. That's all doable.

The more difficult challenge will come from departments that are not represented on the committee and that don't trust their colleagues in other disciplines to understand their fields. The chief research officer must listen to these concerns and then try to accommodate them through careful selections. Also, if the appointment term is three years, for example, each discipline should ultimately have a member on the committee as membership turns over. Furthermore, each member should be an active researcher who commands the respect of the other faculty members. Additional guidelines common to most university committees like this also apply. For example, the committee must be balanced along ethnic and gender lines. Importantly, nontenured faculty members should not be included; funding decisions can cause hurt feelings, insulted pride, and the consequent potential for retaliation somewhere along the tenure process.

In general, the chief research officer strongly prefers to decide who will serve on this committee. And, in that ideal world, he or she would choose the members without the need to consult with deans and the faculty members. After all, one might think, "Isn't it enough just to have a faculty committee participate in funding decisions? Let me decide who's on it." In the real world, however, this single-handed approach exposes the committee to potential charges of bias, misrepresentation, and a litany of other complaints from individuals who are unhappy with its funding decisions. Thus, a transparent selection protocol that engages the deans and the faculty members must be devised.

The easiest way to generate names of potential committee members is to ask each dean, in consultation with his or her faculty members, to nominate three or more acceptable, qualified individuals from the particular school or college. Using the division model, if the college spans more than one division, it may nominate members for each. The chief research officer then has the task to evaluate these nominations and ultimately assemble the committee. To maintain the integrity of the process, the chief research officer should not yield to the temptation to pick somebody not nominated by a dean. If the deans fail to nominate enough acceptable candidates, then they should be asked to submit more names. By involving the deans in this way, the chief research officer garners their respect and commitment to the process. Moreover, this builds a first-line defense against any charges that the committee membership was rigged or biased. An associate research officer should be the nonvoting chair of the committee. Why not the chief research officer? Because the chief research officer must be impartial and uninvolved in the committee's deliberations in the event of an appeal.

Ideally, there will be an equal number of members from each division on the research committee. This may disturb some disciplines that have more faculty members than the others. "We have twice as many faculty members, so why don't we get twice as many committee members?" The answer is that the chief research officer's domain is the entire university campus—all disciplines—and the composition of this particular committee must reflect that. Yes, the strategic plan may identify high-priority areas, and this will probably lead to inequalities in the amount of money distributed to the various disciplines. But the composition of the research committee is not the venue for producing these funding inequalities. They will arise from the chief research officer's allocation formula. That topic will be discussed in more detail below.

If the selection process is not convincingly transparent and inclusive of faculty input, challenges to the research committee procedure may arise from the faculty, especially in universities with a tradition of strong faculty governance. In fact, they may arise anyway. Conceivably, the faculty may wish to elect members of the research committee. Alternatively, as the duly recognized body representing the faculty members, the faculty senate may claim that they should choose the committee members. Experienced chief research officers will vigorously resist these efforts. The rationale is that the research committee members must be active researchers themselves if they are to be trusted to make sound decisions about their colleagues' research efforts. There is always the chance that candidates with marginal research credentials will be elected or chosen by the senate, even in elite universities. This rationale is always tricky for the chief research officer to espouse publicly because of the clear risk of offending faculty members. There is no universal strategy for countering these arguments. The university's culture and the chief research officer's persuasive skills will determine the outcome.

> K: You're pushing the importance of faculty buy-in again in this context. Is that why you belabor what are otherwise pretty standard procedures for appointing a committee?
>
> Smith: Yes. These periodic institutional awards are very important to faculty members. If you break the commonsense rules when setting up the research committee, the result is what you might expect: demoralizing disappointment and anger.
>
> K: Can you trust a faculty committee to fund only the most meritorious projects?
>
> Smith: No matter who distributes the money, some decisions will be questioned. That's inevitable. The important point here is to share authority with the

faculty members. In that sense, they also share responsibility for their university's research well-being.

Competitions

The orthodox chief research officer will allocate funds for distribution to the faculty members via a competition. However, before anything else, the chief research officer must decide the purpose of this effort. The most common goal is to provide small awards—"mini-grants"—to the faculty members in all disciplines to be used as "seed money" to launch a new research project; "bridging money" to keep a program active during a hiatus between grants; "expansion money" to enable program growth; "emergency money" to cover the unexpected loss of grant funding; and "transition money" to enable an orderly phase-out of a research program. How big is a mini-grant? The maximum award is usually in the neighborhood of $25,000 to $50,000. This certainly isn't enough to fund a full-scale research project in most disciplines, but these awards are definitely welcomed by the faculty members. However, by keeping the maximum awards relatively small, resources can be awarded to a larger number of faculty members. That is important because mini-grants spread evenly across campus keep the overall research "hum level" up—or, mixing metaphors, they strengthen the university's research muscle tone. Their academic value is further amplified when they are used to support undergraduates in the research, which supports the educational mission.

Alternatively, the chief research officer may constrain a competition to a particular field. And this is where high-priority areas defined in the strategic plan can be singled out for special attention. For example, if molecular neuroscience is a high priority, then eligibility to apply to this competition will be limited to proposals in that area. Often, the allowable budget in these targeted competitions is considerably larger than for mini-grants. Of course, the amount will vary from case to case, but awards exceeding $1 million would not be dramatically unusual. There are two lines of thought about these larger awards. One approach is to limit the maximum targeted award to values in the $100,000 to $250,000 range in order to spread the available funds among more recipients. Another thought is to set the maximum much higher—in the million-dollar range—to ensure sufficient resources to have a major impact. If the project fails with that level of funding, at least it wasn't because of inadequate institutional support. Both arguments have merit, so the chief research officer must make a decision based on how much money is available, how many awards are desirable, and other case-specific variables.

Who is eligible to apply? The quick answer is any tenured or tenure-track faculty member. Just as quickly, however, somebody will come forward who is not in that category but who is permitted to submit grant applications through the university. The argument would be, "I bring in grant money that benefits the university and that you accept willingly. But now you won't allow me to compete for institutional support? What kind of reward is that?" This is a valid point. Therefore, a more thoughtful answer is, "Any individual who has been granted authority to submit extramural grant applications through the university." In many universities, these are individuals holding positions defined by the governing board's policy: tenured and tenure-track faculty members, clinical faculty members or researchers not on the tenure track, and maybe certain adjunct appointees. Seldom does it include postdoctoral fellows or graduate students. This is because they are in training positions and may not be expected to remain at the university for the duration of a grant award.

A related question is whether research committee members may apply to the competition. The answer must be yes; otherwise, there would be a strong disincentive to serve on the committee. However, this breeds a conflict of interest within the committee: how can they fairly judge their colleagues? To resolve this conflict, applications submitted by committee members should be reviewed separately by the chief research officer. The associate research officer should be consulted to ensure that the review criteria and rigor match those of the committee as closely as possible. The chief research officer's decisions need not be shared with the committee until they have completed their deliberations. Incidentally, this process for reviewing committee members' applications should be well known to the campus as a whole before the competition to minimize charges of unfairness or bias toward (or against) committee members.

The allowable budgets may also vary with the competition's purpose and the award's duration. Because the chief research officer seldom controls "longitudinal," long-term salary funds, salary requests may be limited to only one semester or the summer. Longer term commitments are generally not feasible without the provost's assistance. Some universities, such as the University of Wisconsin-Madison, do not allow partial funding of a faculty member's salary in a research award—it must be all or nothing. The rationale is that teaching, even if it is at a reduced load, will interfere with a faculty member's research effort. The value of the research award is maximized if the faculty member can devote full time to the project. Also, because of their probable multipurpose use (teaching, personal, research, and so forth), computers are not allowed in proposal budgets by some institutions. They are considered a departmental obligation. If there is a looming deadline to spend the funds, then equipment (perhaps exceeding a certain cost) may be the preferred allowable item. It can often be bought and paid for within a reasonably short period of time. ("Short" in this context means within a month or so.)

Now, the research committee comes into the scene. Having decided these programmatic issues, the chief research officer calls a meeting and charges the committee with running the competition. If the competition targets a specific discipline or range of disciplines, then only the appropriate subcommittee is convened. For example, if the target is molecular neuroscience, then only the life sciences subcommittee will be involved in the competition; the others will not participate. As chair of the committee, the associate chief research officer provides the operational link with the research office and general staff support. In the case of campus-wide mini-grants, the committee separates into its several divisional subcommittees, which then are responsible for the proposals in their fields. Ideally, the subcommittees will interview each applicant personally. However, if this is impractical because of a large number of applications, for example, then the committee should refrain from any interviews. To maintain fairness and integrity, the committee must either interview every applicant or none of them.

After deliberations are completed and each subcommittee has rank-ordered its potential winners, in most universities the whole committee then reconvenes to decide on the final winners. Under the associate chief research officer's guidance, the allocation of available funds to the various divisions' nominees may be adjusted to account for differences in the number of eligible faculty members, the actual number of applications, the average request size, and other factors. The number of winners may also vary by disciplinary division. For example, the arts and humanities may have more winners because their average awards are generally smaller than those in other divisions. After all of this is settled within the committee, the decisions will emanate from the committee as a whole as a recommendation to the chief research officer. This is important because it reinforces the unified campus research ethos.

Should the committee adjust the proposals' budgets? There are mixed opinions on this. In some universities, the committee retains the freedom to make adjustments (usually downward) during its deliberations. A reviewer might comment, "I would like this grant better if its budget were only half as much." The main reason is to spread the money further. In these situations, the associate research officer must vigilantly caution the committee members not to make capricious, unjustifiable budget reductions. In contrast, some universities do not make adjustments in the requested budget; they fund the entire amount (less any expenditures that are categorically excluded, such as food or computers, for example). The rationale is that the committee simply does not have the requisite expertise to judge what an appropriate budget might be for many proposals.

Most applicants will expect a summary of the reviewers' comments, especially if they were not among the winners. Thus, the committee should prepare a brief (one or two paragraphs) critique for each application. Usually, they accompany the formal notification letter, which is signed by the chief research officer.

One more point about reviews warrants mentioning. The call for proposals announcing the competition will presumably state the review criteria. An example might read like this: "The Office of the Vice President for Research is prepared to allocate $1 million dollars in grant support to stimulate individual investigator research efforts at the University. The funds will be awarded on a competitive basis. Proposals will be judged by the Research Committee on the basis of scholarly and/or creative merit, the potential for completion for any ongoing project, and/or the potential for attracting further support."

The applicants will then address these criteria ("scholarly and/or creative merit, the potential for completion for any ongoing project, and/or the potential for attracting further support") while preparing their proposals. Importantly, the reviewers (members of the research committee in this case) should not be provided additional criteria for judging the proposals. They should base their judgments only on what has been told to all applicants in the call for proposals. Introduction of any other post hoc review criteria would be unfair to the applicants. For the sake of uniformity or scoring ease, the reviewers may be given evaluation forms to fill out. However, these forms must not introduce new criteria—inadvertently or on purpose.

Inevitably, there will be appeals. They should be directed to the associate chief research officer who chaired the research committee. The basis will probably be that the reviewers were unfamiliar with the proposal's topic and, therefore, unqualified to judge its merits. Unfortunately, this may be more or less true in some circumstances. However, this should not be a basis for overruling the committee's recommendation. These in-house competitions cannot be run with the deep pool of expertise needed to ensure that every proposal is read by an expert in the topic; the university does not have the resources available to the NSF or NIH. Some appeals may say that new information (preliminary results) is now available that the committee didn't have at the time of its deliberations. That, too, is not an appealable basis. The only allowable appeals should be based on procedural errors by the committee. What might they be? The reviewer had a conflict of interest, all other applicants were interviewed but not this one, the committee discussed the proposal with the applicant's chair or dean, and so forth. In these cases, the associate chief research officer should reconvene the committee and ask them to consider the merits of the appeal. They should submit their findings to the chief research officer, who will make the final judgment. There is no avenue for further appeals; the chief research officer's decision is final.

Noncompetitive Support

The chief research officer typically reserves a pool of funds to distribute noncompetitively. There are myriad uses for this money. They include start-up funds for new faculty members; cost sharing for grant proposals; emergency funding for researchers who have lost a major grant; money for remodeling laboratory space, sponsoring a conference or seminar series, supporting faculty travel; and on and on. If the research committee has been allocated generous funds to distribute competitively, the chief research officer generally has the flexibility to make these noncompetitive funding decisions without the need for extensive consultation. Nonetheless, these expenditures must always be well justified and transparent. Indeed, the "best practice" is to tabulate and account for the entire research office budget and expenditures on a Web site accessible to the university community, if not the general public.

What should not be supported? Usually, it is unadvisable for the chief research officer to fund proposals that were unsuccessful in the research committee's competition. That undermines the committee's authority and compromises its effectiveness. Some might argue, "If the chief research officer doesn't abide by the committee's decisions, then why have the committee in the first place?" But there may be extenuating circumstances that the chief research officer cannot ignore. Perhaps the faculty member is being recruited by another university or some such situation. In those cases, the chief research officer may make the award. But this should be a rare exception and not a general habit. A related situation arises when a faculty member requests special consideration for support because of his or her perceived value to the university, as in, "I've brought all of this fame and money to the university; the least you can do is grant my request for money." Again, there may be unusual circumstances that merit an award. Also, the chief research officer should avoid using research funds for office-related operational costs. The research money should always be invested with the goal of increasing research capacity. In that context, it is bad practice to divert resources to cover operational costs because of budget overruns, budget cuts, or just plain mismanagement. All in all, the chief research officer should understand these general guidelines but retain the right to be inconsistent if that is necessary to achieve the goal of enriching the university's research environment.

Occasionally, for some compelling reason, the chief research officer may prefer not to use an in-house university research committee. Competitions for particularly large awards (such as $1 million) that involve numerous faculty members serve as a prime example. In these cases, it may prove challenging to get competent internal reviewers who don't have a conflict of interest, especially in smaller institutions. Moreover, some governing boards may be uneasy with a research committee review because of the diffuse accountability; it's hard to hold a committee responsible if things go wrong. One solution is to explain these difficulties to the research committee and then, to maintain the integrity of a competition, have the applications reviewed only by experts external to the university. They would submit their recommendations to the chief research officer, who would then be responsible for the final decision. If things go wrong, the board knows where to look: in the direction of the chief research officer.

Start-up Packages for New Faculty Members

Predictably, negotiations between a job candidate and the university administration (usually the department chair) will focus on the start-up package. This can be a critical moment for the prospective faculty member and the university. The candidate wants as much as he or she can get, and the administration wants to conserve its resources. In some cases, this is a make-or-break point of the deal. If the university offers too little, the applicant may withdraw. Moreover, if the candidate ultimately accepts the position but has a lingering annoyance because the start-up request was not fully funded, this dissatisfaction can devolve into a more general sense of underappreciation by the university. Further efforts to make this faculty member happy may be fruitless. Consequently, it is usually in the university's best long-term interest to err on the generous side.

What's in a typical start-up package? An incoming assistant professor is expected to establish an independent research career prior to coming up for tenure. In many universities, that expectation includes attainment of a national reputation in his or her discipline. Ideally, the start-up package would provide sufficient support to achieve this goal. However, that seldom occurs in reality. Generous packages are usually sufficient for the investigator to generate the preliminary data needed for an extramural-research grant application. They include funds for supplies, equipment, travel to professional conferences, a graduate student, and two or three years of summer salary. In addition, there may be provisions for a reduced teaching load for one or two years and space renovations. Some private universities and medical schools often guarantee only a fraction of the salary; the faculty member must generate the remainder from grants. In these cases, the start-up package may also include sufficient funds to cover two or three years of full salary support if the faculty member fails to generate it from extramural sources. The actual amount of the package varies case by case. In the biomedical sciences, it may easily exceed $1 million. And it can be much higher for more senior appointees.

After making the job offer, the departmental chair will ask what it takes "to bring you here." And the candidate is asked to prepare a list of items needed in the start-up package, along with estimated prices. Initially, the chair corrects for salary discrepancies and any institutional discounts that are offered by many vendors. These discounts can be substantial—sometimes in the 50 to 70 percent range. What happens next depends on the university's culture. In a few cases, the chair manages all of the money needed for start-up requests and finalizes the deal. More commonly, the department, the college dean, and the chief research officer jointly consider the request, and each contributes to the final offer. The split among these three offices varies. By the way, the provost may become indirectly involved if the dean needs more money. In this general context, start-up requests are seldom referred to the research committee for a decision. That usually takes too long, and there are often other factors in the package that should be handled only by the chair.

From a managerial perspective, it is always better if the funding for start-up packages, or for that matter, any other noncompetitive award to a faculty member, is split among two or more sources. For example, the chief research officer should never be expected to pick up the full cost of a start-up package; the department chair and the dean should contribute as well. This is an important point. If the chief research officer provides all of the funding, then the award is a "free good" as far as the chair and the dean are concerned; therefore, it has no value for them, and they do not have a vested interest in seeing it well spent. It is far better when the chair and the dean have "something on the table." Then they also have an interest in the outcome of the investment. Of course, for this to work, the chair and the dean must have sufficient funds available to participate. That is where the provost comes in again. Working with the chief research officer, the provost must ensure that the dean has adequate discretionary funds available and that these funds extend to the department as well. As far as the provost is concerned, there is really only one pool of money in the university's operating budget; therefore, this is really a matter of how funds are allocated. The chief research officer may receive less from this pool in order to give more to the deans. That is acceptable if it enables the dean and the chair to participate in start-up packages, for this is in the chief research officer's better interest.

One more note: the chair may control some funds, such as F&A reimbursement, that are normally distributed to the faculty members. However, he or she may be required to hold back some of these funds for a start-up package. That is also reasonable from a managerial perspective, for it also draws the departmental faculty members to the table because now they, too, have a vested interest in the newly recruited faculty member's success. That is, they have sacrificed their own resources to help their new colleague get started. Yes, they may complain that they have been deprived of money that they deserve. To mitigate complaints, the chair should explain the rationale carefully and clearly.

The role of the chief research officer goes well beyond passively contributing funds. It is not unusual for a chair, and even a dean, to shy away from the most promising candidate because "we can't afford somebody like that." In those cases, the chief research officer may be able to step forward and guarantee the additional funding needed to go after the promising candidate. And he or she should do that if the money is available. If start-up funds become scarce, the chief research officer should actively work with the provost and the chief financial officer to find what is needed to provide the start-up commitment. One common strategy is to schedule payment of an expensive start-up package over several years, thus reducing the immediate financial burden. Using the power of persuasion and of the purse, the chief research officer should continuously insist that the university pursue the best candidates for every position.

The start-up resources should be available for the new faculty member's use immediately after arrival on campus. Institutional integrity is at stake here. If funding for a start-up package is delayed more than a week or so, the new faculty member may begin to doubt the university's sincerity. And a prolonged delay (more than several months) can wreak havoc on the new faculty member's research plans. Several months may not seem like a long time within the usual six-year time frame before tenure decisions are made, but it can cut deeply into the much shorter time available to get an extramural grant.

The most toxic shortcoming is the failure of the university to provide adequate research space to newly arrived faculty members. All the money in the world won't be of much help if there's no place to do research. The chief research officer should periodically monitor the new faculty member's access to promised start-up resources and play an active (if not proactive) role in resolving any problems.

> K: You stress the importance of institutional integrity in start-up negotiations. Why would a university not honor its commitments?
>
> Smith: In the vast majority of cases, I'm sure that it isn't intentional. But there are many anecdotal stories about promises not kept.
>
> K: You would think that word would get out, and prospective applicants would avoid those universities.
>
> Smith: I agree. But it doesn't work that way. There are usually many more applicants than available faculty positions, so classic market forces seldom come into play in university hiring processes.

Transferring Grants and Equipment from Another Institution

Faculty members recruited from another institution may have active research grants that they want to bring with them. That is always good news for the chief research officer, for two reasons. First, this will be a welcome addition to the overall research environment (and expenditures) on campus: the more faculty members with grants, the better. Second, this may lessen the financial burden of the start-up package. The new faculty member may be able to bring equipment purchased with grant funds.

Most granting agencies have explicit guidelines explaining what happens when the principal investigator moves from one institution to another. The NIH and NSF have identical policies. The NSF says it succinctly: "When a PI/PD plans to leave an organization during the course of a grant, the organization has the prerogative to nominate a substitute PI/PD or request that the grant be terminated and closed out. In those cases where the PI/PD's original and new organizations agree, NSF will facilitate a transfer of the grant and the assignment of remaining unobligated funds to the PI/PD's new organization."[4]

When the grant is transferred, equipment purchased using grant funds also transfers to the new university. In NIH terms, "If the new organization is approved by the PHS awarding component to continue the grant activity, then the grant will be awarded and any equipment purchased with grant funds and still needed for the grant project would be expected to transfer to the new grantee organization, which would assume title. If the original grantee does not voluntarily agree to relinquish equipment with the grant, HHS may require transfer of the equipment as specified in 45 CFR Part 74.34(h)."[5] The bottom line is that, if the original university agrees, the grant and any equipment bought with it can be moved to the new institution. Even the moving costs can be paid with grant funds.

Why would the original university agree to this transfer? Who wants to lose a grant? Within the realms of academe, there is an unwritten code of etiquette. And one understanding is that a university will generally not interfere with a departing faculty member's ability to continue a productive research program at another institution—even if there are bad feelings involved. Furthermore, the old university may not have any other investigator qualified to take over the grant. Conversely, why would the original university not agree to transfer the grant? If the grant is large, such as a program project or a center grant, with many faculty members as co-principal investigators, the university may assert that the program is so woven into the institutional fabric that it would be not only difficult but also unreasonable to transfer. The awarding agency usually respects those arguments. But for individual investigator awards, transfers are basically routine events. Executing these transfers from one university to another generally falls into the chief research officer's lap.

Incidentally, these policies pertain to the entire duration of a grant. For example, if the award is in its twentieth year, all equipment purchased since year one can be moved. However, they do not apply to inactive grants; equipment bought with funds from a grant that is no longer active falls into the same category as equipment bought with nongrant funds.

How about equipment purchased by the original university using nongrant or inactive grant funds? That's trickier. Unless the equipment is old and falling apart, many universities balk at releasing it in this category when a faculty member leaves. And that makes sense, especially if it was bought with institutional funds. Indeed, some universities have specific policies that prohibit giving away any of its assets, including equipment. However, for the departing faculty member, there is still hope. Most universities are willing to sell this equipment to the new institution at a fair price. The depreciated value is generally termed "fair." All university business offices have a depreciation schedule for university property. For example, computers usually lose all value after three or four years, but microscopes retain value for up to twenty years. For public universities, these schedules are often set by the state. So, if the new faculty member wants some of this equipment, the usual procedure is for the chair to contact his or her counterpart at the old university and to negotiate a sale price. Sometimes, there are case-specific reasons for the dean, the chief research officer, or even the provost to handle the negotiations.

Since most universities use similar depreciation schedules, it is generally not hard to come to some agreement. In fact, the old university may be willing to offer a discount on top of the depreciated price just to get rid of the equipment; these discounts can be substantial—in the 50 to 70 percent range. Except for some very general items, such as centrifuges, scintillation counters, audiovisual equipment, and high-end computers, the old university may see little value in used or specially modified equipment. This can be a tremendous bargain for the new university. The new faculty member gets to keep his or her valued equipment, and the new university has been spared the cost of replacing it at current prices.

Here's an important technical note: in all of this discussion, the word *equipment* most often applies to any item valued at $5,000 or more. That is the federal government's threshold, and most universities have adopted it, although they may add additional items that are unusually subject to theft or inappropriate private use (computers, cameras, television sets, and so forth). Significantly, the $5,000 threshold applies to the current depreciated value. Federal guidelines require the university to maintain proper inventory records of any equipment valued at more than $5,000; thus, these so-called capital equipment items are inventoried, an identifying sticker is placed on them, and their location is verified annually. When an item's depreciated value drops below $5,000, it is removed from this inventory list. From that time on, the item becomes essentially invisible to the institution. Of course, the institution has a record of these items. But now they enter the same category as all noninventoried items, including lab and office supplies (pipette tips, paper clips, etc.). When a faculty member moves from one institution to another, it is generally acknowledged and accepted that he or she may take all of these noninventoried items to the new university with no questions asked.

With such expensive start-up packages, it is usually more economical for a university to do everything it can to retain faculty members that they have already invested in. Commonly, it is far less expensive to keep somebody than to replace him or her. Retention packages rarely exceed more than an occasional 20 percent pay raise and maybe $200,000 or $300,000 in equipment. And new equipment can often be shared with other faculty members. In fact, the institution could probably offer much higher retention packages and still come out ahead financially. Thus, from a financial perspective, the institution should aggressively mount retention efforts. From a managerial perspective, retention efforts also signal to the faculty members that the institution values them. And that is an immensely important message to convey. Of course, most seasoned administrators recognize the need to guard against faculty members who fish for outside employment offers with little intention to accept them, simply as a means for getting a lucrative retention offer.

Research Enhancement Funding

To maintain their productiveness, faculty members need occasional injections of institutional-research funding. Even individuals with multiple research grants require periodic boosts along the way. This doesn't need to be a lot. As every researcher knows, several thousand dollars now and then can have a huge impact on productivity. Chief research officers whose background has not been in a field that normally attracts large research grants should never assume that an investigator already has enough money. They might think, "You've got lots of grant money. Why do you need more?" That attitude would be just as misguided as if a chemist, for example, were to second-guess an historian's need to visit a library in England. "Can't you get the same books here?" In general, it is advisable to trust the faculty member to know what is necessary to succeed professionally.

In-house competitive grants provide one avenue of support. If at all possible, these competitions should be scheduled regularly so researchers can plan ahead. The chief research officer can also expect to get unsolicited requests for support throughout the year. When they arrive, these requests should be routed through the research committee to avoid any perception of favoritism on the part of the chief research officer. Some universities schedule occasional research committee meetings to consider these out-of-competition requests; others establish a standing subcommittee to look at them. These are smart practices, for they relieve the chief research officer from being overwhelmed by one request after another. A few munificent universities routinely honor any request less than one or two thousand dollars.

Travel money provides another avenue of support. Many universities award travel support to faculty members (and sometimes graduate students) to attend professional meetings where they are presenting a talk or poster. Ideally, these funds would be available to faculty members once per year, and they would cover the entire cost (registration, lodging and meals, and transportation). Depending on the university's resources, this support may be reduced to once every two years or so, and the amount may be capped at some upper limit. Again ideally, international and domestic travel would be treated the same. However, because it costs more and may be subject to more intense scrutiny by auditors and other budget analysts, international travel may be awarded less frequently. Ultimately, it is in the university's better interests to have a generous travel-award policy. Every time a faculty member makes a presentation, it is an advertisement for the university. There are subtle—even subliminal—benefits to that. For example, more name recognition could tip the scale positively in some external grant review. Or it may attract better graduate students.

There are also publication fees to consider. In some disciplines, most journals charge a fee to publish a paper. Traditionally, European journals charged a low fee per page (page charge), but high subscription rates. This encourages library usage. In contrast, American journals charged high fees but low subscription rates. This encourages individual subscriptions. This difference in philosophy and price structure has begun to even out with the advent of open-access journals and online subscriptions. But the costs remain. In all cases, the author must bear these costs, although some publications will waive them if the author can get a signed statement from an institutional official (for example, a department chair) that funds are unavailable for this purpose. As members of the broader academic community, universities generally try to support scholarly journals by paying these fees if at all possible. Fortunately, most granting agencies allow use of their funds to pay these charges. Occasionally, a faculty member will ask the chief research officer to pay these publication costs. The request may be sent back to the departmental chair, but the chief research officer usually pays the bill if nobody else will. Again, it's in the university's better interest because publications raise the institution's visibility.

In this context, if a faculty member is selected to be the editor of a scholarly publication, he or she may approach the chief research officer for money to hire staff support (if the journal won't provide assistance) or, more likely, to buy a reduced teaching load. For the same reason—namely, institutional visibility—this kind of request is generally honored without question.

> K: You put a lot of value in institutional visibility. Is it really that important?
> Smith: I think so. Name recognition and familiarity can be important in so many subtle ways. We usually tend to favor ever so slightly the things, people, and places we know.
> K: Why not just hire a public relations firm to do a professional job?
> Smith: Most universities do. Take a look at all of the slick brochures touting a university's research achievements or the sophisticated Web pages featuring university researchers. It's all an expensive, well-planned public relations operation, and most universities take it very seriously.

Bridge Support

Sooner or later in most researchers' careers, they lose a grant. A competitive renewal is not funded, and the money runs out. And that can seriously disrupt even the most promising research efforts. Therefore, many universities provide funding to keep the program afloat long enough for the investigator to regain extramural support via reapplication to the granting agency. This is known as "bridge support," for it bridges the funding gap. This is an important component of any chief research officer's faculty-development portfolio because it helps sustain the faculty member's research momentum and protects the university's investment in that individual.

There are several mechanisms for awarding bridge support. Which method is used depends on the available resources. The easiest to administer is simply for the chief research officer to make the award in response to an investigator's plea. As a matter of policy, the department chair and the dean should be expected to participate in the final package; their contributions may be limited to student or faculty salary support. This ad hoc method requires the chief research officer to include a "bridge reserve" in the office budget. The major challenge is to know more or less how much may be needed during the course of a year. Past experience is the best guide for estimating how much may be needed, of course. However, because of the high importance of this support to the overall institutional research infrastructure, a cautious chief research officer will always add a cushioning amount to these estimates.

An alternative method is to make a priori awards. In this case, faculty members submit an application to the chief research officer prior to any funding decisions by the granting agency. These applications may be reviewed during a regularly scheduled mini-grant competition by the research committee. A bridge-support award may be made contingent on failure to get a grant renewed and perhaps the resubmission of a proposal to the granting agency during its next scheduled review cycle. So, if the competing renewal is successful, the university doesn't pay; the money stays with the chief research officer. However, if the grant is not renewed, then the university activates the bridge award. This method has been used successfully for many years at the University of Wisconsin-Madison, for example. The advantage is that faculty members of the research committee participate in the decision making, thus reinforcing their role in university governance. And that is always healthy. Also, if an award is contingent on the submission of a revised renewal application by a certain date, the faculty member is motivated to keep seeking extramural grants. The major drawback is that it requires additional bookkeeping.

The duration of the bridge award may vary from case to case. But, as a rule of thumb, it extends to the date when a grant would be awarded if the application were resubmitted for the agency's next review cycle. This is usually nine to twelve months. The amount of the bridging award also varies from case to case. The standard guideline requires the faculty member to prepare a budget with the least amount of money needed to keep the project going. That may include little more than one or two graduate student or technician salaries and supplies—about a $50,000 investment. If the researcher is on soft money, he or she may also require personal salary support, which will raise the budget considerably. Whether the bridge award can be renewed for a second iteration will depend on the specific case.

Faculty Retraining

Unfortunately, some faculty members' research programs become stagnant, for any of a number of reasons. Productivity stalls, and the faculty member can no longer write a competitive extramural-grant application. Can these moribund research careers be saved? Maybe, but it isn't easy. And the chief research officer may play a pivotal role in these efforts.

Who takes the lead? Usually the department chair initiates the discussions. Many universities have periodic post-tenure reviews of all faculty members. Those whose research productivity has fallen may be required to prepare a personal-development plan in consultation with the department chair. Or, the chair may request a plan ad hoc if it appears to be warranted. The chief research officer may be called into these discussions, for a couple of reasons: he or she presumably has experience in these matters and money to help support the retraining plan.

The most practical remedy involves giving the faculty member a leave of absence for professional-development reasons (a sabbatical) to work and to retool in a supportive environment, such as somebody else's laboratory—preferably at another institution. Often that is coupled with the requirement to generate one or two publications and to submit a grant application within a reasonable window of time (a year or two). It would be unrealistic to require the unproductive faculty member to write research papers or submit grant proposals without also providing some means to regain momentum. If nobody else steps forward, the chief research officer should take the initiative to propose a hands-on retraining program in these cases. Of course, the chief research officer may be asked to contribute to the cost of these professional-development leaves because they ultimately benefit the research community. As always, these costs should be shared among two or more offices. And it is not unreasonable to expect the faculty member to pay some of the costs personally (for example, travel or lodging); that ensures that he or she also has a stake in the overall effort.

Alternatively, faculty members whose research program has become unproductive may be encouraged to devote more time and effort to teaching and service. This can be a very good solution in many cases. Certainly, it is less expensive in the short run. If these individuals take on more teaching responsibilities, that may allow other faculty members to teach less, thus potentially increasing their research productivity. In the best of all worlds, this shifting between teaching and research would occur throughout a faculty member's career. When his or her research program is unusually productive, the chair would arrange for a reduction in teaching responsibilities; those duties would be reassigned to another faculty member whose research productivity is particularly low at the time. Of course, the major risk is that the increased teaching load would make it that much more difficult for an unproductive researcher ever to restart a competitive research program.

Faculty Departures

When a faculty member leaves the university, several issues arise that may involve the chief research officer. If the individual is leaving to take a job at another institution, questions about transferring grants and equipment will usually make their way to the chief research officer. This is the flip side of transfers into the university, which were discussed earlier. The question is, "Should we allow the grant to be transferred or not?" If it is large and has several co-principal investigators, then the answer is usually no; it would affect too many other faculty members, and the university has the expertise and the skilled researchers to continue the research without the departing faculty member. And that answers the question about equipment bought using grant funds: it stays. It is then the chief research officer's responsibility to contact the granting agencies, who usually must approve a change in the principal investigator. If the grant is an individual-investigator award, the transfer to the new university is seldom contested and the equipment goes with it. This can have unanticipated repercussions, however. If some of the transferred equipment had been used regularly by researchers in other laboratories, the chief research officer will undoubtedly be asked to help buy replacements. This has the potential to be very expensive.

The more difficult issue to deal with is graduate students. If the faculty member departs suddenly—in university time, that means with less than about three or four months' notice—then accommodating the so-called orphan students can be challenging. The department chair and the graduate dean usually help to arrange for new faculty advisers. However, the chief research officer may be asked to contribute to their salary support for a limited period of time—perhaps one or two semesters. These requests are seldom denied. Annoyingly, the departing faculty member may also request the chief research officer to cover his or her travel expenses back from the new university on one or more occasions to "check in" on the orphaned students' progress. The answer is almost always, "No, let the new university cover that," although the chief research officer may lose a few minutes of sleep pondering the situation.

An even more difficult matter involves research data such as laboratory note-books, tissue samples, and data bases. More likely than not, a departing researcher will believe it is appropriate to take along all of his or her research records. This can pose a serious problem for the university because it is obligated to ensure access to raw data that must be retained for at least three years under the terms of many federal grants and contracts.[6] Moreover, the institution may require these data in legal actions against any infringement of intellectual property. A researcher departing the university on unfriendly terms is quite unlikely to take a positive view of institutional claims to data. For these reasons, many universities have established explicit policies governing the rights and obligations of the institution and the researchers in the management and retention of research data. The Council on Government Relations (COGR) provides a thorough analysis of institutional data retention requirements.[7]

> K: *What do you do if an unproductive faculty member has given up and doesn't want to retool?*
>
> Smith: *Not much. It is extremely difficult to fire tenured faculty members if they meet their teaching obligations—even if they are convicted felons.*
>
> K: *Don't post-tenure reviews usually specify some requirement that the faculty member comply with a proposed plan?*
>
> Smith: *Yes. But practically speaking, very few faculty members ever fail a post-tenure review. In my experience, the usual pass rate is in the neighborhood of 98 percent or higher. This is especially true if the department chair or other departmental faculty members control the review process and don't want to punish a colleague.*

K: Then why do it?

Smith: At least they offer some motivation. That's better than nothing. Nobody wants to fail one of those things. It's embarrassing.

Notes

1. *Stanford University, The Founding Grant with Amendments, Legislation, and Court Decrees* (Stanford, Calif.: Stanford University, 1987), p. 14.
2. Calif. Const. art. 9, §9a (1868).
3. Hawaii Const. art. X, §6 (2000).
4. National Science Foundation (NSF), "Disposition of a Grant When a PI/PD or co-PI/co-PD Transfers from One Organization to Another Organization," in Proposal and Award Policies and Procedures Guide (Arlington, Va.: NSF, 2009), p. II-3.
5. National Institutes of Health, "Frequently Asked Questions: Equipment Under NIH Grants," 2010, http://grants.nih.gov/grants/policy/equipment_faqs.htm (accessed January 7, 2011).
6. Office of Management and Budget, Executive Office of the President, Circular No. A-110, 2 C.F.R. Pt. 215, §53.b (2010), p. 92.
7. Council on Government Relations (COGR), *Access to and Retention of Research Data: Rights and Responsibilities* (Washington, D.C.: COGR, 2006).

CHAPTER 7

Centers and Institutes

K: *Chief research officers are usually asked how they will foster interdisciplinary research. How do you go about that?*

Smith: *That's a question asked in every job interview. There is no easy answer because faculty members are usually so independent. You can't just force them to work together on an interdisciplinary problem.*

K: *But there must be some effective strategy for encouraging collaborations.*

Smith: *Of course, there is always money. That's usually a powerful incentive—if there's enough on the table. But another institutional incentive is the establishment of interdisciplinary centers and institutes. They can be very effective incubators of creative cross-disciplinary interactions. And the chief research officer can play a major role in their effectiveness.*

Interdisciplinary Research

Historically, universities have been organized into departments that specialize in traditional core pedagogical subjects, such as history, English, chemistry, mathematics, and the like. And these departments have hired faculty members qualified to teach these subjects. *Pari passu*, their scholarly activities focused on these departmental specializations. This traditional academic structure has continued into the modern universities, where these departments retain their organizational primacy. Occasionally, a department will split into two or more separate departments to accommodate varying aspects of the core discipline. An example is the bifurcation of a biology department into an ecology, evolution, and behavior department and a cell and molecular biology department. Creation of a totally new departmental discipline occurs much less frequently; the few examples include departments of computer science and biochemistry. Otherwise, the chemistry department continues to hire chemists who do research on chemistry, the history department continues to hire historians who do research on history, and on and on.

Faculty members and university administrators recognize that this historically based compartmentalization potentially stifles creativity. "Wouldn't it be exciting if chemists, biologists, and physicists could work together at the interface of the three departmental disciplines?" they ask. Yes, it would be exciting, and that's where centers and institutes enter the academic stage. They are the university's foremost venue for interdisciplinary scholarly activities, and universities generally encourage their establishment.

That introduction raises an additional question: What actually defines centers and institutes? Exact definitions are a bit difficult to achieve because the terms "centers" and "institutes" are used somewhat imprecisely at many universities. The one element in common to all institutions is that centers and institutes are interdisciplinary. As an administrative unit, they bring together faculty members from different departments and disciplines, with the hope that this union will generate novel academic contributions. These units are not limited to research; the center or institute may be an instructional or service unit, as well.

The next question is, What's the difference between a center and an institute? It all depends on the university, its customs, and its tendency to worry about things like this. Although there are no formal, standard definitions, institutes are most commonly larger in scale than centers. In fact, institutes may have centers embedded within them, but usually not vice versa. Some universities follow a variation on this definition based on scale, by stating categorically that institutes involve faculty members from different colleges and schools, whereas centers involve individuals from different departments within a single college or school. For universities seeking formal definitions of the terms, this marks a crisp distinction.

Many universities have explicit policies defining their centers and institutes, but realistically they are very difficult to enforce. Centers and institutes are inherently interdisciplinary, and the composition of their membership may be expected to evolve with time. Indeed, that is a favorable sign of success. For example, a center for marine biology may have been established in the college of arts and sciences, and at that time, only faculty members in that college joined the center. But a few years later, several faculty members in the college of agriculture became interested in marine aquaculture and were invited to join the center. And perhaps a newly appointed professor of chemical engineering who studies bacterial biofilms has also expressed an interest in joining the center because his or her research is related to marine microbiology. So what may have started out as a center located strictly within a college grew gradually by incorporating faculty members from other colleges. But now with faculty members from different colleges, the center should, by definition, metamorphose into an institute. Because of administrative inertia, however, that may not happen. And, when all is said and done, it probably isn't all that important. After all, membership may revert to only arts and sciences faculty members in another several years, and then it would be a center again.

There is an additional organizational unit occasionally used in a university setting—namely, a laboratory. In a sense, a laboratory is a diminutive center, with a much sharper focus on some academic topic. It may be housed entirely within a department or, like centers and institutes, cross departmental boundaries. However, because of their limited scale, laboratories are usually not included in policies or in discussions concerning centers and institutes.

In a totally different dimension, some universities use the term "center" for much larger organizational units. The best example is a "center for health sciences," which on numerous campuses includes schools of medicine, nursing, pharmacy, and other allied health sciences. Each of these schools may be a locus of tenure for faculty members. And the center may also include a university hospital and its associated clinics. Although these centers fit the interdisciplinary criterion for being a center or institute, they transcend the usual definition. Indeed, some of these large, multischool centers are separate legal entities. An example is the Texas Tech Center for Health Sciences, a self-standing university legally distinct from its namesake, Texas Tech University. Most of the subsequent discussion here about centers and institutes does not apply to these mega-centers.

Atavistically, membership in an academic center or institute is generally secondary to an appointment in a traditional department. Thus, centers and institutes as a rule cannot recruit and hire new tenure-track or tenured faculty members. Only the established departments have that authority. This is because most board policies stipulate that faculty members be hired for teaching, research, and service—their departmental duties include all three of these required activities. However, centers and institutes have narrower expectations for their members; they are usually established to serve only one of these requirements but not all three. Thus, an individual hired into a center or institute could not meet the broader tenure criteria set by the governing board.

Consistent with their loosely defined status, these centers and institutes always exhibit exceptions to the general rule. Some universities allow centers and institutes to teach courses in their interdisciplinary topic, for example. They may even have the authority to confer degrees, including the Ph.D. And, of course, voluntary outreach and other service activities sponsored by the center or institute are certainly allowable. In this sense, these entities possess many of the attributes of a department; however, faculty members generally do not receive credit from their primary department for these center- or institute-based endeavors. Just because a faculty member teaches a course under the auspices of a center or institute, he or she cannot expect to teach one less course for the home department. This situation often breeds chronic low-level tension between the centers and institutes and the mainstream academic departments.

Two operational questions arise. If the university encourages participation in centers and institutes, why wouldn't a dean or provost step in and insist that the faculty members get credit for teaching and service through a center or institute? That might seem to be not only fair but also in the university's best interests. But if credit for teaching above and beyond a faculty member's departmentally assigned responsibilities were granted, then the department would have to hire additional personnel to cover that faculty member's teaching load. And that costs money, which would probably have to come from reallocation. In a similar vein, if the teaching, research, and service activities performed under center or institute auspices satisfy the governing board's workload requirements, why couldn't the center or institute hire its own primary faculty members? Again, in most cases that would involve reallocating resources from the existing departments, and as most provosts know all too well, reallocations can be unpopular and extremely difficult to accomplish.

Although they may function like departments by offering courses, granting degrees, and performing outreach service, centers and institutes seldom transform into a formal department. There are three underlying reasons that doesn't happen. The first two reasons, not surprisingly, involve money. Unless new money has become available through additional state support, a major endowment, or a long-term grant or contract, changing a center or institute into a formal department would require reallocation of existing resources. And that would undoubtedly encounter formidable resistance from those who would lose funding in the deal. In addition, and more important in the long run, departments are more expensive to operate than centers and institutes that rely on volunteer efforts. That alone is a powerful deterrent to conferring departmental status on a center or institute. The third reason is less mercenary and more practical in nature. Establishing a new department usually requires a lot of time-consuming effort to design curricula, develop budgets, and many other tasks. Accrediting associations must often approve any new plans like this, and preparing the necessary paperwork adds to the bureaucratic load. Moreover, many states have coordinating boards for higher education that must also approve any new academic department. And that requires even more work—analyzing demand for the program, comparing the new department with others like it in the state, and myriad other reports and analyses. Only the most dedicated faculty members want to spend their time doing that.

Organizational Structure

Because of their interdisciplinary nature, centers and institutes serve as breeding grounds for fertile, new ideas; thus, universities encourage their establishment. Ideally, a new center or institute originates with faculty members who have common interests, who find it beneficial to organize themselves as an identifiable unit within the university. The proposal to establish a center or institute states its relevance to the university's academic, research, or service mission; its potential benefits to the institution; and its consistency with the university's strategic plan.

In this ideal scenario, the administration welcomes the initiative and agrees to provide adequate resources to ensure that the center or institute can operate comfortably for five years. At that time, the center or institute will undergo a rigorous review, and if it is judged to be successful, it is allowed to continue with institutional support for another five years. In contrast, if it is found not to live up to expectations, it will be dissolved, and the university's resource commitment is redirected to a newly proposed center or institute. In this ideal world, if the center or institute faces dissolution, at least it won't occur because of inadequate institutional support; it will occur because the programmatic theme was not as promising and fertile as originally thought. Through this idealistic process, the university continually refreshes its investment in interdisciplinary, creative scholarly endeavors—reinforcing the successful ventures and winnowing out the weaker ones.

But, as usual, the real world introduces interesting variations on this ideal situation. The least variable aspect is that, with few exceptions, centers and institutes originate from the faculty members and not the administration. Adequate financial support from the institution is much less certain. Some universities limit the number of centers and institutes, and provide "reasonable" baseline support—office staff, laboratory space, and so forth. At the University of Hawaii, for an extreme example, several institutes receive budgets and tenure-track faculty positions exceeding those of many mainstream departments. For whatever reason, other universities provide little or nothing. And some universities fund some institutes and centers but not others. In other words, there are no generalizations in this regard.

When it comes to performance reviews, there are equally disparate practices. Nearly all universities mandate periodic evaluations—usually every five years or so. Some universities assiduously perform these mandatory reviews, with most reviewers from outside the university. Again, that is the ideal. At the other pole, some universities fall woefully behind schedule and only with great effort manage to conduct occasional performance evaluations. As the number of centers and institutes increases, of course, the logistic challenges and expenses of conducting timely center and institute reviews also increase. In many universities, centers and institutes seem to sprout up like mushrooms after a summer rain, and this simply compounds accountability issues. But then again, experienced chief research officers and provosts will usually not become distressed about these deviations from the ideal model, thinking "this is just the nature of interdisciplinary centers and institutes. They come, they flourish, or they flounder. Then the next creative idea comes along, and a new center or institute arises."

At most universities, the chief research officer is responsible for the overall administration of centers and institutes, including those with teaching or service missions. Because of their importance to the university's scholarly mission—its research vitality—this is a major responsibility. As a result, the chief research officer has the requisite authority to authorize the establishment and dissolution of a center or institute, although in some institutions the provost's approval may be required as well. Furthermore, the chief research officer oversees periodic evaluations of center and institute performance. Thus, he or she is ultimately responsible for their sustainability.

If the university provides resources, such as an operating budget, then further approvals may be required from the chief executive officer and even the governing board. One reason for these higher level authorizations is that the governing board retains ultimate responsibility for the university's budget, and the policies may limit the delegation of budgeting authority. Also, the governing board may retain its authority to approve all academic endeavors, including not only departments and degree programs but also centers and institutes. These approvals constitute formal university recognition of the center's or institute's existence. That recognition is quite important to the centers and institutes, for it confers a de facto commitment to their success—regardless of whether significant institutional financial support follows. In practical terms, it also means that these centers and institutes must conform to university policies and regulations.

Although the chief research officer has general authority over the establishment and dissolution of centers and institutes, he or she usually is not responsible for operational oversight. If that's the case, then to whom does the center or institute report? Now, the organizational structure becomes a bit murkier. Logic might dictate that if all of the center faculty participants have primary appointments in one college, then the center should report to the dean of that college. That's easy and straightforward. If faculty members are from more than one college, then all else being equal, the center or institute should report to the dean with the most representation. Sometimes, however, programmatic issues override this representational reporting arrangement and the center or institute reports to a "minority" dean. As an example, the majority of faculty members in an institute for water resources may have primary appointments in a college of agriculture or engineering. However, the institute concentrates on water law. Thus, it might be more appropriate to have it reporting to the dean of the law school.

Unfortunately, these canonical reporting lines via a dean to the provost may not necessarily apply. Several factors complicate the easily drawn reporting lines. At the outset, newly formed centers or institutes often request to report directly to the chief research officer, thus bypassing a dean. The faculty participants may argue that a dean, no matter how enlightened he or she may be, simply cannot impartially represent the interests of a diverse, interdisciplinary group. They will argue, "Only the chief research officer can provide that broad-minded leadership." Alternatively, the center or institute faculty members may suspect that they will receive a greater share of their grant-generated indirect-cost funds under the aegis of the chief research officer. (In fact, that is often true.) Furthermore, a center or institute may originate in part out of some faculty members' frustrations with a particular dean; they look to the chief research officer for refuge. In parallel with these complicating factors, centers and institutes that were established for a purely teaching mission may wish to report directly to the provost. As most senior faculty members know, meetings to discuss forming a new center or institute can claim an inordinate amount of time spent on figuring out the optimal reporting line. They debate, "Which dean will give us the best deal? And which one will most likely leave us alone?"

Ideally, centers and institutes should not report directly to the chief research officer. If at all possible, they should remain in the mainstream academic reporting line, and that involves reporting to a dean. There are several reasons for this. For starters, if a center or institute reports to a dean, then he or she has a vested interest in seeing it succeed. That is significant because deans control faculty positions and recurrent academic budgets; the chief research officer doesn't. If a center or institute convincingly needs a new faculty member to boost its scholarly productivity, the dean is in a position to provide the needed resources. The best that a chief research officer can do in these cases is to provide short-term support, such as a year or two of salary, start-up funding, or a needed piece of equipment. Also, the dean has the authority to mediate any tensions (such as teaching credit) that may arise between the departments and the center or institute. Importantly, a center or institute may require office space for secretarial or fiscal staff. And within the college, the dean controls space assignments. Another more pragmatic reason is that the chief research officer may not have the time or the expertise to provide good leadership. Therefore, it is generally in the center or institute's best interests to report to a dean. Of course, there will be exceptional cases that require oversight by the chief research officer. But those should be rare and well justified.

Within the center or institute, the usual rules of governance apply. The director is selected by the members, usually by an election, and is appointed formally by the individual to whom the center or institute reports—usually a dean. As always, the director should be encouraged to develop a succession plan. And in most cases, the center or institute should prepare a strategic plan that is compatible with the university's overall plan, along with benchmarks for judging successful implementation of the plan.

> K: *I understand the logic behind your assertions that a center or institute should report to a dean. But a dean's job is to promote his or her specific college. So how can you reasonably expect a dean to provide unbiased and effective leadership for a cross-disciplinary center or institute with members from several colleges?*
>
> Smith: *That's a very good point. And that's why larger centers and institutes with representation from several colleges often report directly to the chief research officer. However, there are inherent disadvantages to this organizational structure that not everybody appreciates until they become a problem.*
>
> K: *Couldn't the university solve this dilemma by giving the chief research officer resources like a few faculty positions and space to support interdisciplinary centers and institutes?*
>
> Smith: *Sure. Some universities do that on a limited scale, and that's very good. But without these resources, the chief research officer has to rely on the*

power of persuasion to convince a dean to provide unbiased support for other colleges represented in a center or institute.

Soft-Money Centers and Institutes

So far, only university-recognized centers and institutes have been considered. They have been approved by the chief research officer or other top-level authority and may even receive financial support from the university. In most institutions, though, there is another genre: the soft-money center or institute. These arise in the context of a gift or grant award. Several federal funding agencies award grants explicitly to establish a center or institute. Examples include the NSF engineering research centers and the NIH designated cancer centers. As a condition of the award, the principal investigator establishes the center or institute, which exists for the duration of the award. When the grant terminates, the center or institute ceases to exist unless the university chooses to continue it for some programmatic reason. In these soft-money cases, the university implicitly recognizes and approves the creation of the center or institute when it accepts the award. However, in general, further approval by the chief research officer is not required unless the university also contributes to the unit's funding—which occurs rarely.

On a cautionary note, bear in mind that often these awards and their associated centers and institutes merit publicity. The chief research officer must ensure that the governing board knows about the award and the center or institute in advance of any press release. Board members can become quite annoyed when they learn about these things in the newspaper or on television.

Unlike the university-recognized centers and institutes, the soft-money centers and institutes do not report to a dean. They report to the principal investigator, who has full authority over the academic program and operation. He or she may also appoint another individual funded by the grant to serve as director. Although the principal investigator has programmatic authority, it should be remembered that the chief research officer bears the ultimate institutional responsibility for these soft-money centers and institutes.

In this context, not uncommonly a group of faculty members will form a center or institute on its own, completely bypassing university policies concerning the establishment and approval processes. Often the raison d'être is fund-raising. They will say, "It looks better to potential donors if we have a center business card." Likewise, a principal investigator on his or her initiative may use an award as the basis for founding a center—with or without university approval. (Nowadays, it is very easy for an enterprising principal investigator to print an official-looking center or institute letterhead and business cards under the chief research officer's radar screen.) Because they have not been endorsed officially by the university, these centers and institutes usually fall outside the usual regulations governing centers and institutes. And they do not lie on any particular reporting line other than to the founders. Nonetheless, they are often included in a list of university centers and institutes when it is for publicity reasons. Indeed, many universities tout their large number of centers and institutes because that contributes to their prestige as a major, thriving research institution. However, a closer look may reveal that a much smaller number of them have undergone formal approval. But few people care very much about this technicality.

Funding

Ironically, despite their important role in the university, centers and institutes as a rule receive little institutional support. Of course, there are always exceptions, but in general they must raise their own operating funds through gifts, grants, and contracts. Occasionally, a university may provide funding for secretarial help and perhaps several graduate-student stipends, but that is usually the limit. Consequently, university policy commonly allows faculty members—including research faculty members not on tenure track—to submit grants through the center or institute, with the implicit understanding that this somehow benefits the unit.

Predictably, the director will argue that the center or institute should receive any revenue generated by grants administered by the center or institute. This includes indirect-cost distributions, salary savings, fees, and so forth. Equally predictably, the center and institute faculty affiliates' home department chairs will reply that they have some claim to these funds; they will argue, "After all, we bear the administrative costs of processing the faculty members' personnel actions such as payroll, graduate student records, upkeep and utilities of his or her laboratories and office," and on and on. The dean may have to step in and reconcile these conflicting claims.

For his or her part, the chief research officer can help mediate these disputes preemptively by requiring principal investigators to document for the sponsored research office how grant-generated revenue (such as indirect-cost reimbursement) will be distributed prior to submitting the grant application. And the director and dean must sign-off on this document, thus acknowledging an agreement. Other than that, the chief research officer should resist the temptation to intervene in disputes involving center or institute management, if at all possible.

Similarly, if the center or institute offers instructional courses, it usually expects to receive any tuition revenue that is normally returned to the generating unit— just like the mainstream academic departments. Again, there will be conflicting claims on that money because the instructor's home department may expect reimbursement for processing his or her personnel matters. The dean (or deans) must reconcile these differences.

More frustrating, the center or institute may become entangled in a curious administrative web if, as a matter of state or institutional accounting policy, so-called nonacademic units (that is, anything other than a formally recognized academic department) do not have instructional budgets. In that case, there is nowhere to put the money where it is accessible to the center or institute. The only remedy to this vexing situation is to change the underlying policy, which may or may not be easily doable.

Performance Reviews

Like all other academic programs, centers and institutes typically undergo periodic performance reviews. The usual time frame is once about every five years. Unlike standard departments, however, these evaluations examine whether the center's or institute's continued existence is in the best interests of the university and its overall academic program. Thus, there is a lot at stake.

To avoid potential conflicts of interest, the chief research officer typically initiates and oversees the review. Initially, he or she notifies the director and the university official to whom the center or institute reports (usually a dean) that a review will occur, and he or she specifies what documents and information must be prepared beforehand. The most important item is a comprehensive, information-based self-study. In addition, the chief research officer appoints a review team. Nominations may be solicited from the center or institute director and the dean. It is not unusual for the chief research officer to select independently one or two members from outside the university. In the ideal but often extreme case, especially when an unbiased in-house review seems difficult to achieve, the entire team may be brought in from outside the university. The reviewers evaluate information submitted in the self-study that examines achievement of their missions and strategic plan goals. This is usually followed by a site visit.

Incidentally, who pays for these performance reviews? University policies in general require that the program under review pay the full costs. These costs include any secretarial or other routine office-related costs and external reviewers' honoraria (typically $500 to $1,000), plus travel, lodging, and meal expenses. Therefore, under this general policy, the centers and institutes cover the costs of performance reviews. If they don't have funds available for this purpose, then the dean to whom the center or institute reports pays for the review, including the external site visitor's expenses. Of course, the chief research officer pays if the center or institute reports to him or her.

Following the review, the centers or institutes are generally assigned active or probationary status. In the former case, they continue to exist and will be reviewed again in cycle (after another five years, for example). In the latter case, centers or institutes assigned probationary status will be reviewed again after a shorter period specified by the chief research officer. This is usually three years or so. During this period, the center or institute must address concerns expressed in writing by the review committee. Failure to meet this condition can lead to dissolution.

Many reviewers succumb to the temptation of suggesting that the center or institute needs additional institutional support to thrive or to achieve greatness. They will say, "If it just had another million dollars, the center could step up to the next level." Unfortunately, this kind of commentary is not helpful to the chief research officer. Axiomatically, any academic unit, including the university as a whole, can benefit from more money. Stated whimsically, when asked by the chief research officer "How much money does it take to run this center?" the director's real answer is simply "How much do you have?" As in most educational endeavors, more money buys additional resources and, by inference, enhanced quality. Therefore, to predicate the review on additional funding compromises its value, for it puts the chief research officer in a difficult position: if he or she is not prepared to provide the recommended funding, then why bother reading the review at all? Thus, chief research officers should instruct the review committee a priori to concentrate on the performance achieved or achievable solely with the available resources.

> K: *You're pretty harsh on that point. The performance review is not the place to ask for more money. But take that a step further. A review committee is expected to recommend further areas of improvement and maybe promising directions to follow. Isn't it implicit that money will be needed to follow these recommendations?*
> Smith: *Maybe. But the center or institute must figure out how to accomplish its goals within its budgetary constraints. The group shouldn't be forced into the situation where they can't meet the review's recommendations without additional funding—especially if there's little chance that they can get the money.*
> K: *If budgets are tight, as they always seem to be, are you suggesting that the review process is a waste of effort?*
> Smith: *No. Stripping away these budgetary concerns, a review nearly always helps. At the very least it requires a self-study, which, if thoughtfully prepared, can be of great value to the center or institute, regardless of the quality. By the way, if the self-study is not thoughtfully prepared, the center or institute director should be reprimanded and probably replaced.*

Dissolution

The time may come when a center or institute no longer contributes to the university's mission. When this occurs, it is in the university's better interests to dissolve the center or institute. Dissolution poses its own set of challenges. As most experience administrators know, closing an academic unit, regardless of size (for example, a center, department, or college) can be extremely difficult and unpleasant. Usually, there are few easy ways of going about this. But there are several ways to ease the pain.

The originating recommendation to dissolve a center or institute may come from several possible sources. The center or institute director may propose its dissolution. If the faculty members endorse, or at least do not contest, this recommendation, dissolution is reasonably straightforward. Alternatively, a committee may recommend dissolution of a center or institute after a regularly scheduled performance review. From an institutional perspective, these are the two most desirable sources, for they conform to the principles of faculty governance.

The least desirable pathway to dissolution arises when the dean or the chief research officer decides that the center or institute is not performing up to the university's expectations and that its dissolution is in the university's best interest. In these cases, the chief research officer should document the center or institute's perceived shortcomings and ask the director for a rebuttal within a reasonable time period (for example, a year). If the director's response contradicts this decision to close the center or institute, the chief research officer should launch a performance review, following the same procedures as the regularly scheduled reviews. The chief research officer should then follow the review committee's recommendations, which may involve closure or some other remedial action. It is highly advisable for the chief research officer to follow these principles of faculty governance and not attempt dissolution singlehandedly.

The chief research officer can expect to receive telephone calls, e-mails, and letters opposing the closure of even the smallest center or institute. These may come from not only university personnel but also members of the general public, and even state and local governments. The diversity of a center or institute's constituency can sometimes be quite amazing. Anecdotally, after a performance review recommended closure of the University of Hawaii's small Center for Southeast Asian Studies, a donor offered a $25,000 gift to the center, praising its merits to the community. Now, what should the chief research officer do? Turn down the gift (which universities do not like to do) or reverse the decision to close the center? In this case, the closure decision was reversed and the center continued to exist.

If it is to be dissolved, the head of the center or institute will develop a written plan providing for appropriate personnel actions (such as notification of reassignment or layoff), accommodation of students in a degree-granting program, and disposition of any property or assets. All of this takes time, and should not be rushed. Usually, the chief research officer works closely with the deans of the colleges impacted by the closure to ensure an orderly process. And, of course, the university's human resources personnel will be involved.

Service Centers

Service centers stand partly under the definitional umbrella of centers and institutes. The term "service centers" usually applies to a facility that provides a specific service to the general university community. Common examples include biotechnology centers that make available DNA sequencing and synthesis, transgenic animal centers, imaging centers that offer various sophisticated microscopes, survey centers that conduct sample surveys and opinion polls, and high-performance computing centers. Like the academic centers, they are certainly interdisciplinary because researchers from many different departments on campus use their services. However, unlike academic centers, their mission is to support the academic enterprise, not lead in scholarly pursuits. Moreover, the staff members are seldom faculty members.

Service centers derive financial support from various sources. If they're fortunate, the institution provides some measure of support, such as the salary (often partial) of one or two key staff members, telephone bills, and maybe a part-time fiscal officer. Institutional F&A funds are a typical source of the money, which is appropriate because these costs are usually included in the F&A rate calculations. Since this amount is seldom sufficient to operate the service center, however, most of them charge fees for their services. Fee schedules are based on the actual costs of running the center—personnel salaries (plus fringe benefits), materials and supplies, utilities, and related items. The goal is simply to recover costs incurred in providing a service. For this reason, these centers are sometimes called "recharge centers."

If federal grant funds are used to pay these fees (which they often are), then according to OMB circular A-21:

> The costs of such services, when material, must be charged directly to applicable awards based on actual usage of the services on the basis of a schedule of rates or established methodology that
> (1) does not discriminate against federally supported activities of the institution, including usage by the institution for internal purposes, and
> (2) is designed to recover only the aggregate costs of the services. The costs of each service shall consist normally of both its direct costs and its allocable share of all F&A costs.[1]

In other words, the fees are based on the actual costs of running the facility averaged over several years (for example, three) and, importantly, the same fees must be charged for accounts paid by federal grant funds as by other sources of money. (In other words, prices can't be raised just because a customer has lots of NIH grant money). In addition, centers and institutes usually factor in depreciation of major equipment. Revenue gained from this depreciation component of the fees is often deposited into a reserve account that is used to buy replacements for fully depreciated equipment.

In the eyes of the Internal Revenue Service (IRS), these service center fees are income. However, because the university, and therefore the service center even if it is a separate legal entity, is a nonprofit organization, this income is exempt from federal taxation—that is, as long as the services generating the fees are associated with the university's overall mission. If this is not the case, then according to the federal tax code, the university may be subject to the so-called unrelated business income tax on fees collected for services unrelated to the university's mission. For example, if a university's biotechnology center analyzes DNA sequences strictly for research projects conducted by faculty members, then these services fall within the university's research mission. However, if the center also analyzes DNA sequences for private companies or even local government agencies (such as a public health office), then these services do not fall within the university's mission. This is considered unrelated business, and the revenue from these customers may be subject to federal and perhaps state income tax. As the IRS states it, "Unrelated business income is the income from a trade or business that is regularly carried on by an exempt organization and that is not substantially related to the performance by the organization of its exempt purpose or function."[2] The phrase "regularly carried on" is critical in this context. An occasional unrelated service does not raise the specter of the unrelated business income tax. However, if these unrelated services are a regular aspect of the service center's operations, then the fees are taxable.

Even if the institution does not provide direct financial support to the service center, it provides a subsidy in the form of free real estate, utilities, insurance, publicity, and other less fungible assets. This implied support has a monetary value that can be estimated. University users generally don't pay for this subsidization. However, the fee schedule for nonuniversity customers most likely includes these subsidized costs. Therefore, they pay considerably higher fees than university customers for the same services.

University service centers often compete with private businesses. And this competition can be quite disruptive. One illustration is in the realm of DNA synthesis. About fifteen years ago, many universities established DNA-synthesizing facilities to provide faculty members with small, tailor-made pieces of DNA ("primers") needed for a powerful new technique known as polymerase chain reaction (PCR). These were costly facilities to set up; they required expensive equipment and well-trained personnel. Nonetheless, they quickly became indispensible to many researchers. Initially, there was no meaningful competition from the private sector; the university centers had a virtual monopoly. After a lag, however, several private companies entered this market and offered the same product at a lower price, even with shipping costs. And, they often had faster delivery times and better quality control. Consequently, many researchers turned to these companies for the product, thus relegating the university's DNA synthesis center to a minor player in the business. This drove up the expenses of maintaining the university's facility. To break even, user fees would have to be increased, but that would further push away customers, thus exacerbating the problem.

Ultimately, this kind of problem becomes the chief research officer's dilemma. Pour more money into the university's service center to remain competitive with the private sector or phase it out? Of course, the solution to this problem varies according to the university's unique situation. As a rule of thumb, however, it is generally advisable to withdraw from the market if the private sector can reliably provide a comparable product at a better price. In these cases, the university's assets can be reinvested in a newer emerging service or a product that promises to enrich the academic community.

> K: *Couldn't the university require researchers to use its service centers rather than commercial businesses?*
>
> Smith: *Yes, that happens but sometimes subtly. For example, a university may have its own "store" that sells routine laboratory chemicals and supplies, compressed gases, notebooks, computer supplies, and so forth. Because of a university's large overhead and limited market, the prices may not be competitive on all items, but the university may direct all purchases of these stocked items to its own store.*
>
> K: *Why would the university maintain a service center like that if the same products could be obtained less expensively from private vendors?*
>
> Smith: *Convenience mainly. Before the days of overnight express deliveries, online purchasing systems, and credit cards, these university service centers were indispensable and well worth the premium prices. Nowadays, the convenience argument is much less compelling. Nonetheless, many researchers still depend on a campus-based supplies center for emergency needs when even overnight delivery is too slow, regardless of price.*

Notes

1. Office of Management and Budget, Executive Office of the President, Circular No. A-21, 2 C.F.R. Pt. 220, App. A §§J.47.b.(1)-(2) (2010).
2. Internal Revenue Service (IRS), *Publication 598 Tax on Unrelated Business Income of Exempt Organizations* (Washington, D.C.: IRS, 2010), p. 3.

CHAPTER 8

Sponsored-Research Services

K: Most faculty members at a research university are expected to apply for grants to support their research. How do you help them do this?

Smith: That depends on the institution, of course. But there's every reason to do as much as possible to help get the grant applications out the door.

K: Can the university actually help improve a proposal's chances of being funded?

Smith: Yes, in many ways. That's all a part of a chief research officer's job.

Office for Sponsored Research

Nearly all universities conducting research—large and small—have an office that administers their sponsored research. It is called the "sponsored research office," "research services office," or some variation on that theme, and it reports to the chief research officer. Typically, these offices have a director and a well-trained staff. Indeed, these individuals are generally quite skilled in research-management issues, as well as in people management. They interact daily with faculty members who are often under severe time pressures to meet the deadline for a grant application and, consequently, they must deal regularly with stressful situations.

The director of the sponsored-research office, who reports to the chief research officer, usually bears a heavy institutional responsibility. This responsibility derives from federal expectations that recipients of grants and contracts will designate an official "who, on behalf of the proposing organization is empowered to make certifications and assurances and can commit the organization to the conduct of a project."[1] Because the grant proposal is formally submitted by the governing board, each institution appoints an authorized organization representative (AOR), also called the signing official (SO), who is the board's designated representative in matters related to the application and the award. The director of the sponsored research office (not the chief research officer) usually holds this title. Only this person is authorized to sign the final application on behalf of the university. And, as NIH puts it:

> In signing a grant application, this individual certifies that the applicant organization will comply with all applicable assurances and certifications

referenced in the application. This individual's signature further certifies that the applicant organization will be accountable both for the appropriate use of funds awarded and for the performance of the grant-supported project or activities resulting from the application.[2]

There are national organizations that provide a forum for professional training and development in the field, such as the National Council of University Research Administrators (NCURA)[3] and the Society of Research Administrators International (SRA).[4] Furthermore, as testimony to the skills and knowledge required in this profession, in 1993, the SRA formed the Research Administrators Certification Council, "whose role is to certify that an individual, through experience and testing, has the fundamental knowledge necessary to be a professional research or sponsored programs administrator."[5]

To be effective, the chief research officer must have a good understanding of the administration of sponsored research. Many faculty members become familiar with the fundamental mechanics of this, especially as they submit more complicated grant applications. A chief research officer with that kind of background is generally familiar with the basic procedures of getting a grant application out the door and submitting required reports. But, as they say, "the devil is in the details." Thus, the chief research officer should seize any opportunities to learn more about grants administration. One good way is to attend meetings of the Council on Government Relations (COGR), a national organization of research universities whose

> primary function is to provide advice and information to its membership and to make certain that federal agencies understand academic operations and the impact of proposed regulations on colleges and universities. [The] COGR helps to develop policies and practices that fairly reflect the mutual interests and separate obligations of federal agencies and universities in research and graduate education.[6]

Research Corporations and Foundations

Some universities outsource the administration of their sponsored research to an affiliated corporation. These are separate legal entities, most often a 501(c)(3) non-profit organization. These corporations, which may also be called "research foundations," have a separate governing board, although the university's chief research officer may be an ex officio member. They operate in two possible ways. In one version, grants and contract applications are submitted through the university— thus, they are awarded to the university as well. But the university then turns them over to the corporation via a contractual arrangement for subsequent administration.

All personnel paid using grant funds are employees of the corporation, not the university. Furthermore, the corporation processes all purchase orders and other grant-related expenditures.

The Research Corporation of the University of Hawaii (RCUH) is a good example of this arrangement.[7] Although the state legislature established RCUH, it exempted the corporation from state personnel and procurement guidelines. There is an interesting history behind this. The university operates several oceanographic research vessels. If they needed to hire a crew member or replace a lost anchor in some remote location in the Pacific Ocean, they could not wait the long time usually needed to comply with state personnel and purchasing guidelines. To solve this problem, RCUH was created so that the University of Hawaii could contract them to administer its sponsored research. The RCUH management fee is, as of 2009, 2.5 percent of the awards' modified total direct costs (MTDC), which is the base amount that the federal government uses to calculate F&A reimbursement.

The second way to outsource the research administration is for the corporation to submit to the granting agencies the grant and contract applications on behalf of university researchers. In these cases, the awards are given to the corporation. Although the corporation administers the awards through its office for sponsored research, it contracts with the university (and, therefore, the principal investigator) to conduct the actual research. To fund the research projects, the corporation pays the awarded direct costs to the university. The California State University campuses' research foundations and the University of Georgia Research Foundation (UGARF) are good examples of this type of organization. In addition to administering all of the university's grants, contracts, and gifts, UGARF oversees technology transfer and economic-development endeavors.[8] It even funds and administers competitive mini-grant programs and other faculty-development initiatives. Although it is a separate 501(c)(3) corporation, UGARF is tightly integrated into the university's research office. Indeed, the chief research officer is also the UGARF executive vice president.

Most research corporations administer all their university grants and contracts in either of these two ways, although there are exceptions whereby the university might choose to retain full control over a particular award. Because they are generally not subject to state personnel and procurement rules, private universities seldom have the need for a separate research corporation.

One further point about research corporations merits attention. Often, granting agencies limit the number of proposals for a specific funding opportunity that may be submitted by an institution. Like UGARF, if the research corporation (or foundation) "acts as the fiduciary entity for private contracts and grants for several campuses within the same multi-campus college or university system, and if the campuses are distinct . . . then [it] may submit up to one proposal on behalf of each campus."[9] Can the corporation submit independently of the university, thus doubling the number of proposals that may be submitted? The answer is no.

Although the research corporation is a separate entity, with no students or faculty of its own, according to the NSF, it supports the activities of the university and cannot be considered an organization with interests distinct from the university. Thus, research proposals submitted by the research corporation count toward the limit on institutional proposals.

Award Support

The administration of sponsored projects is typically broken down into two phases: before (pre-) and after (post-) an award is received by the institution. Pre-award services focus on the submission of a grant application and corollary negotiations with the granting agency prior to receiving notification of the actual award. After an award has been received, its financial management and reporting requirements are administered by post-award personnel. In some universities, both pre- and post-award services are in the same office that reports to the chief research officer. This facilitates communication between the two sections. However, other universities place the post-award management under the direction of the chief financial officer. The rationale is that all personnel dealing with fiscal affairs should report to the chief financial officer who generally has more expertise in that area. In the latter case, the two offices must conscientiously work together closely because of the overlap between pre- and post-award administrative issues. The chief research officer and the chief financial officer must be particularly diligent about the assignment of responsibilities when the offices have separate reporting lines, especially when it comes to matters of regulatory compliance. Otherwise, things may "fall through the cracks," with potentially damaging consequences.

Pre-Award Services

The services that are provided pre-award typically include notifying faculty members and staff about funding opportunities and various sponsor policies and procedures. In its simplest form, this may amount to little more than forwarding calls for proposals issued by various funding agencies via a university-wide e-mail list serve. Or, the office for sponsored research may prepare a summary listing of grant opportunities for e-mail distribution. In addition, its staff may participate in various Web-based services that list funding sources and deadlines; Community of Science (COS) is a popular example.[10] Schools and colleges may supplement these services with their own listings of discipline-specific grant opportunities.

Some universities also provide help in preparing grant applications. This includes assistance with organizing materials, getting proper assurances, constructing a budget, fine-tuning the writing style, and myriad other proposal details.

Research service personnel who have been trained in grant writing may hold periodic workshops during which the techniques of preparing a proposal are discussed. In that context, federal agencies offer similar workshops; indeed, the NSF holds regional grants conferences at various host institutions throughout the year—at no cost to the attendees.[11] Particularly aggressive universities go a step further: they make "house calls." In these cases, the office for sponsored research will equip one or more fully trained staff officers with cell phones. In response to a call for help, they go to the office of a researcher who is having difficulties preparing a grant application. This service may be available after normal business hours, especially when a major NIH or NSF deadline is near.

When a proposal is to be submitted to a granting agency, it must first be vetted by pre-award service personnel. Ultimately, the principal investigator bears the responsibility for the accuracy and completeness of the application. Nonetheless, the office for sponsored research generally provides the applicant with expert assistance in meeting these obligations. In particular, they ensure that the proposal conforms to all agency compliance regulations. In that capacity, they include assurances that the proposed project has been reviewed and approved by committees or officials with oversight for the use of human subjects, animals, biological agents and toxins ("select agents"), controlled substances, items to be exported to foreign countries, radiation and radioisotopes, and laboratory and environmental biosafety, to name the most prominent. In addition, the budget is usually checked to ensure that salary calculations are accurate, proper effort is reported, subcontracts are correctly entered, and F&A costs are calculated accurately.

Furthermore, pre-award personnel check for any sponsor-mandated limitations on the publication of research results, ownership of intellectual property, participation of foreign nationals on the project, and third-party liability. Most universities consider any of these limitations unacceptable. All potentially conflicting financial interests or other conflicts of interest are discussed with the applicant. The ultimate goal is to bring the proposal into conformance with the granting agency's guidelines, to ensure that it will not be returned without review because something is missing or for some other technical reason. Most faculty members complain about these many detailed requirements ("too much bureaucratic paperwork"), but they readily appreciate the office's assistance in gathering the necessary assurances.

In addition, most offices for sponsored research submit the applications on behalf of the university. This is more than just a helpful service to the principal investigator. It also ensures that no changes are made to the proposal after the AOR has signed-off on it. They send paper applications directly to the granting agency. (The principal investigator usually pays the shipping expenses.) Since the advent of online, Web-based submissions (for example, the NSF's FastLane and the NIH's eCommons and Grants.gov), personnel in the office for sponsored research oversee the actual electronic submissions. Indeed, the AOR may have exclusive authorization to submit the proposal. Some third-party vendors, such as Cayuse,[12] offer software systems designed to simplify the somewhat cumbersome electronic application process.

Pre-award officers also help investigators who wish to change the scope of an award. According to NIH policy, "change of scope" refers to the following situations:[13]

* Change in the specific aims approved at the time of award.
* Substitution of one animal model for another.
* Any change from the approved use of animals or human subjects.
* Shift of the research emphasis from one disease area to another.
* A clinical hold by FDA under a study involving an IND or an IDE.
* Application of a new technology, e.g., changing assays from those approved to a different type of assay.
* Transfer of the performance of substantive programmatic work to a third party through a consortium agreement, by contract, or any other means. If the third party is a foreign component, this type of action always requires NIH prior approval.
* Change in key personnel.
* Purchase of a unit of equipment exceeding $25,000.

Significant modification of the budget for the original award also constitutes a change of scope. According to the NIH, "significant" rebudgeting occurs when expenditures in a single direct-cost budget category change by more than 25 percent of the total costs awarded. For example, if the award budget for total costs is $200,000, any budget modifications that total more than $50,000 in a budget category are considered "significant rebudgeting." And finally, the NIH considers any changes in budgeted costs for research patient care a change of scope. The NSF's policies are more or less similar.[14]

When any of these situations occurs, the principal investigator must inform the program director for the federal agency when seeking approval for the change of scope. Because the grant is awarded to the institution, the AOR (the "signing official," in NIH jargon) must co-sign the written request. The OMB's circular A-110 provides specific guidelines for all federal granting agencies in this regard.[15]

In 2008, the OMB revised its circular A-110 to adopt less stringent guidelines first proposed in 2000 by the Federal Demonstration Project (FDP), which is a cooperative initiative among ten federal agencies and ninety-eight institutional recipients of research funds. These revisions provided what is known as "expanded authority" to participating institutions. Now, the university simply has to request this expanded authority, and it will be granted if the institution agrees to abide by the spirit of the guidelines for management of federal grants. This expanded authority waives the requirement for agency approval to carry forward grant funds from one year to the next (except in the final year), to award up to a one-year extension of the grant's duration (with no additional funds), to transfer funds between direct and indirect cost categories of the grant budget, and to transfer funds among direct-cost categories for grants in which the federal share exceeds \$100,000.[16] Most federal agencies (including the NIH and NSF) and universities have adopted these relaxed guidelines.

Another useful revision is the university's authority to expend grant funds up to ninety days before receiving the actual notice of grant award. This allows an investigator to get started promptly after learning that the award is forthcoming. Most directors of offices for sponsored research insist on receiving written notification from the granting agency that the award letter will arrive within the ninety-day period. This caution is well justified because, until the official notice of grant award has been received, the federal agency is under no obligation to make the award and, therefore, to reimburse any advance expenditures. Consequently, if an advance exceeds several hundred thousand dollars, the chief research officer must exercise particular caution.

Parenthetically, advanced funding raises another issue—namely, the "float." Technically, most granting agencies, including those of the federal government, pay universities on a reimbursement basis. Therefore, the university covers the costs of a research project and then submits a bill to the agency for those expenses. So, there is a lag between expenditures and revenue—a cash-flow problem, so to speak. This is known as the "float." To ease this burden on the university, the federal government allows the institution to estimate its grant-related expenditures in advance and to receive this advanced funding via a monthly letter of credit "draw down" from the federal treasury. Thus, technically, the federal government covers its portion of the float. As in any business, the university must not abuse this system by exaggerating its estimated expenses and therefore drawing down more than is needed to cover the actual expenses. Most universities make conservative estimates, thereby assuming responsibility for only a fraction (very small, it is hoped) of the float.

However, as research expenditures increase year after year, the amount of the float grows as well; it can easily become tens and even hundreds of millions of dollars. This occurs especially if the institution has numerous nonfederal grants and contracts that do not provide this advanced funding. Private universities and some public universities can accommodate this float by running an operational deficit at the end of a fiscal year. The pending reimbursement is treated as an account receivable. However, some states prohibit universities from running a deficit; the books must balance at the end of a fiscal year—otherwise, the university's chief executive officer risks going to jail. With this powerful incentive, the university must somehow cover the float from its available cash resources. These resources may include rainy-day funds, bond-repayment reserve accounts, and any other pool of money. This is mainly a problem for the university treasurer, but the chief research officer may become involved because of its link to research.

In fact, the chief research officer may be expected to contribute money under his or her own control to a reserve account that provides coverage for the float.

F&A (Indirect) Cost Policies

At the pre-award phase, the office for sponsored research checks the F&A (indirect) cost component of the budget. The default policy is to collect the maximum amount allowable by the granting agency. For most federal agencies, that is the university's negotiated rate. Ideally, all other sponsors would be expected to pay the negotiated rate as well. However, some granting agencies limit the amount of F&A costs allowable in the budget, and usually this is less than the federally negotiated full rate. In some federal and nonfederal grants, F&A costs are not an allowable item; the F&A rate is effectively zero. Examples include federal equipment or facilities grants and some training grants. Thus, none can be included in the proposal's budget. And, of course, the university may not rebudget one of these awards in an attempt to recover F&A costs without agency approval.

Most universities accommodate these F&A cost limitations in the following way. If the granting agency has a documented policy limiting the allowable F&A rate to a specific amount (which may be zero), and applies that policy uniformly to all grants, then the university will accept that limitation without question. This is consistent with the overall policy that the institution collects "the maximum amount allowable by the granting agency." Thus, there is no need for the principal investigator to request a reduction or waiver from the negotiated rate in these cases. The office for sponsored research will generally have a record of various granting organizations' allowable F&A amounts on file. However, the staff may need to contact the granting agency occasionally to verify the continuation of this limitation. Also, they may ask the principal investigator to provide documentation of a sponsor's policy, and the principal investigator must comply.

This accommodation procedure is not beyond abuse. There is always the possibility that a granting organization will yield to an unscrupulous principal investigator's request for a letter simply to satisfy the office for sponsored research—even though the organization has no specific policy. The chief research officer and staff of the research office are usually wary of this, and in suspicious cases they will contact the organization directly for verification.

There are gray areas in this arena. Technically, federal agencies must allow full recovery of the federally negotiated F&A costs. However, some members of Congress may informally discourage any F&A cost payments from specific awards, such as those arising from funding an earmark. Or a principal investigator may assert that, "the program officer doesn't want the university to claim any F&A costs on this project." Unfortunately, there are seldom any documented policies governing these kinds of requested exceptions to federally negotiated F&A costs. This causes difficulties for the office for sponsored research because it must then somehow determine exactly what the "official" policy is. And this may require multiple, time-consuming telephone calls and e-mails. In very rare cases, the chief research officer simply decides that it is not in the university's better interest to pursue these questionable cases; he or she will conclude, "I give up. It's not worth the money."

Occasionally, for programmatic reasons, principal investigators request an exceptional waiver of F&A cost collection by the university. If the sponsor's maximum grant budget is so small (for example, less than about $10,000) that the project cannot be accomplished if the full negotiated F&A amount were deducted, then a reduced rate may be acceptable. This case would be more compelling if there were the potential for the grant to spawn larger awards in the future. It is not difficult to envision other extenuating circumstances that must be considered on a case-by-case basis.

This kind of case raises a policy question: why would a university encourage faculty members to apply for grants that are so small that they require an F&A cost waiver just to accomplish the project goals? The answer is that the university seeks to keep as many faculty members active in research as possible. This practice maintains morale and, importantly, provides research opportunities for students. Ideally, the best policy is not to "top off" research grants with university funds; investigators should apply for the amount needed to conduct the project. Ultimately, however, the institution doesn't benefit from discouraging any faculty member from going after grants—no matter how small they might be. And, more important, they don't want to inadvertently encourage them to submit proposals through some other organization outside the university just to hang onto more of the grant's F&A reimbursement.

The chief research officer's response to these entire-waiver requests will depend on how much F&A funding is under his or her control—or the university's control, for that matter. In private universities and public institutions that have budgetary authority over all F&A funds, then, a waiver amounts to a cash contribution to the project. Technically, a waiver means that the institution is subsidizing the project's cost. From that perspective, all other faculty members are subsidizing the waiver recipient's research project because the waived funds would otherwise have been available for general distribution. In those cases, many chief research officers prefer to deny the waiver request to maintain policy consistency, but in compelling situations, to give the investigator the comparable amount of money from some other account. This preserves the principle of collecting full F&A reimbursement but provides the requested institutional support.

If the state keeps a sizable fraction of the F&A cost reimbursement, or restricts its availability to the faculty members in some way, then the chief research officer has less incentive to uphold the "full recovery" policy. He or she may ask, "Why should I? The state just keeps the money anyway, and we never see it." In those cases, waivers may become far more prevalent. Ultimately, that is bad management that emanates from equally bad public policy.

Cost-Sharing

Some granting agencies require the university to share in the costs of the proposed research. This lowers the award cost to the agency and enlists the institution's vested interest in the project. Both are worthy reasons for sharing the costs. However, this practice discriminates against the less wealthy universities that may not be able to afford the investments, and according to critics, also imposes a financial hardship on even the wealthier universities. They claim, "We should be competing on the basis of the proposal's quality, not the university's monetary contribution." Furthermore, "if the agency wants the work done, then let them pay for it. Why should we have to pick up part of the tab?"

In response to these objections, in 1986, the NIH dropped mandatory cost-sharing on most but not all of its research initiatives. According to their policy, matching or cost-sharing may be required by the NIH under only one of the following conditions: the requirement is based in statute (matching or cost-sharing) or program regulations (cost-sharing).[17] Note: "matching" here refers to a requirement specified in statute. For example, the program's authorizing statute may require matching or cost-sharing without necessarily specifying the exact amount. When the requirement is included in program regulations, and not in statute, the requirement may be stated as a percentage of actual, allowable costs.

Since 2007, the NSF has adopted a similar policy. Indeed, according to their 2011 grant proposal guide, "Inclusion of voluntary committed cost sharing is prohibited."[18] Like the NIH, the NSF requires cost-sharing when it is mandated by either federal statute or in the announcement for a specific program.

Matching and cost-sharing requirements usually appear only when the institution's financial support and commitment is deemed foundational to program success. Specifically, "Factors that may justify the inclusion of programmatic mandatory cost sharing requirements include, but are not limited to, capacity-building, linkages with industry, procurement or support for facilities or permanent equipment, and long-term sustainability."[19] These factors include items that provide a tangible benefit to the institution beyond the activities supported by the grant or that have a clear potential to generate income. For example, cost-sharing of 30 percent is required for the NSF's major research-instrumentation grants because of the anticipated broad usage of the awarded items. Interestingly, the comparable NIH program, the NCRR's shared-instrumentation grants, does not require cost-sharing.

Note that the NSF's cost-sharing policy normally applies only to Ph.D.-granting and nondegree-granting institutions. Universities that do not grant Ph.D.s need not cost-share. Furthermore, the NSF specifically states that they may tailor the cost-sharing requirements to take into account the type of institution, its size, level of other research support, population served, and so forth. The chief research officer at smaller institutions should take advantage of this negotiating opportunity.

Contributions toward cost-sharing may be drawn from any nonfederal source, and may be cash or in-kind. The most common source is faculty salaries.

For example, faculty may report 50 percent effort on the project but include only 20 percent of their salary on the grant budget. The university can claim the other 30 percent of the salary as its contribution to cost-sharing. Other sources include subsidized services offered by shops and cost centers (for example, animal care) if a service is provided to the project at less than actual costs, as well as third-party contributions (for example, equipment or software) and any other source of unrestricted income.

Several other details warrant mentioning. If the granting agency reduces the proposed budget by more than a certain amount (such as $10,000), then the amount of required cost-sharing is usually reduced proportionately. Also, to repeat an important point, federal money cannot be used for cost-sharing on a federal grant unless the granting agency specifically allows it. The F&A reimbursement is not considered federal money in this case, so it can be used. Moreover, an institution may voluntarily reduce the amount of F&A costs to less than its entitled reimbursement and claim the amount of the reduction as cost-sharing. Beware, though: any cost-sharing in the grant budget that is above and beyond what is required ("voluntary cost-sharing") becomes a condition of the award (if the granting agency allows this kind of cost-sharing). And the university must honor this commitment. Consequently, the chief research officer must be very careful when evaluating a researcher's request to contribute voluntary cost-sharing because it presumably makes the proposal more competitive in the reviewer's eyes. Granting agencies routinely assert that voluntary cost-sharing does not play a role in the review process. Finally—and this is very important—as a matter of policy, most institutions do not voluntarily cost-share if it is not required.

> K: I can envision a faculty member arguing that voluntary cost-sharing will make a proposal more competitive. After all, it shows institutional commitment to the project.
> Smith: Yes, that is usually a difficult argument for the chief research officer to counter. However, you have to believe the granting agencies when they say that it doesn't play a role.
> K: It might be a small investment that leads to a big return if the grant is awarded.
> Smith: I admit that it's tempting. But, it's probably wiser not to cost-share any more than necessary. It's a dangerous precedent to set because cost-sharing can become an expensive expectation. At least with NSF, voluntary cost-sharing on most grants is no longer permissible.

Post-Award Services

After the official notice of the grant award is received, management of the grant passes into the post-award phase. The transition point is not crisply defined at all universities. Some pre-award offices perform what other universities consider post-award activities. Nonetheless, the standard post-award office typically monitors expenditures to ensure that they fall within the approved budget and helps the principal investigator to prepare and submit the required progress reports, including invention reports. In addition, the office provides financial status reports to government and private sponsors, generates invoices, deposits revenue, and collects outstanding receivables for sponsored projects. It also reviews transactions, maintains equipment inventories, and coordinates audits.

The post-award office prepares for the required annual audits. If an institution expends more than $500,000 in federal funds during a fiscal year, then it must conduct an audit according to guidelines documented in OMB circular A-133.[20] For most universities, it is not difficult to exceed that threshold because not only NIH, NSF, and other federal research grants but also some categories of federally funded student financial-aid programs are included. The institution hires and pays the auditing firm. However, the costs (which can be hundreds of thousands of dollars) can be reimbursed by the federal government via F&A cost recovery. The auditors examine suspected problem areas, as well as randomly selected transactions. The chief research officer should pay close attention to these audits, for he or she may be held accountable for any findings. Indeed, if material weaknesses are identified by the auditors, the chief research officer may face serious questions about the institution's grant-management procedures.

Finally, the post-award office closes out an award when the grant expires. This involves submitting final progress, invention, and financial reports. And they are due ninety days after the grant terminates. All records of the grant and its activities must be retained for three years.

Effort Reporting

Effort reporting is one of the more challenging responsibilities of the post-award office. Universities must assure federal and most other granting agencies that the assignment of time and associated salary and fringe-benefit costs for the projects they sponsor is fair, consistent, and timely. In simpler terms, if an investigator commits 50 percent of his or her effort to a particular sponsored project in the grant application, then he or she must truthfully devote that much time to the project if the grant is awarded. Stated differently, if the investigator derives 50 percent of his or her salary (plus fringe benefits) from a grant budget, then he or she must devote at least 50 percent effort to that project. The university files periodic assurances that these obligations are being honored with the sponsoring agencies. This is the so-called effort reporting, and it is a serious concern for chief research officers.

Technically, circular A-21 does not use the term "effort reporting." But in many words, in several contexts, it documents the requirement for institutions to account for effort and salary support relative to commitments made in the grant. For example, "At least annually a statement will be signed by the employee, principal investigator, or responsible official(s) using suitable means of verification that the work was performed, stating that salaries and wages charged to sponsored agreements as direct charges, and to residual, F&A cost or other categories are reasonable in relation to work performed."[21]

Furthermore, the institution must have a payroll system in place to match the effort on particular projects or assignments to the salary paid for that effort. According to circular A-21:

> The method must recognize the principle of after-the-fact confirmation or determination so that costs distributed represent actual costs, unless a mutually satisfactory alternative agreement is reached. Direct cost activities and F&A cost activities may be confirmed by responsible persons with suitable means of verification that the work was performed. Confirmation by the employee is not a requirement for either direct or F&A cost activities if other responsible persons make appropriate confirmations.[22]

These directions raise two questions for the institution to answer. First (and less interesting to the chief research officer), how does the institution file these assurances? The federal government does not prescribe a standard method for filing them. However, it presents specific criteria for an acceptable method and provides examples to follow. A majority of universities employ an after-the-fact procedure. Salaries and wages are initially distributed to activities based on estimates of the individual's planned effort. Periodically (for example, quarterly), investigators must file reports documenting the actual effort—a so-called labor distribution report—of all personnel working on each specific project. An individual's labor distribution must be adjusted for any significant changes in actual effort, and the actual effort must then be certified on an after-the-fact basis. The post-award office is generally responsible for collecting these reports and making any necessary adjustments.

Second (and more interesting to the chief research officer), who is the "responsible person" for confirming the effort? In fact, a third question also arises: what constitutes a "suitable means of verification?" Circular A-21 does not provide answers to these latter two questions. Therefore, each institution must develop its own procedures in this context. The COGR provides sage advice in an informative analysis of university effort reporting:

> Institutions will be at risk when using liberal interpretations of either "responsible persons/officials" and/or "suitable means of verification that the work was performed." A department administrator should never be put in a position to sign an effort report, unless he/she has received definitive and verifiable confirmation from the individual that performed

the work, or from an individual that has specific knowledge of the work. Also note, an oral verification from a faculty member to an administrator will most likely not pass the test of "suitable means of verification." Verification, at a minimum, should be accompanied by some form of written correspondence and documentation.[23]

The COGR continues, stating that direct knowledge is a:

useful standard for defining "responsible persons/officials with/using suitable means of verification." Direct knowledge could encompass the individual performing the work, or a direct supervisor or an administrator (with sufficient and verifiable knowledge of the work being performed). In short, any individual at the institution who has sufficient and verifiable knowledge, including an understanding of another individual's regular duties and responsibilities, would qualify as a "responsible person/official with/using suitable means of verification."[24]

Most universities rely on the principal investigator to certify the effort reports. He or she is the "responsible person." And his or her "means of verification" is direct knowledge based primarily on visual observation—he or she can see what people are working on.

Effort is a slippery thing to capture, especially in the university context. At first grab, the term refers to the percentage of the total obligation to the university, which may include teaching, organized research, departmental research, administration, committee work, and other activities devoted to the particular research project. That's relatively easy to comprehend. But things become a bit more evasive when calculating the "total obligation to the university." How many hours is this per week? For most professions, the usual answer is forty hours of work per week. But faculty members, students, and research staff often work many more hours per week. To simplify matters, the total university effort for all activities (teaching, research, service, clinical duties, and so forth) must be 100 percent, regardless of how many hours are actually worked per week. Therefore, if a faculty member works an average of fifty total hours per week and an average of ten hours per week on a particular sponsored project, the correct effort percentage for that project would be 20 percent. The hours of work per week may exceed forty, but the total effort cannot exceed 100 percent.

The amount of effort dedicated to a particular activity may vary throughout the year. For example, during a heavy teaching semester, research effort may decrease. However, this will be compensated by increased research effort at other times during the year, such as in the summer. The annual effort report is based on the average throughout the reporting period.

Often, investigators will submit several grant applications, with the expectation that they won't get them all. In these cases, total committed effort on paper may exceed 100 percent. That is permissible. However, if enough grants are actually awarded to bring the actual effort above 100 percent, then the investigator must promptly reduce that actual effort to 100 percent or less. When an effort report indicates that a salary distribution during the reporting period was incorrect and did not match the commitment, a so-called confirmation of effort distribution, which involves a cost transfer from one account to another, may be required to update the original distribution. According to the COGR:

> From a technical standpoint, this type of transaction does not fall within a strict definition of a cost transfer, but rather is a mechanism to finalize provisional charges (estimates) from the prior accounting period. Though this may be seem to be merely a difference in terminology, there is value in the distinction. Excessive cost transfers are sometimes synonymous with poor internal controls, while confirmations of effort distribution should not be characterized in the same manner.[25]

Ultimately, the federal guidelines articulated in circular A-21 are quite appreciative of the university setting. For example, they state that, "In the use of any methods for apportioning salaries, it is recognized that, in an academic setting, teaching, research, service, and administration are often inextricably intermingled. A precise assessment of factors that contribute to costs is not always feasible, nor is it expected. Reliance, therefore, is placed on estimates in which a degree of tolerance is appropriate."[26]

As a rule of thumb, the federal agencies will allow as much as a 5 percent margin of error in effort committed in a grant proposal and that actually reported after the fact. However, if the university bases its effort reporting on that tolerance level, it must state this explicitly in the effort report.

Failure to submit accurate, well-documented, and verifiable effort reports can have serious consequences. From 2003 to 2006, seven institutions paid more than $1 million in fines for improper salaries charged, effort commitments, and effort reporting. For example, because of faulty effort reports, Northwestern University paid a $5.5 million fine and the University of South Florida returned $4.1 million to the federal government. This is serious money. In fact, the False Claims Act provides incentives for whistleblowers to initiate charges of improper effort reporting; they can receive between 15 and 20 percent of the settlement, plus attorneys' fees. These whistleblower claims are known as *qui tam* suits, and they can be very lucrative for the person filing the charges, as well as their attorneys. Consequently, there have been numerous *qui tam* suits brought against universities.

The chief research officer has responsibility for complying with federal effort-reporting requirements. At best, the chief financial officer shares some of this burden. Consequently, most experienced chief research officers pay close attention to institutional discussions about effort reporting. And they provide regular training opportunities for all research personnel in the principles and practicalities of proper effort reporting.

> K: *These seem to be quite punitive consequences for improper effort reporting, especially since there is an acknowledged imprecision to these reports in the university environment.*
>
> Smith: *I agree; they are hefty fines. And chief research officers can lose their jobs for failing to keep on top of this. However, from the government's perspective, a grant is to perform research on a specific project with well-defined goals. Taking the salary money but working on something else is seen as nothing less than theft.*
>
> K: *All of this appears to be pretty tricky because the pre-award office monitors the effort commitment in the grant proposal, but the post-award office keeps track of the actual effort spent on the project. This must be inherently awkward.*
>
> Smith: *It sure is. The need for such close cooperation between pre- and post-award offices is a major reason for having them both report to the chief research officer.*

Notes

1. National Science Foundation (NSF), "Definitions," in *Proposal and Award Policies and Procedures Guide*, Introduction, § D.1.a, 2010 (Arlington, Va.: NSF, 2010), p. II-3.
2. National Institutes of Health (NIH), "Award Management," 2010, http://grants.nih.gov/grants/managing_awards.htm (accessed January 9, 2011).
3. National Council of University Research Administrators, "Educational Programs," 2011, http://www.ncura.edu/content/educational_programs/ (accessed January 9, 2011).
4. Society of Research Administrators International, "Home," 2011, http://www.srainternational.org/sra03/index.cfm (accessed January 9, 2011).
5. Research Administrators Certification Council, "Home," 2010, http://www.cra-cert.org/index.html (accessed January 9, 2011).
6. Council on Government Relations "COGR Home," 2011, http://www.cogr.edu/ (accessed January 9, 2011).
7. Research Corporation of the University of Hawaii, "Home," 2009, http://www.rcuh.com/wps/portal/RCUH (accessed January 9, 2011).
8. University of Georgia Research Foundation, "Overview," 2011, http://www.ovpr.uga.edu/ugarf/ (accessed January 9, 2011).
9. National Science Foundation (NSF), "FAQs Regarding Academic Research Infrastructure, Recovery and Reinvestment (ARI-R^2), Program Solicitation NSF 09-562–Part 1, Question 13," 2009, http://www.nsf.gov/pubs/2009/nsf09051/nsf09051.jsp#muear (accessed January 9, 2011).
10. Community of Science, "COS Funding Opportunities," 2010, http://fundingopps.cos.com/about/fundingopps.shtml (accessed January 9, 2011).
11. National Science Foundation (NSF), "Outreach Activities," 2010, http://www.nsf.gov/bfa/dias/policy/outreach.jsp (accessed January 9, 2011).
12. Cayuse, "Solutions," 2011, http://www.cayuse.com/ (accessed January 9, 2011).
13. National Institutes of Health (NIH), "Prior-Approval Requirements, Change of Scope," 2003, http://grants.nih.gov/grants/policy/nihgps_2003/NIHGPS_Part7.htm (accessed January 9, 2011).

14. National Science Foundation (NSF), "Grantee Notifications to NSF and Requests for NSF Approval," in *Proposal and Award Policies and Procedures Guide, Part II – Award and Administration Guide,*§§ II.B.1.a-h, (Arlington, Va.: NSF, 2010), pp. II-2-4.

15. Office of Management and Budget, Executive Office of the President, Circular No. A-110, 2 C.F.R. Pt. 215, §§25.(a)-(m). (2010).

16. Ibid. §§ 25.e.(1)-(4).

17. National Institutes of Health (NIH), "Post award: Matching and Cost Sharing," in *NIH Manual 4302-202* (Bethesda, Md.: NIH, 2008).

18. National Science Foundation (NSF), "Cost Sharing," in *Proposal and Award Policies and Procedures Guide Part I: Proposal Preparation & Submission Guidelines,* § II.C.2.g(xi), 2010, (Arlington, Va.: NSF, 2010), pp. II-17.

19. National Science Board, *"Investing in the Future: NSF Cost Sharing Policies for a Robust Federal Research Enterprise"* (Arlington, Va.: National Science Foundation, 2009), p. 21.

20. Office of Management and Budget (OMB), *Circular A-133, Audits of States, Local Governments, and Non-Profit Organizations,* § 200.a (Washington, D.C.: OMB, 2007), p. 8.

21. Office of Management and Budget, Executive Office of the President, Circular No. A-21, 2 C.F.R. Pt. 220, App. A, § J.10.c.(1).(e) (2010).

22. Ibid., § J.10.b.(2).(b), p. 116.

23. Council on Government Relations (COGR), *Policies and Practices Compensation, Effort Commitments, and Certification* (Washington, D.C.: COGR, 2007), p. 47.

24. Ibid.

25. Ibid., p. 38.

26. 2 C.F.R. Pt. 220, App. A, § J.10.b.3.(c), p. 116.

CHAPTER 9

Research Ethics

K: *I've read about several high-profile research misconduct cases recently. How do you respond to those situations?*

Smith: *It is disheartening to read about those cases. But they happen. All research universities have policies and procedures to deal with them.*

K: *Is the chief research officer responsible for administering these, too?*

Smith: *Yes, usually. In many respects, the chief research officer sets the standard for responsible behavior. From that perspective, he or she is the "conscience of the university."*

Ethics and Compliance

Most universities have a code of ethics that all members of their community—students, staff, faculty members, administrators, and governing board—are expected to embrace. University ethics codes vary slightly in format and specificity, but they all share a common focus on integrity and honesty. Moreover, the universities presume that members of their academic communities know these expectations and honorably strive to abide by them. In research universities, the ethics code usually contains a section pertaining specifically to the ethical conduct of research and scholarship. A good example of a research ethics code comes from the University of California:

> All members of the University community engaged in research are expected to conduct their research with integrity and intellectual honesty at all times and with appropriate regard for human and animal subjects. . . . The University prohibits research misconduct. Members of the University community engaged in research are . . . expected to demonstrate accountability for sponsors' funds and to comply with specific terms and conditions of contracts and grants.[1]

Significantly, as this example illustrates, in university settings the topic of research ethics extends beyond commonly accepted norms of honesty and integrity in the conduct of research and financial accounting. It also encompasses compliance with, as stated above, "specific terms and conditions of contracts and grants." That entails the ethical use of research materials, such as animals, human subjects, and dangerous substances.

The NIH amplifies this directive:

> NIH requires grantees to establish safeguards to prevent employees, consultants, members of governing bodies, and others who may be involved in grant-supported activities from using their positions for purposes that are, or give the appearance of being, motivated by a desire for private financial gain for themselves or others, such as those with whom they have family, business, or other ties. These safeguards must be reflected in written standards of conduct.[2]

At a minimum, these ethical standards must pertain to financial interests, including gifts, gratuities, and personal favors, nepotism, and personal comport. Most universities have these guidelines embedded in their overall institutional ethics policy.

In federal jargon, research codes of ethics go by the term "responsible conduct of research." According to the Office of Research Integrity, the responsible conduct of research encompasses standards of behavior in nine core areas: data acquisition, management, sharing, and ownership; mentor/trainee responsibilities; publication practices and responsible authorship; peer review; collaborative science; human subjects; research involving animals; research misconduct; and conflict of interest and commitment.[3] The acceptable ethical standards for each area in this expansive list are codified at various sites in federal legislation, and compliance with them is a legal requirement for institutions receiving federal funds.

Therefore, in the context of research administration, ethical expectations include what is referred to as "regulatory compliance," which means conforming to the ethical rules and regulations set by the institution, state, and federal agencies. Failure to comply with them can have serious adverse consequences for individuals and the university as a whole. Indeed, people can lose their jobs and go to jail, and the federal government can suspend all payments to the university. Compounding that, some grant-related expenditures can be disallowed, forcing the university to return the money that has already been spent. Because of these severe possibilities, all institutions have mechanisms in place to oversee regulatory compliance.

If a university executive, including the chief research officer, learns about misconduct either directly or indirectly, he or she must do something about it. Failure to act on a known compliance violation is not an option. Indeed, it would be a breach of fiduciary responsibility and could have adverse consequences for the executive. Therefore, the chief research officer must investigate any reports of misconduct. In addition, many universities' honor codes require all personnel to report any perceived case of misconduct to a supervisor or other appropriate individual, such as a compliance officer.

Assignment of Responsibilities

Needless to say, each individual is responsible for his or her personal adherence to conventional standards of ethical behavior. These are the generally accepted, unwritten rules of right and wrong, good and bad, just and unjust. These ethical standards may or may not be prescribed in university policies. Regardless, they are presumed to apply to all university personnel in every aspect of behavioral conduct.

Ultimately, however, in a sponsored-research environment, the question of who bears the responsibility for ensuring ethical compliance with codified rules and regulations will arise. The thread of responsibility weaves its way from the governing board down through the administration to the chief research officer. According to the NSF and NIH, the "grantee" has full responsibility for conduct of the project and compliance with all award terms and conditions. Officially, the grantee is the governing board. But, in most universities, it delegates this responsibility explicitly to the chief research officer. As a typical example, the University of California, Berkeley, states that "The Office of the Vice Chancellor for Research is responsible for the coordination of research oversight activities for the campus. . . . The Vice Chancellor for Research has direct responsibility for assuring the humane use of animals in research, the safety of human subjects in research, the management of financial conflicts of interest that arise in research-related activities, and the management of misconduct in science."[4]

The NIH assigns responsibility for institutional certification of ethical compliance to the authorized organization representative within the university's research enterprise: "This individual's signature on the grant application further certifies that the applicant organization will be accountable both for the appropriate use of funds awarded and for the performance of the grant-supported project or activities resulting from the application."[5] The NSF has a similar requirement for an authorized institutional official to certify that the institution has a plan to provide appropriate oversight in the responsible and ethical conduct of research.[6] Commonly, the director of the office for sponsored research serves as the "authorized organizational official" (or signing official). He or she typically reports to the chief research officer, so the ultimate institutional responsibility remains with the chief research officer.

Some institutions have a designated compliance officer and even a separate compliance office. In most cases, these compliance officers report to the chief research officer. Regardless of the reporting line, however, the chief research officer remains responsible ex officio for ethical regulatory compliance at the institutional level. This is a major responsibility that requires close attention because the university's integrity and standing in the community are at stake.

Responsibilities of the Principal Investigator

The thread of responsibility continues beyond the chief research officer to the individual researchers—specifically the principal investigator. Since the chief research officer cannot possibly administer each grant or contract to ensure full compliance, the principal investigator understandably must be entrusted with this obligation. Indeed, most universities have policies assigning ethical compliance responsibilities explicitly to the principal investigator. For example, this straightforward assignment of responsibility was delivered to Stanford faculty members by the university's president, John Hennessy, in a letter stating that principal investigators (PIs) "are responsible for the intellectual direction of research and scholarship and for the education and training of students. In carrying out these critical tasks, PIs are also responsible for compliance with laws and regulations that touch on all aspects of the research enterprise."[7] The NIH goes further in defining the principal investigator's responsibility. The principal investigator "is a member of the grantee team responsible for ensuring compliance with the financial and administrative aspects of the award."[8] Thus, by accepting an award, the principal investigator acknowledges assumption of this responsibility.

Importantly, however, in the eyes of the federal agencies, institutional assignment of responsibility to the principal investigator "does not alter the grantee's full responsibility for conduct of the project and compliance with all award terms and conditions."[9] In other words, the federal agencies will hold the chief research officer accountable for regulatory noncompliance. However, the institution may hold the principal investigator accountable for an offense. Therefore, the principal investigator cannot presume that some institutional official, such as the chief research officer, will be the only person held accountable for compliance issues in conjunction with his or her individual research projects.

The need for understanding the assignment of responsibilities unambiguously arises in many situations. When they are held accountable for a breach in compliance, some faculty members may respond that the administration is responsible; they will say, "That's what you're paid to do" or "That's what my F&A costs pay for." Their defensive truculence is understandable but misdirected. Alternatively, members of the administration may presume that faculty members know the various rules and regulations and therefore comply with them. They will say, "That's the principal investigator's job, not ours." Again, the administrators would be correct but misdirected. Their job is to support the principal investigator, who bears the responsibility for his or her project, in these compliance efforts.

Confusion can occur within administrative units, as well. For example, post-award personnel may presume that pre-award staff members are responsible for some compliance issue and vice versa. This can occur with vexing regularity if the institution does not have a detailed assignment of responsibilities. A damaging breakdown in the assignment of compliance responsibilities occurred between the University of Hawaii and its research corporation, RCUH, in the early 1990s, for example. Audits uncovered several serious material weaknesses that resulted in a disastrous cessation of federal funding for several days. Because they paid RCUH to administer their grants, the university researchers assumed that the corporation bore the compliance responsibility. Conversely, because the grants were awarded to the university, RCUH assumed that the university was responsible for compliance. The lesson is that responsibilities must be crystal clear within and between organizations.

Responsibilities of the Chief Research Officer

If the principal investigator is responsible for regulatory compliance in the conduct of his or her research program, what constitutes the chief research officer's institutional responsibility? Basically, the university must provide the principal investigator with adequate infrastructural support to enable his or her individual compliance efforts. This is accomplished via working committees and offices serving various research activities, such as the use of animal and human subjects, and training programs to educate researchers about ethical compliance. As the governing board's delegate, the chief research officer has the authority and the responsibility to provide this infrastructural support to the principal investigators. Therefore, if an investigator fails to comply with regulations, the chief research officer will be asked, "How did you allow that person to fail?"

In this context, the federal granting agencies require the university to establish committees to oversee compliance in at least four research-related activities. They include the use of human subjects, the care and use of animals, biosafety, and radiation safety. In addition, many universities have other committees to oversee ethical issues in conflicts of interest, stem-cell research, laboratory safety, and other institution-specific activities. Usually, these are faculty committees appointed by either the chief executive officer (ex officio) or the chief research officer, who provides staff support. They report to the chief research officer.

With the aid of these committees and office staff, the chief research officer monitors compliance. The committees generally review research protocols prior to submission to a federal granting agency. In their review, the committees usually detect and correct compliance failures. Committee approval is required before a grant proposal can be submitted. It is not uncommon for members of the committee or research office staff members to visit various laboratories, either on a random basis or in response to concerns voiced by other individuals. The deans should always be informed in advance about these visits. Despite the temptation to "catch somebody in the act of noncompliance," unannounced surprise visits always tend to erode confidence in the chief research officer. If issues of noncompliance are found in these visits, often they can be resolved on the spot through the power of persuasion. However, if difficulties arise, then the chief research officer should inform the dean, who may then choose to resolve the issue through the chair. In all cases, protocol must be honored; the chief research officer should not approach the faculty member without first informing the dean, who then presumably informs the chair.

The chief research officer's institutional responsibilities also include an educational component. If they are responsible for ethical compliance within their research project's realm, researchers (including students) must understand the dimensions of this responsibility. For starters, every principal investigator must understand the "terms and conditions" of a grant award. According to the NSF, "The grantee is responsible for ensuring that the Principal Investigator(s) or Project Director(s) receives a copy of the award conditions, including: the award letter, the budget, these general terms and conditions, any special terms and conditions and any subsequent changes in the award conditions."[10] This somewhat obvious directive may occasionally require a reminder to the principal investigator about the need to read the terms and conditions embedded in the award document's fine print.

In this educational framework, federal granting agencies mandate institutions to provide investigators and students with proper training in the responsible conduct of research, which includes compliance issues. According to the NSF, the institution must "provide appropriate training and oversight in the responsible and ethical conduct of research to undergraduates, graduate students, and postdoctoral researchers who will be supported by NSF to conduct research."[11] Moreover, universities are encouraged to provide this instruction to all graduate students and postdoctoral trainees, regardless of source of support. Consequently, most universities have established programs that provide periodic training in the federal rules and regulations and what constitutes acceptable compliance for both new and established researchers.

Institutional plans for providing this instruction must be included in all NIH applications for grants involving student or postdoctoral training. Proposals lacking this plan will be returned without review. Fortunately, the NIH offers guidelines for these plans:[12]

> While there are no specific curricular requirements for instruction in responsible conduct of research, the following topics have been incorporated into most acceptable plans for such instruction:
>
> > a. conflict of interest – personal, professional, and financial
> > b. policies regarding human subjects, live vertebrate animal subjects in research, and safe laboratory practices
> > c. mentor/mentee responsibilities and relationships
> > d. collaborative research including collaborations with industry
> > e. peer review
> > f. data acquisition and laboratory tools; management, sharing and ownership
> > g. research misconduct and policies for handling misconduct

h. responsible authorship and publication
i. the scientist as a responsible member of society, contemporary ethical issues in biomedical research, and the environmental and societal impacts of scientific research.

The chief research officer and the graduate dean (who may be the same person) typically organize and sponsor these courses. Many universities use an interactive, online training course on the responsible conduct of research offered by a nonprofit organization, the Collaborative Institutional Training Initiative (CITI).[13] (Membership fees are currently $1,750 per year.) This course partially fulfills the NSF's requirement for training in the responsible conduct of research. Supplementary instruction is generally provided once per year by institutional personnel. Notably, the National Academy of Sciences, the Council of Graduate Schools, and the Department of Health and Human Services have published instructional guides for the training programs in the responsible conduct of research.[14]

In the realm of regulatory compliance, the chief research officer's role usually goes beyond research. It extends to instruction and other campus activities, as well. There are two underlying reasons. The first reason is pragmatic. Some instructional and student service programs use human subjects and animals. Rather than establishing separate oversight procedures (at additional expense) for those two units, it is much easier simply to let the chief research officer handle them. The second reason is managerial. If more than one office shares oversight, this introduces the risk that something may fall through the cracks because of confusion about who handles what. This undesirable possibility becomes much less probable under a single leader—namely, the chief research officer.

When addressing situations of noncompliance, chief research officers should take a pro-active lead. If the investigator pleads that compliance was impossible because of inadequate funding, then the chief research officer should offer to help find adequate resources to solve that problem. For example, if noncompliance is simply a matter of not having a biosafety hood, the chief research officer may agree to contribute (along with the faculty member, the chair, and the dean) to the cost of purchasing the required unit. In that context, it would be unreasonable to order a shutdown of the laboratory until the situation is corrected. On the other hand, if radiation safety is compromised owing to sloppy lab techniques, the chief research officer may require the researchers to attend training sessions on the proper handling of radioactive materials. If this fails to correct the situation, then the chief research officer may be compelled to bar all access to radioisotopes until the investigator agrees to a remedial plan. In fact, the threat of losing access to radioactive materials may be sufficient to trigger remediation; as they say, "nothing motivates like fear." Obviously, the correct action will vary with the case. But the best strategy, if at all possible, is to provide the resources necessary to bring a research program into compliance.

> K: *The principal investigator has authority over the conduct of a grant-funded project. Yet the chief research officer ultimately bears responsibility for the project's regulatory compliance. Don't we have an uncoupling of responsibility and authority here?*
>
> Smith: *Of sorts. However, the grant is really awarded to the governing board, and the principal investigator is designated as the individual responsible for carrying out the project. The board retains the authority to revoke that designation—that is, to change principal investigators. Or at least to petition the granting agency for a change if they felt that it was necessary for some reason.*
>
> K: *Are you saying that the governing board has the authority to enforce compliance by the principal investigator?*
>
> Smith: *Yes, and they delegate this authority to the chief research officer. So, authority and responsibility remain intact at the board level.*

Research Misconduct

Universities and granting agencies prohibit research misconduct. So, it is useful to know what they're talking about. According to the Federal Policy on Research Misconduct, which applies to all federal granting agencies:[15]

> Research misconduct is defined as fabrication, falsification, or plagiarism in proposing, performing, or reviewing research, or in reporting research results:
>
> a) Fabrication is making up data or results and recording or reporting them.
> b) Falsification is manipulating research materials, equipment, or processes, or changing or omitting data or results such that the research is not accurately represented in the research record.
> c) Plagiarism is the appropriation of another person's ideas, processes, results, or words without giving appropriate credit.
> d) Research misconduct does not include honest error or differences of opinion.

In other words, research misconduct is the old-fashioned "cooking the data." Plus plagiarizing, which everybody understands.

These sins have been around for a long time. Indeed, the "father of modern statistics," R. A. Fisher, claimed that the "father of modern genetics," Gregor Mendel, may have fudged his data (which were published in 1866) that ultimately became the cornerstone of modern evolutionary theory.[16] For example, in his theory, Mendel expected the ratio of heterozygous to homozygous peas to be 2:1.

In his experiments, Mendel reported that out of 600 peas, 399 were heterozygous and 201 were homozygous. After a statistical analysis of the raw data, Fisher asserts that this is implausibly close to the expected value. Fisher concludes that, "Although no explanation can be expected to be satisfactory, it remains a possibility among others that Mendel was deceived by some assistant who knew too well what was expected. This possibility is supported by independent evidence that the data of most, if not all, of the experiments have been falsified so as to agree closely with Mendel's expectations."[17] Fisher's analysis and conclusions have been debated over the years, but they demonstrate a problem inherent to scientific inquiry—the compulsion to match experimental data with theory. More recent attention, for example, has focused on fraudulent claims in stem-cell research, with widely publicized retractions of papers published in major journals.

Particular attention now centers on the doctoring of photographic images. With the advent of digital photography and image-processing software, such as Photoshop, it has become commonplace to adjust image quality. Many adjustments are simple: alter contrast, brightness, "gamma," and so forth. Others are more sophisticated: background subtraction, superimposition, cutting and pasting, and smoothing boundaries, to name a few. Researchers want to publish beautiful images that portray their results, and they routinely adjust contrast and brightness. Reviewers and journals expect no less. However, clear cases of fraudulent data due to inappropriate image processing have attracted considerable international attention. Most journals now have guidelines limiting these kinds of image processing, and some insist on reviewing the original, unaltered photographs prior to publication. The general rule is to allow some enhancement (brightness and contrast), but, importantly, information may not be added or subtracted in the process. But what constitutes "information" in these cases? A bright background that detracts from the meaningful data? A few spots that are unrelated to the object of interest? And to confuse the issue, statisticians talk routinely about dropping outliers. All of these cases pose challenges for publishers, committees investigating misconduct, and chief research officers.

In this context, some journals caution authors to maintain access to their original research results. For example, the Society for Neuroscience, publishers of the high-impact *Journal of Neuroscience*, advises that, "The retention of accurately recorded and retrievable results is essential for the progress of scientific inquiry. Moreover, errors may be mistaken for misconduct when primary results are unavailable. Primary data should remain in the laboratory and should be preserved as long as there may be a reasonable need to refer to them."[18] This might seem like a condescending piece of advice; however, as the society points out, it could save considerable embarrassment resulting from a misconduct allegation.

A less obvious, but quite serious, form of misconduct occurs when an investigator misrepresents his or her qualifications to perform the research in a grant application. Of course, falsifying academic credentials falls in this category, as does deliberately exaggerating the extent of training necessary for the project.

The office for sponsored research should monitor this. However, it is exceedingly difficult to ferret out misrepresentations without imposing unrealistic credential verification requirements on the principal investigators.

Plagiarism also haunts the research community, especially with the explosion of information available on the Internet. The ease of "cutting and pasting" the information from one site to another, and of spreading ideas through the electronic medium, lends itself to plagiarism. Cultural differences complicate the matter. For example, occurrences of apparent plagiarism may occur more frequently among foreign students and scholars. Because they often have limited command of the English language, they may either inadvertently or willfully use text lifted from a copyrighted source as an expedient. They might think, "I could never write that thought as beautifully as it appears in the journal. So why try?" A case like this may not be an honest error, but it may require compassionate judgment.

To avert clear-cut cases of plagiarism and similar types of misconduct, the university should carefully coach all students (domestic and foreign) and visiting scholars who may be new to academe's standards of intellectual honesty in the proper use of citations. The chief research officer and the graduate dean should take the lead in this effort early in every graduate student's matriculation. And, of course, all university administrators and faculty members must lead by example.

Investigations of Research Misconduct

Most universities have standard operating procedures for handling breaches in their ethics code, including alleged research misconduct. By and large, they follow guidelines similar to those promulgated by the federal government. According to the Office of Science and Technology Policy:

> A response to an allegation of research misconduct will usually consist of several phases, including: (1) an *inquiry*—the assessment of whether the allegation has substance and if an investigation is warranted; (2) an *investigation*—the formal development of a factual record, and the examination of that record leading to dismissal of the case or to a recommendation for a finding of research misconduct or other appropriate remedies; (3) *adjudication*—during which recommendations are reviewed and appropriate corrective actions determined.[19]

Federal agencies rely on the university to take the lead in this response except in unusual cases. Indeed, if an allegation is made directly to the granting agency, the agency will usually refer it to the university on the premise that it is in a better position to conduct inquiries and investigations than are the federal agencies. Therefore, universities have protocols for reporting and investigating potential cases of research misconduct. Of course, they will vary from one university to the next, but they all follow the federal template. It should be noted that the federal government always retains the right to launch its own inquiry or investigation if it determines that the institution is not prepared to handle the process according to federal policy or that the agency needs to step in to protect the public interest, including public health and safety.

The Department of Health and Human Services' Office of Research Integrity and NIH provide sample procedures for dealing with research misconduct.[20] At the outset, all members of the university community are responsible for reporting instances of misconduct in research or scholarly activity. Initial allegations should be discussed with a direct supervisor. For example, students report potential cases first to their faculty adviser or, if that is not feasible because of a potential conflict, then to the department or program chair. Staff or faculty members' allegations follow a similar pathway: first, inform the chair or the dean if the chair may be compromised. Since ethical issues are often not black and white, these initial discussions usually deal mainly with information gathering and establishing facts to decide whether there is sufficient concern to warrant a more detailed examination of the case. If there is, then a formal, signed allegation of misconduct or fraud should be filed by the person making the allegations with the dean, who initiates an inquiry to be conducted by a small committee of faculty members.

Some agencies refer to an institutional research integrity officer (RIO). Although federal policy does not require it, some universities appoint a research integrity officer to oversee misconduct inquiries and investigations. This individual may also be an administrator with other responsibilities (such as an associate research officer) or a faculty member. In these cases, the research integrity officer, not the dean, assesses research misconduct allegations to determine if they merit a formal inquiry. Furthermore, the research integrity officer may appoint the inquiry review committee. Even if the research integrity officer is also a lawyer, however, it is imperative to limit his or her responsibilities to an investigative role.[21] He or she should not offer legal advice; that is strictly the chief legal counsel's domain. Likewise, the research integrity officer should not become involved in mediating dispute resolutions. As the investigator representing the institution, he or she is placed in a de facto adversarial position and may be perceived as biased by the accused. The perception of bias may compromise the inquiry's integrity, thus requiring the process to begin anew under different leadership.

The goal of an inquiry is to gather further information and facts to determine whether the allegation warrants a formal investigation. Inquiry procedures depend on the circumstances of the allegations, but almost always include notification of the individual against whom the allegation is made. All persons involved in the inquiry are expected to make diligent efforts to protect the identity of the accuser. If the process reaches the investigative phase, the right of the accused to confront the complainant may require revealing the identity of the person bringing the allegations.

The chief research officer's staff becomes involved if the inquiry finds that an investigation is warranted. Caveat: allegations of fiscal mismanagement or improprieties should also be directed to either the chief financial officer or the university's auditor. The chief research officer will ultimately decide if research misconduct has occurred. Therefore, he or she must maintain an informed but unbiased position throughout the process. So, the case is typically assigned to another individual, such as an associate research officer, who leads the investigation at this stage. Alternatively, some universities have a standing ethics committee to which the allegations are referred. In some situations, the investigation leader in consultation with the ethics committee may appoint an ad hoc committee comprising faculty members who have sufficient acquaintance with research and scholarship in the discipline in question to assess the allegation. In appointing the investigating committee, the investigation leader tries to select impartial experts and to avoid any real or apparent conflicts of interest. For example, the director of the technology-transfer office should not be in the investigative chain if the case involves a university patent.

This committee investigates the charges and hears testimony from the concerned parties. According to federal policy, a finding of research misconduct requires that "a preponderance of the evidence establishes that: (1) research misconduct . . . occurred (respondent has the burden of proving by a preponderance of the evidence any affirmative defenses raised, including honest error or a difference of opinion); (2) the research misconduct is a significant departure from accepted practices of the relevant research community; and (3) the respondent committed the research misconduct intentionally, knowingly, or recklessly."[22]

All three of these criteria must obtain for misconduct to have occurred. The term "preponderance of evidence" is crucial in this regard. It means that misconduct most probably occurred, but the evidence need not be "beyond a reasonable doubt." According to federal policy, the rationale is that "preponderance of the evidence" constitutes the uniform standard of proof for establishing culpability in most civil fraud cases and many federal administrative proceedings. From the federal perspective, there is no basis for more stringent standards in research misconduct cases. Universities may impose a higher level of proof, but they must report misconduct cases to the federal agencies according to the federal guidelines—namely, a "preponderance of evidence."

If the accused leaves the university before the investigation is complete, the process must continue. According to the Office of Research Integrity:

> The termination of the respondent's institutional employment, by resignation or otherwise, before or after an allegation of possible research misconduct has been reported, will not preclude or terminate the research misconduct proceeding or otherwise limit any of the institution's responsibilities . . . If the respondent, without admitting to the misconduct, elects to resign his or her position after the institution receives an allegation of research misconduct, the assessment of the allegation will

proceed, as well as the inquiry and investigation, as appropriate based on the outcome of the preceding steps. If the respondent refuses to participate in the process after resignation, the RIO [research integrity officer] and any inquiry or investigation committee will use their best efforts to reach a conclusion concerning the allegations, noting in the report the respondent's failure to cooperate and its effect on the evidence.[23]

In the end, the investigative committee submits a report to the investigation leader documenting its findings as to whether or not the allegations have sufficient basis in fact for the university to consider disciplinary action against the individual. If the committee judges that disciplinary action is warranted, it will also make a recommendation to the investigation leader concerning what action should be taken. Possible disciplinary actions include issuing a formal reprimand, requiring special administrative arrangements to ensure compliance with applicable regulations, restricting particular research activities, removing the individual from the graduate faculty, and filing a formal charge of unfitness for continued employment at the university, to name the most prominent.

Following the investigation, the investigation leader forwards the committee's findings and recommendation to the chief research officer, who decides what actions should be taken. This is the adjudication phase. Usually, he or she follows the committee's recommendations. If the chief research officer (called the "deciding officer," in the Office of Research Integrity sample protocol) determines that a faculty member should be formally charged with unfitness for employment, the further disposition of the case will follow established governing-board procedures. In addition, the chief research officer will take interim administrative actions to protect federal funds and patients and to ensure that the purposes of the grant or contract are being carried out.

Any person who has been found by these procedures to have committed misconduct in research or scholarly activity has the right to appeal that finding. A good route is via the provost, who has presumably not been involved in the proceedings to this point. An appeal does not allow for repeating the investigative review of the facts of the case with the hope that the committee will come to a different opinion a second time around. It must be based strictly on procedural matters. For example, an appeal is warranted if it can be shown that the investigative committee did not consider all available evidence; did not provide the accused with due process; or made the determination in an arbitrary, capricious, or prejudicial manner. In considering the appeal, the provost may act alone or involve others. The provost's decision will be final.

Following a conclusive finding of no research misconduct, the chief research officer should make an effort to restore the reputation of the accused. How this is done will depend on the particular situation and the wishes of the accused. Certainly, any individuals who participated in the investigation or knew of it should be notified about the final outcome. In some cases, that may require a public relations announcement from the university. And all reference to the allegation should be removed from personnel files. If there is any indication that the allegations or any aspects of the investigation were not made in good faith, the chief research officer will determine whether any administrative action should be taken against those who failed to act in good faith.

All federal granting agencies have mandatory-notification policies in cases of research misconduct. Therefore, if the investigation involves a project funded by any of these agencies, the chief research officer should inform them at the immediate onset of an investigation and should continue to provide updates throughout the course of the investigation. If research misconduct has occurred, the granting agencies will issue a response that may call for retraction of any relevant publications, termination of clinical trials, debarment of the researcher, repayment of some or all grant expenditures, and so forth. The chief research officer represents the university in these discussions. Importantly, his or her primary goal at this point is to protect the university's reputation.

Federal policy also calls for institutional policies that protect the rights of the individual who makes the allegations (the whistleblower) and the person against whom the allegations were made. Consequently, university policies contain these provisions. Moreover, they specify ways to protect the rights and responsibilities of everybody involved in an investigation. This includes the explicit expectation of strict confidentiality throughout the process. Although these conditions may seem to be self-evident, the chief research officer should make these policies and expectations clear to all participants at the very beginning of any inquiry or investigation.

Three further comments bear mentioning. First, throughout these proceedings, specific deadlines must be set for each step. And, as they say, "time is of the essence." Indeed, federal policy sets time limits for each step.[24] Failure to meet the deadlines is not an option, for it could become the basis of an appeal based on procedural error. Conversely, the accused may forfeit the opportunity to appeal if deadlines aren't met. Second, e-mail is not suitable for any correspondence in these matters. It is far too easy to forward them inappropriately and sometimes indiscriminately. Telephone calls, hard-copy letters, and personal communication are the rule. Third, and most important, legal counsel should be involved at every step of the process. Indeed, any communication with the accused—written or oral—should be cleared first with legal counsel. Investigations of this sort can become quite contentious, so the legal implications of every action must be considered a priori. As a corollary to this, it may be advisable in some cases to have an attorney on the investigative committee, either a faculty member (from a law school, for example) or an ex officio consultant.

K: By informing the granting agency before the outcome of an investigation, couldn't you prejudice them against the accused regardless of the veracity of the allegations? And couldn't that hurt the chances of a successful competitive grant renewal regardless of the outcome?

Smith: Yes, unfortunately that's a possibility. But the law is the law, and it says that you have to keep the granting agency informed no matter what. It's up to the agency to keep all of this confidential until the outcome has been decided. So, potential grant proposal reviewers should never know about this unless misconduct has been established.

K: Would you be inclined to offer advice to the accused on any aspect of the case? For example, should he or she be looking for another job or hiring a personal lawyer to defend against the allegations?

Smith: No. I would resist the temptation to offer advice on anything related to the case, no matter what. You have to be very careful here, because you never know if this case will end up in court, and anything that I may have said can be held against the university.

Conflicts of Commitment

Traditionally, university faculty members are hired to perform teaching, research, and service. In that capacity, they are expected to devote their university work efforts to official functions of the institution and to use institutional resources only in the interest of the university. These generic expectations apply to nearly all other workplaces, so universities are not unique in this respect. However, unlike employees in many other settings, faculty members are routinely encouraged and rewarded for engaging in activities outside the usual workplace setting—namely, the campus— ranging from serving on peer-review panels to writing books to founding start-up companies based on university-owned patents. Moreover, academic custom allows faculty members about eight hours per work week (20 percent time) for nonuniversity ventures such as consulting. Collectively, these various external activities can become the source of a conflict of commitment.

Simply stated, a conflict of commitment occurs when an employee's primary professional allegiance no longer benefits the employer. In the case of faculty members, this most often involves time allocation. For example, outside consulting cannot exceed the permissible limits imposed by university policy—usually eight hours per week. Compensation is not an issue in these cases; universities seldom regulate outside earnings. Most universities have well-documented policies related to conflicts of commitment that define their guidelines clearly, so there is seldom any administrative confusion about what is permissible.

In the research realm, conflicts of commitment occur mainly when a faculty member launches a company based on university research that requires his or her attention during the critical start-up phase. These situations can pose complicated ethical dilemmas when the university holds a financial interest in the company. In addition, a technology-transfer officer may inadvertently spawn a conflict of commitment by encouraging a faculty member to devote more and more time to a potentially lucrative invention. The chief research officer must monitor these situations to ensure the integrity of both the faculty member and the institution.

Because they involve conditions of employment, the provost generally resolves conflicts of commitment. As a matter of protocol, they are usually referred to the dean for resolution. Often the resolution requires the faculty member to take a reduced employment level or temporary leave of absence from the university. The chief research officer may play a muted role if the conflict arises from a faculty member's preoccupation with a patent-related issue or a start-up company, for example. Because the chief research officer has an inherent conflict of interest in these cases, he or she may be asked for information but should not participate in any decision making. That should be left to the provost or dean.

Financial Conflicts of Interest

Financial conflicts of interest can be far more insidious. Before going any further, it is useful to know exactly what is considered a financial conflict of interest. In its simple form, this phrase refers to an individual's private financial interests or his or her family's interests that may influence the individual's professional actions, decisions, or judgments in pursuing research. In its report on institutional conflicts of interest, the Association of American Universities (AAU) summarizes the obvious: "The bias such conflicts may conceivably impart not only affects collection, analysis, and interpretation of data, but also the hiring of staff, procurement of materials, sharing of results, choice of protocol, involvement of human participants, and the use of statistical methods."[25] From an operational perspective, this definition of financial conflicts of interest should be modified by adding the clause "in the eyes of an observer"—that is, a financial conflict of interest exists if it reasonably appears to exist.

The federal agencies provide a much more explicit definition. A "significant financial interest" is described as anything of monetary value, including salary or other payments from private for-profit organizations for services such as consulting fees or honoraria in excess of $10,000 annually. The definition also subsumes equity interests such as stocks or stock options in excess of $10,000, as well as intellectual property rights such as patents, copyrights, and royalties.[26] However, this definition of financial interests is modified by several exceptions that are particularly relevant in a university setting. Exclusions include salary, royalties, or other remuneration from the institution; any ownership interests in the institution, if the institution is an applicant under the SBIR and STTR programs; income from seminars, lectures, or teaching engagements sponsored by public or nonprofit entities, and income from service on advisory committees or review panels for public or nonprofit entities.[27]

Nearly all universities have policies covering financial conflicts of interest. Many derive from state or state-mandated policies. And, of course, it is the right thing to do from a commonly accepted ethical perspective. However, there is another strong motivation to establish these policies: if an institution accepts federal grants, it must have a written policy that defines financial conflicts of interest and describes institutional procedures for dealing with them. Furthermore, according to federal guidelines:

> No employee, officer, or agent shall participate in the selection, award, or administration of a contract supported by Federal funds if a real or apparent conflict of interest would be involved. Such a conflict would arise when the employee, officer, or agent, any member of his or her immediate family, his or her partner, or an organization which employs or is about to employ any of the parties indicated herein, has a financial or other interest in the firm selected for an award.[28]

For example, the NIH states that "Grantees are required to adopt and enforce policies that minimize the opportunity for improper financial gain on the part of the organization, its employees, and organizations and individuals with whom they may collaborate, and that limit the potential for research results to be tainted by possible personal financial or other gain."[29]

Some universities apply more stringent guidelines. For example, they require reporting all equity interests and salary, royalties, or other payments obtained from nonuniversity sources by the employee and his or her spouse and dependent children—not just those exceeding $10,000, as in the NIH guidelines. Beware: when a university sets guidelines that are more stringent than those established by the federal agencies, then in the eyes of the federal agencies, the university will be held accountable to abide by their more restrictive guidelines.

Universities have three options for responding to an individual's financial conflict of interest: manage, reduce, or eliminate it. The most prevalent way to manage a financial conflict of interest is to assign an independent group such as a standing or, more likely, an ad hoc committee to monitor the research project with the specific goal of averting any bias in the conduct of the research arising from the financial conflict of interest. Some universities include one or two members from outside the university. This managerial group reports to the chief research officer and has the authority to recommend procedural changes in the administration of the research project if they detect bias caused by the financial conflict of interest.

A related remedy is to reduce the financial conflict of interest. This may require modification of the research plan to minimize participation of the conflicted individual with any aspect of the project associated with the financial conflict of interest. For example, aspects of the grant that could conceivably be affected by the financial conflict of interest will be administered by somebody other than the conflicted researcher.

Finally, the institution may simply choose to eliminate the financial conflict of interest. The conflicted individual may be removed as a participant in a portion or even the entire project. Alternatively, the individual may choose to divest the conflicting financial interest or at the very least to place it into a blind trust. If none of these options proves doable, the institution may decide to decline the grant. The COGR presents informative case studies that illustrate these various ways to address financial conflicts of interest.[30]

Federal agencies require institutions to disclose all "significant financial interests" that would reasonably appear to be affected by the research for which funding is sought. According to the NIH, "Prior to the Institution's expenditure of any funds under the award, the Institution will report to the PHS Awarding Component the existence of a conflicting interest (but not the nature of the interest or other details) found by the institution and assure that the interest has been managed, reduced or eliminated."[31] The conflicting interest must be managed, reduced, or eliminated, at least on an interim basis, within sixty days of that report. Similarly, the NSF requires institutions that employ more than fifty persons to maintain "an appropriate written and enforced policy on conflict of interest."[32] Note: in this context, they mean financial conflicts of interest. The agencies may not require submission of a plan to manage conflicts of interest along with a grant proposal, but they usually reserve the right to request access to the plan at any time. Therefore, universities have responded by developing these policies, generally following the templates provided by the federal regulations. Moreover, several prominent national associations have prepared quite useful guidelines for managing financial conflicts of interest that are worth reading, including the Council on Government Relations and the Association of American Universities.[33]

Particularly stringent policies regarding financial conflict of interest apply to researchers using human subjects. The Association of American Medical Colleges states this quite succinctly: "financial interests in human subjects research are distinct . . . because the perception is widespread that they may entail special risks. Specifically, opportunities to profit from research may affect—or appear to affect—a researcher's judgments about which subjects to enroll, the clinical care provided to subjects, even the proper use of subjects' confidential health information."[34] Because human health is at stake, the Department of Health and Human Services has imposed a punitive remedy if a financial conflict of interest has not been properly reported. Specifically, the investigator must disclose the conflict in every public presentation of the research project.

At first glance, this may not seem like a very meaningful additional requirement. But it is. This says that if an investigator fails to disclose and resolve a financial conflict of interest pertaining to a study of human subjects, he or she must tell the audience about this conflict in any public forum. That disclosure is chilling news to many researchers because, on the one hand, it could raise doubts—maybe subliminal—about the veracity of any results, especially if they're favorable to the investigator's financial interests. On the other hand, many universities encourage or require all investigators, whether they're working with human subjects or not, to disclose financial conflicts of interest in any public forum, including talks and publications. And, most journals now require all authors to declare any financial conflicts of interest.

The key element of all individual financial conflict of interest policies is disclosure. Ostensibly, disclosure enables an objective assessment of an individual's conflict of interest. In that sense, it establishes confidence. Stated very practically, a researcher might say, "If I disclose a conflict of interest and you still want to work with me, then I no longer have a problem." Legally, a priori disclosure significantly reduces the risk of civil and criminal penalties consequent to a financial conflict of interest. Thus, all faculty members must disclose any significant financial conflict of interest to the university at least annually. These are generally reviewed by the dean, the chief research officer, the research integrity officer, or an ethics committee, who will be looking for financial conflicts of interest. Importantly, financial conflicts of interest are not inherently bad—however, failure to disclose them is. As the COGR points out, "It is not possible, nor is it necessary, to eliminate all perceived, potential, or real financial conflicts of interest. The existence of a conflict is not necessarily a problem; it is how individuals and institutions respond to conflicts that may be problematic."[35]

Federal agencies require universities to document their enforcement mechanisms for financial conflict of interest and sanctions that may be applied, if necessary. Moreover, they must be informed if the institution cannot adequately manage a conflict. Significantly, the NIH retains the right at any time to review institutional financial conflict of interest procedures and all records related to compliance concerning an NIH-funded grant. If the NIH judges that a particular conflict of interest will bias the objectivity of the NIH-funded research because the institution has not adequately managed, reduced, or eliminated the conflict of interest, it may suspend funding or terminate the project. Therefore, all matters concerning financial conflicts of interest should be well documented and available for inspection by the granting agency. These records must be retained for at least three years after the final resolution of any action or termination of the grant, whichever is longer.

As a footnote, consider that scholarly conflicts of interest are often akin to financial conflicts of interest. These are sometimes called "scientific conflicts of interest." They occur when scholarly impartiality is compromised by potential professional or personal gains to the researcher. A common case might arise when a faculty member reviews a grant application or manuscript submitted by a direct competitor. Despite all conscious efforts to control any negative bias, the reviewer may subconsciously render an unfair critique. Therefore, most granting agencies and journals require individuals with a scholarly conflict of interest to recuse themselves from reviewing under these conditions.

Financial considerations may lurk in the dark shadows of a scholarly conflict of interest. Indeed, that is often the case. For example, preventing a competitor from winning a lucrative grant may enhance a reviewer's own chances of getting an award and its attendant financial benefits, such as summer salary and credit toward a promotion and pay raise. As another example, a reviewer may use information read in a manuscript under review to enhance the commercial prospects for his or her invention. In cases like this, there have been quite significant financial consequences for both parties. Because of their potential relationship to financial conflicts of interest, scholarly conflicts of interest must be resolved with the same prompt and thorough care. And, unfortunately, they must always be investigated with the old cynical adage in mind: "follow the dollar."

Institutional Conflicts of Interest

In addition to individual researchers, institutions and their officials may have financial conflicts of interest. These occur when the institution or members of its upper administration, including the governing board, have a relationship with a company that has a financial interest in a university research project. For example, if a member of the governing board has an equity stake in a company that has awarded a grant to fund a faculty member's research project, there is an institutional financial conflict of interest. This becomes clearer when it is remembered that the grant is awarded officially to the governing board. Another example is when a university "holds equity positions or has royalty arrangements, *and* the equity or royalties are derived from university inventions, startups, or other university technology transfer."[36] Might this bias the university's oversight of these money-making research projects? Similarly, institutional conflicts of interest arise if senior administrators or members of the governing board have a relationship with companies that do business with the university. For example, if a member of the governing board also sits on the board of a chemical supply company, he or she could influence a researcher's decision about where to buy laboratory chemicals.

These perceived financial conflicts of interest at an institutional level pose the same risks to the university's integrity as individual conflicts of interest. Therefore, most universities have policies that address these institutional financial conflicts of interest. Many of these policies are embodied in state law and in the governing board by-laws. Normally, the chief research officer usually does not become involved in their enforcement. But he or she should be aware of these possible financial conflicts of interest in the research realm and diligently report to the chief executive officer any failures to comply with policies governing them.

Incidentally, most state ethics commissions provide free, confidential legal advice about how conflict-of-interest laws apply in specific situations. The chief research officer should encourage the use of this service as a way to avert preemptively an embarrassing conflict of interest.

In the context of institutional financial conflicts of interest, the University of California, Los Angeles, has issued an interesting and provocative proclamation:

> The University must also take steps to ensure that decisions about hiring University faculty are not driven exclusively by the availability of research support, but rather primarily by the opportunity to support scholarship in areas important to the advancement of knowledge. Where the University has a potential or actual financial stake in the work of particular research-ers, decisions about hiring and promotion of such individuals must not be influenced by those economic considerations. Rather, positive academic actions in such cases need to be based entirely on the application of appropriate academic standards.[37]

This is a bold statement. Many universities, including not just the elites, openly declare that they will hire only new faculty members who already have extramural grants. Furthermore, many departments and colleges have guidelines that specify the number of extramural grants a candidate must have to get tenure or a promotion. The rationale is obvious: they want only well-funded investigators. This is because these individuals have proved that they can submit competitive proposals. They aren't dead wood. But could the university also be interested in the financial gains (such as F&A cost recovery) brought in by their grants? That would certainly taint its academic integrity. This is a question for the university's faculty members to consider and to answer.

Consider one final footnote about financial conflicts of interest: as most seasoned investigators and research administrators know, federal officials (such as NSF or NIH program directors) are prohibited by law from accepting any gifts from potential or current grant recipients. They cannot accept even a purchased cup of coffee. To offer a gift of any sort simply causes embarrassment. The chief research officer may need to inform junior staff members or young investigators about this regulation. Conversely, university personnel including the chief research officer should not accept gifts of more than "nominal" value from vendors or contractors.

Organizational Conflicts of Interest

Federal procurement laws define an additional dimension of ethical behavior—namely, organizational conflicts of interest. These occur when a contractor such as the university has interests that "may diminish its capacity to give impartial, technically sound, objective assistance and advice, or may otherwise result in a biased work product" or "may result in its being given an unfair competitive advantage."[38] Or, more succinctly, an organizational conflict of interest arises when the institution cannot give the federal government impartial advice.

Within a university setting, organizational conflicts of interest generally lie within the chief financial officer's realm of responsibility. He or she must certify to the federal government that the institution has a comprehensive conflict-of-interest policy that covers all federal contracts and grants. These include grants and subcontracts embedded within a research grant.[39]

Generally, the chief research officer plays only a marginal role in the management of organizational conflicts of interest. However, he or she must be aware of the requirement to disclose and remedy any apparent or proposed conflict. In a large research university, these can be peculiarly evasive. For example, a researcher in the biology department may have a federally funded research grant to study the deleterious effects of a particular pesticide on an endangered frog species, while a member of the chemistry department may have a consulting contract from the pesticide's manufacturer to improve the product's toxicity. Technically, both the grant and the contract are awarded to a single entity—the university. Therefore, the university is studying two opposing aspects of the pesticide. In the eyes of the law, this constitutes an organizational conflict of interest in violation of the federal acquisitions regulations that must be resolved. But the university's two research groups—biologists and chemists—may be unaware that they're both working on two opposing aspects of the same compound. Because the chief research officer oversees all research on campus, he or she may have the best chances of detecting this kind of organizational conflict of interest.

> K: It seems to me that the university has to walk a thin line in all of this. It encourages the faculty to be entrepreneurial, but the university must enforce potentially discouraging financial conflict of interest policies.
>
> Smith: Yes, this can be a bit tricky. That's why it is so important to use committees to review disclosures for potential conflicts of interest. This is a prime case of the need for faculty members to make judgments of their colleagues.
>
> K: Why is that so much better than having a single, unbiased chief research officer make the decisions? After all, it's a matter of enforcing university policy.
>
> Smith: In a sense, the chief research officer has a subtle conflict here. He or she wants two things: to maximize research expenditures—help faculty members get and keep as many grants as possible—and to help faculty members commercialize their research products. A committee tends to neutralize those two forces that might influence a chief research officer's judgment.

Notes

1. University of California, "Statement of Ethical Values," 2005, http://www.ucop.edu/ucophome/coordrev/policy/Stmt_Stds_Ethics.pdf (accessed January 10, 2011).

2. National Institutes of Health (NIH), "Standards of Conduct," in *National Institutes of Health Grants Policy Statement* (Betheda, Md.: NIH, 2003), p. 44.

3. Department of Health and Human Services, Office of Research Integrity, "Responsible Conduct of Research (RCR) Education," § V.A, 2009, http://ori.dhhs.gov/policies/RCR_Policy. shtml (accessed January 10, 2011).

4. University of California, Berkeley, "Research Compliance: A Faculty Handbook," Research Administration and Compliance, 2010, http://rac.berkeley.edu/compliancebook/introduction. html (accessed January 10, 2011).

5. National Institutes of Health, "Grantee Staff", NIH Grants Policy Statement, § 2.1.2, 2003, http://grants.nih.gov/grants/policy/nihgps_2010/nihgps_ch2.htm#grantee_staff (accessed January 11, 2011).

6. National Science Foundation (NSF), "Certification Regarding Responsible Conduct of Research (RCR)," in *Proposal Award Policies and Procedures Guide Part I - Proposal Preparation & Submission Guidelines*, § II.C.1.e (Arlington, Va.: NSF, 2010), p. II–4.

7. Stanford University, "Principal Investigator Responsibilities at Stanford University," Letter from John Hennesy, 2000, http://www.stanford.edu/dept/DoR/PIship/pres_letter.html (accessed January 10, 2011).

8. NIH, "Grantee Staff" § 2.1.2.

9. National Science Foundation (NSF), Grantee Responsibilities and Federal Requirements in *Grant General Conditions (GC-1)*, § 1.d (Arlington, Va.: NSF, 2009), p. 4.

10. Ibid., p. 3.

11. NSF, "Certification Regarding Responsible Conduct," p. II–4.

12. National Institutes of Health (NIH), "Instructional Components," Update on the Requirement for Instruction in the Responsible Conduct of Research, 2009, http://grants.nih.gov/grants/ guide/notice-files/NOT-OD-10-019.html (accessed January 10, 2011).

13. Collaborative Institutional Training Initiative (CITI), "CITI Course in the Responsible Conduct of Research," 2011, https://www.citiprogram.org/Default.asp (accessed January 10, 2011).

14. National Academy of Sciences (NAS), *On Being a Scientist: Responsible Conduct in Research* (Washington, D.C.: National Academy Press, 1995); P. D. Tate and D. D. Denecke, *Graduate Education for the Responsible Conduct of Research* (Washington, D.C.: Council of Graduate Schools, 2006); N. H. Steneck, *ORI Introduction to the Responsible Conduct of Research*, rev. ed. (Washington, D.C.: Department of Health and Human Services, 2007).

15. Department of Health and Human Services, "Public Health Service Policies on Research Misconduct, 42 CFR 93," *Federal Register*, 70, no. 94 (2005): 28369–400.

16. R. A. Fisher, "Has Mendel's Work Been Rediscovered?" *Annals of Science*, 1 (1936): 115–37.

17. Ibid., p. 132.

18. Society for Neuroscience, "Policy on Ethics," 2011, http://www.sfn.org/index.cfm?pagename= guidelinesPolicies_PolicyonEthics (accessed January 10, 2011).

19. Office of Science and Technology Policy, "Federal Policy on Research Misconduct; Preamble for Research Misconduct Policy," *Federal Register*, 65, no. 235 (2000): 76260–4.

20. National Institutes of Health (NIH), *Sample Policies and Procedures for Responding to Allegations of Research Misconduct* (Bethesda, Md.: Office of Research Integrity, 2009); NIH, "Public Health Service Policies on Research Misconduct," 42 C.F.R. Part 93, *Federal Register* 70, no. 94 (2005): 28390–2.

21. L. N. Geller, "Exploring the Role of the Research Integrity Officer," *Science and Engineering Ethics*, 8 (2002): 540–2.

22. NIH, *Sample Policies and Procedures*, § VII.D.1, p. 15.

23. Ibid, § XI.A, p. 20.

24. NIH, "Research Misconduct," § 93.311, p. 28391.

25. Association of American Universities (AAU), "Report on Individual and Institutional Financial Conflict of Interest," in *Task Force on Research Accountability Report and Recommendations* (Washington, D.C.: AAU, 2001), p. 2.

26. National Institutes of Health (NIH), "Responsibility of Applicants for Promoting Objectivity in Research for Which PHS Funding Is Sought," 42 C.F.R Part 50, Subpart F, § 50.603 (2000).

27. Ibid.
28. Office of Management and Budget, Executive Office of the President, Circular No. A-110, 2 C.F.R. Part 215, § 215.42 (2005).
29. National Institutes of Health (NIH), "Public Policy Requirements, Objectives and Other Appropriation Mandates," NIH Grants Policy Statement, § 4, 2010, http://grants.nih.gov/grants/policy/nihgps_2010/nihgps_ch4.htm#research_misconduct (accessed January 11, 2011).
30. Council on Government Relations (COGR), *Recognizing and Managing Personal Conflicts of Interest* (Washington, D.C.: COGR, 2002).
31. NIH, "Public Policy Requirements," § 4.1.10.
32. National Science Foundation (NSF), "Grantee Standards, Conflict of Interest Policies" in *NSF Proposal and Award Policies and Procedures Guide Part II-Award & Administration Guidelines,*" § IV.A.1, (Arlington, Va.: NSF, 2010), p. IV–1.
33. Council on Government Relations (COGR), *Approaches to Developing an Institutional Conflict of Interest Policy* (Washington, D.C.: COGR, 2001); AAU, "Financial Conflict of Interest."
34. American Association of Medical Colleges (AAMC), *Protecting Subjects, Preserving Trust, Promoting Progress–Policy and Guidelines for the Oversight of Individual Financial Interests in Human Subjects Research* (Washington, D.C.: AAMC, 2001), p. 3.
35. Council on Government Relations (COGR), *Recognizing and Managing Personal Conflicts of Interest* (Washington, D.C.: COGR, 2002), p. 5.
36. AAU, "Financial Conflict of Interest," p. 10.
37. University of California, Los Angeles, "Financial Conflicts of Interest in Research: Statement of Principles," Memorandum, Office of the Chancellor, 2011, http://www.research.ucla.edu/researchpol/memos/memo_coi.htm (accessed January 11, 2011).
38. Federal Acquisition Regulation, Organizational Conflicts of Interest, 48 C.F.R. Chapter 20, Part 2009, § 209.570-2 (2005).
39. Circular No. A-110, 2 C.F.R. Part 215, § 215.42, p. 87.

CHAPTER 10

Hazardous Materials

K: Every now and then, I read about lab workers who became seriously ill after exposure to highly toxic agents. What controls do universities have to guard against this?

Smith: The federal government has various policies that govern how universities should protect human health. And the chief research officer is usually held accountable for their enforcement.

K: Aren't individual researchers responsible for their own safety? After all, if they adhere to good lab practices, there shouldn't be a problem.

Smith: I agree; all the policies in the world can't make up for sloppiness and carelessness in the lab. Nonetheless, the chief research officer can be held accountable for mishaps—right or wrong. So, universities put a lot of effort into teaching good lab practices.

Biosafety

Biosafety is the realm of potentially hazardous biological agents, such as infectious agents, bloodborne pathogens, recombinant DNA molecules, and genetically modified organisms. Containment is the rule of law. If not contained properly, these materials can cause serious health risks not only for individual researchers but also for entire communities. Therefore, the federal government has established a series of rules, regulations, and "best practices" to minimize the health risks through proper containment. Enforcing compliance with these biosafety rules and regulations poses a subtle and potentially complex challenge to the chief research officer.

Of course, the existence of hazardous biological agents has been known since the days of Louis Pasteur (1822–1895), who demonstrated that infectious microorganisms cause disease. This is the so-called germ theory. Pasteur's demonstration paved the way for research into ways of controlling infection and containing the infectious agents. In that regard, his seminal discovery spawned what became the field of biosafety.

Two subsequent events defined modern standards for biosafety. The first was the development of techniques to introduce recombinant DNA into microorganisms in the early 1970s. This powerful technique revolutionized biotechnology, but it also carried the potential for creating novel, toxic organisms. Recognizing this possible threat to the environment and health, pioneers in the field met in Asilomar, California, to assess ways to contain new life forms derived by recombinant biotechnology. In the 1975 Asilomar Conference on Recombinant DNA Molecules, guidelines for containing recombinant organisms were developed, and these became the template for subsequent biosafety rules regulating the emerging biotechnology disciplines. The conference attendees' basic conclusion became the backbone of modern biosafety:

> Although our assessments of the risks involved with each of the various lines of research on recombinant DNA molecules may differ, few, if any, believe that this methodology is free from any risk. Reasonable principles for dealing with these potential risks are: (i) that containment be made an essential consideration in the experimental design and, (ii) that the effectiveness of the containment should match, as closely as possible, the estimated risk. Consequently, whatever scale of risks is agreed upon, there should be a commensurate scale of containment.[1]

They continued with recommendations for matching the types of containment based on the different levels of risk associated with an experiment.

The second pivotal moment was the aftermath following the September 11, 2001, attack on the World Trade Center in New York City. This event raised the specter of other terrorist acts, including biological terrorism. Indeed, a week later, bioterrorism became a very real threat as anthrax attacks were waged against various targets around the country. The need for containing toxic agents reached the crisis stage, and biosafety regulations were further redefined. These stringent guidelines now shape federal and university policies for handling hazardous materials.

With that as a backdrop, federal biosafety guidelines have been promulgated by the NIH, the Centers for Disease Control (CDC), the Department of Agriculture (Animal and Plant Health Inspection Service, APHIS), and the Occupational Safety and Health Administration (OSHA). Some states have additional regulations governing waste materials and other biosafety aspects. To simplify things, many universities produce a biosafety manual that summarizes the myriad federal rules and regulations. But even those so-called summaries often reach medical textbook size—big. So, the novice chief research officer faces the daunting task of figuring out where to start, what to read first, and, more practically, who is responsible for what.

The best place to start is the *NIH Guidelines for Research Involving Recombinant DNA Molecules* (the *NIH Guidelines*).[2] This document lays out the basic policies that every institution must follow if it receives NIH or NSF funding for research using recombinant DNA. Specifically, "As a condition for NIH funding of recombinant DNA research, institutions shall ensure that such research conducted at or sponsored by the institution, irrespective of the source of funding, shall comply with the *NIH Guidelines*."[3] Furthermore, it encourages voluntary adoption by other institutions. Since the use of recombinant DNA is so prevalent in modern natural sciences research, most universities must adhere to these guidelines. A complementary document published by the CDC and NIH, *Biosafety in Microbiological and Biomedical Laboratories* (BMBL),[4] provides more general coverage of biosafety regulations and good laboratory practices. The BMBL has become the standard reference describing the principles of biosafety for the research laboratory.

At their core, most biosafety regulations are built on the framework developed at the Asilomar Conference that classifies the potential health hazard of biohazardous agents based on the different levels of risk associated with their use in research. According to the *NIH Guidelines*, they are:[5]

> Risk Group 1 (RG1) Agents that are not associated with disease in healthy adult humans
>
> Risk Group 2 (RG2) Agents that are associated with human disease which is rarely serious and for which preventive or therapeutic interventions are *often* available
>
> Risk Group 3 (RG3) Agents that are associated with serious or lethal human disease for which preventive or therapeutic interventions *may be* available (high individual risk but low community risk)
>
> Risk Group 4 (RG4) Agents that are likely to cause serious or lethal human disease for which preventive or therapeutic interventions are *not usually* available (high individual risk and high community risk).

The *NIH Guidelines* contains a long list of various microorganisms that are assigned to each of these groups. Thus, a researcher can simply look up the risk group for a particular microorganism that he or she wants to study. If the microorganism is not on the list, NIH must assign it a risk group rating before any research using it can proceed.

Following the Asilomar Conference recommendations, the necessary facilities to contain these microorganisms are also categorized according to a matching 1 to 4 biosafety level (BSL) scale. Like the risk group ratings, the criteria for the biosafety level categories are infectivity, severity of disease, transmissibility, and the nature of the work being conducted. The *NIH Guidelines* and *BMBL* describe the microbiological practices, safety equipment, and facility safeguards for the corresponding level of risk associated with handling a particular agent. To paraphrase *BMBL*'s list of facility ratings:[6]

> Biosafety level 1 (BSL-1) is the basic level of protection and is appropriate for agents that are not known to cause disease in normal, healthy humans.

Biosafety level 2 (BSL-2) is appropriate for handling moderate-risk agents that cause human disease of varying severity by ingestion or through percutaneous or mucous membrane exposure.

Biosafety level 3 (BSL-3) is appropriate for agents with a known potential for aerosol transmission, for agents that may cause serious and potentially lethal infections and that are indigenous or exotic in origin.

Biosafety level 4 (BSL-4) is for exotic agents that pose a high individual risk of life-threatening disease by infectious aerosols and for which no treatment is available.

Thus, the facilities generally needed to contain organisms in risk groups 1 (RG1) through 4 (RG4) are in the biosafety level 1 (BSL1) through 4 (BSL4) categories, respectively.

In principle, all research universities should have the capability to construct BSL-1, BSL-2, and BSL-3 facilities. Levels 1 and 2 can usually be met with standard, commercially available biosafety cabinets and laboratory air-handling systems. However, construction of a BSL-3 facility generally requires construction designs prepared by architects and engineers skilled in this level of biocontainment. Major remodeling of an existing BSL-2 facility to meet BSL-3 criteria involves sealing all vents, electrical outlets, and other nooks and crannies where microorganisms might dwell, designing clean and dirty rooms for changing clothes, easy-access autoclaves, back-up air-handling systems, and other nontrivial modifications. All of that can become quite costly; the design stage alone can easily cost $1 million. Nonetheless, most major research universities now have at least one BSL-3 facility. Temporary BSL-3 facilities can be erected much less expensively using tentlike hoods and HEPA filtration systems, but they are unsuitable for general, long-term use.

On the other hand, universities cannot readily construct BSL-4 facilities. They are major projects that require quite sophisticated, fail-safe engineering designs. Design and construction costs may be as high as hundreds of millions of dollars. Consequently, there are only about fifteen BSL4 facilities in the United States.

In the *NIH Guidelines*, separate facility plans have been developed for plants (P), large animals such as farm livestock (N), and large-volume (more than 10 liters) and other large-scale projects.[7] Each of these follows the same biosafety-level 1 to 4 scale. For example, the level 1 facilities are coded BSL-1-P, BSL-1-N, and BSL-1-large scale, respectively.

All BSL-3 and BSL-4 facilities must be certified by NIH-accredited certifying agents. Likewise, biosafety cabinets, which are the primary means of containment developed for working safely with infectious microorganisms, must be certified annually. This can be done in the field. A nonprofit, nongovernmental organization, NSF International (which is not affiliated with the National Science Foundation), began a program for accreditation of certifying agents,[8] but a variety of organizations now offer accreditation programs. Many universities have accredited certifiers on their staff.

To ensure compliance, the *NIH Guidelines* requires institutions conducting recombinant DNA research to appoint an institutional biosafety committee. The chief research officer may appoint the committee members, although it is not uncommon for the chief executive officer to sign the appointment letters ex officio. Committee membership is tightly defined by NIH: "The Institutional Biosafety Committee must be comprised of no fewer than five members so selected that they collectively have experience and expertise in recombinant DNA technology and the capability to assess the safety of recombinant DNA research and to identify any potential risk to public health or the environment."[9] They must have expertise in recombinant DNA technology of animals, plants, large animals, and large-scale volumes depending on whether that kind of research occurs in the university. And, of course, they must have expertise in containment and biosafety. Moreover, there must be two members not affiliated with the university "who represent the interest of the surrounding community with respect to health and protection of the environment (e.g., officials of state or local public health or environmental protection agencies, members of other local governmental bodies, or persons active in medical, occupational health, or environmental concerns in the community)."[10]

The Institutional Biosafety Committee reviews all recombinant DNA research associated with the institution. Generally, all research using RG-2, RG-3, and RG-4 organisms must be approved by the committee before the project can begin or a grant application supporting the project can be submitted. In their oversight capacity, the biosafety committee assesses the containment levels, facilities, procedures, practices, and training and expertise of personnel involved in the research. Furthermore, it ensures that all recombinant DNA research projects comply with the *NIH Guidelines* and reports any significant research-related cases of noncompliance, accidents, or illnesses to NIH's Office of Biotechnology Activities (OBA). And the committee develops a plan for handling emergencies, such as accidental spills or personnel contamination. Importantly, the committee may not authorize the initiation of experiments that are not explicitly covered by the *NIH Guidelines* without prior NIH approval.

In addition, the *Guidelines* requires the institution to appoint a biological safety officer if it engages in large-scale research or production activities involving viable organisms containing recombinant DNA molecules or in BSL-3 or BSL-4 level research. The biological safety officer's primary responsibility is to ensure proper laboratory procedures through periodic inspections and technical advice to researchers. This individual serves ex officio on the institutional biosafety committee and as a liaison between the committee and the chief research officer.

Optimally, the biological safety officer reports directly to the chief research officer, thus connecting biosafety and animal care organizationally. This is "optimal" because of the widespread use of recombinant microorganisms to modify an animal's innate genetic composition. Examples include transgenic "knock-out" and "knock-in" mice. To ensure that the right and the left hands know what's going on, biosafety and animal-care officials must coordinate their respective recombinant DNA and animal-care monitoring activities. Failure of the two offices to communicate can have serious adverse consequences. Many universities have an environmental health and safety office, and in some cases the biological safety officer may report to that office instead of the chief research officer. This suboptimal reporting arrangement may have arisen prior to the advent of recombinant technologies. Regardless of the history, this particular reporting configuration warrants a thorough review for its effectiveness.

The chief research officer has two main functions in the biosafety arena. The first is to appoint the institutional biosafety committee and the biological safety officer according to criteria posted in the *NIH Guidelines*. Caveat: if either of these report to an environmental health and safety office, the chief research officer may simply be asked to nominate qualified individuals. The second is to provide adequate training and education in biosafety procedures and techniques to members of the biosafety committee and to principal investigators conducting research involving recombinant DNA. Outside consultants are often brought in to supplement in-house trainers.

Training opportunities for the principal investigator are particularly important because he or she carries a heavy burden. According to the *Guidelines*, "On behalf of the institution, the Principal Investigator is responsible for full compliance with the *NIH Guidelines* in the conduct of recombinant DNA research. . . . The Principal Investigator is responsible for ensuring that the reporting requirements are fulfilled and will be held accountable for any reporting lapses."[11] Therefore, the principal investigator must provide adequate training for all laboratory personnel. As *BMBL* states, "Workers are the first line of defense for protecting themselves, others in the laboratory, and the public from exposure to hazardous agents."[12] And the chief research officer must provide any needed support—usually financial—to encourage these efforts. Indeed, to support the principal investigators he or she should actively sponsor periodic biosafety training programs that focus on good laboratory techniques. Ultimately, the chief research officer may be held accountable for a mishap if it can be shown that inadequate training contributed to the accident.

Genetically Engineered Crops

One area of biosafety that has concerned chief research officers at numerous universities merits separate attention, and that is genetically modified organisms (GMOs). These are organisms whose DNA has been altered through recombinant DNA technologies. Although the term GMO refers to any organism, it usually refers to those higher phylogenetically than bacteria—namely, plants and animals.

Most attention has focused on genetically modified agricultural crops. Soybeans, papayas, corn, cotton, and other crops have been modified using genetic engineering to resist various herbicides or pests. Other food crops, such as rice and carrots, have been modified to improve nutritional content. Despite their benefits to modern agriculture, these modified agricultural products evoke considerable opposition from opponents who fear that they may alter the natural balance of nature and possibly trigger unexpected, adverse environmental and health consequences. Some indigenous populations also express concerns because they consider tampering with a food crop to be a violation of their religious beliefs. For example, some Native Hawaiians object to university genetic-engineering research on their sacred food crop, taro.

The tremendous influence of genetically modified crops on modern agriculture is exemplified by Monsanto's Roundup Ready product line. In 1996, Monsanto introduced a remarkable genetically modified crop, Roundup Ready soybean seeds. Prior to this introduction, many farmers would spray their fields with the Monsanto herbicide Roundup to control weeds prior to planting the soybean crop. After the crop had been planted, Roundup could not be used further because it would kill not only the weeds but also the soybeans. Using recombinant DNA technology, Monsanto developed soybeans that were resistant to Roundup, namely Roundup Ready soybeans. Now, the farmer can apply Roundup, plant the modified soybeans, and then reapply Roundup whenever weed growth threatens the soybean crop. As always, the weeds die, but unlike unmodified soybeans, the Roundup Ready soybeans are unaffected by the Roundup. This is very clever bioengineering and marketing. The farmer now buys both the herbicide Roundup and the herbicide-resistant Roundup Ready soybean seeds from Monsanto. Nowadays, roughly 80 percent of the world's soybeans are Roundup Ready. Capitalizing on this success, Monsanto has engineered six additional Roundup Ready crop varieties.

More recently, Monsanto has developed a genetically modified variety of corn, MON 810, which is engineered to produce a toxin to kill insects. Because its long-term effect on naturally occurring insect populations and their related ecosystem remains uncertain, this crop has become a lightning rod for negative public concern in Europe. Indeed, several countries have banned its use. Because plant seeds and pollen can easily cross borders (via the wind or animal vectors), regulatory control resides in the executive branch of the European Union, the European Commission.

Although public concerns are not so vehement in the United States, genetically modified crops are highly regulated by state and federal agencies. Under the Coordinated Framework for the Regulation of Biotechnology, three federal agencies oversee their use: the Department of Agriculture (USDA), the Environmental Protection Agency (EPA), and the Food and Drug Administration (FDA). The USDA's Animal and Plant Health Inspection Service (APHIS) regulates field-testing of agricultural biotechnology products, including genetically engineered plants, microorganisms, and invertebrates. In APHIS parlance, they are known initially as "regulated articles." If their release does not pose risks to agriculture or the environment, APHIS may approve their use. After several years of field tests showing that the unconfined release does not pose a significant risk to agriculture or the environment, an applicant may petition APHIS to change the classification to "nonregulated" status, thus facilitating commercialization of the product. At this point, the "unregulated" organism can be moved and planted without further APHIS authorization. If a plant is engineered to produce a substance that prevents, destroys, repels, or mitigates a pest, it is considered a pesticide and is subject to regulation by the EPA. All food applications of crops, including those crops that are developed through the use of biotechnology, are regulated by the FDA to ensure that foods derived from new plant varieties are safe to eat.

Most colleges of agriculture have sizable research programs studying genetically modified crops, and monitoring procedures for containing these organisms comes under the purview of the institutional biosafety committee. The dean of agriculture and the chief research officer are often drawn into public discussions about the pros and cons of GMOs. Indeed, when genetically engineered bovine growth hormone was first introduced to Wisconsin dairy cattle to increase milk production, the University of Wisconsin chief research officer was pulled right into the heart of a heated debate. These discussions became quite emotional for many partici-pants, especially those who protested the use of "unnatural" milk-production stimulants. Thus, the chief research officers at universities with agriculture colleges (such as the Land Grant universities) should devote the time needed to become familiar with GMO issues. The USDA and the United States Department of Energy, which sponsored the federally funded Human Genome Project, have succinct introductions to the topic.[13]

Select Agents

There is one further aspect of biosafety that can be of great concern to the chief research officer—namely, select agents. Following the 2001 anthrax attacks, which resulted in five deaths, the U.S. government enacted legislation controlling the access and use of so-called select agents. These are any biological organisms or toxins that could potentially pose a severe threat to human, animal, or plant health. In more detail, they are:

> any microorganism (including, but not limited to, bacteria, viruses, fungi, rickettsiae, or protozoa), or infectious substance, or any naturally occurring, bioengineered, or synthesized component of any such micro-organism or infectious substance, capable of causing death, disease, or other biological malfunction in a human, an animal, a plant, or another living organism; deterioration of food, water, equipment, supplies, or material of any kind; or deleterious alteration of the environment.[14]

The Department of Health and Human Services (HHS), specifically the CDC, regulates select agents that may affect human health. In parallel, the Department of Agriculture, specifically APHIS, regulates agents that pose a severe threat to animal or plant health. These are called "high consequence livestock pathogens and toxins" and "plant pathogens." Each agency maintains a list of these agents, and those that appear on both lists and therefore pose a threat to human health, animal health, and animal products are called "overlap agents."

Any institution that uses select agents must register with either the CDC or APHIS, depending on whether the agent poses a threat to human or animal and plant health. In the case of overlap agents, the institution may register with either federal agency. Furthermore, the institution must appoint a "responsible official" who oversees all administrative aspects of select agent usage. He or she must be approved by the Department of Health and Human Service secretary. By law, this individual must have the authority and responsibility to act on behalf of the institution. Commonly, the university's biological safety officer serves in this capacity. All communications between the institution and the CDC or APHIS go through the responsible official. That includes registration issues, permission to possess and to use select agents, all disposal records, and reports of any loss, theft, or other unexpected breach of security involving select agents. Moreover this individual must provide annual training programs in biosafety, containment, and security procedures to individuals with access to select agents and conduct annual inspections of select-agent facilities. In addition, the responsible officer develops the facility's security plan in case of an "incident," such as an accident, loss or theft, or natural disaster.

All researchers who will have access to select agents must undergo a security-risk assessment by the attorney general. Furthermore, they must be well-trained in laboratory procedures appropriate for the use of select agents. If they meet these qualifications and have a legitimate need to study select agents, they are added to the university's registration, which must be approved by the HHS secretary. Only these approved individuals have access to the select agents. Unapproved staff, such as housekeepers, workmen, and so forth, must be escorted at all times by an approved person while in the facility. Project principal investigators bear full responsibility for the conduct of the research project, training subordinate staff, and proper record-keeping.

Incidentally, failure to keep adequate records or to abide by registration terms of select agents can have very serious consequences. These include large fines and possible jail time. Indeed, there have been highly publicized cases of unaccountably missing select agents that have had ruinous consequences, including jail time, for the principal investigator's career.[15] Therefore, the principal investigator and the responsible officer must monitor laboratory practices and record-keeping systems routinely to ensure full compliance with federal regulations.

> K: You said that select agents can be of great concern to the chief research officer. But the responsible officer seems to bear full responsibility here.

Smith: Yes, that's true. The responsible officer has well-defined responsibilities. But when something goes wrong, the chief research officer quickly becomes deeply involved because of the potential impact on the university's reputation as a responsible research institution.

K: And how about the principal investigators? Aren't they ultimately responsible for select agents under their control?

Smith: Yes. As always, the principal investigators have "first-order" compliance responsibility. However, higher level officials representing the institution—in this case, the responsible officer—will be held accountable if there is a mishap.

K: Once again, however, there appears to be an uncoupling of authority and responsibility.

Smith: Not necessarily. By accepting the authority to conduct the project, the principal investigator also accepts the responsibility for compliance with all rules and regulations. That is usually stated in the notice of grant award. For the responsible officer, the coupling is explicit in the law. The chief research officer's authority and responsibility focus primarily on the institution's integrity as a trustworthy custodian of select agents. He or she always retains the authority to suspend or terminate a research project if the principal investigator misuses select agents.

Radioactive Materials

Radioactivity is an elusive, invisible threat to human health. Excessive exposure causes serious illnesses that can lead to death. This was manifest in a most gruesome way following the atomic bomb explosions during World War II. However, radiation has been used for good purposes for many years in medical clinics (for example, x-ray machines) and in university laboratories. Nonetheless, even in these well-controlled settings, overexposure to radiation can have serious health-related consequences.

Therefore, the federal government has established licensing procedures that regulate exposure limits, permissible possession amounts, and radioactive waste disposal.[16] These regulations pertain to all uses of radioactive materials, ranging from nuclear weapons to biochemical assays. Thus, to some faculty members' consternation, users at nuclear weapons laboratories and in university science laboratories adhere to the same general guidelines.

Licenses are issued by the Nuclear Regulatory Commission (NRC). However, to streamline the process, the NRC has entered into agreements with many states (the so-called agreement states) that delegate licensing and enforcement to state agencies if they agree to follow the NRC guidelines. As of 2009, thirty-six states have entered into this kind of agreement. The NRC and the states coordinate the regulation of radioactive materials through the National Materials Program.

This program "covers activities solely carried out by NRC and 36 Agreement State programs, such as licensing, inspection, response to incidents, staffing and training, and enforcement and investigation. It also covers activities that can be shared by each program such as rule and guidance development, development of orders to enhance security of radioactive materials, event evaluation for generic implication and issues, and program evaluation."[17]

Licenses may be granted to individuals or organizations. Individual licenses are rare within the university setting. Normally, the institution is the applicant for either a so-called limited license or a broad license. The major difference is that proposed users are reviewed by the NRC or the institution, respectively. Applicants for a limited-scope license generally submit the specific training and experience of each proposed user and the facilities and equipment available to support each proposed use to the NRC for review and approval.

Applicants for a broad-scope license normally submit a description of the institution's internal review process and the criteria that will be used to approve users and uses. Unlike limited-scope licenses, which typically identify specific isotopes that may be possessed, the broad-scope license generally authorizes the possession and use of a wide range of radioactive materials. An applicant for a broad scope license must show that appropriate personnel, equipment, and facilities are available. Individual users are not named on the license, nor are radioisotopes limited to specified uses. Because they have numerous different research projects using a variety of isotopes, most research universities have a broad-scope license.

Importantly, broad licenses require the establishment of an institutional radiation safety committee that conducts the required internal review process. The NRC delegates administration of the license explicitly to this committee. A broad scope license allows the radiation safety committee to review proposed methods of use and to permit individuals to use material under the provisions of the broad scope license. Stated differently, individual users and methods of use are authorized by the institution's radiation safety committee.[18] With this delegation, the committee has the authority to establish policies and procedures, approve investigator access to radioactive materials, monitor and enforce safety procedures, order and receive radioactive materials, and transfer and dispose of them.

The radiation safety committee is usually composed of faculty members knowledgeable in radioactive materials, appointed by the chief research officer or, alternatively, an environmental health and safety officer that oversees radiation safety. As in other university-wide committees, the chief executive officer may sign the appointment letter ex officio. Committee members' qualifications are reviewed by the NRC, and if they are judged acceptable, they are named in the university's license as the individuals responsible for the oversight and review of the institution's radiation safety.

The broad license also requires institutions to appoint a radiation safety officer. This individual, who may report to the chief research officer, works closely with the radiation safety committee in the approval of faculty and laboratories for radioactive material use. In this role, the radiation safety officer serves as the chief administrative officer overseeing the procurement and use of radioactive materials.

The NRC requires each licensee (through the committee) to "develop, document, and implement a radiation protection program commensurate with the scope and extent of licensed activities and sufficient to ensure compliance with the provisions of this part."[19] Moreover, "The licensee shall use, to the extent practical, procedures and engineering controls based upon sound radiation protection principles to achieve occupational doses and doses to members of the public that are as low as is reasonably achievable."[20] This latter concept, "as low as reasonably achievable," which is commonly referred to by its acronym, ALARA, lies at the heart of most NRC radiation safety guidelines. The goal is to minimize possession amounts.

As in all research activities, the principal investigator is ultimately responsible for radioactive material use in his or her laboratory. That entails training all lab personnel in proper techniques for handling radioactivity. The chief research officer should help in this regard by supporting periodic training sessions, including regular workshops. Furthermore—and this is very important—the chief research officer should always bear in mind that the university has only one license. Thus, if the actions of one principal investigator jeopardize this license, all users of radioactive materials in the research community may suffer the consequences. For that reason, an alert chief research officer will devote particular attention to a laboratory that recurrently violates radiation safety regulations. Similarly, the radiation safety committee will generally suspend the principal investigator's permission to purchase and to use radioactive materials until compliance problems are resolved.

Hazardous Waste

Research universities generate a lot of waste. Laboratories, in particular, must dispose of radioactive, chemical, and animal-carcass waste, and proper disposal can cause problems for a lot of people. Radioactive materials constitute a major component of all laboratory waste. Most universities have well-documented hazardous waste procedures that comply with federal and state regulations, and compliance is most commonly monitored by the environmental health and safety officer. The chief research officer seldom becomes deeply involved in hazardous waste management, but he or she should be familiar with some of the basic challenges because, if something goes wrong, it may impact the university's research environment.

Like most people, university researchers have a reasonable notion about what constitutes hazardous waste. *Waste* has the customary meaning—anything that is no longer useable, and it is hazardous when it poses a threat to human, animal, or plant health. Things like radioactivity, poisonous chemicals, and the like fall into this category. But, from a legal perspective, a researcher's notion of what constitutes hazardous waste isn't specific enough.

Legally, the EPA considers hazardous waste to be anything that appears on one of their four lists of hazardous waste materials and any other waste that is ignitable, corrosive, reactive, or toxic.[21] For laboratories, the most relevant EPA listings are those for spent solvents, which are itemized on the so-called F-list, and discarded commercial chemical products, which are itemized on the so-called P- and U-lists.[22] States may classify additional items as hazardous waste. The chief research officer may not need to know these lists by heart, but he or she should ensure that the individual researchers know which of their laboratory wastes are considered hazardous.

Hazardous waste generated in a laboratory can be accumulated within the laboratory until a certain threshold amount is reached, such as fifty-five gallons. In this context, the laboratory is termed a "satellite accumulation area." The waste is generally collected periodically from the various satellite accumulation areas and taken to a designated site on campus that is equipped to handle emergencies, such as spills, fire, and natural disasters. The amount generated per month and accumulated over time determines what the EPA calls "generator status." The two categories are "small quantity" or "large quantity." Although some hazardous waste can be treated—or neutralized—on site, most of it is shipped to facilities off campus for proper disposal or containment.

Hazardous waste must be handled according to rigid EPA and state regulations. To simplify this process for universities, the EPA has launched a program of "performance-based standards." This program allows facilities the flexibility to choose the appropriate manner in which to manage their hazardous wastes in order to meet regulatory requirements. It was developed in part to account for the diversity among college and university operations and practices. This diversity of programs for managing wastes, including hazardous wastes, is also "reflective of logistical considerations including campus size, space, personnel, and other resource differences among colleges and universities."[23] Management by performance-based standards is not mandatory, but many universities have adopted this option.

The best strategy is always to minimize the amount of hazardous waste generated. Some forms of radioactive waste can be reduced through normal radioactive decay. If the isotope has a half-life less than sixty-five days (for example ^{32}P, and ^{125}I), most laboratories store the waste for ten half-lives, when only 0.1 percent of the original radioactivity remains. Buying small quantities of most chemicals also has the potential to reduce hazardous-waste generation. Working with the environmental health and safety office, the chief research officer should continually provide training programs and material for researchers at all levels, including graduate students and staff in ways to minimize hazardous waste. Moreover, records of all training opportunities must be kept for EPA inspection.

Failure to abide by the regulations may have serious financial and criminal consequences. The EPA personnel may conduct unannounced compliance inspections at any time. Common deficiencies include improper or poorly labeled containers, excessive amounts, and inadequate training records. An illustrative case occurred several years ago at a well-known university that had been accumulating bottles of hazardous chemicals in a storage room. These came from discontinued laboratory courses, departed faculty members' laboratories, and other various sources. The EPA discovered them and ultimately fined the university over $1 million for these compliance violations. The fine was paid from F&A funds, which would otherwise have been available for other research initiatives.

> *K: Are individual researchers usually required to pay for their hazardous-waste disposal?*
>
> *Smith: No. Granting agencies generally expect the university to pay. This is an allowable F&A cost, so the university recoups some of the money from the federal government.*
>
> *K: How can the university be sure that individual researchers dispose of waste properly? For example, how does it know that some toxic waste isn't just dumped hastily into the sink where it can pollute public drinking water?*
>
> *Smith: Most researchers learn proper disposal procedures as students. Nonetheless, the chief research officer routinely organizes workshops to train researchers in waste management procedures. And, of course, we all drink the same water.*

Notes

1. P. Berg et al., "Summary Statement of the Asilomar Conference on Recombinant DNA Molecules," *Proceedings of the National Academy of Science*, 72 (1975): 1981–84.
2. National Institutes of Health (NIH), *NIH Guidelines for Research Involving Recombinant DNA Molecules* (NIH Guidelines), (Bethesda, Md.: NIH, 2009).
3. Ibid., § 1-D, p. 10.
4. Centers for Disease Control (CDC) and National Institutes of Health (NIH), *Biosafety in Microbiological and Biomedical Laboratories* (BMBL), 5th ed. (Washington, D.C.: U.S. Government Printing Office, 2007).
5. NIH, *Guidelines*, p. 37.
6. CDC/NIH, BMBL, pp. 25–6.
7. NIH, *Guidelines*, pp. 17–19.
8. NSF International, "Biosafety Accreditation," 2010, http://www.nsf.org/ (accessed January 11. 2011).
9. NIH, *Guidelines*, § IV-B-2-a-1, p. 23.
10. Ibid.
11. Ibid., § IV-B-7, p. 26.
12. CDC/NIH, BMBL, p. 15.
13. J. Fernandez-Cornejo and M. Caswell, "The First Decade of Genetically Engineered Crops in the United States," *Economic Information Bulletin*, 11 (2006), pp. 1–30; Department of Energy, "Genetically Modified Foods and Organisms," Human Genome Project Information, 2008, http://www.ornl.gov/sci/techresources/Human_Genome/elsi/gmfood.shtml (accessed January 11, 2011).

14. Department of Health and Human Services (DHHS), "Possession, Use, and Transfer of Select Agents and Toxins," *Federal Register*, 70, no. 52 (2005): 13294–325.

15. Department of Commerce, "Action Affecting Export Privileges"; in the matter of Thomas Campbell Butler, *Federal Register*, 71, no. 178 (2006): 54265–66.

16. U.S. Nuclear Regulatory Commission (NRC), Standards for Protection Against Radiation, 10 C.F.R. Part 20 (2010).

17. U.S. Nuclear Regulatory Commission (NRC), "National Materials Program," 2009, http:// nrc-stp.ornl.gov/materials/nmpbkgrd090604.pdf (accessed January 11, 2011).

18. U.S. Nuclear Regulatory Commission (NRC), "Consolidated Guidance About Materials Licenses Program-Specific Guidance About Licenses of Broad Scope," *NUREG*, 1556 (1999), p. 8–17.

19. U.S. Nuclear Regulatory Commission (NRC), Radiation Protection Programs, 10 C.F.R. Subpart B, § 20.1101.(b) (2010).

20. Ibid., § 20.1101.(a).

21. Environmental Protection Agency (EPA), "Wastes—Hazardous Waste," 2010, http://www. epa.gov/osw/hazard/index.htm (accessed January 11, 2011).

22. Environmental Protection Agency (EPA), "Listed Wastes," 2010, http://www.epa.gov/osw/ hazard/wastetypes/listed.htm (accessed January 11, 2011).

23. Environmental Protection Agency (EPA), "Waste—Hazardous Waste Frequent Questions," 2010, http://www.epa.gov/osw/hazard/generation/labwaste/lab-faqs.htm (accessed January 11, 2011).

CHAPTER 11

Restricted Research

> K: Compliance with all of these regulations appears to be quite a burden for a researcher.
>
> Smith: It is, and for the chief research officer, as well. Fortunately, most researchers recognize the need for them. But there are even more regulatory restrictions that impose further constraints on research.
>
> K: I hope that they are justified.
>
> Smith: Some of them are by-products of the times we live in. I suppose that we shouldn't complain too bitterly, though. History is full of various constraints placed on scholarly expression.

Export Controls

Hazardous materials come in many guises. In addition to those that threaten human health directly, there are more subtle and potentially more devastating agents: those that threaten national security or economic prosperity. Therefore, to protect national security, the federal government has export controls that govern the shipment, transmission, or transfer of certain items or pieces of information to foreign persons or countries. The scope of these controls was expanded by the Patriot Act that was passed following the 2001 attack on the World Trade Center.[1]

Three government agencies enforce export controls: the International Traffic in Arms Regulations (ITAR) of the State Department, the Export Administration Regulations (EAR) of the Commerce Department, and the regulations of the Office of Foreign Assets Control (OFAC) of the Treasury Department.[2] They regulate exports of military items (munitions; any space-related technology such as satellites, software with military applications, and so forth); dual-use items (those with both commercial and military applications); and monetary assets and services to embargoed or sanctioned countries such as Iran and Cuba, respectively. If something falls into one of these regulated categories, it may not be exported without a license granted by the regulating agency. Obtaining a license may take several months. On a cautionary note, failure to abide by these export-control regulations carries severe penalties, both monetary and criminal.

"How do I know if a particular item is controlled?" The answer depends on the regulatory agency. If the item has been designed, modified, or enhanced for military use, ITAR determines whether it requires an export license. They have a munitions list that tabulates controlled exports,[3] although the agency readily asserts that there is no fully comprehensive catalogue and that they must be contacted for further guidance. Notably, ITAR also regulates some aspects of global positioning system (GPS) technology because it regulates satellites with military applications. Universities are more likely to deal with dual-use items (both military and commercial applications) and, therefore, with the Department of Commerce (EAR), which regulates about 90 percent of the exports. They, too, have a Web-accessible list of controlled exports.[4] It is extensive and reasonably comprehensive. Likewise, OFAC has a list of "specially designated nationals and blocked persons."[5] If an item appears on any of these lists, it is advisable to call the agency for explicit information.

Deemed Exports

The word *export* carries the usual meaning—to send or take something out of the country. But the regulating agencies extend this definition to include not just the straightforward shipping out of the country but also the access of foreign persons in the United States to restricted items. The word *access* is used quite liberally in this context. It may involve handling an item or, very significantly, little more than just seeing a controlled item, much less being able to scrutinize it in private. In these cases, the item is deemed to have been exported, since the foreign person could presumably convey (that is, export) information about the item to somebody outside the country. Thus, those items that have been accessed by a foreign individual are so-called deemed exports, and they are subject to the full array of export controls. For example, if a foreign student is allowed to see blueprints of a communications satellite, presumably he or she could convey this information (from memory) to somebody outside the country by telephone, e-mail, or any other means. Therefore, the blueprints become a deemed export and are subject to export-control laws because the student has the opportunity to receive technical information about the satellite via his or her eyes and could transmit (that is, export) this information outside the country.

The term "foreign person" requires further definition as it is used in the export lexicon. As Stanford elegantly puts it, "A 'foreign person' is anyone who is not a 'U.S. person.'"[6] So, who is a "U.S. person?" This is a U.S. citizen, a permanent resident alien of the United States who is holding a green card, or an alien who has been admitted as a refugee or granted asylum.[7] Significantly, a foreign or U.S. "person" may also refer to an organization such as a university. The general rule is that only "U.S. persons" are eligible to access controlled items, information, or software without first obtaining an export license from the appropriate agency.

Thus, according to these definitions, foreign students or other university employees without green cards are all potential recipients of a deemed export.

Universities come under particular scrutiny in this regard, for two major reasons. First, as more and more industrial research is performed through grants and contracts to university researchers, correspondingly more products of this university-based research enter the global economy—and that means more exports. Second, universities employ many foreign nationals in their research enterprise, and they represent potential conduits for transferring controlled items out of the country. For these reasons, a tension has developed within academe. These controls conflict with traditional academic freedoms to disseminate research results freely, without restrictions, and to employ people without discrimination based on nationality. Deemed exports pose a particularly vexing challenge in this regard because their inclusion in the export-control law clearly limits opportunities for foreign nationals to participate fully in some research activities.

In this deemed-export context, keeping an accurate, up-to-date inventory of its export-controlled items can pose a daunting challenge for a research university. Many institutions have tens of thousands of equipment items in various laboratories, and not all of them are on an official inventory because their new or depreciated value is less than the federal threshold for inventory record-keeping ($5,000). To complicate matters, some items contain internal components such as lasers that fall under export controls. Luckily, many vendors inform customers that an item may fall under export controls. And presumably, most researchers know if they are dealing with potentially controlled munitions. Nonetheless, researchers may be unaware that a piece of equipment or component part is subject to export controls and unwittingly allow foreign persons access to it. Therefore, to be on the safe side, the chief research officer should periodically inform researchers about the need to identify any potentially controlled items in their laboratories.

Fortunately, ITAR and EAR grant three export-control exceptions to universities.[8] These exceptions apply only to information transfer (deemed exports), not to shipment of actual goods. The first exception is for deemed exports arising from "fundamental research" in science and engineering. What makes research "fundamental?" The term means that the results of the basic or applied research are ordinarily published and shared broadly within the scientific community. By inference, any sponsor limitations on hiring foreign nationals to participate on a project de facto violate the "shared broadly" clause and therefore invalidate the fundamental research exclusion. There can be no restrictions on publication of fundamental research, although there can be limited-duration prepublication reviews by research sponsors to prevent inadvertent divulgence of proprietary information provided to the researcher by the sponsor or to ensure that publication will not compromise the patent rights of the sponsor. Universities usually allow that. Thus, as COGR puts it, "when the fundamental research exemption applies, research may be conducted with the participation of foreign nationals, and research information and results may be disseminated inside or outside the United States without the need to obtain a license from either the Department of Commerce or the Department of State."[9]

From a pragmatic perspective, universities generally assume that a deemed-export license is not required if foreign students and researchers simply use controlled research equipment for fundamental research purposes. This assumption becomes problematic when researchers require access to technical information about the equipment to use it properly. Conservatively, the controlling department (State or Commerce) should be consulted a priori in these questionable situations to avert potentially unpleasant legal disputes.

The second and third exceptions are closely related. Information that is in the public domain is excluded from export controls. The public domain includes materials that can be accessed in libraries, bookstores, Web sites, patents, conferences, and seminars in the United States, as well as other generally accepted venues available to the public at a reasonable fee. The rationale is that this information is freely accessible anyway, so export controls would be meaningless. In addition, educational information presented by instruction in catalog courses and associated teaching laboratories is excluded from export controls by EAR but not ITAR. After all, why control access to information that is readily available by taking a university course?

Universities, and the chief research officer in particular, pay close attention to these export controls. In particular, ITAR requires each institution to appoint an "empowered official" who is authorized to sign and process applications for export licenses on behalf of the university. The primary university officer (and the empowered official) in this role is usually the sponsored-research director who monitors grant proposals for potential export-control issues and helps principal investigators negotiate terms with a granting or contracting agency that mitigate exposure to controls. The COGR provides useful guidance in these negotiations.[10]

It is important to guard against private agreements about export-control issues between a principal investigator and a research sponsor. If a researcher agrees informally to abide by fundamental-research guidelines, but then violates them— willingly or inadvertently— the institution and the investigator may face serious legal consequences.

Another concern has to do with subcontracts. If a subcontract contains any restrictions on the free dissemination of research results, the fundamental-research exclusion may be lost. So, most universities try to eliminate that restriction before accepting the subcontract. The less desirable alternative is simply to apply for an export license. Some aspects of the project may proceed before the license is approved (which may take up to six months), but anything subject to the export restrictions must be delayed until the license has been acquired. A similar case could arise if a research project requires procurement of an item that is subject to export controls. The vendor may insist that the university refrain from publishing any technical aspects of the item, thus breaching the fundamental-research exclusion.

This conflict might be resolved via nondisclosure agreements. Ultimately, the institution has the option of applying for an export license to address control issues.

The Government Accounting Office (GAO) also pays close attention to export controls. In a 2006 report to Congress entitled "Export Controls: Agencies Should Assess Vulnerabilities and Improve Guidance for Protecting Export-Controlled Information at Universities," the GAO stated: "To improve their oversight of export-controlled information at universities, we are recommending that the Secretaries of Commerce and State direct their export control entities to strategically assess potential vulnerabilities in the conduct and publication of academic research through analyzing available information on technology development and foreign student populations at universities."[11] Not surprisingly, their primary concern is deemed exports because of the many foreign nationals in the universities' research enterprise. That chilling report underscores the need for the chief research officer to ensure diligent oversight in this area. Not all export-control issues are black and white; there are many gray areas that are open to interpretation. Thus, legal counsel often becomes involved to assist in resolving questionable areas. The COGR presents and analyzes numerous case studies that provide guidance in these matters.[12]

> K: *You seem to worry a lot about export controls. Is this really such a big problem on most campuses?*
> Smith: *No, not really. But you only need one mistake to incur a huge penalty.*
> K: *If a principal investigator violates the export control law—knowingly or not—who pays the fine?*
> Smith: *The one with the "deep pockets." That's most probably the university. That's why the chief research officer needs to keep on top of all this. The university can usually afford the cost of sponsored-research staff to check for export-control violations before they occur, but they may not be able to afford the cost of a huge penalty. The cost transcends money; it involves a tarnished reputation as well. Furthermore, nobody wants to go to jail, if it comes to that.*

Classified Information

On many university campuses, the phrase "classified research" evokes painful memories of unrest during the Vietnam War years. And even today, any attempt by a chief research officer to raise the topic for open discussion can awaken an otherwise dormant anxiety among students and faculty members. Yet ironically, many institutions conduct classified research with little or no opposition.

To understand this duality, it helps (as always) to begin with definitions. "Classified research" covers any research that entails access to classified information.

And classified information is information that the sponsor (usually the federal government) has declared in need of protection against unauthorized disclosure for the sake of national security. There are three classification levels: confidential, secret, and top secret. They apply to information that could cause "damage," "serious damage," and "exceptionally grave damage," respectively, to the national security.[13] These levels must be clearly marked on classified material. "Derivative classification" refers to the incorporation, restatement, or modification of classified information in some new form. It retains the original material's classification level, and researchers who prepare derivative-classified information must mark the material with the appropriate classification level.

Any federal agency may classify information. The federal government recognizes the Department of Energy, Nuclear Regulatory Commission, Central Intelligence Agency, and Department of Defense as "cognitive security agencies" (CSAs) who provide general supervision of industrial security services. The Department of Energy and the Nuclear Regulatory Commission oversee items concerning nuclear energy, and the Central Intelligence Agency oversees items pertaining to intelligence sources and methods. The Department of Defense is responsible for all other classified items and is the cognitive-security agency for most universities. Furthermore, it serves as the executive agency with oversight of contractors (including universities) and others requiring access to classified information. The Department of Defense also maintains the guiding document for classified information, the *National Industrial Security Program Operating Manual.*[14]

To access classified information, an institution (called a "contractor") must have a facility security clearance, known simply as a "facility clearance." This is issued by the Department of Defense. For institutions with multiple facilities, the main campus must have a facility clearance; the cognitive-security agency will determine whether other off-campus facilities also require clearance. The clearance pertains only to the level of classified information required. Therefore, the facility will not be cleared to access top secret material if it requires only secret or confidential information.

The facility-clearance process requires the institution to appoint a U.S. citizen employee as the "facility security officer." Typically, this individual reports to the chief research officer, although within the university the chief executive officer may be expected to make this appointment ex officio. The facility security officer supervises and directs security measures necessary for compliance with all federal regulations regarding classified information.

In addition, every employee who requires access to classified information must receive a "personal security clearance." Significantly, only U.S. citizens are eligible for a security clearance, although limited access may be permitted in rare cases "where the non-U.S. citizen possesses unique or unusual skill or expertise that is urgently needed to support a specific U.S. Government contract involving access to specified classified information and a cleared or clearable U.S. citizen is not readily available."[15] Moreover, the number of requested personal clearances must be limited to the minimal number of employees necessary for operational efficiency, consistent with contractual obligations. Thus, a university cannot establish a pool of cleared investigators. A potential employee may apply for a personal security clearance up to thirty days prior to the employment date. Ultimately, the cognizant security agency (the Department of Defense) determines eligibility for a personal clearance.

Clearances are valid for access to classified information at the same or lower level of classification as the level of the clearance granted—confidential, secret, or top secret. And they permit access only on a need-to-know basis. Simply possessing a clearance does not automatically authorize an individual to view all material classified at or below that level. The individual must present a legitimate need to know—a requirement to access the information—in addition to the proper level of clearance. For example, although a chief research officer has a personal security clearance, he or she may not have access to all classified information on campus unless there is a defensible reason.

Significantly, senior management personnel must obtain a personal security clearance at the facility-clearance level. That includes members of the governing board, the chief executive officer, and the facility security officer. Typically, it also includes the chief research officer. However, with cognizant security-agency approval, the governing-board members may be excluded from this requirement and, therefore, any access to classified information disclosed to the institution. Except in unusual circumstances, most governing-board members request this exclusion, and it is granted routinely. In this context, the university must report any change in leadership affected by these clearance exclusions to the cognizant security agency for reapproval. Thus, any changes in governing-board membership must be reported, and the exclusions must be reapproved by the cognizant security agency. Technically, the facility security officer is responsible for filing these and all other reports to the cognizant security agency.

Universities with a facility clearance are responsible for safeguarding classified information in their custody or under their control. By extension, individuals are responsible for safeguarding classified information entrusted to them. The extent of protection afforded classified information must "reasonably foreclose the possibility of its loss or compromise," and the *National Industrial Security Program Operating Manual* provides extensive guidelines for providing this security.[16] Pragmatically, in most cases a vault or reinforced filing cabinet located in a secure room suffices. And only a few people—perhaps the facility security officer and the chief research officer—know the combination or possess a key. Separate guidelines regulate the security of electronic data transfer. Approximately once per year, the cognizant security agency will conduct a site visit to inspect these facilities.

Individuals receiving a personal security clearance must understand their responsibilities for safeguarding classified information. Thus, the institution is obligated to provide adequate training. This includes advice on record-keeping and reporting any breaches of confidentiality to the cognizant security agency. The facility security officer has the responsibility to provide this training.

Prior to receiving access to classified information, an individual with a personal security clearance must sign a "classified information nondisclosure agreement" with the federal government. The agreement certifies that the individual has received proper indoctrination concerning the nature and protection of classified information. Furthermore, the agreement declares that:

> I will never divulge classified information to anyone unless: (a) I have officially verified that the recipient has been properly authorized by the United States Government to receive it; or (b) I have been given prior written notice of authorization from the United States Government Department or Agency . . . responsible for the classification of the information or last granting me a security clearance that such disclosure is permitted. I understand that if I am uncertain about the classification status of information, I am required to confirm from an authorized official that the information is unclassified before I may disclose it, except to a person as provided in (a) or (b), above.[17]

This nondisclosure agreement effectively prohibits unauthorized dissemination of classified information, including derivative information. Thus, classified research restricts publication of some or all of the results and procedures obtained using classified information and typically restricts the kinds of personnel working on the project under rules established by the sponsoring agency.

Classified Research

These restrictions on publication and personnel form the kernel of opposition to classified research—or synonymously, "research of a classified nature"—within the university community, for they violate the age-old adherence to academic freedom that entitles faculty members to full freedom in research and in the publication of the results. That violation of academic freedom is why most universities have policies prohibiting classified research on campus. The prohibition may be stated quite simply. The University of Oregon provide a clear-cut example:

> No classified research shall be conducted at the University or with University facilities or equipment. Applications for research grants will not be accepted when all or any portion of the intended research is classified, or if there is a reasonable likelihood that all or any portion of the intended research will become classified in the future. If all or any portion of the research underway becomes classified, the research will be terminated within a reasonable time unless a successful appeal is made to seek declassification.[18]

Alternatively, the prohibition against classified research may be embedded in a more general policy excluding any research that entails restricted publication. Stanford provides an example: "No research on a thesis or dissertation should be undertaken if, at the time the topic is set, there is any substantial possibility that it will lead to a secret thesis or dissertation."[19]

Other universities have similar prohibitive declarations but leave a door open for accepting classified research contracts. For example, the University of Texas at Austin leaves an opening for accepting some classified contracts:

> The University of Texas at Austin shall not accept any classified contract which restricts freedom to acknowledge the existence of the contract, to identify the sponsor, and to disclose the general purpose and scope of the proposed research in sufficient detail to permit informed discussion regarding its appropriateness within the University. The University shall accept only those classified contracts under which there is a reasonable expectation that the investigation will yield significant new literature at an early date.[20]

Likewise, the University of Wisconsin-Madison leaves the door open for classified research on an exceptional basis if it serves a "greater good":

> As policy, the University will not undertake research with restrictions on openness or academic freedom on its campus. [However,] The University recognizes that, in a very few instances, the best interests of society will mitigate against broad participation in research and open exchange of information. In such cases, the Vice Chancellor for Research may grant exceptions to this policy. Exceptions will be very rare and will require that the research is critically important to the University's mission and serve a demonstrable greater good. If these conditions are not met, the University will decline or discontinue the research or, if an acceptable off-campus site is available, consider moving it to such off-campus site.[21]

Despite these assertions against classified research, many universities conduct substantial amounts of classified research, ostensibly because it is in the national interest. How can they reconcile this with policies that explicitly disapprove of classified research? The usual way is to move it off-campus, thus eliminating the need to have classified facilities on campus and greatly reducing any participation of students in the research projects. This is illustrated in the University of Wisconsin policy. Johns Hopkins University, which administers a huge classified research portfolio at its Applied Physics Laboratory, documents this policy clearly:

> Classified research will not be carried out on any academic campus of Johns Hopkins University . . . Any member of the research community

at Johns Hopkins who is planning to participate in a project conducted under the auspices of the University that may involve classified research must first obtain approval from her/his divisional research administration office on behalf of the University before submitting a proposal for the project. This approval must include a plan for a non-academic site where the expected research will be conducted.[22]

The University continues that, "An exception to this policy is the Applied Physics Laboratory, which is not an academic division, and has a distinct mission that makes it an appropriate venue for classified research."[23]

Other universities maintain the same practice: conduct classified research at a facility located off-campus, out of the academic mainstream. In this context, some universities establish a separate legal entity to manage a classified research facility, such as the University of Chicago's Argonne National Laboratory. In a curious variation on this off-campus solution, the University of Hawaii's flagship Manoa campus balked at accepting a large U.S. Navy classified research contract, so the university system office intervened and accepted the contract, thus removing it organizationally from a campus academic mainstream. In addition, all classified research was restricted to off-campus facilities, including university-operated ships.

A corollary to these prohibitions against conducting classified research on campus is a university's refusal to acknowledge any student thesis or faculty member's tenure or promotion dossier based on classified research. As an example, at Johns Hopkins "Research programs using classified materials cannot be used to satisfy the criteria for completion of academic degree requirements, faculty or scholarly appointments, or promotions."[24] Importantly, most universities have a clause that recognizes the possibility that a project may unexpectedly generate results that must become classified. In those cases, when classification was not known a priori, the project is generally moved off-campus as quickly as practical, and at least the nonclassified results may be admissible in a thesis (subject to necessary security regulations).

Some research universities' policies remain silent on the topic of classified research. This implicitly leaves open the opportunity to accept contracts of a classified nature. Because of the inherent restrictions on academic freedom and free dissemination of research results, the chief research officer at these institutions should consult with the provost and the chief executive officer, and inform the faculty senate before accepting any of these awards. Furthermore, some members of the university community may have moral objections about university involvement in classified military-related research projects. As a matter of courtesy, the chief research officer should address these concerns before accepting classified research contracts of a military nature.

Notice that in all of these cases, the chief research officer plays a pivotal role in determining the extent of classified research, whether on or off the campus. Some universities, however, require the chief executive officer or even the governing board to make the final decision to allow classified research on campus. As at the Universities of Texas and Wisconsin, the participation of a faculty committee in making these determinations is highly advisable. Indeed, since these are fundamental matters of academic freedom, not to mention emotional volatility, only a very naïve or overly self-confident chief research officer would make these decisions without formal faculty involvement. Moreover, any decision should be made public. Secrecy at this stage would simply make a difficult situation worse.

Universities generally permit researchers access to information generated by a classified research project conducted by some other entity. In those cases, the investigator must obtain a security clearance. For example, a researcher may require access to information sent by a classified satellite for a project of considerably larger scope—beyond simply the nature of the information. Although the information may be classified, it is peripheral to the main project thrust. As Stanford puts it, "the relationship between the classified data and the overall research endeavor must be sufficiently remote so that:[25]

> 1. a member of the research group who did not hold a security clearance would nevertheless be able to participate fully in all of the intellectually significant portions of the project; and
> 2. there is no substantial basis for an expectation that any part of the final results of the research, or any but a trivial part of the research processes, will be subject to restriction on publication more enduring than [90 days].

Also, universities generally permit faculty members to conduct classified research as consultants. However, this must not interfere with normal university duties and must be conducted off-campus. Generally, faculty members must report their private consulting arrangements, including those that are classified, to their dean. The chief research officer should insist on receiving copies of these reports if they include classified research because he or she may be asked to comment on them in some public forum.

Proprietary Research

Proprietary research is closely related to classified research but carries less rigid restrictions on academic freedom. Proprietary research is sponsored research in which the sponsor (usually a business corporation) imposes data-ownership restrictions that limit publication of the results for a defined period of time. This allows the sponsor the opportunity to review the intended publication in advance to ensure that its proprietary information is not revealed. It also allows time to file a patent application prior to publication.

To avoid misunderstandings, a sponsor should always be required to reveal any proprietary information involved in a project to the university before beginning the contracted research. This revelation is generally preceded by the execution of a nondisclosure agreement between the sponsor and the university. It must also be clearly understood a priori by the sponsor that any results or data generated by university personnel during the conduct of the research project belong to the university unless other arrangements have been agreed upon beforehand and they can be presented freely by university students and faculty members. The University of California, Berkeley, has a model policy statement in this regard:

> Sponsored projects allowing access to and/or use of the sponsor's proprietary data or materials will be accepted only if regulations regarding access, use, and protection of such data or materials do not restrict the full dissemination of scholarly findings made under the grant or contract or put the University in a position of assuming financial liability. Proprietary data or materials must be labeled as such by the sponsor before release to University researchers. Sponsor requirements should not proscribe citation of the sponsor name in publications.[26]

The term "restricted research" is sometimes used if proprietary information is not involved, but the sponsor requests a delay in publication until after it has reviewed the results for factual accuracy, time to file a patent, or other defensible reason. In cases of both proprietary and restricted research, the length of delay in publication varies from one university to another, but it usually lies between 60 and 180 days. In general, universities do not accept grants or contracts for proprietary research that specify delays longer than 180 days, at the absolute most.

> *K: You're saying that universities can prohibit classified research on campus but still manage large facilities that engage in it anyway. Isn't that a bit hypocritical?*
>
> *Smith: Yes, it is. But, you can trace this back to about 1950, when the federal government decided to contract much of its research to the nation's universities.*
>
> *K: Do you mean that this inconsistency is acceptable because of its historical origin?*
>
> *Smith: I understand your misgivings. But once again, we live in a real world and in real time. I suppose that I would rather have universities deeply involved in managing classified research facilities than some less accountable organization.*

Notes

1. Uniting and Strengthening America by Providing Appropriate Tools Required to Intercept and Obstruct Terrorism (USA PATRIOT ACT), Public Law No. 107-56, 115 Stat. 272, 107th Cong., 1st sess. (October 26, 2001).

2. Department of State, International Traffic in Arms Regulations, 22 C.F.R. Parts 120–130 (2010); Department of Commerce, Export Administration Regulations, 15 C.F.R., Chapter VII, §§ 730-774 (2010); Department of the Treasury, "Terrorism and Financial Intelligence" Office of Foreign Assets Control, 2010, http://www.treas.gov/offices/enforcement/ofac/ (accessed January 12, 2011).

3. 22 C.F.R. Part 121, §§ 121.1–121.16.

4. Department of Commerce, Commerce Control List, 15 C.F.R., Part 774, § 774.1 Supplement 1 (2010).

5. Department of the Treasury, "Office of Foreign Assets Control, Specially Designated Nationals and Blocked Persons," 2011, http://www.ustreas.gov/offices/enforcement/ofac/sdn/t11sdn.pdf (accessed January 12, 2011).

6. Stanford University, Office of the Vice Provost and Dean of Research, "Export Controls," http://export.stanford.edu/tree/ (accessed January 12, 2011).

7. 15 C.F.R., §734.2(b)(2)(ii).

8. 15 C.F.R., §§ 734.8–734.9; Department of Commerce, "Deemed Export Questions and Answers," Question 16, 2011, http://www.bis.doc.gov/deemedexports/deemedexportsfaqs.html#5 (accessed January 12, 2011).

9. Council on Government Relations (COGR), *Export Controls and Universities: Information and Case Studies* (Washington, D.C.: COGR, 2004), p. 7.

10. Ibid., p. 46.

11. Government Accountability Office, "Export Controls: Agencies Should Assess Vulnerabilities and Improve Guidance for Protecting Export-controlled Information at Universities," GAO-07-70, 2006, http://www.fas.org/sgp/gao/gao-07-70.pdf (accessed January 12, 2011).

12. Council on Government Relations, *Export Controls*, pp. 18–38.

13. Department of Defense, *National Industrial Security Program Operating Manual* (Washington, D.C.: Department of Defense, 2006), pp. C-2–C-5.

14. Ibid.

15. Ibid., p. 2-2-3.

16. Ibid., p. 5-3-1.

17. General Services Administration, "Form: SF312 Classified Information Nondisclosure Agreement," Standard Form 312, 2000, http://www.gsa.gov/portal/forms/download/03A78F16A522716785256A69004E23F6 (accessed January 12, 2011).

18. University of Oregon, "Research: Classified Research," Policy Number 09.00.03, 2010, http://policies.uoregon.edu/policy/by/1/02000-academic/classified-research (accessed January 12, 2011).

19. Stanford University, "Openness in Research (RPH 2.6)," Research Policy Handbook, 2007, http://rph.stanford.edu/2-6.html (accessd January 12, 2011).

20. University of Texas at Austin, "Classified Research Policy," *Original Handbook of Operating Procedures*, chap. 5, Special Programs, Publications, and Projects, Section 5.09, 2010, http://www.utexas.edu/policies/hoppm/h0509.html (accessed January 12, 2011).

21. University of Wisconsin-Madison, "Policy on Open Research and Free Interchange of Information," Graduate School Research Policy Advisory Council, 2010, http://www.grad.wisc.edu/research/policyrp/rpac/openresearch.html (accessed January 12, 2011).

22. Johns Hopkins University, "Policy on Classified and Otherwise Restricted Research," p. 3, 2005, http://jhuresearch.jhu.edu/JHU_Classified_Research%20Policy.pdf (accessed January 12, 2011).

23. Ibid., p. 1.

24. Ibid., p. 3.

25. Stanford University, "Openness."

26. University of California, Berkeley, "Policy Guidelines Governing Openness and Freedom to Publish," Publication Restriction Policies, 1991, http://vcresearch.berkeley.edu/research-policies/policy-guidelines-governing-openness-and-freedom-to-publish (accessed January 12, 2011).

CHAPTER 12

Human Subjects

K: Your discussion of restricted research raises another question: how does the university ensure the ethical conduct for all research on humans?

Smith: This is about the most closely scrutinized aspect of university research. And for the chief research officer, it's one of the more challenging to manage.

K: Who sets the standards for research on human subjects? The university? The federal government?

Smith: The federal government. But you raise an interesting question. You would think that humanity in general would agree on a uniform set of standards for research on fellow human beings. But, as history has shown, this isn't the case. Moral and ethical guidelines vary widely with historical time and culture.

Regulatory Guidelines

In most developed countries, current standards for the responsible conduct of research with human subjects derive from the Nuremberg War Crime trials following the conclusion of World War II. In 1946, twenty-three Nazi physicians were tried by Allied forces for crimes committed against prisoners in concentration camps, including exposure to extremes of temperature, mutilating surgery, and deliberate infection with deadly pathogens. During the trials, a set of ten standards for judging physicians and scientists who had conducted these experiments was drafted, and this is known as the Nuremberg Code. It became the document that defined modern concepts of the basic rights of human subjects in medical experimentation and was adopted by the fifty-one original members of the United Nations. Nowadays, these rights carry over to all other scholarly pursuits involving humans as well, including interviews for social science studies, educational surveys, and other less invasive studies.

Because it is the seminal document, as a prelude to an examination of institutional procedures for safeguarding human dignity during research projects, it is useful to view the Nuremberg Code in its entirety:[1]

1. The voluntary consent of the human subject is absolutely essential. This means that the person involved should have legal capacity to give consent; should be so situated as to be able to exercise free power of choice, without the intervention of any element of force, fraud, deceit, duress, over-reaching, or other ulterior form of constraint or coercion; and should have sufficient knowledge and comprehension of the elements of the subject matter involved, as to enable him to make an understanding and enlightened decision. This latter element requires that, before the acceptance of an affirmative decision by the experimental subject, there should be made known to him the nature, duration, and purpose of the experiment; the method and means by which it is to be conducted; all inconveniences and hazards reasonably to be expected; and the effects upon his health or person, which may possibly come from his participation in the experiment.

The duty and responsibility for ascertaining the quality of the consent rests upon each individual who initiates, directs or engages in the experiment. It is a personal duty and responsibility which may not be delegated to another with impunity.

2. The experiment should be such as to yield fruitful results for the good of society, unprocurable by other methods or means of study, and not random and unnecessary in nature.

3. The experiment should be so designed and based on the results of animal experimentation and a knowledge of the natural history of the disease or other problem under study, that the anticipated results will justify the performance of the experiment.

4. The experiment should be so conducted as to avoid all unnecessary physical and mental suffering and injury.

5. No experiment should be conducted, where there is an *a priori* reason to believe that death or disabling injury will occur; except, perhaps, in those experiments where the experimental physicians also serve as subjects.

6. The degree of risk to be taken should never exceed that determined by the humanitarian importance of the problem to be solved by the experiment.

7. Proper preparations should be made and adequate facilities provided to protect the experimental subject against even remote possibilities of injury, disability, or death.

8. The experiment should be conducted only by scientifically qualified persons. The highest degree of skill and care should be required through

all stages of the experiment of those who conduct or engage in the experiment.

    9. During the course of the experiment, the human subject should be at liberty to bring the experiment to an end, if he has reached the physical or mental state, where continuation of the experiment seemed to him to be impossible.

    10. During the course of the experiment, the scientist in charge must be prepared to terminate the experiment at any stage, if he has probable cause to believe, in the exercise of the good faith, superior skill and careful judgment required of him, that a continuation of the experiment is likely to result in injury, disability, or death to the experimental subject.

The code states most importantly that participation in an experiment must be voluntary, and the procedures and all of the attendant risks must be clearly explained beforehand. Furthermore, medical experiments using human subjects must be based on a scientifically valid research design that could produce fruitful results for the good of society. Additionally, they must evolve from animal studies and generate results unobtainable in any other way. Only qualified investigators may perform the experiments. And the subjects may withdraw from the experiment at any time.

More recently, much broader guidelines were established by the World Health Organization— namely, The Declaration of Helsinki: Recommendations Guiding Medical Doctors in Biomedical Research Involving Human Subjects—and they were endorsed by the World Medical Association in 1964. This declaration has been amended eight times since then. In general, the Helsinki declaration adheres to the Nuremberg principles: "In medical research involving human subjects, the well-being of the individual research subject must take precedence over all other interests."[2] Interestingly, the Helsinki document includes a section protecting the environment: "Appropriate caution must be exercised in the conduct of medical research that may harm the environment."[3] It also reminds authors, editors, and publishers of their ethical responsibilities in the reporting of human subject research results. They add that "Sources of funding, institutional affiliations and conflicts of interest should be declared in the publication. Reports of research not in accordance with the principles of this Declaration should not be accepted for publication."[4] Accordingly, most biomedical journals require authors to sign a statement of compliance with the Helsinki Declaration at the time of manuscript submission.

Even more definitive guidelines for the protection of human subjects of research were promulgated in 1979 by the federal government's National Commission for the Protection of Human Subjects of Biomedical and Behavioral Research, in the so-called Belmont Report. This document supplements the rules embodied in the Nuremberg code and the Helsinki Declaration by interpreting them in the context of three ethical principles: respect for persons, beneficence, and justice. Using these three core principles as a framework, the Belmont Report presents an analysis of various situations that arise when applying the rules for ethical treatment of human subjects. The report draws particular attention to the inclusion of vulnerable or heavily "burdened" individuals in a research protocol. For example, in the context of justice:

> One special instance of injustice results from the involvement of vulnerable subjects. Certain groups, such as racial minorities, the economically disadvantaged, the very sick, and the institutionalized may continually be sought as research subjects, owing to their ready availability in settings where research is conducted. Given their dependent status and their frequently compromised capacity for free consent, they should be protected against the danger of being involved in research solely for administrative convenience, or because they are easy to manipulate as a result of their illness or socioeconomic condition.[5]

The Belmont Report is a good introduction to the subtleties of interpreting the fundamental rules set by the Nuremberg Code and the Helsinki Declaration. The NIH also produced a good resource on the topic, the so-called Graybook, which briefly summarizes the history and the guidelines for research on human subjects.[6]

A noteworthy recent addition to these fundamental guidelines has been the necessity to include diverse populations of individuals in research protocols. For example:

> it is the policy of NIH that women and members of minority groups and their subpopulations must be included in all NIH-supported biomedical and behavioral research projects involving human subjects, unless a clear and compelling rationale and justification establishes to the satisfaction of the relevant Institute/Center Director that inclusion is inappropriate with respect to the health of the subjects or the purpose of the research.[7]

In addition, "It is the policy of NIH that children (i.e., individuals under the age of 21) must be included in all human subjects research, conducted or supported by the NIH, unless there are scientific and ethical reasons not to include them."[8] These policies arose because medical treatments based on testing done historically only in white male adults were found to be inappropriate for women, members of minority groups, and children.

Institutional Assurance

After a lengthy review process that began in 1978, in 1991 the federal government issued formal guidelines for the conduct of research using human subjects.[9]

It adheres closely to the Belmont Report. This set of rules applies to research sponsored by all U.S. government departments and agencies, including the Central Intelligence Agency. Therefore, it is known as the "common rule." Individual departments or agencies, such as the Food and Drug Administration, to name just one example, may add additional regulations, but they all must abide by the common rule.

At the outset, these guidelines call for each institution that conducts research on human subjects to submit an assurance that guarantees compliance with federal policy. This assurance is filed with the federal agency that supports the research project where it is reviewed and approved (or "certified"), if it is judged to be satisfactory. No research project involving human subjects may proceed without an approved assurance on file. Technically, the assurance applies only to federally supported or conducted research. However, in practical terms, it applies to all research using human subjects, regardless of funding source. This inclusivity is embedded in the federal requirements for the assurance: "Assurances applicable to federally supported or conducted research shall at a minimum include . . . a statement of principles governing the institution in the discharge of its responsibilities for protecting the rights and welfare of human subjects of research conducted at or sponsored by the institution, regardless of whether the research is subject to Federal regulation."[10] The key phrase is "regardless of whether the research is subject to Federal regulation."

In 1995, the Department of Health and Human Services, through its Office of Human Research Protections (OHRP), adopted a Federalwide Assurance (FWA). This assurance, which is filed with OHRP, is generally accepted by all government departments and agencies, thus relieving the institution from filing multiple assurances. Importantly, when the federal agency approves (or certifies) an assurance, it has not affirmed that the institution is in full compliance with human subject regulations. The assurance simply documents the university's intentions to comply with federal policy.

Usually the chief research officer oversees preparation and filing of these assurances. That includes signature authority delegated by the chief executive officer on behalf of the institution. He or she is the signatory official. However, with federal encouragement, the chief executive officer may choose not to delegate signature authority to the chief research officer. Thus, at some universities, the chief research officer may not be authorized to sign the assurance. But if the chief research officer is responsible for preparing the assurance, why shouldn't he or she have the authority to sign it? According to OHRP, "The intent in requiring that the Signatory Official be a high-level individual is two-fold. First, OHRP encourages institutions to promote a culture of conscience for the ethical conduct of human subjects research at the highest level within the institution. Second, the Signatory Official should be at a level of responsibility that would allow authorization of necessary administrative or legal action should that be required. OHRP recommends that the Signatory Official not be the chair or member of any IRB designated under the FWA."[11]

In simpler terms, the signing officer must have line authority over individuals who may be involved in research on human subjects in case disciplinary action is ever required. This is a valid reason for the chief executive officer to retain the assurance authority. However, if the chief research officer remains responsible for its implementation, authority (the chief executive officer) and responsibility (chief research officer) become uncoupled. That is not desirable management. A better alternative is for the chief executive officer to delegate signatory authority to the chief research officer, who then serves as the signatory official.

Institutional Review Board

A second major component of federal policy is the requirement for the institutional establishment of a committee, the Institutional Review Board (IRB), to review all proposed and ongoing research projects involving human subjects. Furthermore, the institution must provide adequate space and staff for IRB activities.

What are these activities? By statute, the IRB has the authority to review and approve all human subject research protocols. (A "protocol" is the document submitted to the IRB by the principal investigator that describes the proposed research in detail.) It may also require protocol modifications necessary to gain approval. One of the most important protocol components is the "informed consent" document that prospective subjects must clearly understand and sign voluntarily (if they are able to) prior to participation in the project. The IRB must also review all ongoing research at least annually or more frequently according to the risks to human well-being. It may suspend or terminate approval of research that is not being conducted according to the approved protocol or that incurs unexpected serious harm to the subjects. Federal policy also requires the IRB to provide full documentation of all research protocols involving human subjects, meeting minutes, informed-consent permission forms, and any other correspondence concerning research using human subjects. These records must be maintained for at least three years.

The Health Insurance Portability and Accountability Act (HIPAA) confers additional authority on the IRB. The HIPAA requires patient authorization for the release of protected health information to other individuals, including researchers. The rationale is that an individual's health information is private; it is strictly a matter between physician and patient. Authorization to gather patient data for research may be incorporated into the informed-consent agreement. If a patient's identity cannot be ascertained from the health data (the data have been "de-identified"), patient authorization is not required for research. By statute, an IRB may approve a waiver of the authorization requirement for the use or disclosure of identifiable health information for research if the "use or disclosure of protected health information involves no more than a minimal risk to the privacy of individuals."[12]

The IRB retains the authority to suspend or terminate approval of a project under adverse or unanticipated conditions. Examples include serious or continuing noncompliance with federal common rule regulations or institutional IRB requirements and unanticipated risks to subjects or other related complications. In federal jargon, these problems are called "incidents," and they must be reported promptly to the sponsoring federal agency. Usually, the chief research officer files this report and leads any further discussions with the agency concerning remedial actions.

It should be pointed out that an institution's officials, such as the chief research officer, have the right to further review any protocol approved by an IRB. They have the authority to override IRB approval, thus disapproving the research project. However, they do not have the authority to approve a project that has been disapproved by the IRB.

Federal policy also dictates IRB membership criteria. Since the chief research officer usually selects the IRB members, it is useful to review membership guidelines in more than casual detail. (Parenthetically, the person signing the institutional assurance also signs the official appointment letters.) At baseline, there should be at least five members with varying backgrounds sufficient to review competently all human-subjects research within the university. They should represent the racial, ethnic, and cultural diversity common to the research projects and should possess sensitivity to community attitudes. And they must understand applicable institutional and federal regulations. If the institution regularly conducts research on vulnerable populations, such as children, prisoners, pregnant women, or handicapped or mentally disabled persons, "consideration shall be given to the inclusion of one or more individuals who are knowledgeable about and experienced in working with these subjects."[13] At least one member must be a scientist and one must be a nonscientist. Also, one member (and his or her immediate relatives) must not be affiliated with the institution. On top of all that, the IRB members should not be all male or female or all in one profession (such as medicine). Outside consultants may be brought in on a nonvoting basis if their special expertise is needed. Predictably, no member may vote on a protocol if he or she has a conflict of interest. Adding up all of these membership requirements, the usual IRB has in the range of fifteen to twenty-five members.

According to policy of the Department of Veterans Affairs, alternate members may be appointed to the IRB to substitute for a specific primary member. In these cases, the IRB roster must document which primary member the equally qualified alternate replaces. And, of course, the alternate receives and reviews the same material provided to the regular member.

Notably, the chief research officer must not be an IRB member. Federal policy doesn't prohibit this, but it would constitute a serious conflict of interest. This is because the chief research officer wants to bring in research grants and contracts to the university; thus, he or she may not be unbiased in making decisions about protocol approvals. Indeed, in 1999, the federal government temporarily stopped all federally funded research at Duke University Medical Center. One of the stated reasons was that the director of grants and contracts was a member of the institutional IRB, and this was potentially an inherent conflict of interest.

In most cases, an IRB must review a great many proposals—as many as 300 or so per year is not out of the ordinary. This places serious demands on the membership. Thus, large research institutions may have several IRBs. Indeed, those with sizable health science centers, including affiliated hospitals and clinics, may have as many as six or more IRBs. Ideally, each of these institutional IRBs recognizes the actions of the others, although for historical or other reasons, this may not always be the case. Any frictions between the various IRBs in an institution can pose annoying impediments to researchers, so the chief research officer's goal should be to negotiate university-wide acceptance of its IRB actions. An IRB chair, who is usually a faculty member, feels these time demands most acutely. Therefore, most institutions provide teaching or service relief; typically, the chief research officer provides about 25 percent of the chair's salary to offset teaching or service obligations and a salary supplement of about $1,000 per month. Of course, this will vary from case to case.

A few universities offset these costs of running an IRB by charging for some or all of their services. In these cases, the investigators include these fees in the project's direct-cost budget. How much does it cost per proposal? That can always be estimated in various ways, ranging from the simple to the complex. The easiest way is just to divide the total cost of running an IRB operation by the total number of protocols reviewed. It probably amounts to between $1,000 and $2,000 per proposal. It must be remembered, however, that IRB fees in a federal direct-cost grant budget cannot be included in the institutional F&A rate calculations.

In projects involving investigators at more than one institution, each cooperating institution is responsible for safeguarding the rights and welfare of human subjects under its purview. This requirement has the potential to add further demands on an IRB and duplication of effort. Therefore, with the approval of the granting agency, an institution participating in a cooperative project may enter into an arrangement for joint review by only a single IRB at one or the other partner institutions or make similar arrangements for avoiding duplication of effort. For research performed at foreign institutions, that country's human-subjects protocol review may be acceptable if it complies with all elements of the common rule. In this regard, the NIH has compiled a helpful directory of human-subjects rules and regulations for ninety-two countries.[14]

Regardless of these cooperative arrangements, each institution remains liable for full compliance by its investigators with federal policy. For that reason, most chief research officers (and IRB members) step cautiously into these shared-compliance arrangements. Nonetheless, any reduction in the number of IRBs that must review a cooperative proposal is good news to the principal investigators. Most will say, "There's too much bureaucratic red tape anyway."

Finding enough qualified individuals to serve on the IRBs poses a challenge to the chief research officer. Recruiting clinicians often proves exceptionally difficult because of their time-demanding clinical obligations. Yet they are often the most necessary members when reviewing clinically oriented protocols. And financial incentives are usually ineffective in these recruitments.

Fortunately, the private sector offers some relief. It all started in 1981, when the Food and Drug Administration (FDA) began requiring IRB approval of clinical drug trials. This increased the number of protocols to be reviewed. Academically affiliated IRBs were not prepared to fill this need, so independent IRBs began to emerge. It wasn't until 1995, however, that these independent IRBs were authorized to review and approve federally funded research projects. Currently, there are about twenty independent IRBs, and twelve of them belong to the Consortium of Independent Review Boards (CIRB), which represents the industry as a whole. In general, they have been well received because they act quickly and have the capacity to review large, multicenter proposals.

One particular independent IRB that has attracted market share in the academic community—the Western Institutional Review Board, Inc. (WIRB)—serves as a good example of the industry. Like the other independent IRBs, this private, for-profit company conducts full-scale IRB reviews on a contract basis. According to the company's publicity, "WIRB can serve as an institution's sole IRB or one of an institution's IRBs for human subjects research, through inclusion on an institution's Federalwide Assurance. WIRB meets all requirements of the U.S. Department of Health and Human Services (HHS) regulations on human subject protection (45 CFR §46), and is able to provide IRB services for federally funded research that falls under the auspices of the Office for Human Research Protections (OHRP)."[15]

A growing number of universities have utilized these privately offered services, although seldom exclusively. Most institutions restrict these outsourced IRB reviews to research protocols funded by nonfederal sponsors. For example, Tufts University, the University of Washington, the University of Florida, and Emery University all allow WIRB review and oversight of research projects that are industry sponsored. Universities may impose further restrictions on a project's eligibility for WIRB review. WIRB has a fee schedule that is generally competitive with a university's IRB review costs; for example, the base fee is $1,750 for the initial review and $850 for an annual review of an approved protocol. In many cases, WIRB bills the project sponsor directly, thus eliminating the need for universities to levy F&A surcharges. Note: if the sponsor refuses to pay these fees, the university will be held responsible. Therefore, the chief research officer should ensure that the investigator has negotiated the sponsor's agreement to pay these costs before contracting WIRB's services.

The for-profit status of the independent IRBs has raised concerns about financial conflicts of interest. Some might ask, "Wouldn't they be inclined to give favorable reviews in order to keep customers happy?" To counter this potential conflict, the NIH prohibits anybody holding equity in the IRB company from participating in the review of a project funded by the Department of Health and

Human Services. Another concern is "IRB shopping." That would occur if an investigator shopped around to find an IRB willing to approve a protocol, comparing one IRB with another. The Veterans Health Administration (VHA) makes it easy to deal with these potential conflicts: they explicitly prohibit the use of commercial IRBs.[16]

These concerns were highlighted in a recent congressional investigation into for-profit IRBs. As part of that study, the House Energy and Commerce Committee set up a sting operation. They "asked the Government Accountability Office to conduct undercover testing of the IRB review process. We wanted to know whether IRBs are rubber stamping research studies, whether clinical researchers are 'IRB shopping' or choosing IRBs based on how quickly and inexpensively they approve studies, and whether governmental oversight of IRBs is adequate."[17]

As part of that effort, the Government Accountability Office (GAO) submitted a fictitious study, led by a fictitious doctor, from a fictitious company to three for-profit IRBs. The study proposed pouring a full liter of a fictitious, non-FDA-approved solution into a woman's abdominal cavity after surgery to help with healing. This bogus protocol was based on a real study of a product that the FDA withdrew from the market because of deaths and infections arising from its use. Two IRBs promptly rejected the protocol: "It is the worst thing I have ever seen." However, one for-profit IRB approved the proposal unanimously. According to congressional testimony "The doctor with primary responsibility for reviewing the study told the other Board members that the protocol 'looks fine' and that the substance to be injected into the abdominal cavity was 'probably very safe.' Nobody at [the] IRB ever reviewed any of the data cited in the proposal to support those claims. If they had, they would have discovered that it didn't exist."[18]

The committee concluded that the IRB company "was more concerned with its financial bottom-line than protecting the lives of patients."[19] The for-profit IRBs weren't the only victims of this sting operation. The GAO also successfully registered a fictitious IRB headed by a dog with the Department of Health and Human Services with "no questions asked." Does all of this mean that one out of three for-profit IRBs are incompetent? Or that the federal government can't tell a dog from a human? No, of course not. Furthermore, there are always two sides to every story. But these cases do point out the need for caution when choosing an independent IRB. The chief research should always exercise due diligence in this regard. As always, caveat emptor—buyer beware.

> K: *Those stories about the for-profit IRBs are certainly disconcerting. Why would a university risk contracting them if they have in-house IRBs?*
> Smith: *It becomes a matter of managing the workload. Large medical centers can have thousands of active clinical trials, and each has to be reviewed annually. Sometimes, the in-house IRBs simply can't handle the volume.*
> K: *I suppose that it's like everything else in commerce. Find a reliable, honest independent IRB and then stick with it.*

Smith: Out of fairness, it bears mentioning that IRBs in the academic setting may also harbor subtle conflicts of interest. Because many of the members are from within the institution, they may be biased either for or against specific colleagues for any of a number of reasons that can be imagined. We're still dealing with human beings, no matter what the setting.

Accreditation

In addition to concerns about independent, for-profit IRBs, other factors arise affecting IRB effectiveness at protecting human subjects in the academic setting. Although federal policy and its underlying framework—the Nuremberg Code, Helsinki Declaration, and Belmont Report—spell out specific standards for the protection of human subjects in research, the ultimate approval authority lies in the hands of the local IRBs. Understandably, they reflect the cultural milieu of the surrounding communities. And cultural and societal standards vary considerably from place to place across the country. How can uniformity in the implementation of federal policy be achieved under these circumstances? Compounding this inherent variability, many large clinical trials now enroll thousands of patients in university-affiliated facilities from around the country. Moreover, many institutional IRBs are overworked; their members must review numerous consent forms, protocols, renewals, and so forth on top of their other professional obligations. What assurance is there that these busy IRBs adequately evaluate all materials presented to them? These questions demanded answers.

Public concerns about humans in medical research multiplied in the late 1990s. In March, 1999, the federal government, through the Office of the Protection of Research Risks (OPRR), ordered a shutdown of about four hundred projects using human subjects at the Los Angeles Veteran's Administration hospital associated with the University of California, Los Angeles, because of serious deficiencies in human-subjects protection. In May 1999, the OPRR and the Food and Drug Administration (FDA) suspended human-research programs at seven other universities because of apparent noncompliance with federal regulations.

A tragic death punctuated the need to provide some kind of oversight program for protection of human research. In September 1999, Jesse Gelsinger, an eighteen-year-old research volunteer, died in a gene-transfer experiment at the University of Pennsylvania because of a deadly immune reaction against the experimental intervention. After the fact, it became apparent that previous difficulties with this procedure in both animal and human studies were not disclosed adequately and that the informed-consent form had been altered after it had been signed. Furthermore, the principal investigator and the university had a financial conflict of interest in the trial. Needless to say, the university suffered major embarrassment and financial penalties because of these errors.

To address these concerns, the Institute of Medicine set up a committee to review ways of improving protection programs for human-subjects research. Accreditation was one solution. Two accreditation associations emerged. The first was the National Committee for Quality Assurance (NCQA). It contracted with the Veterans Health Administration to accredit its human-subjects protection programs. In 2002, another association, the Association for the Accreditation of Human Research Protection Programs, Inc. (AAHRPP), was launched. Its founding members include the Association of American Medical Colleges (AAMC), the Association of American Universities (AAU), the Association of Public and Land-grant Universities (APLU), and other prestigious academic organizations. In 2005, the NCQA withdrew from the human-subjects accreditation business, leaving AAHRPP as the sole accreditor. Many research universities have now sought AAHRPP accreditation, and it appears to have been accepted as a desirable goal. By the way, AAHRPP charges fees based on the number of protocols reviewed annually. For 1,000 protocols, the current application fee is about $20,000, and the annual renewal fee is about $9,000.

The AAHRPP accredits an organization's entire human-subjects protection program, not individual components. Therefore, if a university has eight IRBs, the AAHRPP accredits the entire group as one unit. If an institution also contracts to WIRB for additional reviews, the AAHRPP would not concentrate on that component of a university's IRB ensemble because AAHRPP accredits WIRB as a self-standing organization. In AAHRPP's words, "The academic institution applies for accreditation as a whole unit regardless of the number of IRBs or separate schools within the university."[20] In large, multicampus systems, such as the University of California, each campus (for example, UCLA or UCSF) may apply individually. Furthermore, "Organizations may also share resources to form a single comprehensive Human Research Protection Program."[21] Thus, two or more universities may combine their human-subjects protection programs and apply as a single entity. But they need to have a common set of policies and procedures. For example, the Universities of Michigan at Dearborn and Flint combined their human-subjects protection programs with the much larger Ann Arbor program, and AAHRPP accreditation covers all three campuses as a unit. This consolidation may appeal to smaller, less research-intensive institutions.

Accreditation requires adherence to fifteen standards that basically follow the guidelines spelled out in the common rule. They are grouped into three domains: the organization, the IRB, and the researchers. The application process requires an institutional self-assessment of its human-subjects protection programs and self-identified potential improvements, a site visit, and an evaluation by AAHRPP's council on accreditation. Full accreditation must be renewed every three years, supplemented by annual reports that inform AAHRPP of major changes or problems related to the institution's human research protection program.

What are the benefits of AAHRPP accreditation? Presumably, the accreditation process stimulates the institution to improve its human-subjects protection program. As an additional benefit, AAHRP asserts that accreditation provides a competitive edge in attracting research sponsors: "Sponsors and other funding agencies recognize that accredited organizations have more efficient operations, provide more comprehensive protections, and produce high-quality data. Increasingly, accreditation is expected to be a condition of research support."[22] Furthermore, they claim that "Federal agencies acknowledge the value of accreditation. They have begun seeking accreditation for their own HRPPs and using accreditation status to guide decisions. Regulators are more likely, for example, to target non-accredited organizations for inspections. With its commitment to quality and accountability, accreditation also is a viable alternative to further regulation."[23]

Are all of these claims true? That remains open to debate. Clearly, however, there is a growing trend toward reliance on accreditation to boost public confidence in human-subjects protection programs in both industrial and academic settings. For example, one of the world's largest pharmaceutical companies, Pfizer, Inc., announced in 2009 that:

> Pfizer continues to support voluntary accreditation and other measures to improve confidence in human subject protection. Last year, Pfizer adopted a policy of only using central IRBs that had received accreditation from the Association for the Accreditation of Human Research Protection Programs (AAHRPP). In addition, we recently benchmarked our own policies and operations, including our IRB review practices, against those set forth by AAHRPP and are the first pharmaceutical company to have obtained accreditation from AAHRPP (for our phase I research units).[24]

Should a chief research officer push for institutional AAHRPP accreditation and thus incur yet another hefty annual fee? As more and more sources of research funding require AAHRPP accreditation, it appears as if there will be little choice in the matter in the near future. So, the direct answer to the question is yes, AAHRPP accreditation is worth the investment.

There is another accrediting association specifically for IRB personnel—namely, Public Responsibility in Medicine and Research (PRIM&R). This nonprofit corporation certifies IRB professional personnel through its Certified IRB Professional (CIP) program. According to PRIM&R, "The certification program is designed specifically for individuals participating in and/or overseeing the daily operations of IRBs. Professionals from institutional IRBs, independent IRBs, and industry, as well as other institutions focused on either biomedical or social/behavioral/educational research, may be eligible. IRB administrators, staff, chairs, and institutional officials are, therefore, all appropriate candidates for certification."[25] To be eligible for certification, these individuals must have had at least two years of experience working with an IRB during the past seven years.

Certification requires passing an exam on IRB issues consisting of 250 multiple-choice questions. The exam is given twice yearly and costs about $400. Every three years, certification must be renewed. Reexamination is one way to do this. Another option, which is available once every six years, is to "complete 30 documented hours of continuing education in human subject protections, applied research ethics, and topics listed in the CIP body of knowledge."[26] PRIM&R also offers workshops and formal courses on the protection of human subjects, which can be counted towards the continuing education requirement.

Given the subtle complexities of IRB reviews and decision making, many chief research officers encourage (and pay for) IRB personnel, including faculty members, and other personnel engaged in human subjects research to attend training opportunities. PRIM&R's offerings are quite popular and well recognized. Another well-known training source is the nonprofit Collaborative Institutional Training Initiative (CITI).[27] CITI, which was founded in 2000 as a collaborative effort between the University of Miami and the Fred Hutchinson Cancer Research Center, provides Web-based training programs covering many different aspects (called modules) of the protection of human subjects in research. Institutions subscribe to CITI for a fee (currently $1,500 per year), and then any number of individuals within the institution may use the CITI course site. The fee also entitles the member institution to add modules with content specific to their institutional protection programs. That's why CITI is so popular. Indeed, many universities require all individuals involved in human-subjects research to complete the CITI basic modules covering their research (for example, biomedical) and to complete the refresher course module every two or three years.

Expedited and Exempt Reviews

Federal policies allow for an expedited review of proposals that carry no more than minimal risk or that request only minor modifications of an already approved protocol. The expedited reviews may be carried out by the IRB chair or one or more experienced IRB members designated by the chair. In this capacity, these individuals act on behalf of the full board, so they possess the full authority of the IRB with one exception: they cannot disapprove a project. Only the full IRB can do that. OHRP maintains a list of research categories eligible for expedited review.[28] Most of the procedures eligible for expedited review are noninvasive. Examples include the collection of hair and finger-stick blood samples, voice recordings, x-rays, and normal use of an over-the-counter drug. Importantly, in these cases the requirements for informed consent still apply.

If a research protocol qualifies for expedited review, it may also qualify for an informed consent waiver. The IRB may waive the requirement if the research involves only minimal risk to the subjects, the waiver or alteration will not adversely affect the rights and welfare of the subjects, and the research could not be conducted easily without the waiver.

In addition, some uses of human subjects are exempt from IRB review. These include studies conducted in an educational setting, such as comparing teaching methods and testing (achievement, aptitude, and so forth), provided that individual subject identities are not revealed. As long as individual subjects are not identifiable, this also includes studies using existing data sets and pathological or diagnostic specimens that are available to the public. Data obtained for some other purpose, such as medical treatment, may also be exempt if they are coded in a way that conceals subject identity. The rationale is that the patient is not exposed to greater risk through this piggybacking of research onto a treatment protocol. Further exemptions include evaluations of public-service benefits and of taste and foods—as long as the food is "wholesome." Individual investigators are not empowered to decide if their research protocol is exempt from IRB review. The IRB must make that decision; usually the chair has that authority.

Interestingly, in vitro research on established human cell lines, including human embryonic stem cells, does not normally require IRB review. According to the Department of Health and Human Services (HHS):

> HHS-conducted or supported research that involves neither interactions nor interventions with living individuals or obtaining identifiable private information is not considered human subjects research. Accordingly, in vitro research and research in animals using already derived and established human cell lines, from which the identity of the donor(s) cannot readily be ascertained by the investigator, are not considered human subject research and are not governed by the HHS or FDA human subject protection regulations. . . . IRB review is not required for such research.[29]

However, if these cells are used in a protocol involving humans, such as transplantation or some other therapy, this clearly falls under the federal guidelines as research using human subjects and requires full IRB review. In this context, biological material from autopsy cases or deceased patients does not require IRB approval, but certification or proof of the patient's death is required for the exemption.

Backing up a step, established cell lines must have come from a donor. Thus, the original investigator who derived the cell line must have obtained IRB approval to collect the cells from the donor in the first place. And if the cells were deposited in a repository, the repository (such as American Type Culture Collection, ATCC) most probably must have IRB approval to receive them. For example, the repository IRB sets the conditions under which data and specimens may be accepted and shared. One important condition would be that the identities of the donor-subjects cannot be ascertained by any subsequent recipients. To cement these assurances in place, OPRR recommends a written usage agreement for recipient investigators according to the following template:

> Recipient acknowledges that the conditions for use of this research material are governed by the cell repository Institutional Review Board (IRB)

in accordance with Department of Health and Human Services regulations at 45 CFR 46. Recipient agrees to comply fully with all such conditions and to report promptly to the cell repository any proposed changes in the research project and any unanticipated problems involving risks to subjects or others. Recipient remains subject to applicable State or local laws or regulations and institutional policies which provide additional protections for human subjects.[30]

In simpler terms, "This research material may only be utilized in accordance with the conditions stipulated by the cell repository IRB. Any additional use of this material requires prior review and approval by the cell repository IRB and, where appropriate, by an IRB at the recipient site."[31] Most repositories incorporate these recommendations into material transfer agreements or other contractual arrangements containing assurances that the recipient investigator will use the cell lines in accordance with all state and federal laws, including the common rule.

> K: I find it curious that human cell lines are exempt from IRB review. Many of them have been around for years. And investigative methodologies have become so much more powerful since then. Things like DNA sequencing. How do we know that the donor would ever have approved of these modern procedures using his or her cells?
>
> Smith: That is a good question. In fact, this has become the topic of considerable debate within the bioethics community.
>
> K: Shouldn't these original consent forms be re-examined in today's context?
>
> Smith: That, too, has been debated. But no consensus has emerged. Part of the problem is that there are so many different human cell samples—millions and millions of them. It would take an impractical amount of work to renew all of these consent forms.

Human Research Protection Programs

In their guidelines, the Department of Veterans Affairs (VA) extends beyond the common-rule requirements for an assurance and an IRB. It also requires establishment of a more comprehensive approach to protecting human subjects. This approach is manifest as a "human research protection program" (HRPP). As the VA puts it, "A HRPP is a comprehensive system to ensure the protection of human subjects participating in research . . . The objective of the system is to assist the institution in meeting ethical principles and regulatory requirements for the protection of human subjects in research."[32.]

Many research universities, including those with no affiliated VA medical center, have implemented HRPPs. Indeed, AAHRPP's first accreditation standard (Standard I-1) requires institutions to have an HRPP: "The Organization has a systematic and comprehensive Human Research Protection Program that affords protections for all research participants. Individuals within the Organization are knowledgeable about and follow the policies and procedures of the Human Research Protection Program."[33] And just to make sure that the program is sufficiently funded, they add (Standard I-2) that "The Organization ensures that the Human Research Protection Program has resources sufficient to protect the rights and welfare of research participants for the research activities that the Organization conducts or oversees."[34] Thus, most major research universities have established an HRPP under these broad guidelines.

What does an HRPP look like? Neither the VA nor AAHRPP specify exactly what form they take. Technically, the HRPP is composed of a number of individuals, offices, and committees. In general, they include the chief facility officer (such as a medical center director), chief research officer, compliance officer, the IRB, the institutional biosafety committee, the radiation safety committee, and others. Collectively, they represent all aspects of the enterprise involved in research on human subjects. The VA has explicit criteria for HRPP composition:

> The HRPP consists of a variety of individuals and committees such as: the Medical Center Director, Associate Chief of Staff (ACOS) for Research and Development (R&D), the Administrative Officer (AO) for R&D, compliance officers, etc., the R&D Committee, the IRB, other committees or subcommittees addressing human subjects protection (e.g., Biosafety, Radiation Safety, Radioactive Drug Research, Conflict of Interest), investigators, IRB staff, research staff, health and safety staff (e.g., Biosafety Officer, Radiation Safety Officer) and research pharmacy staff.[35]

Ultimately, the chief facility officer must ensure effective coordination of these various individuals, offices, and committees.

From a university's viewpoint, an institution-wide HRPP is headed by the chief research officer via authority delegated by the chief executive officer (the medical center director, in the VA system). Beyond that, the HRPP appears somewhat amorphous because of its decentralization. Various aspects of human-subjects protection fall under the purview of various committees or offices that report to the chief research officer, such as IRBs, radiation safety (for example diagnostic x-rays and radiation therapy), biosafety (for example, gene therapy), and conflicts of interest. In addition, academic programs may play a meaningful role. One less obvious example might be the statistics department, which might provide expertise in the design of a drug trial, a behavioral survey, or other experiment involving human subjects. In its broadest form, the HRPP also includes other high-level administrators, such as the provost and chief financial officer, who ultimately oversee faculty members (including those in clinical settings) and financial resources, respectively. To coordinate all of these activities and individuals into a cohesive and effective plan, many chief research officers establish a standing

HRPP committee; the directors of the various offices comprising the program (such as IRB chairs, biosafety officer, inter alia) sit ex officio on the committee.

The HRPP has become an integral part of most university Federalwide assurances. In that context, as well as the more explicit AAHRPP standards (Standard I-5), the HRPP must be evaluated regularly to ensure that it meets its goals effectively. According to AAHRPP: "The Organization measures and improves, when necessary, compliance with organizational policies and procedures and applicable laws, regulations, codes, and guidance. The Organization also measures and improves, when necessary, the quality, effectiveness, and efficiency of the Human Research Protection Program."[36]

Therefore, the chief research officer must develop an appropriate evaluation procedure. This entails regularly scheduled audits, surveys, and reviews. The university auditor can play a major role in this effort. Also, a professional evaluator may provide needed expertise and skills to ensure compliance with this standard. In addition, the VA requires HRPP accreditation; this is done by AAHRPP.

Stem-Cell Research

The federal government restricts any research that creates or destroys a human embryo. Those restrictions extend beyond the prima facie notion of creating Frankenstein-like creatures or committing some macabre act. These restrictions apply to research on stem cells, which lie at the core of modern regenerative medicine.

Stem cells are remarkable. They retain the capability to differentiate into any body part. And this capability can be controlled under laboratory conditions to repair tissue ravaged by disease or injury, test new drugs, and diagnose diseases. Thus, biomedical research using stem cells has mushroomed during the past decade. But all of this is not without serious controversy. Many people object quite strenuously on moral grounds to stem-cell research, and this has led to rigid oversight by federal agencies.

To understand the source of this controversy, it helps to trace stem cells through normal human development. After the female egg is penetrated by the male sperm, a single fertilized cell is formed. This single cell then divides into two, then into four, eight, sixteen, and so on. After about seven divisions, the resulting 128 cells are organized in a spherical body, known as the blastocyst, with an outer layer of cells that become the uterus and an inner cluster of about 100 cells, the "inner cell mass." These cells in the inner mass are the embryonic stem cells that ultimately differentiate into the wonderfully complex human embryo. But, full differentiation takes time. It takes about six weeks for brain-cell activity to appear, and as everybody knows, a full nine months before a baby takes its first breath of air.

The human embryonic stem cells (hESCs) used in biomedical research and clinical treatment are derived from embryos created clinically for in vitro fertilization.

In this procedure, which has been used routinely for many years, clinicians remove several eggs from a woman's body and fertilize them with the father's sperm in a laboratory setting. The fertilized eggs, which are now embryos, are allowed to divide several times, and then one is re-implanted into the woman's uterus, where it develops normally until birth. Usually, several eggs are fertilized in this way to ensure that at least one will survive in the laboratory for the re-implantation. The remaining embryos are frozen for ultimate disposal. Stem cells used in research are obtained from these frozen remaining, excess embryos that are destined for eventual disposal.

And that's where the debate begins. Some individuals assert that life begins at conception; therefore, they consider it immoral to destroy an intact embryo regardless of its origin. Other individuals avow that life begins at the first sign of electrical brain activity—six weeks after fertilization, if not later. Therefore, in their opinion it is perfectly reasonable to harvest the stem cells from leftover embryos from in vitro fertilization. And others believe that life begins at birth. The debate ends with the fundamental question: when does life begin? There is no universally accepted answer to that question.

Against this diverse backdrop of beliefs, the federal government regulates the use of human embryonic stem cells in research funded by NIH. The guidelines issued in 2009 begin with a defining assertion: "For the purpose of these Guidelines, 'human embryonic stem cells (hESCs)' are cells that are derived from the inner cell mass of blastocyst stage human embryos, are capable of dividing without differen-tiating for a prolonged period in culture, and are known to develop into cells and tissues of the three primary germ layers. Although hESCs are derived from embryos, such stem cells are not themselves human embryos."[37] This last point is critical and bears repeating: "stem cells are not themselves human embryos."

The regulations then continue to lay down guidelines pertaining to all federally funded human embryonic stem cell research. Basically, only cells from sources that have been approved by the NIH may be used if federal funding is involved. The NIH maintains a registry listing eligible cells.[38] If researchers develop a new human embryonic cell line that is not on the registry, they may not use these cells without prior NIH approval. To obtain this approval, the applicant must provide assurances that the cells were derived from human embryos that were "created using in vitro fertilization for reproductive purposes and were no longer needed for this purpose" and "donated by individuals who sought reproductive treat-ment . . . and who gave voluntary written consent for the human embryos to be used for research purposes."[39] The guidelines provide extensive informed-consent criteria to ensure that the donors' decisions to donate embryos for research had no influence on the in vitro fertilization treatment and that there was no financial quid pro quo. Applications to use cells obtained from foreign countries must meet these same standards.

Therefore, according to these guidelines, research involving human embryonic stem cells listed in the NIH registry may proceed without further NIH authorization, and federal funds may be used to support this research. However, if the human embryonic cell lines are not listed on the NIH registry, federal funds may not be used for any aspect of the project—not personnel, supplies, nor other expenses. That includes equipment acquired (even partially) with federal grant funds unless (and this is important) the grant has terminated and the university has retained unrestricted title to the items.

Significantly, none of these federal regulations applies to research funded from nonfederal sources. These NIH guidelines apply only if federal funds support the research project in any way. If the research is supported entirely by nonfederal funds, then human embryonic stem cells from any source may be used without the need for NIH approval. In these cases, most universities segregate research on the NIH nonapproved cells into a separate laboratory room where there are no items purchased using federal money. That may result in wasteful duplications, but it minimizes the risk of violating federal laws.

The NIH policy allows faculty and staff with portions of their salaries paid with federal funds to conduct human embryonic stem-cell research on cells not listed in the NIH registry during time that is uncommitted to federal projects. However, the salary portion allocated to this nonfederal effort and all other expenses must be paid using nonfederal money. For example, if an investigator receives 75 percent of his or her salary from the NIH, effort on a project using nonapproved human embryonic stem cells must not exceed 25 percent. As a corollary, faculty and staff members paid solely with federal funds are restricted from conducting any research involving cell lines not listed in the NIH registry.

Incidentally, stem-cell lines remain the property of the individual stem-cell providers, as listed on the NIH stem-cell registry. Therefore, researchers may need to negotiate their rights and responsibilities concerning resulting data, publications, and potential patents with the providers. The chief research officer should actively provide advice and counsel to university investigators in these negotiations to avert potential disagreements about these issues after research has begun.

There is an additional, potentially serious impediment to research using human embryonic stem cells. It derives from the so-called Dickey amendment. This is a rider that has been attached to an appropriation bill every year since 1995 that prohibits the use of NIH funds for the creation of human embryos for research purposes or for research in which human embryos are destroyed.[40] Thus, technically it precludes NIH funding for the derivation of stem cells from human embryos. However, the NIH has consistently interpreted this as not applicable to human embryonic stem cells because, according to their guidelines, stem cells "are not themselves human embryos." Furthermore, the NIH states that:

> This long-standing interpretation has been left unchanged by Congress, which has annually reenacted the Dickey Amendment with full knowledge that HHS [the Department of Health and Human Services] has been funding hESC research since 2001. These guidelines therefore recognize

the distinction, accepted by Congress, between the derivation of stem cells from an embryo that results in the embryo's destruction, for which federal funding is prohibited, and research involving hESCs that does not involve an embryo nor result in an embryo's destruction, for which federal funding is permitted.[41]

Proponents of human embryonic stem-cell research have sought to block the Dickey amendment, but so far they have not succeeded. Thus, this potential restriction remains on the horizon.

There are further restrictions on use of human embryonic stem cells derived from other sources, such as somatic nuclear transfer (a precursor to cloning), parthenogenesis (asexual reproduction), and in vitro fertilization embryos created solely for research purposes. In addition, human embryonic stem cells may not be transplanted into nonhuman primate blastocysts because they could possibly develop into a living hybrid organism. And, similarly, human embryonic stem cells may not be introduced to nonhuman animal germ cells (egg or sperm), again because of the potential for human-animal hybrids (also known as chimeras).

Between 2001 and 2009, federal regulations were far more rigid. They allowed federal funding of research using only about twenty-one suitable cell lines. To get around this crippling restriction, some states established their own (nonfederal) agencies to fund stem-cell research. The largest of these is the California Institute for Regenerative Medicine, which provides $3 billion in funding for stem-cell research at in-state institutions. Although federal oversight is not required, the State of California requires "that research involving the derivation and use of human embryonic stem cells, human embryonic germ cells, and human adult stem cells, including somatic cell nuclear transplantation, shall be reviewed by a stem cell research oversight committee."[42] Also, some universities launched special initiatives with nonfederal funds to support their human embryonic stem cell researchers. The most celebrated is WiCell, which was created in 1999 by the University of Wisconsin-Madison as a separate nonprofit organization to manage and distribute stem cells patented by the university. To ensure a complete separation of nonfederal and federal funds, WiCell is located off-campus.

Because of federal regulations and public sensitivity to the use of human embryonic stem cells, many universities have a stem cell research oversight (SCRO) committee. Typically, any research project involving the use of human embryonic stem cells must be approved by the committee prior to the project's beginning. The chief research officer or an associate research officer chairs this committee. Other members generally include faculty members familiar with stem-cell research, an ethicist, and somebody not associated with the university. Legal counsel may also serve on the committee. Note: if patients are not involved, research using human stem cells is exempt from IRB review.

Parenthetically, it should be noted that, because of the legal impediments and public concerns, alternatives to human embryonic stem cells are being actively pursued in the research community. In a major breakthrough, techniques for converting adult human cells, such as those derived from skin, to stem cells fully capable of differentiating into all different organs of the body were announced in 2007. These are called induced pluripotent stem cells (iPS cells), and they appear to possess most of the properties of stem cells derived from embryos. Not surprisingly, they have generated considerable excitement because this procedure sidesteps many of the NIH limitations and assuages public concerns about using embryonic tissue. Nonetheless, some restrictions remain, mainly those prohibiting the introduction of induced pluripotent stem cells into some nonhuman tissue.

> K: At the beginning you said that research using human subjects was the most scrutinized aspect of university research. I see what you mean.
>
> Smith: Yes, and we haven't covered all aspects of this. For example, we haven't even gotten into the Food and Drug Administration's guidelines for clinical trials.
>
> K: Shouldn't the chief research officer know about that?
>
> Smith: Yes. Clinical trials are part of the university's research mission. Fortunately for the chief research officer, most clinical trials are administered by medical schools, and they have well-trained personnel who ensure compliance with institutional and federal regulations.
>
> K: Are these clinical trial regulations different from what you've been discussing so far?
>
> Smith: Not really. There are a few technical additions, but by and large, all regulations come back to those ten basic principles in the Nuremberg Code as elaborated in the Belmont Report.

Notes

1. *Trials of War Criminals before the Nuremberg Military Tribunals under Control Council Law No. 10* (Washington, D.C.: U.S. Government Printing Office, 1949), pp. 181–82.
2. World Medical Association (WMA), "Declaration of Helsinki—Ethical Principles for Medical Research Involving Human Subjects," p. 1, 2008, http://www.wma.net/en/30publications/10policies/b3/17c.pdf (accessed January 12, 2011).
3. Ibid., p. 2.
4. Ibid., p. 4.
5. Department of Health, Education, and Welfare, National Commission for the Protection of Human Subjects of Biomedical and Behavioral Research, "The Belmont Report: Ethical Principles and Guidelines for the Protection of Human Subjects of Research," Part C.3, 1979, http://ohsr.od.nih.gov/guidelines/belmont.html (accessed January 12, 2011).
6. National Institutes of Health (NIH), "Guidelines for the Conduct of Research Involving Human Subjects at the National Institutes of Health," 2004, http://ohsr.od.nih.gov/guidelines/GrayBooklet82404.pdf (accessed January 12, 2011).
7. National Institutes of Health (NIH), "NIH Policy and Guidelines on the Inclusion of Women and Minorities as Subjects in Clinical Research–Amended, October, § II.A 2001, 2001," http://grants.nih.gov/grants/funding/women_min/guidelines_amended_10_2001.htm (accessed January 12, 2011).

8. National Institutes of Health (NIH), "NIH Policy and Guidelines on the Inclusion of Children As Participants in Research Involving Human Subjects," 1998, http://grants.nih.gov/grants/guide/notice-files/not98-024.html (accessed January 12, 2011).

9. National Institutes of Health (NIH), Protection of Human Subjects, 45 C.F.R. Part 46 (1991).

10. Ibid., § 46.103.b.(1).

11. Department of Health and Human Services, "Assurance Process – FAQs," http://answers.hhs.gov/ohrp/categories/1563 (accessed January 12, 2011).

12. Office for Civil Rights, U.S. Department of Health and Human Services, "HIPAA Administrative Simplification, Regulation Text 45 CFR Parts 160, 162, and 164," 2006, http://www.hhs.gov/ocr/privacy/hipaa/administrative/privacyrule/adminsimpregtext.pdf (accessed January 12, 2011).

13. Department of Health and Human Services, 45 C.F.R. Part 46, § 46.107.a. (2011).

14. Office for Human Research Protections (OHRP), Department of Health and Human Services, "International Compilation of Human Research Protections," 2011, http://www.hhs.gov/ohrp/international/intlcompilation/hspcompilation-v20101130.pdf (accessed January 12, 2011).

15. Western Institutional Review Board, "History of WIRB," 2010, http://www.wirb.com/content/about_history.aspx (accessed January 12, 2011).

16. Veterans Health Administration (VHA), "Requirements for the Protection of Human Subjects in Research," *VHA Handbook 1200.05* (Washington, D.C.: Department of Veterans Affairs, 2010), p. 15.

17. U.S. Congress, House Energy and Commerce Committee, "Institutional Review Boards that Oversee Experimental Human Testing for Profit," 2009, http://democrats.energycommerce.house.gov/Press_111/20090326/stupak_open.pdf (accessed January 12, 2011).

18. Ibid.

19. Ibid.

20. Association for the Accreditation of Human Research Protection Programs (AAHRPP), "Who Is Eligible for Accreditation?" 2011, http://www.aahrpp.org/www.aspx?PageID=15 (accessed January 13, 2011).

21. Ibid.

22. Association for the Accreditation of Human Research Protection Programs (AAHRPP), "The Benefits of Accreditation," 2011, http://www.aahrpp.org/www.aspx?PageID=12 (accessed January 13, 2011).

23. Ibid.

24. Pfizer, Inc., "IRB Accountability," p. 2, 2009, http://media.pfizer.com/files/research/research_clinical_trials/IRB_Accountability.pdf (accessed January 13, 2011).

25. Public Responsibility in Medicine and Research (PRIM&R), "Certified IRB Professional (CIP) Eligibility," 2010, http://www.primr.org/Certification.aspx?id=234&ekmensel=c580fa7b_48_80_234_2 (accessed January 13, 2011).

26. Council for Certification of IRB Professionals, "Recertification Guidelines for Certified IRB Professionals (CIP)," p. 2, 2006, http://www.primr.org/uploadedFiles/PRIMR_Site_Home/Certification/CIP/CIPRecertbyContinuingEdPacket.pdf (accessed January 13, 2011).

27. Collaborative Institutional Training Initiative (CITI), "Home," https://www.citiprogram.org/Default.asp (accessed January 13, 2011).

28. National Institutes of Health (NIH), "Protection of Human Subjects: Categories of Research That May Be Reviewed by the Institutional Review Board (IRB) Through an Expedited Review Procedure," *Federal Register*, 63, no. 216 (1998): 60364–67.

29. Office for Human Research Protections (OHRP), Department of Health and Human Services, "Guidance for Investigators and Institutional Review Boards Regarding Research Involving Human Embryonic Stem Cells, Germ Cells and Stem Cell-Derived Test Articles," p. 3, 2002, http://www.hhs.gov/ohrp/policy/stemcell.pdf (accessed January 13, 2011).

30. Office for Human Research Protections (OHRP), Department of Health and Human Services, "Issues to Consider in the Research Use of Stored Data or Tissues," 1997, http://www.hhs.gov/ohrp/policy/reposit.html (accessed January 13, 2011).

31. Ibid.

32. Veterans Health Administration (VHA), "Requirements," p. 5.
33. Association for the Accreditation of Human Research Protection Programs (AAHRPP), "Domain I: Organization," 2010, http://www.aahrpp.org/www.aspx?PageID=318 (accessed January 13, 2011).
34. Ibid.
35. VHA, "Requirements," p. 5.
36. AAHRPP, "Domain I."
37. National Institutes of Health (NIH), "National Institutes of Health Guidelines on Human Stem Cell Research," *Federal Register*, 74, no. 128 (2009): 32170–75.
38. National Institutes of Health (NIH), "NIH Human Embryonic Stem Cell Registry," 2011, http://grants.nih.gov/stem_cells/registry/current.htm (accessed January 13, 2011).
39. NIH, "NIH Guidelines," p. 32171.
40. Omnibus Appropriations Act 2009, Public Law No. 111-8, Division F, Title V, § 509, 123 Stat. 524, 803, 111th Cong., 1st sess. (March 11, 2009).
41. NIH, "NIH Guidelines," p. 32173.
42. State of California, SCRO Committee Review and Notification, 17 CA ADC § 100070 (2010).

CHAPTER 13

Animal Use and Care

K: Are the regulations covering animals in research as stringent as those for humans?

Smith: Not yet. But they've become a lot more rigorous during the past several years.

K: I've read about violent protests by opponents of research using animals.

Smith: Yes, there have been some explosive confrontations. Emotions can be quite volatile in this regard. And the chief research officer is drawn right into the middle of these situations.

Sources of Animals

To appreciate the culture and history of legislation regarding the welfare of research animals in the United States, it helps to know a priori where the animals come from. Laboratory animals are "big business." Roughly 20 or 30 million animals (mostly mice and rats) are used annually. Popular lore has them coming from unscrupulous dealers who snatch beloved pet dogs and cats from backyards, neighborhood streets, and overfilled animal shelters such as the Humane Society. Or it is thought they come from breeding colonies like puppy mills, where dogs are bred with one goal in mind—selling them for a profit to a medical research laboratory. Are these anecdotes true? To a small extent, yes. That sums up, in overly brutal terms, where research animals come from. But there's much more to the story.

Jumping ahead a bit, it should be noted that federal legislation requires all suppliers of research animals to hold a license issued by the U.S. Department of Agriculture (USDA). Research animal breeders and suppliers fall into two license classes: A and B. Class A includes breeders "whose business involving animals consists only of animals that are bred and raised on the premises in a closed or stable colony and those animals acquired for the sole purpose of maintaining or enhancing the breeding colony."[1] These animals are called "purpose bred" or "colony bred;" they are born and raised under controlled conditions for one purpose—research. Most (about 75 percent) research animals are purpose bred.

One reason is that they can be bred with specific characteristics achieved through selective breeding and genetic engineering. These animals, ranging from mice and rats to dogs and cats to large farm animals, are available from numerous commercial suppliers. Incidentally, individuals who sell fewer than twenty-five purpose-bred dogs or cats per year are exempt from these licensing requirements.

Class B is for dealers "whose business includes the purchase and/or resale of any animal. This term includes brokers, and operators of an auction sale, as such individuals negotiate or arrange for the purchase, sale, or transport of animals in commerce. Such individuals do not usually take actual physical possession or control of the animals, and do not usually hold animals in any facilities."[2] So, class B dealers are really brokers; they don't breed animals, they acquire and then resell them. The animals are often obtained from city or county animal shelters. Thus, they are called "random source" animals. Random-source animals generally cost less than purpose-bred animals, and they do not come from genetically defined breeding stock. From that perspective, a main virtue of random-source animals is their genetic diversity, which is desirable in some biomedical experiments. For the record, purpose- and random-bred dogs currently (2011) cost about $500 and $100, respectively.

Because they deal with random-source animals, class B dealers have historically attracted public attention as potential thieves of household pets. And there have been notorious cases of illicit acquisitions. However, to thwart pet theft, class B dealers may not legally obtain dogs and cats from unlicensed individuals who did not breed and raise the animal on their own premises. However, there is always the possibility that a pet may somehow land in an animal shelter (via a dogcatcher, for example) and then be acquired by a class B dealer before the owner can retrieve it. To minimize the possibility of this scenario, in 1990, Congress passed a pet-protection law that requires facilities such as animal shelters and dealers to wait between five and ten days before selling an animal for research purposes. Specifically, the animal shelter "shall hold and care for such dog or cat for a period of not less than five days to enable such dog or cat to be recovered by its original owner or adopted by other individuals before such entity sells such dog or cat to a dealer."[3] Moreover, the facilities and dealers must mark every animal with some means of identification and keep thorough records of its disposition.

Despite these legal protections, a cloud of suspicion lingers over class B dealers. These suspicions are fueled by occasional high-profile arrests of dealers who allegedly flout federal regulations. And these cases ultimately catalyzed federal animal-welfare legislation.

The Cultural Context

Unlike public opinion about the use of humans in research, attitudes about animals in research have been in a state of flux during the past forty years. In the case of human subjects in research, the governing principles were established during the Nuremberg trials, and there have been no major changes since then. In sharp contrast, the governing principles for the care and use of animals in research have been evolving at a fast rate—at least in the United States. The major piece of legislation, the Animal Welfare Act,[4] has been amended six times and may be amended again during the lifetime of this book. Furthermore, the guidelines for implementing the provisions of this act have been revised off and on. These changes reflect the rapid evolution of public attitudes toward animals in general.

Two axioms underlie current attitudes toward research using animals. The first goes back to the dawn of Judeo-Christian culture: animals serve human needs. This stems from Genesis 1:26, "Then God said, 'Let us make man in our image, after our likeness; and let them have dominion over the fish of the sea, and over the birds of the air, and over the cattle, and over all the earth, and over every creeping thing that creeps upon the earth.'" Subsequent philosophers such as Aristotle, St. Thomas Aquinas, and Descartes built on this notion that animals are subservient to humans, and most people in Western society embrace it today. The second axiom is that animals are sentient; they feel pain. Or, to put it another way, if something is uncomfortable to humans, it must presumably be uncomfortable to animals. Although the exact threshold for animal pain remains somewhat elusive, few individuals disagree with the assertion that animals—at least mammals—feel pain.

Based on these two axioms, public sentiment against the mistreatment of beasts of burden ultimately resulted in laws prohibiting the abuse of domestic animals (mainly, horses, cows, and sheep) in Western societies, including all fifty states, beginning with the Massachusetts Colony in 1641.[5] According to these early laws, animals are just animals, but at least they should be treated with compassion—that is, as long as they serve human needs, including comfort, entertainment, food, and companionship. These animals include horses, cows, sheep, dogs, and cats. Other animals, such as mice, rats, opossums, snakes, coyotes, and so forth don't usually count in this reckoning.

The passage of federal laws regulating the humane care and use of animals lagged far behind these more local ordinances. Ironically, the most vociferous opposition to federal legislation regulating animal care and use came from the biomedical research community. Prominent scientific societies lobbied strongly against federal regulations. Their main concern was that progress in medical research would be slowed considerably if access to research animals such as cats, dogs, and nonhuman primates (mainly monkeys and chimpanzees) were restricted or, at worst, prohibited. They would claim, "It's your dog's health or your child's health. Which will it be?" But times change. Ultimately, their attention shifted from federal regulations governing the humane use and care of research animals to the need for federal protection from those violently opposed to any use of animals in research.

The first major piece of federal legislation was the Laboratory Animal Welfare Act of 1966. Despite the title, the law concentrated heavily on the buying, selling, and transport of animals used in not only research but also in exhibitions such as zoos and circuses. The major impetus for this legislation came from two highly publicized reports of animal abuse by dog dealers in 1965 and 1966. The first was a *Life* magazine story, "Concentration Camps for Dogs," that featured shocking photographs of emaciated dogs awaiting an uncertain fate.[6] *Life* purportedly received more mail on "Concentration Camps for Dogs" than any story in the history of the magazine—more letters than *Life* got on the Vietnam War.[7] The second story concerned Pepper, a Dalmatian dog, whose picture appeared in a local Pennsylvania newspaper after it and seventeen other dogs (and two goats) were unloaded from a dog dealer's truck. Pepper's owner saw the picture while lying in a hospital bed recovering from a heart attack. Before the dog could be located and retrieved, it was euthanized on the operating table in a New York medical research laboratory. These two stories propelled congressional action.

> K: *I'm surprised that biomedical researchers would argue against regulations for the humane treatment of research animals. Don't they rely on healthy animals for their research?*
>
> Smith: *Yes, of course they do. It's difficult to trust research results obtained from unhealthy animals. But the root issue wasn't health. It was the availability of research animals.*
>
> K: *Animals like dogs and pigs are used routinely in medical school teaching. Was there a concern about the use of animals in teaching, as well?*
>
> Smith: *Indirectly. Public sentiment against the use of animals in research was so strong that many medical-school educators worried that the animal dealers would be shut down, thus cutting off supplies of dogs and cats for teaching and research.*

Welfare Legislation for Research Animals

Although several Western countries had laws prohibiting abuse to domestic animals for centuries, the seminal law promoting the humane treatment of animals explicitly in research was enacted in Britain during the nineteenth century. The so-called Cruelty to Animals Act, 1876, states that "A person shall not perform on a living animal any experiment calculated to give pain, except subject to the restrictions imposed by this Act." The first four restrictions of this document convey the spirit of this and most subsequent legislation:[8]

> (1) The experiment must be performed with a view to the advancement by new discovery of physiological knowledge or of knowledge which will be useful for saving or prolonging life or alleviating suffering; and
>
> (2) The experiment must be performed by a person holding such license from one of Her Majesty's Principal Secretaries of State in this Act

referred to as the Secretary of State, as is in this Act mentioned, and in the case of a person holding such conditional license as is herein-after mentioned, or of experiments performed for the purpose of instruction in a registered place; and

(3) The animal must during the whole of the experiment be under the influence of some anaesthetic of sufficient power to prevent the animal feeling pain; and

(4) The animal must, if the pain is likely to continue after the effect of the anaesthetic has ceased, or if any serious injury has been inflicted on the animal, be killed before it recovers from the influence of the anaesthetic which has been administered

In short, the act imposed restrictions on any experiment calculated to cause pain. Only licensed individuals may perform experiments that cause pain. Moreover, the animal must be anesthetized during the experiment and, as a matter of compassion, killed if the pain is expected to continue after the anesthesia wears off. Importantly, the experiments must be designed to generate new medical knowledge or to confirm the results of previous experiments "alleged" to "be useful for saving or prolonging life or alleviating suffering." They cannot be frivolous exhibitions of animal physiology or anatomy.

It took another ninety years for the United States to pass similar legislation—namely, the 1966 Laboratory Animal Welfare Act. Subsequently, the name was simplified to the Animal Welfare Act, as it is known today. The act originally applied to research animals that were bought or sold by dealers for research purposes. Furthermore, the animals had to cross state lines. However, the original act has been extensively amended, usually during the five-year reauthorizations of the Farm Bill, to broaden its impact. Among other things, the need to cross state lines has been eliminated, which expanded the reach of the law. Although the original bill covered animals housed on the dealer's premises or in laboratories, coverage was amended subsequently to include the animal's entire laboratory stay. Significantly (certainly for the chief research officer), an amendment included in the Food Security Act of 1985 (also called The Improved Standards for Laboratory Animals Act) significantly extended the law's coverage of animal housing and psychological well-being. It also contained provisions aimed at reducing unnecessary duplicative animal research experimentation.[9]

Before going ahead, an important question must be answered: in the eyes of the law what is an animal? The British Cruelty to Animals Act applies specifically to dog, cat, horse, ass, and mule. Ambiguously, it also refers to animals "similar in constitution and habits to a cat or dog" but does not mention any species in that category. Presumably, mice and rats do not fall into that category. Explicitly, "This Act shall not apply to invertebrate animals." The United States Animal Welfare Act applies to dead or living dogs, cats, nonhuman primates, guinea pigs, hamsters, rabbits, marine mammals (such as dolphins), and all "warm-blooded animals" used in research. "All warm-blooded animals" would seem to be an all-inclusive term for birds and mammals.

However, there is a catch; the law explicitly excludes "(1) birds, rats of the genus *Rattus* [the basic laboratory rat], and mice of the genus *Mus* [the basic laboratory mouse], bred for use in research, (2) horses not used for research purposes, and (3) other farm animals, such as, but not limited to livestock or poultry, used or intended for use as food or fiber [for example, beef cattle and woolly sheep, respectively], or livestock or poultry used or intended for use for improving animal nutrition, breeding, management, or production efficiency, or for improving the quality of food or fiber."[10] Only farm animals used explicitly for biomedical research are covered.

Excluding those species is very important for research. Rats and mice are used routinely in modern biomedical research, and livestock and poultry are commonplace at an agricultural college. Why are they exempt? As usual, the answer can be found by following the dollar. Laboratory research uses so many mice and rats that universities argue that the cost of implementing animal-welfare regulations for these animals would impose an unbearable financial burden. And the Department of Agriculture claims that it does not have the necessary personnel to enforce regulations on these species.

The Animal Welfare Act names the Department of Agriculture (USDA) as the implementing and enforcing agency. Through the Animal and Plant Health Inspection Service (APHIS), they published highly detailed regulations.[11] These cover issues such as cage size, feeding regimens, number of animal care employees, and facility cleanliness. The chief research officer seldom becomes involved at this level of exhaustive detail. However, he or she will be held accountable if something goes wrong.

The USDA is required to inspect each facility at least once a year to ensure regulatory compliance, and these inspections can be unannounced. Significant deficiencies usually trigger more frequent unscheduled inspections. Normally, universities are allowed a limited amount of time to correct a violation. However, if conditions are not rectified within a reasonable time, the USDA can fine the institution or close the facility. Even chipped paint on the floor can lead to a fine of thousands of dollars. Thus, the chief research officer should be familiar with at least the level of detail required for full compliance and provide adequate support for animal care staff in their compliance efforts. Indeed, APHIS regulations require the facility to have appropriate facilities, personnel, equipment, and services to ensure proper veterinary care.

At the time (1966), there was some controversy over naming the USDA as the Animal Welfare Act enforcement agency. Why not the Public Health Service (PHS), which includes NIH, since most research animals were used in biomedical fields? The publicly stated reason is that the USDA already had a well-developed team of veterinarians in service nationwide who could readily enforce the law's provisions. Nonetheless, in 1971, the PHS, via the NIH, promulgated its own "Policy for

Humane Care and Use of Laboratory Animals,"[12] which essentially placed the provisions of the Animal Welfare Act in a biomedical research setting. Additionally, as public concerns about the use and care of research animals mounted, the federal government established an Interagency Research Animal Committee that included representatives from numerous federal departments (such as NIH, NSF, the Departments of Agriculture, State, and Interior). In 1985, they produced another defining document, the *U.S. Government Principles for the Utilization and Care of Vertebrate Animals Used in Testing, Research, and Training,*[13] again derived indirectly from the basic tenets of the seminal British Cruelty to Animals Act.

Several months later, Congress passed another law, the Health Research Extension Act of 1985, mandating that all institutions receiving PHS (including NIH, CDC, and FDA) research funds abide by the *U.S. Government Principles.*[14] The NIH Office of Laboratory Animal Welfare (OLAW) is now responsible for implementing and enforcing the regulations; their guidelines are documented in the *PHS Guide for the Care and Use of Laboratory Animals*, commonly referred to as *The Guide*.[15] The PHS policy requires that institutions base their programs of animal care and use on these guidelines. Importantly, they must also comply with the APHIS regulations under the Animal Welfare Act; indeed, compliance with the USDA regulations is an absolute requirement regardless of source of funding.

There are several differences between the PHS and the APHIS (USDA) regulations, but the basic guidelines are generally similar to those of the Animal Welfare Act. A particularly significant difference is that the PHS legislation extends coverage to all vertebrates, including mice, rats, and birds. Furthermore, the PHS guidelines address the use of farm animals, "nontraditional species" (such as armadillos), and wild animals (such as coyotes) used in biomedical research. In these cases, the basic guidelines apply, but they may be modified in case-specific instances.

Although the Animal Welfare Act is the common defining document governing the use and care of animals in research, the existence of PHS- and USDA-specific legislation opened the door to potentially burdensome and confusing enforcement and reporting requirements. To simplify matters, three agencies, APHIS (USDA), the FDA (PHS), and the NIH (PHS) crafted a memorandum of understanding designed to create a "mutually shared perspective on acceptable standards of laboratory animal care."[16] In addition, they agreed to share with each other information about cases of noncompliance and to coordinate "successive evaluations." In other words, if APHIS identified a violation, they shared this finding with the other two agencies. That, of course, raised the stakes as far as the institution (and, therefore, the chief research officer) was concerned, for it raised the prospect of double or even triple jeopardy.

Parenthetically, other federal agencies, such as the Department of Defense, also have agency-specific guidelines. They may differ in minor ways from the APHIS or PHS policy, but ultimately they must all adhere to the tenets of the Animal Welfare Act.

To receive PHS support, an institution must file with OLAW a document that describes its procedures for complying with PHS animal care and use policy—the so-called Animal Welfare Assurance. And OLAW must approve it prior to any grant awards. Moreover, the institution (usually the chief executive officer) must appoint an individual who has the authority to act on behalf of the institution to sign this assurance; this person is called the "institutional official." Often, the chief research officer fills this role, or he or she may delegate this further to a senior member of an animal-care facility management team. Although it is permissible by law, the chief executive officer ought not to serve as the institutional official. He or she seldom has the time needed to fill this role. Regardless of who serves as institutional official, the chief research officer commonly oversees preparation of the assurance and its filing.

An approved OLAW-approved assurance grants the university the right to enforce its own compliance with the Animal Welfare Act. This right is known as "enforced self-regulation." The institution has been granted the opportunity to regulate itself, which is generally welcomed. But, if it fails to self-regulate, the approval of the assurance may be restricted or withdrawn by OLAW. Thus, OLAW enforces self-regulation.

Ultimately, there are three main components of the Animal Welfare Act that regulate the treatment of research animals from a university perspective. First, the law calls for the secretary of the Department of Agriculture to establish minimum requirements "for handling, housing, feeding, watering, sanitation, ventilation, shelter from extremes of weather and temperatures, adequate veterinary care, and separation by species where the Secretary finds necessary for humane handling, care, or treatment of animals" and "for exercise of dogs, as determined by an attending veterinarian in accordance with general standards promulgated by the Secretary, and for a physical environment adequate to promote the psychological well-being of primates."[17]

These standards, which were introduced in the 1985 amendment by the only veterinarian in Congress, Senator John Melcher (D-Montana), initially disconcerted chief research officers and their animal-care staff. The main challenge was to create a physical environment to "promote the psychological well-being of primates." They asked, "How do we know what a primate likes?" Some primates, such as the owl monkey, become quite excitable when anybody disturbs them. The thought was, "Just leave them alone in a bare cage." Others, such as rhesus monkeys, seem to enjoy trees and other things to swing on. Failure to provide legally acceptable accommodations for any of these primate species could have serious financial and legal consequences for the university—and the chief research officer would be held accountable. Nonetheless, the law is the law, so principal investigators and animal-care staff have tried conscientiously to comply with these federal regulations.

The second major component, which is modeled after the seminal British Cruelty to Animals Act, mandates the setting of standards for minimizing pain "with the appropriate use of anesthetic, analgesic, tranquilizing drugs, or euthanasia."[18] Moreover, it requires the principal investigator to consider "alternatives to any procedure likely to produce pain to or distress in an experimental animal."[19] As a final note, no animal may be "used in more than one major operative experiment from which it is allowed to recover except in cases of scientific necessity."[20] This last requirement—only "one major operative experiment" per animal—was received with some consternation from primate researchers, who contended that some animals (which are quite expensive, by the way) could undergo more than one operation without undue discomfort. Fortunately, the law allows exceptions to this and most other regulations if there are compelling reasons.

Institutional Animal Care and Use Committee

The third major component of the Animal Welfare Act of great significance to universities is the requirement for each research facility to establish an institutional committee to oversee animal care and use. In the APHIS guidelines, this committee is called the institutional animal care and use committee (IACUC), and this is the name used in most universities. According to the Act, the committee members "shall be appointed by the Chief Executive Officer of the research facility and shall be composed of not fewer than three members."[21] Some universities delegate this appointment authority to the chief research officer; that is allowable under the law. Alternatively, the chief research officer may recommend a list of members to the chief executive officer, who then signs the formal appointment letter. These IACUC committees, which may go by some variation on this name at various universities, play a pivotal role in compliance with federal regulations governing research animals.

The IACUC membership and responsibilities are spelled out in considerable detail in the Animal Welfare Act. Further details are provided in both the APHIS and the PHS guidelines, which vary in only minor ways. According to the Act, members "shall possess sufficient ability to assess animal care, treatment, and practices in experimental research as determined by the needs of the research facility and shall represent society's concerns regarding the welfare of animal subjects used at such facility."[22] Committee membership is rigidly defined in statute. The committee must include a doctor of veterinary medicine, an individual representing community interests in the proper care and treatment of animals who is not affiliated in any way (for example, through immediate family members) with the university, and no more than three members from the same administrative unit (such as a department) within the university.

The IACUC has the responsibility to review and approve procedures for mitigating pain and distress associated with experimentation and to inspect housing facilities twice a year for compliance with the provisions of the Animal Welfare Act. In addition, it has the requisite authority to "Review, approve, require modifications in, or withhold approval of proposed activities related to the care and use of animals" and "to suspend an activity involving animals if that activity is not being conducted in accordance with the activities approved by the IACUC."[23] The IACUC reports to the institutional official and has statutory authority to make recommendations to the institutional official regarding any aspect of the research facility's animal program, facilities, or personnel training opportunities. All in all, the IACUC has powerful control over what can and cannot be done with animals in the university's research setting. Communications between the IACUC and the federal government (for example, APHIS or OLAW) are through the institutional official.

The IACUC—via the institutional official—must file an "inspection certification report" following each inspection. Also, the institutional official must report ad hoc any deviations from its assurance, any IACUC-imposed suspensions, or other issues of noncompliance that come to his or her attention. But to whom should they report—APHIS or OLAW? Or, for that matter, which of the eleven different oversight offices, if the project is funded by the Department of Defense, should be contacted? This question calls for a clear answer, but none is available. If the issue involves an animal covered by the Animal Welfare Act, then APHIS should be contacted. Officially, this must be in writing. However, from a practical point, the institutional official should also discuss the case by telephone initially to seek guidance about the nature of the report. Since any animal covered by APHIS regulations is also covered by the PHS guidelines, OLAW should also be contacted; again, it is advisable to telephone first to determine whether the report should be filed. Technically, the interagency memorandum of understanding should guarantee that calling just one agency (for example, APHIS or OLAW) is sufficient; that agency will communicate the report to the other agencies. Nonetheless, to be on the safe side, most institutional officials contact both APHIS and OLAW.

Usually, universities hire professional office staff to coordinate IACUC activities. The number of employees, of course, depends on the number of protocols that need to be reviewed. In larger universities, IACUC record-keeping can be quite a daunting task. Among other things, the office usually sends renewal reminders to investigators, receives new and renewal applications, assigns reviewers (from the IACUC membership), prepares the requisite reports to the federal agencies, and performs other administrative chores. To lighten this workload, several commercial firms market software products that automate some of these tasks.

Veterinary Care

The Animal Welfare Act prescribes "adequate veterinary care" for research animals. Thus, APHIS regulations dictate that "Each research facility shall have an attending veterinarian who shall provide adequate veterinary care to its animals."[24] This individual may be part time, but at minimum a well-documented plan for regular veterinary care, including facility visits, must be established. In addition, the attending veterinarian must be vested with the authority "to ensure the provision of adequate veterinary care and to oversee the adequacy of other aspects of animal care and use."[25] And the law stipulates that the veterinarian has adequate resources, including personnel, to provide proper care. The IACUC must include one veterinarian on its roster. Often the attending veterinarian fills this role.

From a practical point, many universities that do not have a school of veterinary medicine retain only the required attending veterinarian. This can lead to some rather interesting situations for the chief research officer. For example, if the university has a polo, equestrian, or rodeo team, the attending veterinarian is often consulted about animal (in this case, horse) health problems. And this, therefore, draws the chief research officer into the picture. Likewise, if the university athletic teams have an animal mascot, such as a dog, goat, horse, or bird of prey, the veterinarian and, therefore the chief research officer, become de facto responsible for its health and well-being. Furthermore, the veterinarian must oversee the health care of animals used in teaching. This expanded responsibility for nonresearch animals is very loosely coupled to authority. The administrative authority for these other programs most probably resides with the provost or the dean of students. Fortunately, these situations seldom provide more than an interesting episode in the overall animal care and use workday.

As a side note, in earlier days, the attending veterinarian may also have served as the institutional official. However, to maintain an effective system of checks and balances, this is no longer permissible. Likewise, the attending veterinarian should not also be the IACUC chair, although this is not specifically prohibited by the regulations.

Training

The Animal Welfare Act requires institutions to provide training opportunities to all researchers working with animals. Therefore, the APHIS stipulates that: "It shall be the responsibility of the research facility to ensure that all scientists, research technicians, animal technicians, and other personnel involved in animal care, treatment, and use are qualified to perform their duties. This responsibility shall be fulfilled in part through the provision of training and instruction to those personnel."[26] According to the regulations, training and instruction of personnel must include guidance in the humane methods of animal maintenance and experimentation, including the basic needs of each species in the facility. The training must cover proper handling and care for the various species of animals used; pre-procedural and post-procedural care of animals; use of anesthetics, analgesics, and tranquilizers for any species of animals used; and aseptic surgical methods and procedures. Furthermore, it must include education in the "concept, availability, and use of research or testing methods that limit the use of animals or minimize animal distress."[27] Information on alternatives to the use of live animals in research and other ways to "prevent unintended and unnecessary duplication of research involving animals" must also be provided as part of the institutional training program.[28]

This is a pretty thorough training mandate. In fact, it sets the required curriculum. And it applies to all individuals, ranging from animal-cage washers to principal investigators. The only individuals eligible for an exception to these training requirements are licensed veterinarians, and only the IACUC may grant these exceptions. Notably, PHS policy has similar requirements that include "training or instruction in research or testing methods that minimize the number of animals required to obtain valid results and minimize animal distress."[29] Moreover, institutional assurance must document the institution's training program for the care and use of animals in PHS-conducted or supported activities.

Consequently, universities insist that those planning to work with animals, either as a care giver or a researcher, must take a formally scheduled training course. Furthermore, they must pass the course, thus becoming certified, before working with animals. Individuals without this certification, including students in a classroom setting, may only work or observe under the direct supervision of a certified animal user. Some universities also allow exceptions to individuals who use animals in their research but do not personally handle them. A prime example would be a researcher who raises antibodies in rabbits; if all experimental procedures (injections and so forth) are done by certified animal-care staff, then the researcher may not need to be certified.

The training curriculum must adhere to the federal guidelines. Furthermore, specific training must be provided for special cases, such as animal surgeries and marine mammal birthing. At many universities, the actual course is developed in-house by the IACUC, the attending veterinarian, and the animal-care staff. In addition, several private organizations offer animal care and use courses. Two examples are the American Association for Laboratory Animal Science (AALAS) and the Laboratory Animal Training Association.[30] They provide certification opportunities for universities that prefer not to develop their own course.

To be thorough, one additional requirement that affects the chief research officer must be mentioned. PHS policy requires institutions to offer an occupational health and safety program to protect animal-care staff and researchers from animal-borne health hazards. According to the *Guide for the Care and Use of Laboratory Animals*, "An occupational health and safety program must be part of the overall animal care and use program. . . . The program will depend on the facility, research activities, hazards, and animal species involved."[31] Moreover, an effective occupational health and safety program must encompass all personnel that have contact with animals. The program should include initial medical evaluations, necessary tests and vaccinations, and adequate training in the hazards and safeguards associated with the job. In addition, most universities provide routine medical examinations for these employees. Although this program may be administered by an environmental health and safety office, the chief research officer usually pays for it.

Accreditation

A single recognized association dominates accreditation of institutions that use research animals—namely, the Association for Assessment and Accreditation of Laboratory Animal Care International (AAALAC). Since its founding in 1965, this private, nonprofit organization has become a prominent component of a university's animal-care program. Indeed, considerable institutional effort and resources are devoted to achieving and maintaining AAALAC accreditation—not to mention the associated fees payable to AAALAC, which range from $5,000 to $10,000 annually. Most universities tout full AAALAC accreditation as positive evidence of their adherence to all federal regulations regarding research animals.

AAALAC uses the *Guide for the Care and Use of Laboratory Animals* as its primary standard for evaluating animal care facilities and programs. This includes not only laboratory animals, such as mice, rats, dogs, and cats, but also farm animals used for biomedical research. In addition, they adhere to the standards set in the *Guide for the Care and Use of Agricultural Animals in Agricultural Research and Teaching* published by the Federation of Animal Science Societies for farm animals used in agricultural research.[32] Formal site visits occur every three years.

Federal agencies such as APHIS and the PHS formally recognize AAALAC accreditation in their policies. For example, the PHS classifies animal-care facilities in two different categories, 1 and 2. Category 1 includes those "accredited by the Association for Assessment and Accreditation of Laboratory Animal Care International (AAALAC). All of the institution's programs and facilities (including satellite facilities) for activities involving animals have been evaluated and accredited by AAALAC." Furthermore, "all of the institution's programs and facilities (including satellite facilities) for activities involving animals have also been evaluated by the IACUC and will be reevaluated by the IACUC at least once every six months."[33] In a footnote, they add that AAALAC is the only accrediting body recognized by PHS. Category 2 includes facilities "evaluated by the Institution. All of the institution's programs and facilities (including satellite facilities) for activities involving animals have been evaluated by the IACUC and will be reevaluated by the IACUC at least once every six months."[34] The only difference between the two categories is AAALAC accreditation; IACUC evaluation is required every six months in both categories. In their reports to OLAW, the IACUC must document which facilities are AAALAC accredited. But the policy does not mention any further consequence to accreditation.

So, if the frequency of IACUC evaluation is the same for both categories, what is the practical advantage of AAALAC accreditation? This is another one of those questions with an elusive answer. Of course, there is the public relations aspect;

it looks good. This may be particularly beneficial with private foundations that might preferentially support an AAALAC-accredited institution—all else being equal. Indeed, several major foundations, such as the American Heart Association, recommend that its grantee institutions have AAALAC accreditation. More stringently, the Department of Defense (DoD) requires AAALAC accreditation for its grantees. "DoD organizations or facilities maintaining animals for use in research, testing or training shall apply for accreditation by the American Association for Accreditation of Laboratory Animal Care (AAALAC)."[35] And a copy of an AAALAC letter confirming the institution's accreditation must be submitted with a DoD grant application that proposes research using animals. Neither the USDA nor NIH has such rigid requirements, although they both encourage AAALAC accreditation in their policies.

Some universities mandate the need for AAALAC accreditation. For example, the University of California system requires full accreditation for its member campuses. Thus, they have no choice in the matter. On the other hand, some universities conscientiously forgo full AAALAC accreditation because of the cost and impracticality of meeting the standards, usually in their farm operations. Also, AAALAC may accredit some but not all of a university's "accreditable units."[36] What does that mean? A university may have separate animal resource centers in each of several different colleges or schools, such as the college of agriculture, the medical school, the veterinary school, or a remotely located farm operation. Each can be an accreditable unit. Thus, to invent an example, the medical school but not the agriculture college may be accredited. In that example, the university would not have "full" AAALAC accreditation.

Taking all of this into account, should the chief research officer encourage his or her university to achieve full AAALAC accreditation? Definitely, yes. The advantages far outweigh the disadvantages. As public attitudes toward the use of animals in research evolve, the university should take every measure to demonstrate its willingness—*desire* may be a better word—to provide humane care and treatment of its experimental animals. Furthermore, the chief research officer should collaborate with the public relations office to ensure widespread publicity about the institution's AAALAC accreditation.

The Animal Rights Movement

The use of animals in research has never been universally accepted as morally permissible. Well back into the nineteenth century, anti-vivisectionists protested the surgical procedures on live research animals. In more recent years, opposition has expanded from vivisection per se to far more general use of animals in research. And, as the number of animals used in research has increased dramatically in the past thirty years, so has the number of opponents grown considerably.

The underlying philosophical issue has also evolved. Ultimately, it goes back to the question about whether animals are property under the dominion of humans. A corollary question is whether humans and animals differ in their fundamental rights. For that matter, the notion of animal "rights" has been marginalized. With what authority can a human assign rights to an animal? As Peter Singer asserts in his influential book *Animal Liberation*, the issue is not about "rights;" it is about "interests."[37] The interests of humans and animals should be considered equally. Pain should not be inflicted on a human because it is not in that person's best interest. Likewise, if an animal can suffer (which most people accept), then inflicting pain or suffering violates the animal's best interests—as it would in the case of humans. It goes beyond that, though. Humans may defend themselves against somebody who intends to harm them. If a human such as a small child is incapable of mounting a defense, another human may provide a defense on his or her behalf. Because animals cannot reasonably defend themselves against humans, it follows that humans may provide a defense on an animal's behalf.

On the basis of this reasoning, activists justify actions to defend animals in situations where they may potentially be exposed to discomfort or harm.[38] Several activists groups, such as People for the Ethical Treatment of Animals (PETA) and the Animal Liberation Front (ALF), have committed acts designed to "liberate" animals or to intimidate researchers who use animals. An effective intelligence-gathering strategy has been for activists to infiltrate an institution's animal-care facility as employees. Furthermore, information about sponsored research projects can be obtained through the Freedom of Information Act. Thus, activists can target specific projects.

Research animals have been set free or taken (in legal terms, stolen) to refuges. In response, the federal government passed the Animal Enterprise Protection Act of 1992, which was amended and, significantly, renamed the Animal Enterprise Terrorism Act of 2006. It states that an individual who "intentionally causes physical disruption to the functioning of an animal enterprise by intentionally stealing, damaging, or causing the loss of, any property (including animals or records) used by the animal enterprise, and thereby causes economic damage exceeding $10,000 to that enterprise, or conspires to do so; shall be fined under this title or imprisoned not more than one year, or both."[39]

The law also prohibits aggravated offenses, which include causing serious bodily injury or death to another person during physical disruption to an animal enterprise. These offenses have penalties ranging from ten years to life in prison. Furthermore, institutions may claim compensation for loss of food production or farm income associated with an offense and, importantly for the university, the cost of repeating any experiments that were interrupted or ruined consequent to an offense.

Despite the law, in more dramatic cases, animal researchers' property, including cars and homes, have been vandalized and even fire-bombed. Although arrests have been made, enforcement of the law is particularly challenging because the groups more prone to violent actions (such as the Animal Liberation Front) are basically leaderless. Individuals self-identify as members and act autonomously. Thus, law-enforcement agencies cannot simply arrest a central organizing group of leaders.

The chief research officer must orchestrate the institution's response to potential threats against its animal-care facilities and researchers. Indeed, this should be a top priority. It involves close cooperation with both campus and local law-enforcement agencies, such as the police and even the Federal Bureau of Investigation (FBI). There are several basic, defensive rules. Obviously, all animal-care facilities must limit access to research personnel—only to those who have a need to enter the facility. Animals should be kept in the secure facility as much of the time as possible. Thus, surgeries and dissections should be conducted within the facility, if possible. If animals must be transported between the facility and a laboratory, this movement should follow routes that avoid public areas such as hospital hallways. These are minimal precautions; each institution will presumably have further specific guidelines. In addition, the National Association for Biomedical Research (NABR) publishes a *Crisis Management Guide* containing useful guidance.[40] By the way, despite NABR's hefty membership fees, most major universities join this organization because of its strong biomedical research support.

In the context of animal-rights activism, a colloquial aphorism conveys sound advice: the best defense is a good offense. One common offensive strategy is to ensure that the institution complies with all federal animal-care and animal-use regulations. Full AAALAC accreditation provides credible testimony to these efforts. Nonetheless, all animal-care personnel and researchers using animals should be reminded regularly via workshops or similar venues about the need for full compliance with the regulations. This is particularly important from a public relations perspective. Also, some activists (often an employee with access to the animal-care facility) report alleged compliance failures. The federal agencies must investigate any reports of noncompliance, and that attracts unwanted negative public attention to the university.

> K: Are the animal rights activists really a meaningful threat to an AAALAC-accredited university?
>
> Smith: Yes. Accreditation simply means that the university is in full compliance with federal regulations. But in the eyes of the animal rights movement, research animals are still captives subject to human oppression despite compliance with federal regulations.
>
> K: Do you agree with that point of view?
>
> Smith: That's a loaded question. Of course, laboratory animals are subject to human domination. Is that morally acceptable? A chief research officer doesn't have the luxury to answer that question negatively. Regardless of personal convictions, he or she has a fiduciary responsibility to protect university assets, including animal-care facilities and research personnel.

Notes

1. Animal and Plant Health Inspection Service (APHIS), 9 C.F.R. § 1.1(2003).
2. Ibid.
3. Animal Welfare Act as Amended, 7 U.S.C. § 2158 (a)(1) (2008).
4. Ibid.
5. Committee on Scientific and Humane Issues in the Use of Random Source Dogs and Cats for Research, *Scientific and Humane Issues in the Use of Random-Source Dogs and Cats in Research* (Washington, D.C.: National Academies Press, 2009).
6. S. Wayman, "Concentration Camp for Dogs," *Life*, February 4, 1966, p. 6.
7. C. Stevens, "Historical Motivation for the Federal Animal Welfare Act," *Animal Welfare Act: Historical Perspectives and Future Directions Symposium Proceedings* (Riverdale, Md.: Working for Animals in Research, Drugs, and Surgery, 1996).
8. Cruelty to Animals Act, United Kingdom, 39 & 40 Vict., Public Acts, c. 77, § 3 (1876).
9. Food Security Act of 1985, Pub. L. No. 99–198, §§ 1751–1759, 99 Stat. 1354, 1645–50, 99th Cong., 1st sess. (December 23, 1985) (codified as amended at 7 U.S.C. §§ 2131 note, 2143, 2146 (2006)).
10. Animal Welfare Act, § 2132(g).
11. APHIS, 9 C.F.R. Parts 1–4.
12. Office of Laboratory Animal Welfare (OLAW), *Public Health Service Policy on Humane Care and Use of Laboratory Animals* (Bethesda, Md.: National Institutes of Health, 2002).
13. Interagency Research Animal Committee, *U.S. Government Principles for the Utilization and Care of Vertebrate Animals Used in Testing, Research, and Training* (Washington, D.C.: Public Health Service, 1985).
14. Health Research Extension Act of 1985, Pub. L. 99–158, § 495, 99 Stat. 820, 875–77, 99th Cong., 1st sess. (November 20, 1985) (codified at 42 U.S.C. § 289d (2006)).
15. National Research Council, *Guide for the Care and Use of Laboratory Animals* (Washington, D.C.: National Academy of Sciences, 1996).
16. "Memorandum of Understanding Among the Animal and Plant Health Inspection Service, U.S. Department of Agriculture, and the Food and Drug Administration, U.S. Department of Health and Human Services, and the National Institutes of Health U.S. Department of Health and Human Services Concerning Laboratory Animal Welfare," 2006, http://grants.nih.gov/grants/olaw/references/finalmou.htm (accessed January 14, 2011).
17. Animal Welfare Act, § 2143.a.2.A-B.
18. Ibid., § 2143.a.3.A.
19. Ibid., § 2143.a.3.B-C.
20. Ibid., § 2143.a.3.D.
21. Ibid., § 2143.a.8.b.1.
22. Ibid.
23. APHIS, 9 C.F.R. § 2.31.c.7–8.
24. Ibid., § 2.33.a.1.
25. Ibid., § 2.33.a.2.
26. Ibid., § 2.32.a.
27. Ibid., § 2.32.c.2.
28. Ibid., § 2.32.c.5.iii.
29. OLAW, § IV.A.1.g.
30. American Association for Laboratory Animal Science, "Certified Manager Animal Resources (CMAR) Certification Program," 2011, http://www.aalas.org/ (accessed January 14, 2011); Laboratory Animal Training Association, "Online Training Program," 2011, http://www.latanet.com/ (accessed January 14, 2011).
31. National Research Council, *Guide*, p. 17.
32. Federation of Animal Science Societies (FASS), *Guide for the Care and Use of Agricultural Animals in Agricultural Research and Teaching*, 3rd. ed. (Savoy, Ill.: FASS, 2010).

33. OLAW § IV.A.2.

34. Ibid.

35. Department of Defense (DoD), Use of Laboratory Animals in DoD Programs, Directive 3216.1 (Washington, D.C.: DoD, 1995), p. 2.

36. Association for Assessment and Accreditation of Laboratory Animal Care International, "Rules of Accreditation," 2011, http://www.aaalac.org/accreditation/rules.cfm (accessed January 14, 2011).

37. P. Singer, *Animal Liberation* (New York: HarperCollins, 1975), pp. 6–8.

38. S. Best, "Gaps in Logic, Lapses in Politics: Rights and Abolitionism in Joan Dunayer's Speciesism," http://www.drstevebest.com/Essays/GapsInLogic.htm (accessed January 14, 2011).

39. Animal Enterprise Terrorism Act, 18 U.S.C. § 43 (2006).

40. National Association for Biomedical Research (NABR), *Crisis Management Guide* (Washington, D.C.: NABR, 2009).

CHAPTER 14

Intellectual Property

K: *Who owns intellectual property generated by university personnel?*
Smith: *That depends on circumstances. Sometimes the creator, who may be a faculty member or a student; sometimes the university itself; and sometimes a granting agency.*
K: *Aren't there well-documented policies governing this?*
Smith: *Yes. They're detailed but ultimately understandable.*

Intellectual Property Rights

In the realm of academe, people create things: new thoughts, new gadgets, new techniques, new theories, and new materials. That's the mission of a research university—to generate new knowledge. With all of these creative new ideas, the question of ownership arises: to whom do they belong? The answer serves as an introduction to the general concept of intellectual property.

Once again, before crafting an answer to this question, it helps to know accurately what constitutes "intellectual property." Most people have an intuitive understanding of the term; it refers to products emanating from some manifestation of mental activity, such as a book, a new software program, a novel way to treat some human disease, or a new technological process. The *Compact Oxford Dictionary: For University and College Students* defines intellectual property more succinctly as "intangible property that is the result of creativity."[1] The convention establishing the World Intellectual Property Organization (WIPO), the definitive United Nations body governing international intellectual property, further declared that:[2]

intellectual property shall include rights relating to:

- literary, artistic and scientific works,
- performances of performing artists, phonograms and broadcasts,
- inventions in all fields of human endeavor,
- scientific discoveries,

- industrial designs,
- trademarks, service marks and commercial names and designations,
- protection against unfair competition,
- and all other rights resulting from intellectual activity in the industrial, scientific, literary or artistic fields.

The items of intellectual property in this list are further divided into two categories: copyright and industrial property. According to international convention:

> The areas mentioned as literary, artistic and scientific works belong to the copyright branch of intellectual property. The areas mentioned as performances of performing artists, phonograms and broadcasts are usually called "related rights," that is, rights related to copyright. The areas mentioned as inventions, industrial designs, trademarks, service marks and commercial names and designations constitute the industrial property branch of intellectual property. The area mentioned as protection against unfair competition may also be considered as belonging to that branch.[3]

Thus, "copyright" relates to artistic creations, such as books, music, paintings, sculptures, and films and technology-based works such as computer programs and electronic databases, including laboratory data. In the university setting, "industrial property" refers primarily to gadgets. Chemical compounds, genes, novel microorganisms, and DNA sequences also fall into this category. Computer programs and some multimedia works often straddle the two categories. Data resulting from scholarly research are also intellectual property. In toto, this compilation of intellectual properties pretty well summarizes the various creative products arising from a university's scholarly endeavors. Note: like any other property, intellectual property may be sold, licensed, assigned, transferred, or given away.

However, the simple term "intellectual property" has interesting overtones. According to the WIPO definition, the term "means the legal rights which result from intellectual activity in the industrial, scientific, literary and artistic fields."[4] Interestingly, this definition refers to intellectual property as "legal rights." What legal rights? In the United States, these derive from the Bill of Rights—more specifically, the Fifth Amendment to the Constitution: "No person shall be . . . deprived of life, liberty, or property, without due process of law."[5] The Constitution elaborates on the word *property* in its assignment of powers to Congress (Article 1, section 8): "The Congress shall have Power—To promote the Progress of Science and useful Arts, by securing for limited Times to Authors and Inventors the exclusive Right to their respective Writings and Discoveries."[6] Internationally, these rights to an individual's creative works are recognized through various treaties. The two major agreements are the Paris Convention for the Protection of Industrial Property and the Berne Convention for the Protection of Literary and Artistic Works.[7]

The Berne Convention treaty calls for member countries to grant "moral rights" to the individual creator of intellectual property. They are the "right of paternity," which is the right to claim authorship of the work, and the "right of integrity," or the right to object to any derogatory action concerning the work, including distortion or modification, that would be prejudicial to the author's honor or reputation. These moral rights are independent of the author's economic rights; they remain with the author forever, even if he or she has transferred the economic rights. Thus, the phrase "intellectual property" extends beyond a mere list of creative products. It conveys the notion of ownership—an individual's right to protect his or her creative endeavors. And, by inference, this is an "unalienable right" of property ownership.

Copyrights

Although the right to ownership is constitutionally guaranteed, manifestation of that right is secured through copyrights and patents. In the case of copyrights, the 1976 United States Copy Right Act grants the authors of "original works of authorship" the exclusive right to reproduce, display publicly, perform, produce derivative works, and distribute the creative item."[8] Significantly, copyright law protects only the form of expression of ideas, not the ideas themselves. The creativity protected by copyright law is in the choice and arrangement of words, musical notes, colors, and shapes. So, copyright law protects the owner against individuals who copy or otherwise use the original work in the same form as that expressed by the author.[9] This principle that ideas and discoveries are not protected but, rather, that the way in which they are expressed is protected by the copyright law is known as the "idea-expression dichotomy."

By law, the work is under copyright protection the moment it is created and fixed in a tangible form that is perceptible, either directly or with the aid of a machine or device.[10] Put an idea in writing on paper or in a computer file, or record it with a tape recorder or camera, and it is automatically copyrighted. This is generally valid for seventy years after the author's death. In addition, the copyright is recognized internationally by the countries—about 180 of them, including all developed nations—that agreed to the treaty of the Berne Convention.

The copyright can be registered formally with the federal government (the Library of Congress) by submitting an application (online or hard copy) and payment of a $35 fee. This establishes a public record of the copyright. Registration is not mandatory, but it confers several legal advantages. Importantly, copyright registration is required before an infringement suit may be filed in court. In that context, it helps to register soon after establishing the copyright. Registration within five years establishes prima facie evidence of the copyright's validity. Furthermore, if registration occurs within three months, statutory damages and attorney's fees may be awarded to the copyright owner in court actions. Otherwise, only actual damages and profits can be awarded to the copyright owner.

Fair Use

In recent years, the term "fair use" is encountered more and more often during discussions about copyright. This refers to the permissibility of using copyrighted material for "purposes such as criticism, comment, news reporting, teaching (including multiple copies for classroom use), scholarship, or research" without permission of the copyright holder.[11] Legally, four factors must be considered when determining whether the use made of a work in any particular case is a fair use:[12]

the purpose and character of the use, including whether such use is of a commercial nature or is for nonprofit educational purposes;

the nature of the copyrighted work;

the amount and substantiality of the portion used in relation to the copyrighted work as a whole; and

the effect of the use upon the potential market for or value of the copyrighted work.

According to the Patent and Trademark Office, the distinction between fair use and infringement may be unclear and not easily defined. There is no specific number of words, lines, or notes that may be taken safely without permission. Furthermore, acknowledging the source of the copyrighted material does not substitute for obtaining permission. In the Internet age, fair use has assumed considerable importance because of the ease of obtaining and distributing copyrighted materials—just cut and paste. The courts judge each case on its own merits. Thus, legal counsel should generally become involved at an early stage of disputed fair use.

Patents

Industrial property, which includes most university inventions, is protected by patents. Formally, these are via "letters patent," which are defined as "the name of an instrument granted by the government to convey a right to the patentee; as, a patent for a tract of land; or to secure to him a right which he already possesses, as a patent for a new invention or discovery; Letters patent are a matter of record. They are so called because they are not sealed up, but are granted open."[13] In simpler terms, an individual must apply to the government for a patent to secure his or her constitutional ownership rights. Thus, the U.S. government established the U.S. Patent and Trademark Office under the Department of Commerce, and this office "shall be responsible for the granting and issuing of patents and the registration of trademarks."[14]

A critical feature of the patent code is the so-called right to exclude. According to the code:

> Every patent shall contain a short title of the invention and a grant to the patentee, his heirs or assigns, of the right to exclude others from making, using, offering for sale, or selling the invention throughout the United States or importing the invention into the United States, and, if the invention is a process, of the right to exclude others from using, offering for sale or selling throughout the United States, or importing into the United States, products made by that process, referring to the specification for the particulars thereof.[15]

In other words, the patent does not grant the right to make, use, offer for sale, or sell or import the invention; an individual can ordinarily do that without any kind of government permission. Of course, the patent does not allow violations of the law in this context. What the patent does offer is the right to prevent (that is, to exclude) anybody else from doing those things: make, use, offer for sale, or sell or import the invention. Thus, the holder of the patent has exclusive rights to the invention. The patent is valid for twenty years after the date on which the application for the patent was filed in the United States. Note: the Patent Office determines whether a patent should be granted in a particular case. However, it is up to the patent holder to enforce his or her rights if the patent is granted.

In return for this right to exclusion, which translates to a legal monopoly, the inventor agrees to place the invention into the public domain for the good of humanity. Without the legal protection provided by patents, the inventor might prefer to keep the invention secret, if for no other reason than to protect his or her monetary investment. Thus, the patent process provides a good way to make the details of new technology publicly available for further improvement by other inventors. Furthermore, when a patent's term has expired, the public record ensures that the invention is not lost to humanity. For these reasons, patents conform to a university's fundamental commitment to make public the results of its scholarly endeavors. Consequently, universities encourage their researchers to patent inventions.

There are three types of patents: utility, design, and plant. According to the Patent Office, utility patents refer to "any new and useful process, machine, manufacture, or composition of matter, or any new and useful improvement thereof."[16] In this context, a utility patent protects the way an article is used and works. Within a university setting, the utility patents predominate; they are the institutional bread-and-butter patents. Design patents protect new, original, and ornamental designs for a manufactured article. They cover the way an article looks. Both design and utility patents may be obtained on an item if the invention revolves around both in its utility and appearance.

The third patent type, plant patents, refers to the invention or discovery and asexual reproduction of any distinct and new variety of plant. Significantly, it is limited to protection of asexually reproduced plant varieties. In the plant world, what does "asexually" mean? According to the Patent Office, "Asexual reproduction is the propagation of a plant to multiply the plant without the use of genetic seeds to assure an exact genetic copy of the plant being reproduced."[17] That means creating a plant involving techniques such as grafting, budding, using root cuttings, layering, bulbs, tissue culture, or division without using seeds. The goal is to establish the stability of the plant, with the offspring genetically identical to the original plant. The plant patents apply to most plants, including fungi and algae. It does not apply to bacteria. Nor does it apply to edible parts of tubers like potatoes.

What about sexually reproduced plant varieties? Plant seeds and genes are covered by utility patents. But there is an additional way to protect sexually reproduced plants—namely, registration as a protected plant variety. This is administered by the USDA's Plant Variety Protection Office. According to the Plant Variety Protection Act, "The breeder of any sexually reproduced or tuber propagated plant variety (other than fungi or bacteria) who has so reproduced the variety, or the successor in interest of the breeder, shall be entitled to plant variety protection for the variety."[18] Upon registration, the breeder has twenty years (twenty-five years for trees and vines) of exclusionary rights (just like patents), starting from the original date of filing. Parenthetically, the federal government retains the right to mitigate this in the event of a national food shortage:

> The [USDA] Secretary may declare a protected variety open to use on a basis of equitable remuneration to the owner, not less than a reasonable royalty, when the Secretary determines that such declaration is necessary in order to insure an adequate supply of fiber, food, or feed in this country and that the owner is unwilling or unable to supply the public needs for the variety at a price which may reasonably be deemed fair. Such declaration may be, with or without limitation, with or without designation of what the remuneration is to be.[19]

Protection of patented and protected plants extends internationally through the International Convention For The Protection Of New Varieties Of Plants.[20]

Patent Applications

An inventor takes two steps leading up to a patent application: conception and reduction to practice. Intuitively, "conception" refers to the inspirational idea for an invention—realizing a novel way to solve a problem or construct a new product. In legal terms, conception must proceed to the stage when no more than routine skill in the art is needed to complete the invention. If creative effort is still required to devise the method for solving a problem, then conception is not complete. It must entail a definite and permanent idea of the complete invention.

"Reduction to practice" can be either actual or constructive. Actual reduction to practice occurs when an invented item is physically constructed or a process is actually performed. In this case, a working prototype demonstrates that the invention actually accomplishes its intended purpose and has a practical use. Technically, an invention does not necessarily have to be actually built or performed to be reduced to practice. It suffices if an individual skilled in the art can duplicate the invention with the information provided in a patent application—and that is a requirement for issuance of patent protection. Thus, an invention is "constructively" reduced to practice when a formal application disclosing the invention is filed with the Patent and Trademark Office. Since the date of an application is the date of constructive reduction to practice, a patent application cannot have a reduction to practice date that is later than its filing date. However, with adequate proof, the date of conception may be established earlier than the filing date. This technicality becomes important when two applicants file for a patent on the same invention.

There are two types of patent applications: nonprovisional and provisional. Nonprovisional patent applications undergo full Patent Office review and establish the filing date. They are the basic patent applications that provide full patent protection. Provisional applications, which apply only to utility patents, are not reviewed. They simply establish the filing date. Furthermore, provisional patent applications expire after one year. Thus, a follow-up nonprovisional application must be filed within that one-year time period to launch the Patent Office review; in these cases, the operational filing date refers to the provisional patent filing date. In either case, the invention is protected by "patent pending" as of the filing date. Incidentally, a patent cannot be enforced until it has been formally granted. Therefore, "patent pending" does not confer legal protection. However, it warns potential infringers that if the patent is issued, they may be liable for damages because patent protection begins retroactively at the filing date.

The provisional applications, which are less expensive than nonprovisional applications, confer two strategic advantages. First, and most important, they give the inventor an additional year beyond the filing date to develop and market the invention. This may lead to changes in the invention that can be incorporated into the final nonprovisional patent application when it is filed. This is advantageous because applications cannot be changed after the nonprovisional filing. During that time, an inventor may also find a company willing to pay the nonprovisional filing fees in exchange for rights to the patent. Conversely, he or she may determine that there is insufficient interest in the product to warrant filing the nonprovisional application. Second, they establish an early filing date; a subsequent nonprovisional application is based on the earlier provisional filing date, thus affording "patent pending" protection from that date. However, the twenty-year patent duration is based on the nonprovisional filing date. For these reasons, many universities favor provisional patents.

To apply for a nonprovisional patent, the applicant must first conduct a novelty search to determine if an idea has already been patented. The U.S. Patent and Trademark Office maintains a searchable database for this purpose.[21] The actual application can then be filed electronically. It contains a description of how to make and use the invention that must provide sufficient detail for a person skilled in the "art" to make and use the invention.

The application also requires a "claims" section. In this important section, the scope of exclusivity sought via patent protection is defined by the patent claims. Stated differently, the patent claims notify the public of the invention's features for which patent protection is being sought. Issuance of the patent conveys the right to exclude others from practicing these defined claims without the patent holder's permission. The claims section often includes drawings or technical data needed to describe the invention in clearly understood terms.

For the inexperienced, preparation of a patent application is seldom a trivial exercise and usually requires the help of an experienced patent attorney. After the patent is issued, a maintenance fee is due 3½, 7½ and 11½ years after the original grant to maintain the patent in force. After the patent has expired anyone may make, use, offer for sale or sell or import the invention without permission of the patent holder, provided that matter covered by other unexpired patents is not used.

Patent applications for products involving DNA sequences require special attention. The Patent Office offers software, PatentIn, to expedite the preparation of patent applications containing nucleic acid and amino acid sequences. PatentIn 3.5 generates sequence listings that comply with all WIPO format requirements.[22]

Patent Office evaluations consider three key criteria. According to patent law, an invention must be "novel, non-obvious, and have utility." Novelty means that no one can patent something that is already known. If the invention has been previously described in a publication, patented, or sold anywhere in the world, it is not novel. The related term "non-obvious" means that the invention could not reasonably have been conceived by somebody "having ordinary skill in the art." In that context, anything known about the invention at the time of the application constitutes "prior art" if it challenges the claim of novelty. The existence of "prior art" renders an invention "obvious" because a person with ordinary skills in the "art" could have reproduced the invention. Thus, a patent would not be issued under these circumstances. Finally, "utility" means that an invention must be functional, operable, and practical; it must have some practical application. Unless the utility is obvious, a successful reduction to practice must include the establishment of a practical use for the invented material.

In the application, the invention's description must be "enabling." In the words of the Patent Office, it must contain sufficient information so "any person skilled in the art can make and use the invention without undue experimentation."[23] That is, it must be complete enough to enable a person skilled in the "art" to actually duplicate the invention by following the description contained in the patent itself. If the disclosure is not enabling, the application will be denied. Or, if the best mode of practicing the invention is not revealed in the filing application and the patent is later challenged in a lawsuit, the patent may ultimately be ruled invalid.

Patents issued by the U.S. Patent Office are valid only in this country. International patent protection requires applications to each country; there is no single multinational patent. Each application can be quite costly, so inventors usually target those countries with the greatest potential market for the invention. The cost can be lowered by taking advantage of an "international search" for prior art administered through a so-called receiving office, which includes the U.S. Patent and Trademark Office, and performed under the auspices of the Patent Cooperation Treaty. The international prior-art search report helps the applicant to determine whether it would be worthwhile filing applications in foreign countries. Furthermore, signatories to the Patent Cooperation Treaty (nearly all countries) honor the international search, thus relieving the inventor of ordering further expensive prior-art searches.

The prior-art criterion raises the issue of public disclosure. In the United States, an invention becomes ineligible for patent protection one year after public disclosure of the invention's details in, for example, a publication. The definition of publication is quite broad. For patent purposes, "published" means any publically available printed, photocopied, typed, microfilmed, or otherwise fixed communication that is accessible to those in the field. This includes standard academic papers, abstracts, master's theses, Ph.D. dissertations, tape recordings, poster presentations, and even Internet communications—all become "printed publications" and therefore public disclosures after they have been disseminated.

Publication establishes prior art. Stating that more positively, an inventor may publish details about his or her invention up to one year before filing a patent application with the U.S. Patent and Trademark Office. In contrast, the rights to foreign patents are lost at the moment of public disclosure or publication (not counting a U.S. filing). Therefore, if an inventor anticipates filing for international protection, he or she must delay public disclosure until after foreign patent applications have been filed.

There is another important issue about timing. In the United States, patents are issued historically on a "first to invent" basis. In the case of competing patent applications, the Patent Office awards the patent to the inventor who first conceived the idea for the invention—even if somebody else filed for a patent at an earlier date. Proving the conception date can be a difficult and costly effort. Publication provides tangible evidence of conception date. However, an inventor can also swear under oath that the conception occurred at some date. To back this up, many universities recommend that their researchers document their research process from conception to reduction to practice by keeping journals written in ink in bound notebooks, with each page dated and signed in the presence of witnesses who understand the nature of the work.

On the other hand, foreign countries use the "first to file" rule. The patent is awarded to the first person to file for the patent, regardless of when it was conceived. Although this system is much easier to administer, it removes the option to publish a year in advance of the application. Nonetheless, the U.S. Congress is currently considering legislation (§515, The Patent Reform Act of 2009) that would change U.S. policy to a similar "first to file" rule, thus standardizing international procedures for filing priority.

Patent applications can become quite expensive and can take a long time to process. The basic filing fees for provisional and nonprovisional applications are, as of 2011, $220 and $330, respectively. But that is just the small tip of a huge iceberg. Nonprovisional applications can easily cost many tens of thousands of dollars in search fees and attorney expenses. Spending $1 million is not unheard of. Furthermore, it can take the Patent Office a few (about two or three) years to process an application. And things can get worse. An infringement suit can readily incur legal bills in the millions of dollars.

> K: *The "first to invent" policy seems very subjective. I'm surprised that it has taken the United States so long to change to the "first to file" rule.*
>
> Smith: *I agree. But universities in general favor the "first to invent" rule. They argue that faculty members usually publish their inventions first and then decide to file for patent protection. So, to accommodate this delay which may be up to one year, universities prefer the "first to invent" rule.*
>
> K: *Why couldn't faculty members in the United States plan ahead and file for a patent prior to public disclosure through publication—just like everybody else?*
>
> Smith: *Universities claim that discoveries coming out of academe are usually quite basic and that it may take some time for peers to evaluate them before they are ready for commercial applications. The twelve-month grace period inherent to the "first to invent" rule provides the extra time needed to vet the invention.*

Transfer of Intellectual Property Rights

The initial copyright or patent owner may transfer all economic rights to a third party. (Moral rights can never be transferred.) For example, an author may sell the copyright of a book to a publishing company. In return, he or she may receive royalties, which are shares of any revenue generated by sales of the book.

There are two types of transfer of intellectual property: assignments and licenses. An assignment transfers ownership of a property right. The new owner may gain some or all rights to the work, depending on the terms of the assignment. A license authorizes a second party to carry out certain acts protected by the copyright or patent. However, the owner of the copyright or patent retains ownership. Usually, a license allows the recipient to exploit the economic rights for a specific period of time and purpose. For example, the author of a novel may grant a license to a publisher to make and distribute copies of his or her work. Licenses may be exclusive— the copyright or patent owner agrees not to authorize any other party to carry out the licensed acts—or nonexclusive, when the copyright or patent owner may authorize others to carry out the same acts. An assignment generally allows the recipient to issue a license. In contrast, a license may not necessarily enable the recipient to grant economic rights to another party via a sublicense without the owner's explicit permission.

In the university context, these transfers play an increasingly greater role. As the owner of most intellectual property generated by its researchers, a university faces the daunting task of taking advantage of these rights through commercialization. For the most part, commercial activities are not in a university's mission. Thus, most institutions endeavor to transfer their copyright and patent portfolios to third parties through what is known as technology transfer, which is the topic of the next chapter.

Ownership

To this point, the right to ownership has been established and secured. But the basic question remains unanswered: who possesses this right to ownership? More specifically, who actually owns the intellectual property generated in a university setting? There are several possible answers, depending on who sponsored or financed the work leading up to creation of the intellectual property.

The first possible answer is straightforward: work done for hire belongs to the employer. This follows a traditional procurement model. Indeed, the U.S. copyright law codifies copyright ownership of works for hire by the employer.[24] For example, if an employee is assigned to develop a drug to treat depression (such as Prozac) and is successful, he or she does not have ownership rights to the drug. The employer paid for the discovery and therefore has ownership rights. For the same reason, if a university hires a researcher to design and build a six-channel amplifier to record brain waves, the university owns any intellectual property rights associated with the instrument. This is standard practice in the industrial and the academic worlds. Likewise, if a university hires an individual specifically to develop a course on accounting principles for online delivery, the university owns the resulting curricular material. It's a matter of law.

In the case of inventions, this ownership principle extends beyond specific work products. If the employee develops intellectual property using university resources, whether or not he or she was hired to create that specific item, then the university generally retains ownership. As Stanford University puts it in their policy, all intellectual property:

> conceived or first reduced to practice in whole or in part by members of the faculty or staff (including student employees) of the University in the course of their University responsibilities or with more than incidental use of University resources, shall be disclosed on a timely basis to the University. Title to such inventions shall be assigned to the University, regardless of the source of funding, if any.[25]

Their phrase "incidental use of University resources" refers mainly to use of major pieces of equipment or facilities. Generally, it does not include use of routinely available computers, software, or reference materials. Many universities have similar policies for inventions. So, if an employee develops an invention while "on the job" using university resources, ownership belongs to the employer—namely, the university. And this applies to all employees—faculty members, staff personnel, and students.

Universities want to retain patent ownership, for several reasons. The first is pretty obvious: they want to protect their monetary investment in researcher salaries, supplies, equipment, and so forth. A second reason is that giving up ownership of inventions may make it impossible for faculty and students to continue to pursue a line of research. If the university were to cede ownership, the owner could conceivably file a broad, blocking patent that would prevent the faculty member and students from using their own technology for further research. Third, ownership by the university maintains a relationship with the inventor. This is often desirable because follow-up work is needed to fully develop the invention, and the inventor has the requisite background and know-how.

There are noteworthy exceptions to this inclusive ownership policy. Stanford, for example, also claims the inventor may place an invention in the public domain if that does not violate any agreements with sponsors and that the "University will not assert intellectual property rights when inventors have placed their inventions in the public domain."[26] The University of Wisconsin-Madison goes a big step further: "The University does not claim ownership rights in intellectual property of its faculty, staff and students produced during research, except as required by funding agreements or other University policies, including the right of the University to use such property for its educational and research purposes."[27]

Traditionally, universities waive any claims to ownership of pedagogical, scholarly, or artistic efforts that were not produced as works for hire. These waived items include dissertations and other scholarly works produced by students as part of their education. In addition, they include textbooks, scholarly books, novels, musical compositions, and unpatentable software. The only catch to the university's waived ownership is that creation of these works must not have made significant use of institutional resources, including nonfaculty employees.

The second possible answer to the original question—who owns the intellectual property generated in a university setting?—is equally straightforward. If a private-sector sponsor such as a corporation funded the research leading to an invention through a grant or contract, then it has ownership rights unless it waives them. Usually these rights are spelled out in the award document. In practice, the office for sponsored research generally examines all grant and contract applications to ensure that ownership rights are well defined a priori. Sometimes, there may be several sponsors of a particular project, opening the door to conflicting ownership claims. Again, the office of sponsored research takes the lead in negotiating a resolution beforehand.

In the case of alliances with corporate partners or other universities where researchers from several institutions (including industry) work on a common project that leads to an invention, a common rule governs ownership: it may be paraphrased as "rights to intellectual property developed by our people belong to us, rights to intellectual property developed by your people belong to you, and rights to intellectual property developed by both of us will be negotiated." Words to this effect generally appear in sponsored research awards and contracts. Usually any negotiations go smoothly. Just in case, however, contracts also contain a section addressing dispute resolution. The most common sticking point here is the locus of any judicial action; both parties prefer their own locality. Universities seldom yield on this point.

Many companies prefer to own the intellectual property that results from the research sponsored at a university. This is true especially if the patented technology required a substantial investment or, naturally, it appears to become a big money-maker. But there is another reason: to prevent the intellectual property from being assigned to a competitor. That would erode their ability to use the invention that they paid for and would put them at a competitive disadvantage. These concerns are perfectly understandable. Thus, universities should always assure corporate sponsors that the results of research that they fund will be available to them. In that context, if a university claims ownership of all patents and software developed using its facilities under a sponsored research agreement, industrial sponsors are commonly granted first options to license patents arising from the research.

K: If a faculty member is hired to teach a specific course, such as linear algebra, and writes a textbook based on his or her lecture notes, isn't that a "work for hire?" Doesn't the university have a claim to ownership?

Smith: You would think so. But universities almost never claim ownership to textbooks. They belong to the author. So, the author gets all of the profit from royalties. If the textbook is a big seller, the faculty member can make a lot of money that way.

K: What if a faculty member requires students to buy his or her expensive textbook? And then the faculty member keeps the profits. Is that considered ethical?

Smith: On close examination, probably not. At best, it borders on a financial conflict of interest. In defense, a faculty member could argue that the students benefit from using a textbook that aligns with the lecture material. To resolve this potential ethical conflict, a few universities require faculty members to give profits made in this way to the university, which then uses the money to improve the instructional offerings in some way. But those universities are sadly in the minority.

The Bayh-Dole Act

Now, for the third possible answer to the question of who owns intellectual property generated in a university setting. If the federal government funded the research in part or *in toto*, then the university has the rights of ownership.

This overall policy stems from a landmark piece of federal legislation, the Patent and Trademark Law Amendments Act, known more commonly as the Bayh-Dole Act.[28] It was enacted in 1980 and amended in 1984. Prior to this law, the federal government retained ownership of intellectual property developed within a university using federal funds. This was based on traditional procurement standards: the government paid for the research leading up to the invention, so it had ownership rights. However, as the number of patents multiplied after World War II, the government accumulated more and more patents than it could license effectively. Indeed, only about 5 percent of the federally held patents were licensed prior to the Act in 1980.[29] And many of these patents originated from university research. Recognizing that the intent of the patent process—making inventions available to the public—was not being met, the federal government ultimately passed the Bayh-Dole Act, ceding its ownership rights to the universities. The result has been remarkable. University patenting increased dramatically, from just 495 issued patents in 1980 to 3,622 in 2007, and this increase has been attributed to passage of the Bayh-Dole Act.[30]

This ownership policy applies to all inventions conceived or first actually reduced to practice in the performance of a federal grant, contract, or cooperative agreement. This is true even if the federal government is not the sole source of funding for either the conception or the reduction to practice. As long as the federal government contributes to the funding—even one penny—the university has rights to the intellectual property. To ensure full compliance with the Bayh-Dole Act, many universities take the position that if a researcher has any federal monies in his or her lab at the time of an invention's conception or reduction to practice, the invention is considered to be federally funded. Notably, however, Bayh-Dole Act policies do not apply to federal predoctoral or postdoctoral training grants.

The university is not required to take ownership. It may waive this right. If the university elects not to accept ownership, the rights revert to the federal government; and if the government also chooses not to claim ownership, the inventor may petition the funding agency to acquire ownership. This latter option—the inventor obtains ownership rights—may seem favorable to the inventor at first glance. However, he or she must file a patent application and pay for all patent-prosecution costs. These can be expensive. Realistically, there must be solid financial reasons the university and the federal government waive ownership rights to a patent. Thus, the inventor may face daunting expenses to prosecute a patent that most probably will not generate much net revenue.

There is one minor catch, the government's so-called march-in rights. Under certain circumstances, the government can require the university to grant a license to a third party, or the government may take title and grant licenses itself. This might occur if the university failed to bring the invention to practical use within a reasonable time, to alleviate health or safety issues, to ensure public use of the invention, or to meet legal requirements.[31] To date (2011), these march-in rights have not been exercised.

Under provisions of the Bayh-Dole Act, ownership comes with some obligations.[32] The university must disclose each new invention to the federal funding agency within two months after the inventor discloses it in writing to the university. To facilitate this reporting to the funding agencies, the federal government provides online capability, the Interagency Extramural Invention Information Management System, iEdison.[33] Corollary to this requirement, the university must have written agreements with its faculty and technical staff requiring them to disclosure any inventions. Most universities require disclosure regardless of funding source.

In addition, the decision whether or not to retain title to the invention must be made within two years after disclosure of the invention to the agency. If public disclosure has occurred via publication or public use of the invention, thus triggering the one-year time period for filing a U.S. patent application, this decision must be made at least sixty days before the end of the allowable filing period.

If it chooses to take the title, the university must file a U.S. patent application within the permissible time period—one year unless publication or public disclosure shortens this period. Federal support must be acknowledged in the application. And, the university must inform the funding agency annually about the invention's status. Furthermore, the university must notify the agency within ten months of the U.S. filing date whether it will also file foreign patent applications. If the university does not intend to file foreign applications, the federal funding agency may then file on its own behalf in the name of the United States.

In compelling cases, the agencies may decide that title should be vested in the federal government. This must be declared in writing before entering into a funding agreement with a university. The agency must also file a Determination of Exceptional Circumstances (DEC) with the Department of Commerce.

There are additional patent-related obligations. If the university elects to retain ownership, it must provide the government a nonexclusive, nontransferable, irrevocable license to the invention. Universities may assign their ownership of inventions only to patent-management organizations, not to other third parties. And, importantly, universities must share with the inventor a portion of any revenue received from licensing the invention. Any remaining revenue, after expenses, must be used to support scientific research or education. In most universities, the chief research officer administers these patent-generated funds.

In all of this discussion about ownership of intellectual property, the role of the chief research officer has been underplayed. In fact, the office for sponsored research, which reports to the chief research officer, plays a major part in the administration of university policies governing intellectual property. Before a grant or contract award is accepted, it is critically important to delineate the rights, obligations, expectations, and roles played by all interested parties. Therefore, the office for sponsored research is responsible for checking all grant and contract proposals for compliance with prevailing intellectual property regulations. Also, the office often negotiates with awarding agencies to bring intellectual-property terms into agreement with university policies.

Generally, if a suitable agreement that conforms to institutional guidelines cannot be reached, the university must be prepared to reject the award; the director of sponsored research has that responsibility and authority. Caveat: the chief research officer retains the authority to override policy-driven decisions, but this authority must be exercised only in the most compelling circumstances. What might those be? Of course, each case stands on its own merits. Nonetheless, examples might include ceding university rights to a corporate sponsor that has recently made a major gift to the university or waiving rights as a start-up recruiting enticement to a newly hired faculty member.

Research Data

Universities usually retain control over raw data, including laboratory notebooks and other primary research records. Thus, a faculty member may not assign these items to a third party. The rationale derives from the university's commitment to dissemination into the public domain of the results of its research efforts through publication. Assignment of raw data to a third party could easily preclude the ability to publish. Therefore, it is not allowed.

The question about who owns raw data arises in a more sinister context, as well. If sponsors retain rights to a study's raw data, the potential for concealing results that they consider unfavorable to their interests lingers in the background. An example might be a drug company that allegedly withholds raw clinical-trial data indicating the ineffectiveness or harmfulness of its product. To address this possibility, "in the fall of 2001, the editors of twelve prominent medical journals collectively announced that they would refuse to publish research on new prescription drugs unless the authors provided assurances that they had unimpeded access to the data and were fully responsible for the paper's conclusions."[34] In general, the chief research officer must diligently reject any research contracts that fail to guarantee full data ownership to the university.

On the other hand, it is certainly permissible to allow third parties access to and use of raw data. Indeed, federal law mandates accessibility to data generated by a federally sponsored research project (that is, a grant). According to OMB circular A-110:

> The Federal awarding agency, the Inspector General, Comptroller General of the United States, or any of their duly authorized representatives, have the right of timely and unrestricted access to any books, documents, papers, or other records of recipients that are pertinent to the awards, in order to make audits, examinations, excerpts, transcripts and copies of such documents. This right also includes timely and reasonable access to a recipient's personnel for the purpose of interview and discussion related to such documents.[35]

Similarly, federal agencies are permitted access to data first produced under a contract. Federal Acquisition Regulations allow the university (the "contractor") to copyright these data (or to patent software), but in return the university grants the federal agency a "paid-up nonexclusive, irrevocable, worldwide license in such copyrighted data to reproduce, prepare derivative works, distribute copies to the public, and perform publicly and display publicly by or on behalf of the Government."[36] A parallel clause grants the same license to software. Thus, "access" does not mean federal confiscation of documents; access comes through a license agreement. As a general rule, research institutions that receive a request for access make the original documents available for review at an institutional site or provide copies of documents requested by the agency.

The general public may also gain access to some types of research data. Under the Freedom of Information Act,[37] interested persons may seek raw data, documents and records possessed by the university, such as material in grant applications, progress reports, and other information generated by federally sponsored research and reported to the funding agency. This provision, known as the Shelby Amendment, is stipulated in circular A-110: "in response to a Freedom of Information Act (FOIA) request for research data relating to published research findings produced under an award that were used by the Federal Government in developing an agency action that has the force and effect of law, the Federal awarding agency shall request, and the recipient shall provide, within a reasonable time, the research data so that they can be made available to the public through the procedures established under the FOIA."[38]

According to COGR, most institutions respond to these requests by first working with the investigator to ensure that any private or protected information is identified to the federal agency so that it can be protected from release.[39] Importantly, preliminary analyses, drafts of scientific papers, plans for future research, peer reviews, communications with colleagues, and physical objects such as laboratory samples are not included. In addition, two other types of information are excluded from this provision: trade secrets and commercial or financial information and certain information that would be considered a clearly unwarranted invasion of personal privacy if it were disclosed. Through these exemptions, certain sensitive institutional data can be shielded from Freedom of Information Act access. Otherwise, the university must provide the requested data to the federal agency that funded the research, which will make them available to the public.

> K: It seems as if a university researcher must relinquish all patents to the university or a corporate sponsor. But what if a faculty member invents something on his or her own time? Evenings, weekends, allowable consulting time. Who owns the patent?
>
> Smith: That depends. If there was a significant use of university facilities, such as lab equipment, then the university has the claim to ownership. Usually it's okay to use an office computer and probably the copy machine, although technically that may not be allowable. Some state laws and governing board policies explicitly prohibit this. So you have to be a bit careful.
>
> K: If a state law or governing board policies prohibits use of any university facilities, including an office computer, for private purposes like writing a novel piece of computer software, isn't the university required to enforce this by claiming the intellectual property rights?
>
> Smith: Of course, the university must comply with state law and governing board policies. But it dare not discourage faculty members from being entrepreneurial even on their own time; otherwise, it risks losing good faculty members to some other university. From an economic perspective, the university also risks losing its investment in the faculty member and bearing the high costs of hiring a replacement. And none of that is in the public or the governing board's interest. The university administrators, including the chief research officer, walk a very tight wire here.

Notes

1. *Compact Oxford English Dictionary: For University and College Students* (Oxford: Oxford University Press, 2006), p. 528.

2. World Intellectual Property Organization, "Convention Establishing the World Intellectual Property Organization, Article 2.viii," 1979, http://www.wipo.int/treaties/en/convention/trtdocs_wo029.html#P50_1504 (accessed January 14, 2011).

3. World Intellectual Property Organization, *WIPO Intellectual Property Handbook: Policy, Law and Use*, 2nd ed. (Geneva:, 2004), p. 3.

4. Ibid.

5. U.S. Bill of Rights, 1789, http://www.archives.gov/exhibits/charters/bill_of_rights_transcript.html (accessed January 14, 2011).

6. Ibid.

7. Paris Convention for the Protection of Industrial Property, 1979, http://www.wipo.int/export/sites/www/treaties/en/ip/paris/pdf/trtdocs_wo020.pdf (accessed January 14, 2011); Berne Convention for the Protection of Literary and Artistic Works, 1979, http://www.wipo.int/export/sites/www/treaties/en/ip/berne/pdf/trtdocs_wo001.pdf (accessed January 14, 2011).

8. Copyright Law of the United States, 17 U.S.C. § 102.a. (2009).

9. World Intellectual Property Organization (WIPO), Understanding Copyright and Related Rights, Ownership, Exercise and Transfer of Copyright (Geneva: WIPO, 2010).

10. Copyright in General, 2011, http://www.copyright.gov/help/faq/faq-general.html#patent (accessed January 14, 2011).

11. 17 U.S.C. § 107 (2009).

12. Ibid.

13. J. Bouvier, "A Law Dictionary Adapted to the Constitution and Laws of the United States of America and of the Several States of the American Union, rev. 6th ed.," 1856, http://www.constitution.org/bouv/bouvier.htm (accessed January 15, 2011).

14. U.S. Patent and Trademark Office, 35 U.S.C. § 2 a.1 (2007).

15. Ibid., § 154.a.1.

16. Ibid., § 101.

17. U.S. Patent and Trademark Office, "General Information About 35 U.S.C. 161 Plant Patents," 2007, http://www.uspto.gov/web/offices/pac/plant/#1 (accessed January 15, 2011).

18. Department of Agriculture, Right to Plant Variety Protection; Plant Varieties Protectable, 7 U.S.C. § 42.a. (2005).

19. Ibid., § 44.

20. International Union for the Protection of New Varieties of Plants, "International Convention for the Protection of New Varieties of Plants," 1991, http://www.upov.int/en/publications/conventions/1991/act1991.htm (accessed January 15, 2011).

21. U.S. Patent and Trademark Office, "Published Patent Application Access and Status Information Sheet for Members of the Public," 2010, http://www.uspto.gov/patents/process/search/access.jsp (accessed January 15, 2011).

22. U.S. Patent and Trademark Office, "PatentIn Instructions and Software," 2009, http://www.uspto.gov/patents/resources/tools/checker/patentinrel.jsp (accessed January 15, 2011).

23. U.S. Patent and Trademark Office, "The Enabling Requirement," in *Manual of Patent Examining Procedures*, § 2164.01 (Washington, D.C.: Department of Commerce, 2010).

24. U.S. Copyright Law, 17 U.S.C. § 101.

25. Stanford University, "Inventions, Patents and Licensing (RPH 5.1)," 1999, http://rph.stanford.edu/5-1.html (accessed January 15, 2011).

26. Ibid.

27. University of Wisconsin-Madison, "Intellectual Property Policies and Procedures for University Research," p. 4, 2005, http://www.grad.wisc.edu/research/ip/ippolpro.pdf (accessed January 15, 2011).

28. Patent and Trademark Law Amendments Act (Bayh-Dole Act), 35 U.S.C. §§ 200–212.

29. General Accounting Office (GAO), Technology Transfer Administration of the Bayh-Dole Act by Research Universities, report to congressional committees, *GAO/RCED-98-126* (Washington, D.C.: GAO, 1998), p. 3.

30. Association of University Technology Managers (AUTM), *AUTM U.S. Licensing Activity Survey, 2007: A Survey Summary of Technology Licensing (and Related) Activity for U.S. Academic and Nonprofit Institutions and Technology Investment Firms* (Deerfield, Ill.: AUTM, 2009).

31. 35 U.S.C. § 203.

32. Ibid., § 202.

33. National Institutes of Health, "Interagency Edison," 2010, http://era.nih.gov/ProjectMgmt/iedison2/flash/iedison_all.htm (accessed January 15, 2011).

34. J. Washburn, *University, Inc.* (New York: Basic Books, 2005), p. 109.

35. Office of Management and Budget, Executive Office of the President, Circular A-110, 2 C.F.R. § 215.53.e (2010).

36. Federal Acquisition Regulation, FAR 52.227-11 (2005).

37. Freedom of Information Act, 5 U.S.C. § 552 (as Amended By Public Law No. 104-231, 110 Stat. 3048, 104th Cong., 2nd sess. (October 2, 1996)).

38. 2 C.F.R. § 215.36 (d)(1).

39. Council on Government Relations, "Access to and Retention of Research Data: Rights and Responsibilities," 2006, http://206.151.87.67/docs/CompleteDRBooklet.htm (accessed January 15, 2011).

CHAPTER 15

Technology Transfer

K: How does the university market its intellectual property?

Smith: Usually the university tries to license its portfolio to private companies, which then commercialize the patent. This raises the whole issue of technology transfer.

K: I suppose that this can be quite lucrative.

Smith: For the lucky few, yes; it is a pot of gold. The royalties from one blockbuster patent can bring in tens of millions of dollars in a year. But there's a lot more to technology transfer than just money—at least there should be.

Office of Technology Transfer

With the passage of the Bayh-Dole Act, universities began to accumulate disclosures for intellectual property. They had no choice in the matter. The law requires universities to disclose all patentable inventions conceived or reduced to practice with federal support to the funding agency.[1] Therefore, to enable compliance with this obligation, the law states further that the university must require its researchers to disclose to the university all patentable inventions. So, disclosures started rolling in. A survey conducted by the Association of University Technology Managers (AUTM) revealed that, in 2008, 191 responding institutions (including 32 hospitals and nonacademic organizations) received a total of 20,115 disclosures.[2] Consequently, on average, a university received about 100 disclosures per year; some universities received 200 or more and, of course, some received many fewer. Moreover, 12,920 patent applications were filed. Thus, nearly 65 percent of the disclosures resulted in patent applications. In that year, 3,280 patents were granted to these institutions. Three universities had over 100 patents issued. These lofty numbers elevate university technology transfer into the realm of "big business."

To administer this trove of intellectual property, most research universities have established offices dedicated to technology transfer. Their responsibilities generally include developing and administering policy on intellectual property, evaluating inventions for possible patent applications, applying for patents, licensing of intellectual property, and enforcing licenses and other agreements on intellectual property. In addition, they may participate in the distribution of patent-generated income. As custodians of the university's intellectual property, the technology-transfer offices also fulfill an important role in marketing patents and copyrighted material through licenses. Working with the inventor, the technology-transfer office seeks business partners to commercialize the university's patented inventions. Indeed, this is the essence of technology transfer—bringing the products of university-based research to the marketplace.

The technology-transfer office also bears the responsibility for complying with the Bayh-Dole Act's record-keeping and reporting requirements. According to the act, the university must disclose "each subject invention to the Federal agency within a reasonable time after it becomes known to contractor personnel responsible for the administration of patent matters, and that the Federal Government may receive title to any subject invention not disclosed to it within such time."[3] In their guidelines, the NIH defines "a reasonable time" as two months.[4] Thus, the university must file the report within two months after a disclosure. In addition, the act requires "periodic reporting on the utilization or efforts at obtaining utilization that are being made by the contractor or his licensees or assignees."[5] Again, the NIH provides further definition to this requirement: "an annual Invention Utilization Report is required for all inventions for which a patent application has been filed or that have been licensed, but not patented (e.g., biological material). The utilization reports must provide the status of development, date of first commercial sale or use, and gross royalties received."[6] Failure to honor these reporting obligations may result in the federal agency exercising its "march-in rights," thus stripping ownership from the university.

These reporting requirements can become quite a major record-keeping chore. And they may come as a surprise to inexperienced research administrators. The chief research officer must diligently ensure that these reports are up to date. It can become a real mess to recover from lapses in timely reporting. To facilitate this reporting to the funding agencies, the federal government provides online capability via the Interagency Extramural Invention Information Management System, iEdison.[7] Currently, eighteen federal agencies participate in this single-interface portal for disclosure and patent-utilization reports required by the Bayh-Dole Act.

And last, but hardly least, the technology-transfer office actively educates faculty members on the patent process, discussing what is and is not patentable and encouraging them to consider disclosure of their intellectual property. This is often a challenging assignment. Many faculty members, especially the older ones, entered academe in its "ivory tower" format; they came from an academic culture that embraced the traditional precept of knowledge for knowledge's sake. Indeed, the university served as a refuge from the world of commerce. Thus, many faculty members have little or no experience with the patent process. Some even consider the notion of commercialization within the academic setting antithetical to scholarship. They posit, "The university is shamelessly selling out for money."

Within this environment, the technology-transfer office must convince a skeptical faculty member that the patent process is truly designed to disseminate scholarly achievements to the general public for society's benefit, as would a publication. And that patents and publications are not mutually exclusive. Moreover, many faculty members benefit from counseling about whether their intellectual endeavors are patentable; they may never have thought about the question. The ulterior motive here is to increase the flow of intellectual property into the university's technology-transfer pipeline. Some technology-transfer offices supplement these persuasive tactics with money. They give a researcher a bonus for every patentable disclosure. For example, the University of Wisconsin's office offers $1,500 if a disclosure results in a patent filing. Amid all of this, the technology-transfer office must convincingly protect the academic missions of the university—education, research, and service—from conflicting business interests associated with the technology-licensing function.

As part of this task to catalyze patentable disclosures, technology-transfer offices often offer funding opportunities for faculty members to enhance commercial aspects of a research product. Typically, this is via a regularly scheduled competition. The competition may be under the auspices of the university research committee, but expertise in the patenting and licensing process is particularly desirable in the review group. Thus, more commonly, successful businessmen are enlisted to participate as reviewers, either as supplementary members of the research committee or, more typically, as a separate self-standing review committee. Incidentally, the chief research officer should always monitor potential reviewers' credentials for potential financial conflicts of interest.

The award size may vary more than the usual research mini-grants because of the targeted goal: bringing a nascent invention a significant step closer to a patent application. Some awards may exceed $100,000, especially if clinical trials are required. In fortunate cases, private corporations, including venture-capital firms or local economic-development organizations, may contribute to this fund, thus alleviating the university's burden. These donations can be quite advantageous to the donors because they gain early-stage knowledge about the university's intellectual property.

With that broad mandate, the technology-transfer offices require staff personnel with expertise in patent law and in marketing—plus good people skills. Therefore, the director routinely has either a legal or a sales background. There are debates within technology-transfer circles about which background is better suited for the position. As in most discussions about the ideal qualifications for a given job (for example, a left-handed versus a right-handed first baseman), there is no simple resolution. A good director can complement his or her own strengths by hiring a patent lawyer or a marketing expert. Both skills will be needed.

Most often, the technology-transfer office reports to the chief research officer, although in a few exceptional cases, he or she will report to the chief financial officer. Some multicampus university systems have pulled the technology-transfer operations into the system administration. In those cases, such as Texas A&M, the system's technology-transfer office serves all campuses collectively; in others, such as the University of California, the system's office supports individual campus offices. And in other cases, the university assigns its intellectual property to a patent-management organization. Two recognizable examples of this organizational structure are the nonprofit Wisconsin Alumni Research Foundation (WARF), which handles all intellectual property for the University of Wisconsin-Madison, and the Georgia Tech Research Corporation.

The ultimate size of the office staff depends on the number of disclosures. As a rule, one licensing professional handles about twenty-five disclosures per year, and a university spawns one disclosure per $2.5 million in annual research expenditures.[8] These data translate to approximately one licensing professional per $60 million in annual research expenditures. Another rule of thumb states that technology-transfer office budgets vary from 0.5 to 1.0 percent of the university's annual research expenditures.[9] The minimal cost of running a technology-transfer office is about $300,000 per year—just enough to pay salaries (plus fringe benefits) for a director, a secretary, and legal fees. The costs of administering technology-transfer efforts are also allowable for F&A reimbursement on federal grants and contracts.

There is an additional hidden cost to running the office—namely, space. Because the technology-transfer personnel must interact with potential licensing customers in the business community, they require professional-looking office space with adequate visitor parking. That last matter—parking—often poses the most difficult challenge, for it exerts pressure on the office to locate off the main campus, or at least on the periphery. However, the technology-transfer personnel must also consult regularly with university researchers to ensure a smooth flow of intellectual capital (in the form of disclosures) into the office. This is best accomplished by having an office in the heart of the campus. And that takes up valuable academic space. Thus, space and facility planners face a conundrum that sooner or later makes its way to the chief research officer's attention. Again, there is no simple resolution, and each institution will arrive at its own, unique compromise.

Does the patent-generated income cover the costs of running the technology-transfer office? For some universities, the answer is definitely yes. In 2007, forty-five universities took in at least $5 million in licensing income, which should have been sufficient to cover most, if not all, of the office's budget—with plenty of money left over to reinvest in the research infrastructure. (Remember: the Bayh-Dole Act requires the university to spend any revenue remaining after expenses have been paid on scientific research or education. That is not benevolent university policy; it is federal law.) New York University earned an astounding $791 million in 2007.[10] The reinvestment of licensing revenue into research has the potential of creating a "virtual spiral," a self-reinforcing cycle of escalating performance. As more licensing revenue is invested in research, the number of disclosures increases, thus increasing the amount of licensing revenue, and on and on. This happy situation is (or should be) the goal of all technology-transfer efforts.

But for many institutions, licensing income does not cover the cost of running the technology-transfer operation. It must be subsidized from the academic budget. Nonetheless, universities sustain the office for several reasons. Pragmatically, there is the need for an office to handle the federal disclosure and patent-reporting requirements. From a more academic perspective, in recent years, many faculty members and students want to create an impact beyond the laboratory and classroom. They look toward commercialization opportunities. To attract and retain these individuals, the university must have a credible technology-transfer operation. It is a competitive matter. Importantly, nowadays universities are looked upon as a driver of economic activity through their intellectual property. The technology-transfer office has become a major interface between the traditional academic institution and the local business community.

> K: *With the potential to earn so much money from their patents, I would think that universities would give the technology-transfer office prime space and budgetary support.*
>
> Smith: *Yes, quite a few universities do that. But it's like playing the lottery; sometimes you win, but most times you lose. And luck plays a major role. In the academic setting, most research is basic by nature, and the potential for lucrative patents is simply unpredictable.*
>
> K: *Nonetheless, you said that forty-five universities earned more than $5 million annually. Those numbers alone would seem to encourage the investment in a top-quality technology-transfer office.*
>
> Smith: *It gets better than that. In 2007, ninety-two universities earned more than $1 million. That's about a third of all academic research institutions in the United States. Regardless, an experienced chief research officer usually tries to dampen expectations of vast wealth from technology transfer. There may be money in it, but for most institutions the amounts will be modest. Realistic goals would be to provide good service to campus researchers and to cover the office's costs. Anything beyond that would be good fortune.*

Ownership Decisions

With disclosures in hand, the technology-transfer office must expeditiously pursue patent applications. Indeed, according to the Bayh-Dole Act, if the university decides to claim ownership, it must file a patent application within one year or less. How does it arrive at a decision to claim or waive ownership?

Looking backwards, the patent process really begins with the disclosure document. It normally contains information about the invention, the inventors, the funding sources, any previous public disclosure through publications, and other related topics. Many universities also ask the inventor to list likely candidates for licensing. The disclosure is reviewed by the technology-transfer office, and it decides whether the university should claim ownership based on the invention's patentability and potential commercial value. This is not a trivial decision to make, for ownership commits the university to filing for a patent. And that costs money—usually about $30,000 for a U.S. patent and at least another $10,000 or more for each international patent.

Universities vary in how they determine whether to accept ownership and pursue the patent. The common element in most cases is an advisory patent review committee that assists in making the decision. These are synonymous with "intellectual property committees." In large organizations, committee members may come entirely from within the technology-transfer office. For example, WARF has an expert staff of licensing professionals who make the decisions collectively. In contrast, most universities (especially those with smaller technology-transfer operations) establish patent review committees with members knowledgeable in patenting and licensing. Membership typically includes faculty members and experts from the private business community. The technology-transfer office director generally selects the committee members, although the chief research officer (to whom the director reports) may retain the appointing authority.

As part of the review process, the inventor is usually interviewed by the technology-transfer staff assigned to the disclosure and, in many cases, by members of the patent review committee. At this meeting, he or she presents the particulars of the disclosure. Questions include: Why is the invention novel? What is its unique niche in the marketplace? and Who are potential licensees? These are informal interviews, but the inventor should be counseled beforehand to come prepared. He or she needs to bring technical sketches, collaborating inventors, and other supporting documents. With this information in hand, the new invention is evaluated not only on technical merit but also on its commercial potential and, not to be overlooked, the enforceability of its patent rights.

Patent Prosecution

If the decision is to accept ownership, then the technology-transfer office files the patent application. For the record, the actual filing procedure and the interactions among the university (the applicant), its attorney, and the patent office are known as "patent prosecution." Patent lawyers generally prepare the applications. Even in the largest technology-transfer organizations, private firms specializing in patent law may be retained. The advantage of a larger firm is that it has individual attorneys with expertise in particular aspects of patent law, such as biotechnology and medical electronics. The inventor usually participates actively in preparing the application. He or she provides not only the requisite technical expertise but also knowledge of the invention's commercial market. The technology-transfer office routinely pays the costs, which can be considerable, of preparing and filing the patent application.

Note: in some cases, the technology-transfer office director may have a professional background in patent law, thus enabling him or her to prosecute patents. Potentially, this could lessen the need for outside legal counsel. At first glance, this might seem desirable because of the cost savings; however, except in the smallest offices, it is not good use of the director's time and effort. Patent prosecution can become quite time-consuming and complicated, and it generally pays to hire experienced outside law firms to handle the application procedures.

If international patents are to be filed, the inventor should be reminded throughout this prosecution process not to make any public disclosure prior to the filing date. "Public disclosure," which invalidates international patent rights, can occur inadvertently when employees from a private company or other researchers visit the inventor's laboratory or meet with him or her at conferences or other venues. To mitigate these risks of accidental public disclosure, prior to formal meetings many universities encourage written agreements—confidential nondisclosure agreements—that document the intention of the parties to maintain the confidentiality of any shared information about the invention. Incidentally, the door swings both ways; many private companies insist on reciprocal nondisclosure agreements, as well, to protect their proprietary information. Most chief research officers and technology-transfer offices routinely enter into these nondisclosure agreements and maintain standard templates for easy preparation.

Licensing

After filing the patent application, the next step is to market the invention to industry. Procedures vary according to specific circumstances, of course. But as a general rule, the marketing arm of the technology-transfer office identifies likely prospects and distributes nonconfidential summaries of university-held patents, including those that are "patent pending," to companies that may be interested in the invention. This may involve quite an aggressive campaign marketing the university's patent portfolio, including presentations via trade-show presentations, slick brochures, and venture-capital fairs. Often, the inventor has previously established relationships with these companies, which may simplify this process. Other primary prospects include venture-capital firms—local, national, and even international—that seek investment opportunities. The technology-transfer office provides further information about the invention to the companies that express interest. If confidentiality is deemed necessary to protect yet-to-be patented property, nondisclosure agreements may be required. After all of this, negotiations continue with interested companies, and everyone hopes this concludes with the sale of a license.

A condition of the Bayh-Dole Act bears mentioning in this context. In their marketing of an invention, universities must give preference to small business firms (fewer than 500 employees), provided that they have the resources and capability for bringing the invention to the marketplace. In particular:

> Contractors are expected to use efforts that are reasonable under the circumstances to attract small business licensees. They are also expected to give small business firms that meet the standard outlined in the clause a preference over other applicants for licenses. What constitutes reasonable efforts to attract small business licensees will vary with the circumstances and the nature, duration, and expense of efforts needed to bring the invention to the market. [This] is not intended, for example, to prevent nonprofit organizations from providing larger firms with a right of first refusal or other options in inventions that relate to research being supported under long-term or other arrangements with larger companies. Under such circumstances it would not be reasonable to seek and to give a preference to small business licensees.[11]

Thus, if a large company has also provided research support that led to the invention, that company may be awarded the license.

Another Bayh-Dole condition merits attention during these licensing negotiations. By statute, licenses must be granted preferentially to businesses that intend to manufacture the product in the United States. Specifically:

> Notwithstanding any other provision of this clause, the contractor agrees that neither it nor any assignee will grant to any person the exclusive right to use or sell any subject inventions in the United States unless such person agrees that any products embodying the subject invention or produced through the use of the subject invention will be manufactured substantially in the United States. However, in individual cases, the requirement for such an agreement may be waived by the Federal agency upon a showing by the contractor or its assignee that reasonable but unsuccessful efforts have been made to grant licenses on similar terms to potential licensees that would be likely to manufacture substantially in the United States or that under the circumstances domestic manufacture is not commercially feasible.[12]

Therefore, if the invention will be sold in the United States by a company holding an exclusive license, it must be manufactured domestically, if at all possible. Importantly, this does not apply in the case of nonexclusive licenses. This "made in the USA" provision captures the original spirit of the Bayh-Dole Act, which is to bolster the American economy. As COGR says, "It was understood that stimulation of the U.S. economy would occur through the licensing of new inventions from universities to businesses that would, in turn, manufacture the resulting products in the U.S."[13]

Market interest ultimately determines whether the university negotiates an exclusive or a nonexclusive licensing agreement. This is a function of the value of the invention to a company and the risks associated with the investment required to develop the new technology. Exclusive licenses are generally negotiated for patents that require significant investment or have high risks of failure to reach the marketplace. Because of their basic nature, many university inventions may require considerably more development before they are marketable, and this may impact the negotiation terms. New drugs requiring extensive clinical trials often fall in this category. In contrast, nonexclusive licenses are generally negotiated for patents that are broad in scope and useful in many different industries. In addition, nonexclusive patents often derive from very basic patents that have the potential to open new market niches in many fields of use. And different "fields of use" can be licensed separately. For example, a novel drug might have several fields of use—diagnostic, therapeutic, veterinary, and so forth.

In this context, there is also a hybrid type of license, an exclusive "field of use" license. The licensee has exclusive rights in a specific field of use. However, the university may continue to grant similar exclusive licenses to the patent in a different field of use. Similarly, exclusive licenses can be awarded for specific geographical regions, such as Europe, Asia, or North America, and even to specified regions within a country or countries. These hybrid licenses are desirable because they open up the technology to many markets.

License Value

How much is a license worth? That question lurks behind the negotiations. Of course, it all depends on the invention's value to the buyer, and that usually comes down to how much the licensee expects to invest to bring a product to the marketplace versus how large it estimates sales and profits will be. Greater investment costs can mean lower monetary compensation for the license.

Typical licensing agreements have up to four different payment options: upfront license commitment fees (like nonrefundable "earnest money"), royalties based on net sales, monetary milestone payments (payable when sales meet certain milestones), and periodic maintenance fees (incentives for the licensee to continue commercialization efforts). In general, license fees usually range from thousands to tens of thousands of dollars, and royalty rates range from 3 to 6 percent of net sales revenue. Milestone and maintenance fees vary considerably, but they may extend into the hundred-thousand-dollar range. Particularly desirable agreements call for the licensee to fund the patent application costs.

Small start-up companies may not have the resources to pay these licensing expenses. Payment of these costs could weaken the company's ability to develop the invention expeditiously. Therefore, rather than requiring money, the university may take equity in the company. Although the amount of equity held by the university will vary from case to case, the amount may be 1 to 5 percent of the company's estimated net worth or market valuation at the time of the deal. Generally, universities do not want to become involved in running a private business, so they sell their holdings as soon as the company has revenues sufficient to cover ongoing licensing expenses—if there is a market for the equities.

Incidentally, in some states, public institutions cannot legally own equities. This becomes a nonissue if a nonprofit foundation handles a university's technology-transfer operations. As a separate legal entity, a foundation can own equities and, more generally, operate outside any other legal constraints specific to public institutions.

During these pecuniary negotiations, experienced technology-transfer personnel resist the temptation to concentrate on long-term financial gain. In the long run, the university's goal is to move its intellectual property into the market-place where it generates revenue but, importantly, also serves the public good. That dedication to public benefit hallmarks the university. So, rather than negotiate the "hard deal" for the sake of increasing future royalty payments, universities often assign higher priority to the licensee most capable of commercializing the technology. From this perspective, a royalty-free license may be granted to another nonprofit research organization simply to enable a researcher to practice the invention for research purposes.

In this overall context, one of the more noticeable mistakes among novice university technology-transfer negotiators is an overzealous insistence on maximizing potential profit. Indeed, in his masterpiece *The Practice of Management*, Peter Drucker also advises against this misdirected approach to business management.[14] The research and teaching missions of the university always take precedence over patent considerations. As Stanford puts it, "While the University recognizes the benefits of patent development, it is most important that the direction of University research not be established or unduly influenced by patent considerations or personal financial interests."[15]

Countless books, newsletters, and workshops provide advice and guidance in patent prosecution and licensing. They're readily available at bookstores and online. In the academic realm, AUTM serves as a reliable source of factual information.[16] Equally helpful is the NIH Office of Technology Transfer, which has model licensing agreements posted on its Web site.[17] Although the chief research officer seldom becomes involved personally in technology-transfer negotiations, he or she may find it necessary occasionally to consult one or more of these in-depth resources—if for no other reason than to talk knowledgeably with interested faculty members and technology-transfer office personnel.

K: Your warnings about overzealous insistence on maximizing profit are interesting. Is that just a personal concern or is it commonplace in the university technology-transfer community?

Smith: In my experience, this opinion is held by most experienced negotiators. Of course, you strike the best deal. But you have to avoid jeopardizing fragile young companies. I'm very cautious about that.

K: Are you implying that settling for less revenue is better than squeezing a small company too hard? Isn't it their problem to figure out what they can and cannot afford?

Smith: Of course, business is business. But I've witnessed deals that gave extensive intellectual-property rights to ambitious small companies in return for promised big royalty payments to the university. For whatever reasons, the companies went bankrupt. Problems arose when their creditors retained claims on the university's intellectual property but had no commitment to pursue commercialization. The inventor, and therefore the university, basically lost all rights to the intellectual property.

Royalty Distributions

Ideally, successful patents will generate revenue, and the licensing agreement will provide for royalty payments to the university. Anticipating this happy possibility, most universities have policies for distributing this patent-generated revenue. And, according to the Bayh-Dole Act, this must be used for research and educational purposes. Many state and institutional policies explicitly reinforce this federal requirement for using patent-generated revenues to support university research efforts.

Commonly, the distribution formula first allocates a portion of the revenue to the technology-transfer office to cover expenses. The remainder goes to the inventor, his or her department and perhaps college, and the chief research officer or the provost, who distributes it in support of the overall university research environment. The exact apportionment varies among universities. For example, Stanford University deducts 15 percent of the gross royalty income to cover the technology-transfer office's administrative overhead and, in addition, any costs assignable to the patent, primarily the patent filing fees. The remaining net royalties are divided one-third to the inventor, one-third to the inventor's department, and one-third to the inventor's school. By comparison, at the University of Wisconsin-Madison, the technology-transfer office (that is, WARF) does not deduct a share of the royalty income; it meets administrative expenses through investment income. The inventor receives 20 percent of the gross royalty income, and the inventor's department receives 15 percent of the gross royalties. Finally, the chief research officer receives the remaining revenues, which he or she then distributes to the faculty members via a regularly scheduled competitive process. Needless to say, if more than one inventor or one department is involved, the royalty shares are divided among them. Income from equity holdings are generally distributed more or less according to the same formula. (By the way, the inventor's royalties may be eligible for special income tax treatment; this is a matter for the inventor and his or her tax counsel.)

Note: the inventor's department and college receive sizable portions as an incentive for them to provide a supportive environment for intellectual property development. This is particularly important because of the subtle undertones of discontent with what are perceived by some faculty members as nonacademic priorities.

If an inventor leaves the university, he or she normally continues to receive royalty payments. On the other hand, if a portion of the royalty payments are specifically allocated for the inventor's research program (and not personal income), these payments remain with the university. They are usually allocated to the departing inventor's college or department, where they continue to be used for research purposes.

Tangible Research Property

To this point, discussion has focused on intellectual property—intangible property that is the result of creativity. Universities tend to generate another commodity—namely, tangible research property. The term refers to unique research products that are more physical in nature than inventive intellectual property. Examples include biological organisms, chemical compounds, DNA molecules, integrated circuit chips, computer software, engineering prototypes, engineering drawings, and other items that can be handled physically and distributed to other parties. They could be boxed and shipped to someone.

Tangible research property developed using federal funds must be shared openly with all other qualified investigators, nationally and internationally. The NIH, for example, requires the sharing of synthetic compounds, cell lines, DNA sequences, and so forth on the premise that this enhances the value of the NIH-sponsored research. Or, as they put it more bluntly, "Unique research resources arising from NIH-funded research are to be made available to the scientific research community."[18] This policy does not apply to human cells that are not commercially available. To enforce compliance with this guideline, investigators are expected to include a specific plan for sharing and distributing unique model organism research resources in their grant applications. The NSF has a similar policy: "Investigators are expected to share with other researchers, at no more than incremental cost and within a reasonable time, the primary data, samples, physical collections and other supporting materials created or gathered in the course of work under NSF grants."[19] On top of these federal mandates, many major scientific journals require authors to abide by these open-sharing principles as a condition for publication.

Because tangible research property is available for public distribution, a researcher generally may take it along when he or she leaves the university. Certainly, it accompanies the transfer of a grant, contract, or other agreement. However, because most tangible research property technically belongs to the university, not the individual researcher, most institutions insist on chief research officer approval of these transfers to a new organization.

Tangible research property may have intangible property rights associated with it. Two examples illustrate this point. A biological organism such as a transgenic mouse may be patented, but it may also be distributed as tangible research property. Likewise, computer software may be either patented or copyrighted, but it, too, may be distributed as an item of tangible research property. If federal funds were used to generate the tangible research property item, any associated intellectual property rights are covered under the umbrella of the Bayh-Dole Act.

At this point, the university may face a dilemma: it must make the property freely available to researchers while protecting its patent rights. A patented resource must still be made reasonably available and accessible to the research community in accordance with the federal-grants policy statements. Thus, to resolve this quandary, alternatives to the use of patents and exclusive licenses should be considered if the invention is useful primarily as a research tool. In those cases, the NIH advises that:

> inappropriate licensing practices are likely to thwart rather than promote utilization, commercialization and public availability of the invention . . . . In determining an intellectual property strategy for an NIH-funded invention useful primarily as a research tool, recipients should analyze whether further research, development and private investment are needed to realize this primary usefulness. If it is not, the goals of the [Bayh-Dole] Act can be met through publication, deposit in an appropriate databank or repository, widespread non-exclusive licensing or any other number of dissemination techniques. Restrictive licensing of such an invention, such as to a for-profit sponsor for exclusive internal use, is antithetical to the goals of the Bayh-Dole Act.[20]

These are strong words to be taken seriously by staff in the technology-transfer office—and, therefore, the chief research officer. To repeat the advice, if the product is useful primarily as a research tool, exclusive licenses are highly discouraged. Caveat: if the product requires further development to optimize its usefulness, exclusive licenses may be suitable if the licensee uses this opportunity to maximize the property's distribution.

Material Transfer Agreements

Often, universities distribute tangible research property without securing intellectual-property protection by using a form of contractual agreement that specifies limitations on the use and further distribution of the item. These are known as "material transfer agreements" (MTAs) and are generally a *sine qua non* when sending research materials to someone outside the university. Formally speaking, a material transfer agreement is a contract that governs the transfer of tangible research materials between two organizations when the recipient intends to use it for research purposes.

The agreement specifies the provider's and the recipient's rights and obligations concerning the tangible research property and any of its derivatives. Material transfer agreements do not grant the recipient rights to intellectual property or commercial use of the item. Furthermore, they limit the use of the transferred materials explicitly to research and generally specify that they cannot be used in human subjects. In this way, research materials such as cell lines, biological vectors, plant germ plasm, and chemical compounds may be shared with other investigators for research purposes while protecting institutional intellectual property rights to the materials. Importantly, most material transfer agreements also stipulate that the individual receiving the material may not transfer it to anyone else (even within the same institution) without the provider's written consent. Indeed, material transfer agreements from the private sector almost universally do not permit a secondary transfer.

Most material transfer agreements contain a clause guaranteeing the recipient's right to publish the results of any research using the transferred material. In fact, NIH policy requires this stipulation:

> Agreements to acquire materials for use in NIH-funded research are expected to address the timely dissemination of research results. Recipients should not agree to significant publication delays, any interference with the full disclosure of research findings, or any undue influence on the objective reporting of research results. A delay of 30–60 days to allow for patent filing or review for confidential proprietary information is generally viewed as reasonable.[21]

Because this requirement conforms to general academic policies concerning the freedom to publish research results, it should be standard language in all university material transfer agreements.

Restrictions in these agreements against commercial use generally apply to the transferred material and any "modifications, unmodified derivatives, or progeny" created by the recipient.[22] These terms refer to a product that incorporates the intact original material. For example, the recipient may insert a novel gene into a unique viral vector; the newly created product (virus plus inserted gene) is a modification of the original material. The commercial-use restrictions do not usually apply to a product derived from the transferred item by the recipient. "Derived" implies that the new product differs from the original material. By this definition, a functional subunit of the original material does not differ from the original material. Therefore, it does not constitute a derived product.

The provider cannot claim so-called reach-through royalty or product rights from a derived product. For clarification, "reach through" means that the provider receives royalties or ownership rights from a product derived from the transferred material by the recipient. In general, material transfer agreements are not suitable for establishing reach-through rights back to the provider. If the university anticipates that a transferred material may generate valuable derivatives, it should file a patent application and transfer the product via a nonexclusive license with explicit "reach-through" terms and conditions. Incidentally, most material transfer agreements explicitly state that the provider retains the intellectual property rights, including the right to patent the material.

Conventionally, transferring research materials from one academic institution to another (including nonprofit organizations) is relatively simple. Most technology-transfer offices provide templates for material transfer agreements. To streamline the process, in 1999, the NIH and AUTM jointly developed a standard agreement known as the Uniform Biological Material Transfer Agreement (UBMTA).[23] It provides boilerplate language governing the transfer, including uniform definitions, ownership, use, and redistribution of the transferred materials, rights and restrictions on commercial access, liability and distribution costs, adherence to federal policies, and the ability to publish research results.

To simplify the process further, the NIH has developed two sample letters based on the UBMTA terms that serve functionally as material transfer agreements: the simple letter and the implementing letter.[24] The simple-letter agreement is designed for routine transfers of material between nonprofit organizations (including universities) for research and teaching purposes. The NIH provides specific guidance for simple-letter usage when their funds are involved:

> The majority of transfers to not-for-profit entities should be implemented under terms no more restrictive than the UBMTA. In particular, Recipients are expected to use the Simple Letter Agreement . . . or another document with no more restrictive terms, to readily transfer unpatented tools developed with NIH funds to other recipients for use in NIH-funded projects. If the materials are patented or licensed to an exclusive provider, other arrangements may be used, but commercialization option rights, royalty reach-through, or product reach-through rights back to the provider are inappropriate.[25]

On the other hand, the implementing-letter agreement is used for the transfer of patentable materials that are likely to be licensed commercially by the provider to the recipient for research and teaching purposes only. In these cases, the implementing letter supplements the UBMTA. In addition, the NIH has prepared a slightly modified "material transfer agreement for the transfer of organisms."[26] The difference is that it contains terms specific to the transfer of animals.

A small group of universities, including Johns Hopkins, Harvard, Stanford, and about fifteen others, have agreed to eliminate the need for a formal material transfer agreement when exchanging materials. According to their master agreement,

"A specific MTA is not required when our investigators and their research colleagues elsewhere are exchanging non-hazardous or non-human biological materials for in vitro research use." Furthermore, "We agree that if materials are transferred without a specific MTA, the transfer will be presumed to be made under the terms stated in the UBMTA even though no written agreement has been signed."[27] Thus, researchers may share tangible research property with relative ease under the implicit assumption that the UBMT applies to the exchange. This is a highly desirable simplification for the investigators, who occasionally overlook the need for a material transfer agreement when sending out or receiving research materials.

When reviewing material transfer agreements for materials coming into the university, the chief research officer commonly looks for several unacceptable stumbling blocks. Two of the more common examples concern ownership and publication. A provider's insistence on ownership of any patentable invention or discovery made using their tangible research property conflicts with usual university ownership policy and the Bayh-Dole Act if federal funding supports the research. To resolve this, universities may offer favorable license rights. Also, restrictions on the right to publish research results are contrary to academic tradition. Reasonable delays (such as three months) to allow the provider an opportunity to review the results usually remove this stumbling block. In general, the chief research officer through the technology-transfer office tries hard to negotiate around potential complications to produce workable agreements because these efforts make a major contribution to the research environment. And, less idealistically, if they fail to iron out troublesome details, researchers may simply make the exchanges on their own initiative—with little patience for perceived administrative red tape.

Cooperative Research and Development Agreements

In the Federal Technology Transfer Act of 1986, the government established the so-called cooperative research and development agreements (CRADAs) as a way to facilitate technology transfer from federal laboratories to nonfederal partners, including universities. Under these agreements, the two parties work on a common project. Unlike a federal grant or contract, with the government providing most of the funding, the university agrees to provide funds, personnel, services, facilities, equipment, and other resources needed to conduct a specific research or development. In return, the federal government agrees to provide personnel, services, facilities, equipment, or other resources toward the conduct of specified research or development efforts—but no funds. Thus, a CRADA is not intended to be a general funding mechanism.

Further limitations apply. The sole purpose of a CRADA cannot be to support post-doctoral fellows or technicians, to obtain funds, or to purchase equipment and supplies. Furthermore, the sole justification of a CRADA cannot be for a federal laboratory to conduct research or tests for the collaborator. There must be mutually beneficial scholarly contributions from both university and federal participants.

With these restrictions, why would a university want to enter a CRADA? The answer revolves around access to intellectual property rights. Importantly, a CRADA guarantees to the university a nonexclusive, paid-up, royalty-free license to make and use any patented inventions that are derived from the project research. Furthermore, the university is granted an option to obtain an exclusive license to the property. Because of these liberal licensing terms, the university gains access to the intellectual property and, therefore, the opportunity to continue research on it. In this way, the university leverages its own research efforts while collaborating in state-of-the-art federal facilities. On top of all that, the university gains access to expertise available at the federal laboratories, which can sometimes be invaluable.

Most federal agencies award CRADAs to university partners. Because these collaborations may detract from their overall research agenda, many agencies can be quite selective in awarding these agreements. In some cases, CRADAs come in various sizes, ranging from a few university investigators working in a federal laboratory (such as at the NIH or the FDA), to large-facility operational contracts, such as the CRADA enabling the University of California's management of the Lawrence Berkeley National Laboratory. And vice versa, universities tread carefully into this territory. For one thing, they must provide the funding. For another, they generally cannot agree to more than very short publication delays. For that reason, the University of California does not allow student participation in the Lawrence Berkeley National Laboratory CRADA project except in unusually justifiable circumstances.

Patents and Faculty Promotion

The exploding numbers of disclosures of intellectual property since passage of the Bayh-Dole Act strongly imply that faculty members are devoting increasingly more effort in this realm. And, by inference, that comes at the expense of other, more traditional academic pursuits—namely, writing scholarly papers, applying for grants, teaching, and community service. Furthermore, many state and local government leaders looking to the university as a driver of economic growth have launched legislative stimulus packages predicated on the commercialization of intellectual property.

Against this backdrop, some universities have endorsed the notion of including the generation of intellectual property as a tenure and promotion criterion. Texas A&M is a prime example. Thus, the number of disclosures, patent applications, or patents issued takes place alongside the number of scholarly publications in a promotion dossier. The mere suggestion of including these factors has sparked sometimes heated debate among faculty members and administrators alike. Proponents argue that commercialization is an integral component of the overall research process. To ignore this is to stay in the dark ages. In contrast, opponents argue that the lure of commercialization will thwart research into basic phenomena. And they quickly raise examples, such as the discovery of the DNA double helix.

Perhaps the most pragmatic argument against the inclusion of intellectual property here is one of time. Typically, it takes several years to prosecute a patent. And it may take years beyond that for successful commercialization of a product. Only then will the patent's impact on the market and society as a whole become known. This time frame exceeds the usual six- or seven-year timeline for tenure and promotion decisions. The counterargument is that patents are thoroughly vetted by campus intellectual property committees, licensed patent examiners, and potential licensees. Not all publications or grant applications undergo such rigorous reviews.

> K: *The universities seem to be going out of their way to facilitate technology transfer. Aren't they implicitly encouraging faculty members to devote more and more effort along those lines?*
>
> Smith: *Yes. The word* implicitly *understates the encouragement. Technology-transfer personnel explicitly encourage development of intellectual property. And university royalty-distribution policies provide further incentive.*
>
> K: *With that encouragement, wouldn't it seem unjust for the university to ignore patents in tenure and promotion decisions? There is an element of hypocrisy here.*
>
> Smith: *You raise a good point. It is hypocritical. Times are changing, however, and I suspect that more and more universities will acknowledge this double standard and ultimately adopt intellectual property as a tenure and promotion criterion.*

Notes

1. Patents, Trademarks, and Copyrights, 37 C.F.R. 401.14 (c)(1) (2010).
2. Association of University Technology Managers (AUTM), *U.S. Licensing Activity Survey: FY2008* (Deerfield. Ill.: AUTM, 2010).
3. U.S. Patent and Trademark Office, 35 U.S.C. § 202 (c)(1) (1980).
4. National Institutes of Health (NIH), "A 20-20 View of Invention Reporting to The National Institutes of Health," *NIH Guide*, 24, no. 33 (1995).
5. 35 U.S.C. § 202 (c)(5).
6. NIH, "A 20-20 View."
7. National Institutes of Health (NIH), "Interagency Edison," 2010, http://era.nih.gov/ProjectMgmt/iedison2/flash/iedison_all.htm (accessed January 15, 2011).
8. AUTM, *Licensing Activity Survey, 2008.*

9. P. H. Weeks, "How to Organize a Technology Transfer Office," in Research Management and Administration, ed. E. C. Kulakowski and L. U. Chronister (Sudbury, Mass.: Jones and Bartlett, 2006), p. 645.

10. Association of University Technology Managers (AUTM), *U.S. Licensing Activity Survey, 2007* (Deerfield, Ill.: AUTM, 2009).

11. 37 C.F.R. § 401.7 (a).

12. 35 U.S.C. § 204.

13. Council on Government Relations (COGR), *The Bayh-Dole Act: A Guide to the Law and Implementing Regulations* (Washington. D.C.: COGR, 1999), p. 2.

14. Peter Drucker, *The Practice of Management* (New York: HarperCollins, 1954), pp. 35-36.

15. Stanford University, "Inventions, Patents and Licensing (RPH 5.1)," 1999, http://rph.stanford.edu/5-1.html (accessed January 15, 2011).

16. Association of University Technology Managers (AUTM), "Technology Transfer Resources," 2010, http://www.autm.net/Technology_Transfer_Resources1/4944.htm (accessed January 15, 2011).

17. National Institutes of Health (NIH), "Forms & Model Agreements," 2009, http://www.ott.nih.gov/forms_model_agreements/forms_model_agreements.aspx#MLA (accessed January 15, 2011).

18. National Institutes of Health (NIH), "Principles and Guidelines for Recipients of NIH Research Grants and Contracts on Obtaining and Disseminating Biomedical Research Resources: Final Notice," *Federal Register*, 64, no. 246 (1999): 72093.

19. National Science Foundation (NSF), "Dissemination and Sharing of Research Results," in *Proposal and Award Policies and Procedures Guide Part II – Award and Administration Guide*, § VI.D.4.b (Arlington, VA.: NSF, 2010), p. VI–8.

20. NIH, "Principles and Guidelines," p. 72093.

21. Ibid., p. 72095.

22. Ibid.

23. Ibid., p. 72094.

24. NIH, "Forms & Model Agreements."

25. NIH, "Principles and Guidelines," p. 72094.

26. NIH, "Forms & Model Agreements."

27. California Institute of Technology et al., "Material Transfer Agreements," 2009, http://www.techtransfer.jhu.edu/bin/i/n/MTA%207-6-09.pdf (accessed January 15, 2011).

CHAPTER 16

Economic Development

K: *With all of its technology-transfer activities, the university begins to look like quite a business enterprise. Does it actively promote this image?*

Smith: *Yes. Universities continually portray themselves as catalysts for economic prosperity. And in most cases, they are right.*

K: *Does this compromise their academic mission?*

Smith: *That's open to debate. Some people think so. But lots of people now view economic development as part of a university's mission—along with teaching, research, and service—especially if it's funded by state tax dollars. In fact, that mission has been thrust on research universities whether they like it or not.*

Public Expectations

The terms "technology transfer" and "economic development" have become inseparable. Indeed, they might as well be one hyphenated phrase: "technology transfer–economic development." A third term can be conjoined, "high-tech." In many conversations, technology transfer implies high tech. And that seeds the fourth term to this concatenation, "university." University, technology transfer, high tech, economic development. Putting these four terms into a proper sentence frames the modern image of a research university: "Through its *technology-transfer* activities, *universities* spin out *high-tech* intellectual capital that stimulates *economic development*." And that leads to a fifth phrase, "high-paying jobs."

These words are so tightly coupled that, in many institutions, the chief research officer's official title includes the term "economic development." For example, at Texas Tech University, the chief research officer's position is formally "vice president for research, technology transfer, and economic development." And this is not unusual. The University of Arizona, Mississippi State University, and many other universities include "economic development" in the chief research officer's title. Regardless of the title, the chief research officer's responsibilities at nearly all research institutions include economic development as a corollary to his or her authority over technology transfer. In this context, economic development generally refers to "local" economic activity—confined mainly to the university's hometown or, at most, its home state.

Where did this semiotic relationship between research universities and economic development originate? The spark was lit with the establishment of the National Science Foundation (NSF) in 1950, when the federal government began to entrust its research to universities. About twenty years later, it was fanned into a small flame in the tinder of "institutional patent agreements" (IPAs) between numerous universities and either the National Institutes of Health (NIH) or the NSF. Under these landmark agreements, negotiated initially by Howard Bremer of the Wisconsin Alumni Research Foundation on behalf of the University of Wisconsin,[1] the participating universities had a contractual right to elect ownership of any invention developed with NIH or NSF funding. Then, according to many observers, the technology-transfer flame was fully ignited by passage of the 1980 Bayh-Dole Act, which essentially codified the institutional patent agreements for all universities and small businesses. Legally, this act changed the presumption of title to inventions made with federal money from the government to the universities and small businesses.

With this impetus, universities have become serious players in the technology-transfer business and therefore in economic development. They have become hubs of high-tech economic activity. According to an analysis of high-tech economies by the Milkin Institute, research universities and institutions:

> are undisputedly the most important factor in incubating high-tech industries. A side effect of the technical capability and scientific research activities of these institutions is the training and education of the skilled labor that will be critical to the expansion and reinforcement of regional high-tech industries. The federal government had an unintended impact on the formation of high-tech clusters around the country through its location of research centers and allocation of grants.[2]

Local communities honor this importance by appointing chief research officers routinely to economic-development boards, chambers of commerce, and other organizations that promote business activity. These appointments often extend beyond community boundaries. Chief research officers often serve ex officio on statewide task forces and related groups mandated to expand economic growth in one or more sectors. As the university's emissary, he or she often serves on a community economic-development board. Commonly, this places the chief research officer at speaker podiums, lunch tables, or festive dinners with government leaders (for example, mayors and governors), corporate executives, and other "movers and shakers."

These economic-development invitations can voraciously devour the chief research officer's time and attention. Indeed, he or she can be drawn into an unfamiliar world, the business world, with many novel temptations—good food, extensive travel, limousines, and the like. Predictably, these activities can be quite distracting. "Mission creep" can beset the office, with economic development displacing more academic responsibilities on the daily agenda. And occasionally, this inattention to other university research issues such as regulatory compliance has cost the chief research officer his or her job.

With all of this recognition, the chief research officer must answer the personal question: What do I have to offer here? Or, more aptly, What does the university have to offer? Clearly, the public expects a lot. And the research university provides a lot. By dint of its research expenditures, the university stimulates the local economy monetarily as an employer and as a purchaser. Since the majority (usually between 65 and 80 percent) of research funding comes from federal sources, the university "imports" money into the local economy. Although some supply and equipment items may be purchased from a national marketplace, much of this money resonates in the local economy. Numerous studies have measured the ultimate multiplier effect—how many dollars enter the economy for every dollar of research expenditures—and the value usually lies between 2.0 and 2.5.[3] Thus, a university that generates $100 million in annual research expenditures pumps at least twice that amount directly and indirectly into the local economy. That becomes a significant factor, especially if the university is located in a small community.

But there's more. Research universities generally tout their contributions to an educated workforce. And this is a powerful magnet for private industry. The challenge, of course, is to retain the university's highly trained graduates in local jobs. Retention of foreign students is particularly difficult, if not hopeless. The value of a highly educated workforce depends to a large extent on the presence of employment opportunities; small towns generally offer fewer prospects, so they benefit less. Nonetheless, the availability of well-educated employees is better with a local research university than without it. (It is not unusual to find Ph.D.-level taxi drivers in some small- to mid-size university towns, such as Madison, Wisconsin.)

Hold up the mirror for a bit. What does the local economy mean to the university's research efforts? As with the earlier vice versa question (what does the university have to offer), the answer is a lot. There are the obvious things, like the availability of a skilled labor force (such as laboratory technicians) and amenities conducive to recruiting desirable students and faculty members (such as good schools and entertainment opportunities). But a more subtle factor equals these in importance to the university's capacity for innovative research: local high-tech industries. Of course, they provide a market for graduates entering the job market, which is an incentive to study and work in fields of interest to the local industries. It goes beyond that, however. Creative research involves risk of failure. Local high-tech job opportunities create alternative career options for an investigator whose imaginative research project fails—an emotional and professional safety net.

In the absence of these local career alternatives, a university researcher may be much less inclined to tackle high-risk, innovative projects. With this in mind, chief research officers actively support all efforts to attract high-tech industries to the local community.

> *K: You make it sound as if the chief research officer spends a lot of time at economic-development events. Does this really benefit the university?*
>
> *Smith: Yes, it does. The chief research officer's presence demonstrates that the university takes its economic impact on the community seriously. That's important for good public relations. Often the university is viewed as an uncaring behemoth isolated from its surrounding communities that just consumes taxpayer money and doesn't pay back through taxes.*
>
> *K: If it's that important, why would you warn that attention to economic development may lead to "mission creep?"*
>
> *Smith: Ultimately, the chief research officer's mission is the maintenance of a healthy research environment within the university. Yes, that includes nurturing supportive relationships with the local community. But for some chief research officers, economic-development activities offer very interesting challenges and opportunities in a nonacademic setting. And that can compromise his or her attention to campus responsibilities.*

Start-up Companies

Newly established companies that commercialize university research products supply the fuel for economic development. Indeed, start-up companies originating as spin-offs from university research efforts constitute an invigorating and highly valued asset to the local economy. (The terms "start-up" and "spin-off" are synonymous in this context.) In 2007, AUTM reported the formation of 543 start-up companies based on university technology.[4] These fledgling businesses, which typically have very few employees, introduce cutting-edge technologies to the local marketplace. And that generates excitement. Many fail. Furthermore, if they succeed, larger corporations may acquire these innovative small companies, thus buying the new technologies. In those cases, the newly acquired companies may be moved out of the community to some other corporate location. Regardless, these spin-off high-tech companies reinforce the university's role as a catalyst for economic development and enhance its public image. They give the university technology focused attention and first priority. Indeed, many university technologies would languish without the impetus provided by start-up companies. When successful, this results in the creation of new wealth, new jobs, and economic growth and development for the community.[5]

In a simple scenario, a start-up company originates from a faculty member's initiative to commercialize an invention arising from his or her research program.

More likely than not, a patent application has been filed by the university, which retains ownership of the invention. With institutional support provided by the business school, the Small Business Development Center (a university-affiliated program funded jointly by the federal and state governments), or the technology-transfer office, the researcher establishes a company by filing the necessary incorporation paperwork with the state. This relatively simple procedure can typically be done online. Initially, the company may amount to little more than the faculty member and perhaps a few colleagues, such as relatives, friends, or members of his or her research group. Rights to the patent can be obtained from the university through a license agreement. Since many of these inventions will require considerable further development before they're ready for introduction to the marketplace, these licenses are often exclusive. In many cases, the university accepts a small equity position in the start-up company instead of upfront license fees, thus allowing the company to invest its money in product development. For the same reason, additional equity may also substitute for royalties.

As a rule of thumb, the university encourages faculty members who founded a company to engage professional managers who have specialized business skills and talent. This is not meant as an insult; it is pragmatic for several reasons. Except in unusual cases, faculty researchers have little experience in running a business. Potential investors recognize this and, therefore, look for an experienced management team. The founding faculty member continues his or her involvement with the company on a consulting basis rather than as an officer, often as chair of the company's scientific advisory committee. This arm's-length arrangement allows the researcher more time to develop and improve the product and to continue his or her faculty role. Most institutions offer help in finding individuals with the requisite business skills. As an incentive, their compensation may come in the form of stock options rather than meaningful salaries.

Financing

Money and experienced business-management talent pose the biggest obstacles confronting a new start-up company. In that apprehensive context, a nascent company has little chance of securing the financing needed to succeed without a solid business plan. Consequently, management's first objective is to prepare a viable business plan. Indeed, a *Nature Materials* article analyzing university start-up companies pointed out, "A competent business team with a reasonable business plan is needed to convert a university spinoff company into a 'real' company. The importance of the business side of a spin-off company increases more or less monotonically from day one."[6]

Therefore, with the business plan in hand, management's second objective is to raise the money needed to operate the company. This poses a significant challenge in the best of cases. Management raises money in what are called "investment rounds." They fall into four basic classes, depending on the development stage of the start-up company: seed, angel, venture, and mezzanine. The financing amount increases and the investment risk decreases with each round.

In the earliest stages of a company's development, when the technologies are new to the market, the founding faculty member and maybe relatives or friends pay initial expenses out of personal wealth. This is the seed round; it is also known as the "friends and family round." (Sometimes it is called the "friends, family, and fools round.") These seed funds, which seldom exceed $100,000 or $200,000, get the company going.

The second round, the so-called angel round, is financed by "angel investors." These are either single individuals or groups of investors (an angel network) who invest their own money. The amount generally falls between a few hundred thousand to a few million dollars. Angel capital fills the gap in start-up financing between seed funding and the third-round funding, venture capital. This gap, when cash flow exceeds available funding, is known as the "valley of death." Thus, angel investors help the start-up company bridge this ominous chasm. Because the investment risk is quite high—investments may be lost totally if the young company fails—angel investors expect potential returns of at least ten to twenty times their initial investment within a five-year period. At that time, they exit via an "exit strategy," which generally depends on a merger or an acquisition.

The third round is the so-called venture round, which features venture-capital firms. These are well-organized groups of sophisticated investors who pool their money into a venture-capital fund and then invest in numerous young companies, thus spreading out the risk. Typically, they provide funding in the $1 million to $10 million range in exchange for equity in the company. Furthermore, these firms participate actively in the company's management; this participation may involve not only managerial expertise but also technical know-how. Often, they prefer to invest in companies located near their headquarters to facilitate this oversight. Because of the high risk involved, venture-capital firms are quite selective in their choice of investments. Moreover, they expect high returns—up to about 40 percent—within about a five-year time frame. Like angel investors, they exit via an exit strategy calling for a merger or acquisition by another company.

Late-stage private funding comes in the fourth round, the mezzanine round. Mezzanine funding provided by investment firms, including large banks, carries a company into its mature stage, marked by a major merger or acquisition or an initial public offering (IPO) of stock to the general public. The amounts may range from tens to hundreds of millions of dollars. Usually this comes as a loan with repayment terms, although the investors may accept equity in some cases. Because of the inherent investment risk, interest rates are higher than for conventional bank loans. Exit strategies include mergers, acquisitions, or IPOs. Occasionally a fifth round of financing, bridge financing, is required to supplement the mezzanine financing en route to the exit.

Some universities help out by investing in start-up companies founded by their faculty members, including those holding equity interests in the company. This usually occurs at the angel round. But there may be restrictive limitations. Stanford University provides an illustrative example:

> The University ordinarily will not invest in such companies if any of the involved faculty members also have line management responsibilities in them, given the potential for apparent or real conflicts of interest. . . . However, Stanford may invest in start-ups in which the extent of its faculty involvement is limited to equity holdings (or rights to equity) and/or advisory roles under the following conditions:[7]
>
> 1. Stanford will not act as a lead investor or syndicating agent. All investments will be as a "passive investor."
> 2. Stanford will not acquire an equity holding greater than 10% of the ownership of the company.
> 3. No Stanford officer is to be a member of the board, or be an officer of the company, or have a personal equity position in the company at the time of Stanford's investment in any of the equity rounds before the company goes public.

Other universities have similar conditions.

In general, universities will participate only if there are other co-investors. The rationale is that these other investors provide additional validation of the company's market analysis, business plan, and management talent. In addition, they help establish the company's value, which is important for subsequent financing efforts. And usually universities limit their investments to between 5 and 10 percent of the company's estimated worth; that translates to 5 to 10 percent of the company's initial stock issue.

The chief research officer generally does not play a major role in these financial activities. Universities have professional staff members who handle this, often in the technology-transfer office. Nonetheless, as the university's representative in numerous economic development forums, the chief research officer is often engaged in discussions about start-up company financing and related topics. Although a technical background is not essential, at minimum he or she must be familiar with basic finance at the level presented in these few paragraphs.

> *K: By investing in their own faculty members' start-up companies, universities begin to look more and more like businesses themselves. Isn't that the kind of "mission creep" that you're talking about?*
>
> *Smith: Some people think so. But, honestly, these small start-up companies face daunting odds when it comes to raising capital. If the university encourages entrepreneurship among its faculty members, providing a financial boost is a reasonable extension of those efforts.*
>
> *K: Isn't that taking money away from the academic programs?*

Smith: Yes, it is. But the same applies to subsidies for the football team or the marching band. At least, a few of these small-business investments have the potential to yield big returns that can be reinvested in academics if the product is a commercial success.

Small-Business Grants

Recognizing the perilous financial challenges confronting small companies, the federal government enacted legislation establishing two parallel grant programs designed to help them: the Small Business Innovation Research (SBIR) program and the Small Business Technology Transfer (STTR) program.[8] Their goals are similar: to boost commercialization of technological innovation through small businesses. (By statutory definition, small businesses have 500 or fewer employees.) Small companies retain the intellectual property rights to technologies they develop under these programs. Each participating federal agency (for example, the NIH) funds grants that fall within its programmatic mission (for example, human health in the case of NIH). In toto, the combined SBIR and STTR programs provide more than $2 billion annually to early-stage technology financing. Nearly half of this comes from the Department of Defense.

Both the SBIR and the STTR programs come in three phases. The first phase (phase I) is for determining, "insofar as possible, the scientific and technical merit and feasibility of ideas that appear to have commercial potential."[9] This is often referred to as the "project feasibility" or "proof of concept" phase. The SBIR and STTR awards are up to $150,000 for a period of six or twelve months, respectively. If the first phase proves project feasibility, firms are invited to apply for a second phase (phase II) grant. These awards, which range up to $750,000 for a two-year period, allow for further development of the concept, usually to the prototype stage. In the third phase (phase III), which follows completion of phase II, small companies are expected to obtain funding from the private sector (such as a venture-capital firm) or non-SBIR, non-STTR government sources to develop the concept into a product for sale. Although phase III is recognized as a component of the SBIR and STTR programs, it is not funded by them. They are saying, "You're on your own" at that point.

The SBIR legislation requires every federal agency with an extramural research and development program exceeding $100 million annually to reserve 2.5 percent of that budget for awards to small-business firms. That includes at least twenty-eight federal agencies, including the NIH and NSF. The principal investigator must be employed by the business on more than a half-time basis. Thus, a faculty member must reduce his or her university appointment to less than half-time to serve as the principal investigator on an SBIR grant.

Parallel STTR legislation requires every federal agency with an extramural research and development budget exceeding $1 billion annually to reserve 0.3 percent of that budget for awards to small business firms for "cooperative research and development." The SBIR and STTR legislative language looks deceptively similar. But STTR differs in two significant ways. The first is readily apparent: the threshold extramural research budget for STTR programs ($1 billion) is tenfold higher than for SBIR programs ($100 million). Consequently, fewer agencies (about thirteen) participate. The second difference lies in the words "cooperative research and development." According to legislation, "cooperative research and development" means "research or research and development conducted jointly by a small business concern and a research institution in which not less than 40 percent of the work is performed by the small business concern, and not less than 30 percent of the work is performed by the research institution."[10] The remaining 30 percent may be used to hire consultants.

In the words of the NSF, the STTR program requires researchers at universities and other research institutions to play a significant intellectual role in the conduct of each STTR project. These university-based researchers, by joining forces with a small company, can spin off their commercially promising ideas while they remain employed at the research institution. Thus, students and other researchers may retain primary (that is, more than half-time) employment with the university. However, the principal investigator (PI) must be employed primarily (at least 51 percent of the time) with the small-business concern at the time of the award. Furthermore, the PI must spend a minimum of two calendar months on an STTR phase I project: "Employment releases and certifications of intent shall be required prior to award."[11]

Importantly, the grant application must be submitted through the business firm, which receives the award. The university's "cooperative" participation is via a subcontract from the business partner.

Federal agencies judge SBIR and STTR proposals competitively on the basis of scientific, technical, and commercial merit. According to the NSF, successful proposals generally "provide evidence of a commercially viable product, process, device, or system, and meet an important social or economic need." Furthermore, they propose "high potential commercial payback, and high-risk efforts." In contrast, "proposed efforts directed toward systems studies; market research; commercial development of existing products or proven concepts; straightforward engineering design for packaging; laboratory evaluations; incremental product or process improvements; evolutionary optimization of existing products; and evolutionary modifications to broaden the scope of an existing product or application are examples of projects that are not acceptable" for either SBIR or STTR programs.[12]

Competition is usually stiff. Although the success rate varies by agency, only about 15 percent or so of the applications for a phase I grant are awarded. On the other hand, 40 to 50 percent of the phase I awardees also receive phase II funding. Many chief research officers, through the technology-transfer or the sponsored-research offices, offer technical guidance in the preparation of SBIR and STTR grant applications. Moreover, many business schools and university-based Small Business Development Centers have entrepreneurship programs that also provide similar assistance to not only faculty members but also small-business owners.

Ethical Conflicts

These fledgling companies often rely on the faculty member and his or her laboratory group for the technology base essential to company formation and growth. This raises ethical conflicts that complicate the scenario.

The first has to do with conflicts of commitment. As full-time employees, faculty members' primary allegiance is to the university. In that capacity, they are expected to devote most of their time and intellectual energies to fulfilling the university's mission—teaching, research, and service. Even if economic development falls within the mission, the faculty member's efforts must benefit the university and not outside ventures. Quantitatively, at most universities, faculty members must spend 80 percent of their time on these university priorities, which leaves 20 percent, or one day per week (assuming a forty-hour work week), for private consulting. That consulting time, plus off-duty hours, weekends and holidays, is available for company business. Failure to abide by the commitment obligations to the employer (namely, the university) can be grounds for dismissal.

The second ethical issue has to do with conflicts of interest. In general, a conflict of interest occurs when an individual's private interests and his or her professional obligations to the university do not coincide. The test is whether an independent observer might reasonably question if the individual's professional actions or decisions are determined by considerations of personal gain. Ultimately, if the faculty member or his or her relatives hold equity in the company, which they most often do, financial conflicts of interest instantly appear on the horizon. Sometimes the appearance may be more or less subtle. For example, if the faculty member were to direct his or her students' research efforts to projects directly impacting the company's well-being, an independent observer might question the objectivity of this guidance—even if the freedom to publish were not compromised.

Most universities require public disclosure of faculty members' financial holdings in a company, with the hope that this will mitigate potential conflicts of interest. Regardless, perceived conflicts of commitment and interest can arise. Their resolution usually begins at the college dean's level, but remediation of difficult cases often ends up at the chief research officer's or the provost's level. If a faculty member's objectivity might reasonably be questioned, the dean or the chief research officer commonly appoints an independent oversight committee to review the faculty member's research program relative to the company's interests. Some universities have standing conflict-of-interest (ethics) committees that routinely monitor a faculty member's relationship with a company in which he or she holds an equity position.

In addition, many universities take a more proactive approach to avert potential conflicts of interest. For example, they may prohibit faculty members from accepting managerial positions in any outside venture, including a start-up company. Moreover, university personnel may not be allowed to sit on the board of directors of a company in which the university has equity holdings. To minimize chances of a conflict of interest, nearly all institutions counsel faculty members to take an unpaid leave of absence from the university if they desire to play a significant managerial role in a start-up company (or any other external entity).

Use of University Facilities for Private Enterprise

By definition, technology transfer in an academic setting involves transferring products developed in university facilities to the private sector. This transition is seldom abrupt. Often, continued product development depends on specialized equipment and facilities not readily available outside the university—at least not at a cost within the budget of a newly established spin-off company. Consequently, entrepreneurial faculty members face the temptation to continue using their university facilities to improve the inventions that spawned a start-up company. And this exposes another facet of conflict of interest: the use of university facilities for private gain. To complicate matters, most states prohibit the use of public facilities such as a state university laboratory for private gain.

Fortunately, there are usually ways to enable private usage of university facilities. The most straightforward solution requires the faculty member—or any other individual—to pay the university for the significant use of its facilities for private, nonacademic purposes. In this context, the chief research officer brokers the contractual arrangements for facility use. The university enters into a lease agreement that allows the use of its facilities, which may include laboratory space, equipment, supplies, personnel, utilities, and other conveniences. The lease rate must be based on prevailing market rates; the university cannot give a faculty member's private business (the lessee) a favorable, below-market lease rate.

How are these lease rates determined? For the most part, estimates come rather easily. Commercial real-estate firms can readily supply the market rates for local office space. And often they can provide reasonable data for laboratory space that contains specialized features such as benches, fume hoods, distilled water, and the like. These estimates can be derived from more or less comparable medical clinic rates, for example. Equipment charges can be drawn from the university's F&A cost calculations, and charges for supplies (such as chemicals, glassware, and compressed gases) can be based simply on expected procurement costs. The only real complications arise when personnel are involved. If company employees (including those with concomitant part-time university appointments) work in university laboratories, liability and insurance issues must be resolved. The university's legal counsel will undoubtedly insist on language relieving the institution of any liability; this is a so-called indemnification and hold harmless agreement. It assigns all risk and liability associated with use of university facilities or equipment to the private user. Incidentally, all lease rates should include F&A costs based on the federally negotiated rate.

Hypothetically, whenever the university enters into an agreement of this sort with a private business, competing companies may also request similar access to institutional facilities. *Ceteris paribus*, these requests must be honored. Otherwise, the university may violate state laws preventing unfair competition. Consequently, many universities add an important condition to their leasing policies: the arrangement must benefit the university academically. Commercializing a university invention or providing student research opportunities fall into that category. Earning rent on underutilized space does not. The chief research officer typically makes the final judgment call about the academic relevance of leases to private concerns. And these decisions are usually quite conservative.

Tax Issues

Allowing private businesses to use university facilities through a lease or other arrangement can have significant tax consequences. In general, they fall under the "unrelated business use" section of the tax code.[13] A particularly relevant situation arises from a university's nonprofit status that allows it to issue tax-exempt bonds for financing building construction. Because the purchasers pay no tax on the income derived from these bonds, the bonds generally pay a lower interest rate. And this reduces the university's cost of constructing the building. However, private business use of a facility financed by tax-exempt bonds may invalidate the tax-exempt status of the bond issue, thus subjecting the interest income to taxation. Consequently, the university must compensate the bond purchasers for the taxes that they now must pay on the interest. Of course, the university considers that undesirable.

Incidentally, the tax code states further that the unrelated business income tax "shall also apply in the case of any corporation wholly owned by one or more such colleges or universities."[14] The IRS comments further: "Consequently, it is immaterial whether the business activity is conducted by the university or by a separately incorporated, wholly owned subsidiary. If the business activity is unrelated, the income in both instances will be subject to the tax."

Therefore, the university cannot escape the tax-code provisions by relegating private use of its facilities to those housed in a building owned by a separately incorporated nonprofit entity that is demonstrably affiliated with the university. For this strategy to succeed, there must be "blue water" between the university and the separate nonprofit entity—that is, the two cannot be linked organizationally in any perceptible way.

Fortunately, the IRS allows some wiggle room in these matters—namely, the so-called safe harbors. For public institutions, private business use is permissible if it does not exceed 10 percent of the amount of the bond issuance; for private universities that are tax exempt under Section 501(c)(3) of the tax code (that is, nearly all nonprofit private universities), the safe-harbor limit is 5 percent. Realistically, these limits are about 2 percent lower because the cost of the bond issuance (about 2 percent of the total) is also considered an unrelated business activity. Importantly, the IRS has ruled that, "to meet the safe harbor, a contract must provide for reasonable compensation for services rendered with no compensation based, in whole or in part, on a share of net profits from the operation of the managed facility."[15]

Before proceeding, it may help to clarify what 10 percent of the amount of the bond issuance really means. The IRS has several methods for calculating the safe-harbor size, based on how the bond funding was used, the nature of the private use, and the square footage. The actual method varies from case to case. In its simplest form, the square footage serves as the baseline. For example, assume that a public university issues $100 million in tax-exempt bonds to construct a 100,000-square-foot research building. Then, 10 percent of the amount of the bond issue equals $10 million, and by inference, 10,000 square feet within the building. So, private businesses may use up to 10,000 square feet of the building without jeopardizing the tax-exempt status of the bonds. (Remember, however, to include the cost of the bond issuance when making these calculations.) Consider another example: assume that a public university issues $50 million in tax-exempt bonds to pay for half the costs of a $100 million, 100,000-square-foot building. The other half was financed by some other source, such as state general-fund money or a donor's gift. Then, most universities assign the unrelated business use to a well-defined portion of the building that was constructed by the private funding. In this example, that would allow 50 percent of the building's square footage for unrelated business use. If more space is required, the unrelated business may occupy an additional 10 percent of the tax-exempt bond-financed portion of the building—5,000 square feet—without affecting the tax-exempt bond status. Case-specific details can complicate this simplicity, so the university's bond counsel should always be consulted before making any decisions that may affect the tax-exempt status. (Note: although this strategy protects the tax-exempt bonds status, the university may still have to pay tax on the unrelated business income.)

Leasing part of a building by a private party clearly constitutes nonrelated business use. However, the IRS has also ruled that a university research project sponsored by an external party (a company) may be considered private business. To the benefit of research institutions, the IRS provides two additional safe harbors where a sponsored-research agreement does not result in private business use and therefore invalidate the tax exemption. They apply only to basic research, which is defined as "original investigation for the advancement of scientific knowledge not having a specific commercial objective." The IRS provides an example of what is not basic research: "product testing supporting the trade or business of a specific non-governmental party."[16] Another example would be clinical trials, which are not basic research.

The first of these two additional safe harbors covers research supported by a single sponsor. This requires that:

> any license or other use of resulting technology by the sponsor is permitted only on the same terms as the recipient would permit that use by any unrelated, non-sponsoring party (that is, the sponsor must pay a competitive price for its use), and the price paid for that use must be determined at the time the license or other resulting technology is available for use. Although the recipient need not permit persons other than the sponsor to use any license or other resulting technology, the price paid by the sponsor must be no less than the price that would be paid by any non-sponsoring party for those same rights.[17]

In other words, the sponsor must pay a fair market price for any license arising from their sponsored project and that price should be determined at the time the technology is available for use (not beforehand). Furthermore, this may be an exclusive license. First options and rights of refusal are permissible as long as the sponsor pays the same license fee as would be charged to a nonsponsor. Conceivably, a sponsor might object: "I paid for the research that developed this product, so why can't I get the license to use it at a discounted price?" To stay within the safe harbor, the chief research officer's reply should be, "We cannot sell the license at a below-market price, but we can sell you an exclusive license."

The second safe harbor applies to cooperative research agreements between industry and university researchers. It addresses situations where the private partner uses a university's bond-financed facilities, thus jeopardizing the tax-exempt status. The criteria for this safe harbor are that the university "determines the research to be performed and the manner in which it is to be performed (for example, selection of the personnel to perform the research)" and "title to any patent or other product incidentally resulting from the basic research lies exclusively with the qualified user"—namely, the university. Furthermore, "the sponsor or sponsors are entitled to no more than a non-exclusive, royalty-free license to use the product of any of that research."[18] Thus, the university has title to any intellectual property generated by the research. Incidentally, the IRS has ruled that this safe harbor also applies to any inventions made with federal support, which are subject to the provisions of the Bayh-Dole Act.

From the university's financial perspective, it is critical to maintain the tax-exempt status of its bonds. Consequently, in cooperative research agreements, most institutions steadfastly negotiate provisions for the use of inventions and facilities by private partners that are consistent with the safe-harbor provisions. Specifically, they require that the nature of the work should fit the IRS definition of basic research and the sponsor should receive no more intellectual property rights than an option for a nonexclusive, royalty-free license or an exclusive royalty-bearing license. In that context, funding support for a research project may not be considered as payment toward a license of future intellectual property.

These tax issues epitomize the aphorism "the devil is in the details." Because the stakes are so high, most experienced chief research officers consult with the university's lawyers and bond counsel whenever they contemplate leasing university facilities to a private entity or departing from the safe harbors in a cooperative agreement.

> K: Why don't universities avoid these problems by using buildings that were constructed without tax-exempt bond funding for privately sponsored research?
> Smith: They would if they could. But on many campuses nearly all university buildings suitable for modern research have been constructed, remodeled, or refinanced using tax-exempt bonds.
> K: But how about buildings endowed by a private donor?
> Smith: That all depends on the donor's commitment. If the donor has agreed to fund all initial costs, then bonding isn't required. However, in many cases the upfront construction costs are financed by a tax-exempt bond issue. The endowment then pays the bond debt over a twenty- or thirty-year period.

Research Parks

Research parks offer an attractive alternative for university development of start-up companies. To frame this attraction, it helps to define "research park." The Association of University Research Parks (AURP) defines a research park as a property-based venture which:

- Master plans property designed for research and commercialization
- Creates partnerships with universities and research institutions
- Encourages the growth of new companies
- Translates technology
- Drives technology-led economic development.[19]

Although they particularly attract small companies, research parks also draw larger businesses. Some larger firms may prefer to locate their research and development branches in a research park because of the proximity to university expertise.

The research parks provide facilities, services, and opportunities tailor-made for young businesses, without the complicating ethical and tax problems associated with the use of official university facilities. Moreover, research parks, which are often located adjacent to campus, are woven smoothly into the university's research fabric. Indeed, according to a survey of 134 research parks conducted by Battelle and AURP:

> The key factor differentiating a university research park from technology or industry parks is the meaningful interaction of the firms in the park with the university. This interaction can include providing internship and employment opportunities for students, sharing facilities and equipment, or conducting collaborative research. In addition, most university research parks have a university presence within the park, which can include research labs, test beds, education and training offerings, or technology transfer offices. Research park tenants, unlike technology or industry park tenants, undertake R&D within their premises in the park; employ greater concentrations of scientific, technical, and professional workers; and generate products or processes that incorporate a significant technological quotient.[20]

The phrase "a university presence within the park" captures an interesting twist in the relationship between a university and its economic-development activities. As universities outgrow their campus, they must lease off-campus space at prevailing fair market value. And where do they often go? They go to the nearby research park, where they can lease state-of-the art facilities with high-bandwidth Internet access. The Battelle and AURP survey revealed that 14 percent of the typical research park tenants are university facilities.

As a general rule, research parks do not make money. Most of them operate on small budgets (less than $1 million per year) and seldom retain significant earnings. Indeed, about half of all research parks do not retain any earnings. According to AURP, "research parks, which are undertaken to diversify local economies and build stronger industry–higher-education partnerships, usually require, at least in the short term, cross subsidization by their partners, communities, and higher-education sponsors."[21] Within the master-planning framework, private developers construct multipurpose buildings in the park to house small businesses, typically with financial help (for example, through tax incentives) from local or state governments. Nearly half of the research parks are affiliated one way or another with a university, which may also provide financial support to the park. For example, the university may offer the land rent-free.

Parks grow slowly. It usually takes many years for them to achieve financial stability. Part of that lag is attributable to the very early stages of many university spin-off companies; often it takes several years to bring a fledgling product to market. A prime example of the difficulties in establishing a viable research park can be witnessed at the new Mission Bay campus of the University of California, San Francisco. Economic factors alone disrupted several potential tenants' plans to locate research programs in the park, thus slowing the fledgling park's promising development. Despite the financial pressures, some research parks have achieved notable success over the years. A prime example is the Research Triangle Park, which was established in 1959 and is surrounded by Durham, Chapel Hill, and Raleigh, North Carolina—homes to three top-tier research universities. A smaller scale research park is affiliated with the University of Wisconsin-Madison. Founded in 1984, it is now self-sustaining, and all profits are returned to the university's research programs. These examples illustrate the need for patience as a research park matures. In the meantime, they serve a very useful purpose for the university's economic-development activities.

Incubators

Business incubators provide a more specialized venue for development of start-up companies unaccompanied by the ethical and tax issues associated with the use of university facilities. Unlike research parks, which accommodate businesses of all sizes, incubators limit their tenants to start-up and very early stage companies. Typically, an incubator building has space and other facilities available for product development, including laboratories. And they provide administrative support, such as accounting, grant management (for example, SBIR and STTR grants), and human-resources services. Importantly, incubators also offer management advice and guidance, often in conjunction with a local Small Business Development Center. These services—facilities, administration, and management guidance—are usually shared among various tenants. Progress in the incubator setting is usually assessed by benchmarks defined in the tenant company's business plan. When predefined goals have been met, the company "graduates" out of the incubator. This usually occurs within about three years.

Like research parks, incubators are generally unprofitable. Indeed, they commonly rely on subsidies from local or state governments and local economic-development boards. Some universities operate their own incubators through their technology-transfer program. Research parks often have incubator programs, which they subsidize. Because small businesses create jobs that usually stay in the community, local economic leaders (mayors, for example) push hard to maintain active incubators. Often, that push is directed toward the university. And the push is matched by a pull for financial contributions from the university (more specifically, the chief research officer) for incubator operations. Ideally, university support is somehow pegged to the number of university-spawned tenants using the incubator services. Realistically, this seldom happens. The call for support usually exceeds that proportional amount, which corresponds to an unfunded spending mandate for the university.

Parenthetically, business incubators do not necessarily command a high funding priority among chief research officers. True, they can provide a nutritive environment for university spin-off companies without serious ethical and tax complications. Moreover, if the incubator helps a product to succeed in the market, the university may gain licensing revenue. However, the chief research officer must weigh these pros against significant cons. In the latter context—namely, the cons—a technology transfer program's success depends on a strong flow of new research ideas into the disclosure stage. Money spent on an incubator, which benefits only a few companies downstream, may be invested more profitably in the university's basic research programs. Investment in the generation of more new ideas, and therefore disclosures, may ultimately have a greater impact on technology transfer than paying the rent for an incubator. In universities with relatively small research productivity, this trade-off requires particular attention.

> *K: If an incubator provides such a nourishing environment for spin-off companies, why wouldn't the university eagerly support it?*
>
> *Smith: Incubators can be a real financial drain for the benefit of only a very few firms. And it's hard to justify taking money from academic programs, which include basic research, for such a limited benefit.*
>
> *K: Why would the university encourage its researchers to commercialize research products and then abandon them at this critical juncture? What are these small companies supposed to do?*
>
> *Smith: In many communities, there are government-sponsored and private-sector business incubators available to fill that gap. We're back to the notion of "mission creep," which must be controlled. The university has to impose some boundaries on its economic-development activities if they drain resources from the core academic mission.*

Notes

1. Wisconsin Alumni Research Foundation, "WARF and Bayh-Dole," 2011, http://www.warf.org/about/index.jsp?cid=26&scid=35 (accessed January 15, 2011).
2. R. C. DeVol, *Growth, Development, and Risks for Metropolitan Areas* (Santa Monica, Calif.: Milkin Institute, 1999).
3. J. J. Siegfried, A. R. Sanderson, and P. McHenry, "The Economic Impact of Colleges and Universities, Working Paper No. 06-W12", 2006, http://www.vanderbilt.edu/Econ/wparchive/workpaper/vu06-w12.pdf (accessed January 15, 2011).
4. Association of University Technology Managers (AUTM), *U.S. Licensing Activity Survey: FY2008* (Deerfield. Ill.: AUTM, 2010).
5. Council on Government Relations (COGR), *University-Industry Relations Brochure* (Washington, D.C.: COGR, 2007).
6. X. Peng, "University Spin-offs: Opportunity or Challenge?" *Nature Materials*, 5 (2006): 923–25.
7. Stanford University, "University Investments in Start-Up Companies Involving Stanford Faculty, (RPH 4.5)," 1994, http://rph.stanford.edu/4-5.html (accessed January 16, 2011).
8. Small Business Act, 15 U.S.C. § 638 (2010).
9. Ibid., § 638.e.4.A.
10. Ibid., § 638.e.7.

11. National Science Foundation (NSF), "Small Business Technology Transfer Program-FY 2011 (STTR) Program Solicitation NSF 10-590," p. 2, 2010, http://www.nsf.gov/pubs/2010/nsf10590/nsf10590.pdf (accessed January 16, 2011).
12. Ibid., pp. 3-4.
13. Internal Revenue Service (IRS), Unrelated Trade or Business, 26 U.S.C. § 513 (2010).
14. 26 U.S.C. § 511 (2)(B); IRS, "Taxation of Unrelated Business Income," § 7.27.4.2.2.2, 2010, http://www.irs.gov/irm/part7/irm_07-027-004.html (accessed January 16, 2011).
15. IRS, "Memorandum number 199932017, UILC: 141.07-00," 1999, http://www.irs.gov/pub/irs-wd/9932017.pdf (accessed January 16, 2011).
16. IRS, "Revenue procedure 2007-47," § 3, 2007, http://www.irs.gov/irb/2007-29_IRB/ar12.html (accessed January 16, 2011).
17. IRS, "Memorandum number 200347009, Index number 141.01-01," 2003, http://www.irs.gov/pub/irs-wd/0347009.pdf (accessed January 16, 2011).
18. IRS, "Revenue Procedure 2007-47," § 6.03.
19. Association of University Research Parks, "What Is a Research Park?" 2011, http://www.aurp.net/mc/page.do?sitePageId=113584&orgId=aurp (accessed January 16, 2011).
20. Battelle Memorial Institute, "Characterization and Trends in North American Research Parks: 21st Century Directions," p. 4, 2007, http://www.aurp.net/mc/page.do?sitePageId=113579&orgId=aurp (accessed January 16, 2011).
21. Ibid., p. 10.

CHAPTER 17

Assessment and Evaluation

K: How do you know whether you've been successful in your job?
Smith: Sometimes that's hard to tell. The obvious hallmark is increased institutional research expenditures.
K: But isn't there more to it than that? How about fields that don't have access to large extramural grants?
Smith: There are other metrics that give a more comprehensive evaluation of scholarly success. But ultimately most observers look primarily at research expenditures.

Evaluation

"How's it going?" That's a standard question asked many times by many people on many occasions. Of course, the answer always depends on what "it" is. For the chief research officer, "it" could reside at several organizational levels: the university's overall research capacity, the research office units' (such as technology-transfer) performance, centers' and institutes' academic productivity, or his or her own individual effectiveness. The formal processes for answering "how's it going"—or, stated less casually, for determining an object's worth or merit—is called "evaluation." This term is coupled tightly with "assessment," and the two words are often used interchangeably.

Before proceeding, it helps to understand clearly what the terms "assessment" and "evaluation" mean. Some dictionaries equate the words *assessment* and *evaluation*. However, in an educational context, they are not necessarily synonymous. For example, according to the National Academy for Academic Leadership:

> Assessment provides faculty members, administrators, trustees, and others with evidence, numerical or otherwise, from which they can develop useful information about their students, institutions, programs, and courses and also about themselves. This information can help them make effectual decisions about student learning and development,

professional effectiveness, and program quality. Evaluation uses information based on the credible evidence generated through assessment to
make judgments of relative value: the acceptability of the conditions
described through assessment.[1]

Within this definitional framework, assessment of research performance tends
to be quantitative in nature. Typical data include numbers of research expenditure dollars, submitted grant proposals, and awarded doctoral degrees. The phrase
"tends to be quantitative" is used purposely because assessment may also consider
qualitative attributes. However, in the research context it routinely involves data
collection to describe a specific topic.

Evaluation compares assessment data to some reference values to judge
the topic's worthiness. Thus, to answer the original question, "how's it going,"
the chief research officer first assesses the situation (for example, looks up the
university's research expenditures) and then evaluates these data to determine if
a priori projections and expectations have been met. For example, he or she compares each department's research expenditures to benchmarks set previously
in the university's five-year strategic plan. The hypothetical question might then
be answered: "It's going well. We assessed last year's research expenditures,
and our evaluation of the data indicates that expenditures in all disciplines
exceeded goals set in the strategic plan." Notably, evaluation refers to some
standards.

Some professional evaluators may disagree with this usage of the terms. They
may prefer to use the words interchangeably. There is nothing wrong with that;
indeed, it conforms to several dictionary definitions. However, because many
authorities distinguish between the two, assessment and evaluation will be
considered as different steps in the determination of a program's merit, with the
explicit caveat that others may use the words synonymously. Therefore, by this
convention, when judging the performance of a university's research efforts and
making decisions based on that performance, information must first be gathered
(assessment) before passing judgment (evaluation). In short, by these definitions
evaluation implies assessment.

Within this definitional context, evaluation boils down to an information-driven
process. To determine if programs or policies are accomplishing their intended
goals, data describing productivity measures are collected—assessment. (How
many peer-reviewed publications per faculty member resulted from a particular
program investment for each of the last five years? And how many have similar
programs at other institutions generated in the same time period?) The information
in these data is deciphered and interpreted—evaluation. (Our faculty members
have consistently published more peer-reviewed papers than their colleagues at
other institutions. Therefore, our scholarly publication incentive policies seem to be
working.) The outcome of this analysis becomes the basis for subsequent decisions
concerning the program or policy.

From a practical perspective, evaluation may occur as an ongoing process or at some end-point, such as the conclusion of a five-year program. These two different time frames define formative and summative evaluation. Formative evaluations examine a program's implementation and progress toward achieving its goals. The organizational structure, personnel productivity, procedures, and related variables are assessed and evaluated periodically, and necessary adjustments are made to improve ongoing performance. Summative evaluations, in contrast, examine the effects or outcomes of a program. They summarize a program's effectiveness by describing whether it achieved its goal. Performance data are assessed and evaluated to determine the program's overall impact. Ideally, a summative evaluation determines "the overall impact of the causal factor beyond only the immediate target outcomes."[2]

So, formative evaluation provides real-time feedback: Are things going okay now? If not, here's why. This allows for continual programmatic adjustments. Usually formative evaluation continues through the duration of a particular program. Summative evaluation looks backwards: Did the program work as intended? If not, here's why it didn't. Although summative evaluation usually occurs at the end of a program, it may also take place at specific times during a program. The terms "formative evaluation" and "summative evaluation" appear in most directives mandating or at least recommending institutional evaluation protocols.

Evaluation has become a standard tool for determining a program's merit. Many accreditation associations, state education boards, and federal-funding agencies require institutions to document detailed plans for integrating assessment and evaluation into their management routine. For example, the NIH states this requirement quite explicitly in its Institutional Development Award (IDeA) grant proposal guidelines:

> An evaluation component is to be included in the application to assess whether the effectiveness of the approach taken will meet the goals or benchmarks for building an effective institutional and statewide scientific network. The application is to describe the development and implementation of the plan for formative and summative evaluations of the network along with strategies for revisions, if deemed necessary.[3]

Furthermore, the NIH requires the use of external evaluators and allows budgeting up to 5 percent of the total direct costs to pay for their services. Likewise, the NSF requires formal evaluation plans for some of its proposals. To help in planning and implementing the evaluation process, they have commissioned a useful tutorial handbook.[4]

From a managerial perspective, evaluation enables university administrators, including principal investigators, to close any gaps between what is—the status quo—and what ought to be, or the strategic goals. As a practical matter, no major decisions should be made without first evaluating reliably assessed information.

By following this simple rule, a chief research officer can always justify a programmatic or policy decision, not only to colleagues and the general public but also to him- or herself.

Institutional Assessment

At the highest organizational level, the institution's research efforts are under constant assessment. Many data are compiled to comply with the Higher Education Act of 1965 (Title IV), which requires institutions that participate in federal student-aid programs to report data on enrollments, program completions, graduation rates, faculty and staff numbers, finances, institutional prices, and student financial aid. These and many other voluminous data are collected regularly by the federal government's National Center for Education Statistics (housed in the Department of Education). It maintains a massive database tabulating numerous university descriptive statistics. These data are generated by their Integrated Postsecondary Education Data System (IPEDS), "a system of interrelated surveys conducted annually, which gathers information from every college, university, and technical and vocational institution in the United States and other jurisdictions (such as Puerto Rico) that participates in the federal student financial aid programs."[5] The IPEDS surveys include annual institutional financial statements, thus providing a good summary of revenue sources and expenditures. Generally, the institutional resources office, with help from the comptroller, completes and submits the IPEDS survey. Although this self-reporting method has an inherent potential for inconsistencies between institutions, the IPEDS database is considered reliable and up-to-date.

In addition, the NSF publishes national research and development expenditures annually, listing universities in rank order. Because the NSF data are used so widely, they are de facto definitive. The NSF generates national statistics describing federal agency funding from in-house sources. However, like IPEDS, the NSF relies on universities to supply their overall research expenditure data, federal and nonfederal, via an annual survey questionnaire that is usually filled out by the sponsored-research post-award accounting office.

Notably, the NSF introduced a new, online survey instrument in 2010. Several significant changes merit attention when reviewing past and future expenditure reports. Unlike the previous survey, the new survey includes clinical trials and training grant research and development expenditure data. Moreover, prior to 2010, these expenditure data were limited to research and development in the sciences and engineering within an institution's academic fiscal year. Non-science and engineering expenditures were reported separately and were cited far less frequently. The survey data now include expenditures in "both science and engineering (S&E) fields and non-science and engineering (non-S&E) fields such as humanities, education, law, and the arts."[6]

On the surface, the entries are quite straightforward: How much of your current fund expenditures for separately budgeted research and development (R&D) came from the following sources?[7] The categories include:

a. U.S. federal government
b. State and local government
c. Business
d. Nonprofit organizations
e. Institution funds
    (1) Institutionally financed organized research
    (2) Cost sharing
    (3) Unrecovered indirect costs
f. All other sources

As part of the report, the NSF asks institutions to categorize their expenditures by discipline, such as physics or biological sciences. According to the NSF, this categorization presents the most likely source of reporting error because the designed fields "do not always translate to an institution's departmental structure, and adjustments must be made by the institution in order to complete the survey."[8]

The NSF data include expenditures from branch campuses, medical schools, agricultural experiment stations, research centers and facilities, and "a university 501(c)(3) foundation established to handle R&D awards."[9] Some university systems, such as the University of California, file separate reports for each campus (UCLA, UCSF, and the rest). Others, such as Pennsylvania State University and the University of Michigan, included expenditures from all campuses in their past reports. (This is noted by the NSF.) However, beginning with the 2010 survey, data from each campus are to be reported separately. Comparisons must account for these reporting differences. In addition, the survey includes research funds subcontracted to another recipient. Significantly, they exclude non-research items such non-research training grants, public service grants, construction or renovation of research facilities, or departmental research that is not separately budgeted.

Expenditure data from each source include both direct and reimbursed indirect (F&A) costs. In addition, the NSF includes unrecovered indirect costs. This category covers all foregone F&A reimbursement—legitimate, recoverable F&A costs that the institution chose not to claim. For example, a university might have waived or reduced an F&A reimbursement claim to meet mandatory or voluntary cost-sharing. Many university accounting systems do not track these uncollected reimbursements. In those cases, they estimate unreimbursed indirect costs by multiplying their negotiated research F&A rate by the corresponding base (usually MTDC) and subtract actual F&A recovery on a project-by-project basis.

Various state agencies and universities also publish expenditure data, but they may not match the NSF statistics exactly. Differences in fiscal-year reporting dates will result in variances. For example, although the federal fiscal year runs

302 Managing the Research University

from October 1 through September 30, the NSF uses July 1 through June 30. The Texas fiscal year, for example, runs from September 1 through August 31. Unlike the NSF, state and university data may exclude items such as unreimbursed indirect costs or funds subcontracted to another recipient. Conversely, unlike many universities' reports, the NSF data do not include the cost of donated research equipment or software. Incidentally, these can be sizable imputed expenditures despite far less lucrative retail worth. It is also worth noting that the NSF and the IPEDS research expenditure data are not comparable. Unlike the NSF's, the IPEDS data incorporate federal appropriations and revenue from independent operations such as federally funded research and development centers.

In addition, some universities also report awards received annually. These numbers will vary considerably from actual expenditures. For example, some awards may be for a multiyear period, but the entire amount is reported when the award first comes in. The actual expenditures occur over the entire multiyear period. Thus, award and expenditure data cannot be compared.

Ultimately, any comparisons of institutional data must recognize these inherent variations and sources of error. A compulsive chief research officer may encounter data variations that defy resolution within a reasonable period of time. In those cases, the best alternative is to rely on the NSF data. Indeed, as a rule of thumb, the NSF data should serve as a standard benchmark. Despite some institutional reporting inconsistencies, they have well-documented reporting criteria and are universally available via the Internet.[10]

Institutional Evaluation

In its simplest form, institutional evaluation usually involves a comparison of research expenditure rankings relative to either a previous year's position or to other universities. For example, "We moved up three positions this year to join the top fifty public universities in research expenditures." And if joining the top fifty was a goal in the university's strategic plan, the evaluation is positive: "Keep up the good work." If this goal was not met—for example, the university dropped in the rankings—the assessment data should be analyzed further to determine which academic units failed to meet expectations.

Several high-visibility publications routinely tabulate various performance data and rank universities on the basis of a single variable, such as research expenditures or composite scores derived from many variables, including overall research expenditures, federal research expenditures, doctoral degrees awarded, and postdoctoral appointees.[11] Generally, they sort their rankings according to public or private and perhaps terminal-degree granting status. For example, using the NSF and other data sets, *U.S. News and World Report* publishes rankings that generate headlines every year.[12] Also, the National Research Council's now-outdated 1995 *Research Doctorate Programs in the United States: Continuity and*

Change and recently updated *A Data-Based Assessment of Research-Doctorate Programs in the United States* continue to be major sources of assessment information.[13] Rankings produced by both of these sources incorporate a subjective measure of academic quality obtained by surveying faculty members across the country for their opinions on various institutions' academic reputation. Although it is less well known among the general public, The Center for Measuring University Performance's annual *Top American Research Universities* annual report has become a standard reference for university administrators.[14] It relies mainly on NSF and IPEDS data and has no subjective component.

Rather than evaluating performance by comparing data obtained from all public or private universities, many institutions limit comparisons to so-called peer groups. Peer institutions are those with similar characteristics, such as enrollment, doctoral degrees awarded, number of faculty members, overall budget, and research expenditures. Comparisons to peers selected using objective NSF and IPEDS data indicate how a university's performance stacks up against statistically comparable institutions.

Three organizations provide services to help identify an institution's peers: the Carnegie Foundation for the Advancement of Teaching, the National Center for Education Statistics (NCES), and the National Center for Higher Education Management Systems (NCHEMS). The widely known Carnegie Foundation publishes broadly defined classifications based on numerous variables derived from IPEDS and NSF data.[15] For research universities, the two major categories are Research University (very high research activity) and Research University (high research activity). Previously, they were known more simply as Carnegie I and Carnegie II classifications. There is a third category, Doctoral/Research University, that includes many smaller or more focused institutions. Although several factors determine a university's classification, annual research expenditures play a major role. Each category contains about 100 institutions. Such large categories limit their usefulness for institutional evaluation. For example, the Research University (very high research activity) category includes both Montana State University and the University of Michigan, two very dissimilar public institutions.

Smaller peer groups more akin to a specific university can be obtained from the National Center for Education Statistics Peer Analysis System and the National Center for Higher Education Management Systems Comparison Group Selection Service.[16] They identify peer groups for individual institutions based on computer sorts of IPEDS data. In both of these services, the user can select the specific variables tabulated by IPEDS that are used to customize the group's characteristics. The usual peer group consists of about eight institutions.

Although these customized peer groups are based on hard data, every member may not represent qualities that the university finds desirable. Therefore, many institutions modify these computer-derived peer groups by adding or deleting specific members. Alternatively, they develop a separate group of benchmark institutions that they aspire to resemble. And this group may not include any peers.

Typically, the benchmark universities are more prestigious in one way or another. In the research context, this probably means more research expenditures, translating to "In ten years, we want to be like our benchmark institutions, not our peer group members." Unlike peer groups, there are no organizations that routinely provide institutional benchmark groups; a university selects *sui generis* benchmark institutions based on its own, unique criteria.

As an aside, universities are prone to setting strategic research goals such as "moving to the next level" or to becoming a "tier 1 institution." In the research context, these are very nebulous goals. The main reason is that there are very few formally recognized levels or tiers. Occasional monographs analyze university research activity and sort the universities into various levels or tiers.[17] However, the Carnegie Foundation provides the only regularly updated major ranking that assigns tiers based on research criteria. The *U.S. News and World Report* sorts universities into four tiers, but they base their rankings on much more than research expenditure data.[18] Thus, it is of limited usefulness for evaluating research level.

Moving from one tier to the next in the Carnegie classifications represents a highly significant change in research activity. For example, the average annual research expenditures for the "very high research activity" (tier 1) and "high research activity" (tier 2) categories are about $302 million and $53 million, respectively (2005 NSF data). Unless a university's ranking lies very close to the border between these two categories, moving to the next level or becoming a tier 1 research institution may prove to be an unreasonable expectation.

Realistically, there is little benefit to challenging an institution's use of the words *level* and *tier* beyond the scope of the Carnegie classifications. The spirit of these aspirations is usually self-evident: the university strives to increase its research capacity and reputation. These are useful goals as long as nobody expects strict accountability for their meaning.

Institutional Performance Indicators

With scores of data measuring every conceivable aspect of university performance, ranging from undergraduate enrollments by major to research expenditures by federal agency to the number of administrative staff members by occupation, the challenge becomes one of interpretation. What does it all mean? For the chief research officer who wants simply to evaluate the effectiveness of his or her initiatives and performance, meaningful information must somehow be extracted from these myriad assessment data. Unfortunately, there is no single statistic (like an average) that summarizes the data.

Clearly, the first step is to evaluate progress toward meeting the goals established in the university's strategic plan. These goals differ among various institutions. However, most plans contain several common elements that are easy to evaluate. Probably the most common is to increase total research expenditures, thus rising in the various national rankings relative to peers. (The ultimate goal is to look more like benchmark institutions.) Although these comparisons are biased heavily toward science and engineering fields, they are easy to comprehend. And, success in these fields is often accompanied by less quantifiable accomplishments in nonscience disciplines.

Another typical strategic goal refers to the number of doctoral degrees awarded, as in "We will increase the number—more are better." Measurements of doctoral degrees awarded reflect the university's overall scholarly effort, not just science and engineering. Therefore, it is often considered a good indicator of research productivity. But these data must be interpreted cautiously. Universities with large, highly funded research programs seldom award correspondingly large numbers of doctoral degrees. For example, two institutions ranked as Research University (very high research activity), the Universities of Michigan and Wisconsin, award about one doctoral degree per $1 million of research expenditures; two others ranked on the lower tier, Research University (high research activity), the University of Houston and Texas Tech University, award about three doctoral degrees per $1 million of research expenditures. Yes, the large research-intensive universities award more doctoral degrees than their smaller counterparts, but the number does not increase in proportion to the research expenditures.

In general, these institutional assessment data should be expressed on a per faculty-member basis whenever that makes sense. The reason is that overall institutional data can be very misleading if one or two highly productive research groups overshadow an otherwise lethargic research effort. For example, a university may have only a few active researchers but they happen to get large grants and publish high-impact papers. A cursory evaluation might not detect an otherwise underperforming faculty. In this context, universities that concentrate resources on only a few lucrative programs to maximize expenditure numbers may accomplish an institutional goal of increased research expenditures, but this strategy may belie the real status of the overall university's scholarly performance.

Therefore, the average amount of research funding generated per faculty member provides a more reliable measure of research productivity than just overall institutional expenditures. In general, faculty at a "very high research activity" university generally garner two to three times as much research funding compared to their "high research activity" colleagues. In many cases, the difference can be much larger; for example, in FY 2009, the federal research expenditures per full-time equivalent faculty member at the University of Texas, Austin ("very high research activity") and Texas Tech University ("high research activity") were $194,526 and $28,269 respectively—nearly a sevenfold difference.[19] (Neither university has a medical school.) An evaluation based on this assessment metric could logically extend to an assessment of the faculty workload, core facilities, administrative support, programmatic strengths, and other factors that might affect a faculty member's capacity to do research. Of course, these data must be examined carefully. Universities with large medical schools may skew the data toward higher per faculty funding because of their access to NIH grants, thus masking areas of underperformance in other schools and colleges. Conversely, universities concentrating on nonbiomedical disciplines may have lower funding per faculty member but highly productive activity.

Similarly, the average number of scholarly publications per faculty member manifests research performance. Publication measurements have become quite sophisticated. With modern tracking systems, the number of times that a publication is cited by others is readily available. Furthermore, the number of times that all articles in a journal are cited can be used to calculate the journal's impact— more citations mean greater impact. With this measurement, the impact of a specific publication can be calculated. Similar impact information can be derived for concerts or exhibits through attendance data. In a sense, evaluations based on these "impact factors" provide the most balanced measure of research performance. They do not bias toward particularly well-funded disciplines, such as the biomedical sciences. Importantly, they incorporate an element of peer review into the data—assuming that citations connote merit.

When evaluating programs designed to increase institutional research capacity, the chief research officer will find a good performance metric in the number of faculty members submitting grant proposals or publishing in a top-tier journal for the first time. An increase in these first-time numbers manifests enhanced scholarly productivity and therefore increased capacity. Indeed, they yield more information about increasing a program's effectiveness than simply tabulating the number of faculty members who have submitted a grant proposal or published in a top-tier, high-impact journal. Those data, which may be quite impressive relative to those of peer institutions, do not indicate whether the university's research capacity has progressed beyond status quo.

Numerous other parameters have been used to evaluate research performance. These include the number of postdoctoral scholars, National Academy of Sciences members, and Nobel Prize winners. Understandably, a university's reputation relates directly to the number of these prestigious appointees. But they may not reflect current research performance. The value placed on these data depends on the institutional goals. Do these goals include elevated prestige? The answer is most probably yes.

> K: You keep coming back to evaluation based on research expenditures. But that metric could give a false indication of a university's overall scholarly performance. Those monetary data may not reveal a university's stellar performance in fields such as the arts and humanities.
>
> Smith: I agree. Focusing on research expenditures can be myopic. However, most people readily understand the meaning of money—that is, research expenditures—but, unfortunately, not scholarly impact. Consequently, many individuals, including legislators and donors, judge a university on

> the basis of research money in the same way that they judge an athletic
> program by the football team's wins and losses.
> K: If research expenditures are the coin of the realm, why shouldn't administra-
> tors concentrate resources on only a few lucrative programs to maximize
> institutional expenditures? That strategy accomplishes the goal—research
> expenditures are up.
> Smith: Some ambitious institutions do just that—invest primarily in the
> "rainmakers." The hope is that "a rising tide raises all ships."

Office Performance

Like all other senior university administrators, the chief research officer's performance is under constant scrutiny. Indirectly, his or her success depends on the
efforts of the various units that report to the chief research officer. These include
the sponsored-research office, animal-care facility, and technology-transfer office,
to name several. Favorable accomplishments by these offices translate into a positive evaluation of the chief research officer's performance. Consequently, his or
her attention focuses on the evaluation of their activities.

As many marketing professionals discovered a long time ago, clients' comments
constitute an informative measure of a service unit's performance. Although
complaints usually outnumber praises—that's a function of human nature—
unsolicited user feedback can be quite informative. In addition, it has become
standard practice to ask users to fill out a questionnaire about the unit's service.
A responsive chief research officer will, of course, acknowledge receipt of any
comments and discuss them with the unit director.

Evaluation of the technology-transfer office adds a quantitative dimension. As
with the other service units, user feedback constitutes an effective baseline
performance metric. However, additional office activities lend themselves to
assessment: how many disclosures, patents, and licenses are processed annually?
And how much revenue was generated? The two evaluation yardsticks—namely,
user comments and quantitative data—may be correlated. Indeed, they probably
are; if the office engenders researchers' confidence, they probably tend to submit
more disclosures. The quantitative data can be evaluated relative to peer and
benchmark institutions and strategic-plan goals. Comparative data from other
institutions are available from AUTM.[20] However, when evaluating these data,
caution must reign. Universities vary widely in the percentage of disclosures
accepted for patenting. The figure may range between 10 and 80 percent, depending on institutional resources and policy. For example, patent-prosecution costs
are quite expensive, and as a matter of fiscal prudence, some universities limit
patent applications to those most likely to generate meaningful income. These
differences must be factored into a comparative evaluation.

More sophisticated (and therefore more complicated) assessment procedures can provide more elaborate analyses of service offices such as sponsored-research, animal-care services, IRB, and biosafety. For example, the average times required to process and submit a grant application or to review and approve an animal-use or human-subjects protocol could be analyzed. But in the absence of specific benchmarks or user complaints, it is questionable whether they would provide any more useful information.

A more powerful evaluation method—namely, constraints analysis—is recommended especially when qualitative assessments indicate user dissatisfaction with a service office's performance. Constraints analysis identifies the single operational constraint—the bottleneck—responsible for suboptimal performance. In this procedure, a working group of individuals familiar with the office (including staff members and, in the research context, the chief research officer) thoroughly analyze the entire system of office operations. Importantly, they focus on all—not just one or a few—aspects of the office processes. Step by step, the group follows all office actions: paperwork processing, decision making, communication, and all other components of the overall operation. By studying the flow and interconnections between individual steps, usually on a blackboard, the group can pinpoint the particular actions most responsible for user dissatisfaction. Metaphorically, the chain is no stronger than its weakest link. Constraints analysis amounts to finding the weakest link in a chain so it can be strengthened. In practice, constraints analysis may identify more than one constraint that limits office performance.

Although the analysis seems simple in concept, it can be tricky to execute. Thus, an individual experienced in constraints analysis usually leads the working group. Most business schools have management faculty with this experience. The principles of constraint theory are well documented in numerous books on management.[21]

After constraints have been identified, the next challenge is to remedy them. In the best-case scenario, they lend themselves to a simple fix. Realistically, however, the solution may not be readily apparent. In those situations, it is advisable to conduct a best-practices study. How do other institutions perform the same constraining operations? In the research setting, the chief research officer typically appoints a working committee to conduct this study. This committee may contain some members from the constraints-analysis working group, but it should also diversify to include individuals from outside the office. Ultimately, the committee determines the best practices at other universities for mitigating potential constraints. The chief research officer thus has the information needed to improve his or her university's performance in this context.

Note: although they are technically not "offices," centers and institutes that report to the chief research officer also undergo periodic assessment and evaluation. However, because of their academic mission, the procedures usually follow those guiding performance reviews of other academic units, such as departments and colleges. In chapter 7, center and institute reviews were discussed in context.

A practical issue merits comment. How should undocumented complaints about office performance be handled? If anecdotal complaints surface, they should not be ignored. The chief research officer should discuss them, off the record, with the office director. Together, they should devise a strategy to mitigate the source of complaints and thus improve performance.

Personal Evaluation

Now, for the most difficult question to answer: How am I doing? The answer to this personal question can be elusive. One possibility arises immediately. If the chief research officer hasn't been asked to step down, then the answer is logically, "You're doing okay." However, as most people know, this can be a fallacious conclusion. Seemingly incompetent and ineffective administrators can defy dismissal for sometimes unfathomable reasons. Thus, a personal evaluation must depend on more objective criteria than simply keeping the job.

Typically, most university administrators must submit a personal assessment and evaluation annually as part of their performance review. These documents itemize accomplishments and progress toward meeting certain goals—usually those elaborated in the university's strategic plan. Not surprisingly, they bias positively. At worst, these self-evaluations offer defensive explanations about why a particular goal has not been met. And why not? Pay raises and promotions lie in the balance. Therefore, truthful as they may be, these self-assessments are not necessarily objective.

Occasionally, the chief research officer serves as principal investigator on grants awarded to the institution. In some cases, he or she writes the proposal with minimal help from colleagues. Success in this venue might constitute objective evidence of good performance, especially if the grant is renewed. At the very least, it reflects skillful writing and grantsmanship. And a chief research officer can justifiably take pride in these successes: they manifest good performance. However, some institutional grants are awarded for reasons related only marginally to the proposal's quality. For example, they may be noncompetitive, formula-driven grants. Or the grant may have been awarded because of a politician's assistance. In that context, a resourceful chief research officer might claim that enlisting political support is also an accomplishment and should not be discounted. And that claim may contain an element of truth.

Major contributions to the university's infrastructure also indicate positive performance. Few accomplishments evoke as much pride as successfully garnering the resources to erect a new research facility. The hallmark contribution is a new building, although other major facilities such as an oceanographic research vessel, a supercomputer, or a large telescope can be equally valuable. The chief research officer seldom works alone to gain these facilities; center directors, deans, provosts, chief executive officers, and politicians all pitch in. And, along with the chief research officer, they all can rightly take partial credit for a success.

Ultimately, one indicator stands out as the most comprehensive, objective measure of a chief research officer's success: institutional performance. This linkage arises from the chief research officer's primary responsibility, which is to maintain and nurture the university's research environment. As a manager, he or she invests resources and provides hassle-free services to support institutional research. Furthermore, as a leader, the chief research officer motivates faculty members to expand their scholarly activities. If he or she has done a good job, the university's research productivity will increase. Quantitatively, this will be manifest in the number of high-impact publications, submitted grants applications, research expenditures, and intellectual-property disclosures. Ideally and most importantly, the chief research officer exemplifies personal integrity and inspires a campus-wide ethos of scholarly accomplishment. These attributes cannot be quantified. They must be felt.

> K: I understand your last comment about a research ethos. Some university campuses just feel exciting.
> Smith: It's always stimulating to be on these campuses. You can feel their pulse racing.
> K: Surely there must be more behind this than just the chief research officer. Doesn't the chief executive officer set the tone?
> Smith: Of course. Leadership comes from the top down. And it extends into many dimensions—teaching, research, community service, and, yes, athletics. Within the research dimension, however, the chief research officer stands up front in the leadership role. It's an exciting and challenging position.

Notes

1. National Academy for Academic Leadership, "Assessment and Evaluation in Higher Education: Some Concepts and Principles," 2007, http://www.thenationalacademy.org/readings/assessandeval.html (accessed January 16, 2011).
2. W. M. K. Trochim, "Introduction to Evaluation," Research Methods Knowledge Base, 2008, http://www.socialresearchmethods.net/kb/intreval.htm (accessed January 16, 2011).
3. National Institutes of Health (NIH), "Evaluation Plan and Milestones," IDeA Networks of Biomedical Research Excellence (INBRE), program announcement PAR-08-150, 2010, http://grants.nih.gov/grants/guide/pa-files/PAR-08-150.html (accessed January 16, 2011).
4. J. F. Westat, The 2002 User Friendly Handbook for Project Evaluation (Arlington, VA.: National Science Foundation, 2002).
5. National Center for Education Statistics, "Integrated Postsecondary Education Data System," 2011, http://nces.ed.gov/ipeds/about/ (accessed January 16, 2011).
6. National Science Foundation (NSF), "Higher Education Research and Development Survey, FY 2010," 2011, http://irdm.uno.edu/reports/docs/NSF_HERD_2010.pdf (accessed January 16, 2011).
7. Ibid.
8. National Science Foundation (NSF), "Survey of Research and Development Expenditures at Universities and Colleges," § 3.d, 2009, http://www.nsf.gov/statistics/srvyrdexpenditures/ (accessed January 16, 2011).

9. NSF, "Higher Education Research and Development."

10. National Science Foundation (NSF), "Federal Science and Engineering Support to Universities, Colleges, and Nonprofit Institutions," 2009, http://www.nsf.gov/statistics/nsf09315/pdf/nsf09315.pdf (accessed Jauary 16, 2011).

11. Institute for Higher Education Policy, "National Ranking Systems," 2010, http://www.ihep.org/research/gcpf-detail.cfm?pc=3&s=63&ss=149 (accessed January 16, 2011).

12. "Best Colleges, 2010 National Universities Rankings," *U.S. News and World Report,* September 1, 2010, http://colleges.usnews.rankingsandreviews.com/best-colleges/national-universities-rankings/(accessed January 16, 2011).

13. M. L. Goldberger et al., eds. *Research Doctorate Programs in the United States: Continuity and Change* (Washington, D.C.: National Academies Press, 1995); J.P. Ostriker et al., eds. *A Data-Based Assessment of Research-Doctorate Programs in the United States* (Washington, D.C.: National Academies Press, 2010).

14. E. D. Capaldi et al., *The Top American Research Universities 2009 Annual Report* (Tempe, AZ.: Arizona State University, 2009).

15. Carnegie Foundation for the Advancement of Teaching, "The Carnegie Classification of Institutions of Higher Education," 2010, http://classifications.carnegiefoundation.org/index.php (accessed January 16, 2011).

16. National Center for Education Statistics, "ExPT and DFR", IPEDS Data Center, 2011, http://nces.ed.gov/ipeds/datacenter/Expt/SelectComparisonInstitution.aspx (accessed January 16, 2011); National Center for Higher Education Management Systems, "Comparison Group Selection Service," 2011, http://www.nchems.org/services/infosvc/comparison.php (accessed January 16, 2011).

17. H. D. Graham and N. Diamond, *The Rise of American Research Universities: Elites and Challengers in the Post-War Era* (Baltimore, Md.: Johns Hopkins Press, 1997).

18. "Best Colleges."

19. Texas Higher Education Coordinating Board, "Federal R&D Expenditures/FTE Faculty Ratio, FY 2009, Texas Public Universities," p. 18, 2009, http://www.thecb.state.tx.us/reports/PDF/2056.PDF?CFID=14905431&CFTOKEN=85846974 (accessed January 16, 2011).

20. Association of University Technology Managers (AUTM), *U.S. Licensing Activity Survey: FY2008* (Deerfield. Ill.: AUTM, 2010).

21. E. M. Goldratt and J. Cox, *The Goal: A Process of Ongoing Improvement* (Great Barrington, MA.: North River Press, 1984).

INDEX